BEFORE I FORGET

Every life has a story
This is mine.

Wynette Alexander-Greene

authorHOUSE®

AuthorHouse™
1663 Liberty Drive
Bloomington, IN 47403
www.authorhouse.com
Phone: 1-800-839-8640

First published by AuthorHouse 8/31/2011

ISBN: 978-1-4567-6111-0 (sc)
ISBN: 978-1-4567-6110-3 (hc)
ISBN: 978-1-4567-6109-7 (e)

Library of Congress Control Number: 2011907430

Printed in the United States of America

Any people depicted in stock imagery provided by Thinkstock are models, and such images are being used for illustrative purposes only. Certain stock imagery © Thinkstock.

This book is printed on acid-free paper.

BOOK I

PART I

"Please leave me alone, I need to sleep, stop that, stop doing that to me".

I thought I was dreaming that a wet, warm tongue was on my nose.

My eye was being licked open. I woke up to realize that it was not a dream; I was being attack by something in my bed. I felt the little warm, wet tongue on my lips, then my ears, to my eyes again, trying to open them. I attempted to push off my attacker with no avail. She jumped with all her weight on my belly, I cry out in pain because some of us know what is in our bladder at four in the morning. She sat on my chest and continue licking at my lips, then my nose.

Worried that I may have peed myself when she jumped on my belly, I threw her across the bed and sat up in the dark, trying to figure out what was happening to me.

'How did I get myself into such bad company?' I didn't see her eyes in the dark, but I knew she was looking at me, waiting to resume her attack. She began to use her teeth.

She started to nibble at my toes, making growling sounds as she pulled the cover off my body. I tried to kick her off my bed but she was too swift.

It's four o'clock her routine wake-up time. Her time was four hours earlier that mine.

1

I said my prayer, ending with, 'don't make me kill this thing in my bed today, Amen'. Trying to avoid a flood, I sat on my throne for some relief. I looked down at my foot where she was sitting on them, waiting like a lioness, for the slightest movement.

"What am I going to do with you? You are only tree months old; you weigh just tree pounds, yet you are putting a hurting in my lifestyle. I have to wake up when you wake up. You refused to sleep into your own bed, you pretend to do so but as soon as I fall asleep, you jump into mine. You are taking control of my life, why should a little Yorkie like you have so much power over a big old woman like me? Tell me Sabrina, what should I do to get rid of you?" upon hearing her name, she looked up at me.

After my bathroom and bedroom duties, I followed my impatient companion to the door. She led the way with waggling tail, stopped ever so often looking back to see if I was following her. Yes, I have become the follower of this 'thing' "I am coming, lead the way". Her waggling tail caused her whole little body to sway from side to side; she was jumping, circling herself and barking at me to open the door and let her out.

That was how my life has changed in the past tree months, with Sabrina in control.

The other members of the family, three dogs and one cat were waiting on the front porch. Six of us made up my family on this paradise island of St Maarten. Onyx, 12 years old black Labrador, Asti, 1-year-old Irish Hound, Prince, 1-year-old Golden Retriever, Snowflake, 12 years old black domestic cat and the 'Terror' Sabrina.

Still dark outside, as soon as the door was opened, the excitement began, Madam Snowflake, high up on the table to avoid being trampled by the excitement, waited for her morning greeting in the form of a head-rub. The three large dogs joined with the 'tree pounder', pushing to see who would be first to get a belly-rub. When I decided that enough was enough, I wanted them to leave me alone, I would say "Who brought all these trash on this po…" Before I could finish my question, everyone disappeared under the table and under the chairs. Each one in his/her hiding place, even Sabrina had hers between the plants, all of them looking at me as if we were playing 'hide and seek'. I used the quiet moment to look at my ten fingers and toes and to assure myself that I am alive. I don't look at the marks and dents on my body. I don't want to be reminded of what my life was all about. I gather my shoes, hat, cane and leaches, as soon as I bend down to tie my shoelaces; they rushed out of their hiding places to give me the usual saliva face wash. It's the start of our daily activities.

I live high up on a hill in the beautiful island of Dutch St Maarten; in the Netherlands Antilles in an area call Belair. The beach is ten minutes walk downhill. Every morning, regardless of the weather (except a hurricane) we wind ourselves down the hill through the empty, quite streets. (With animal names such as Rabbit Hill, Kangaroo Road, Otter Drive and Camel Run) This is our fun time, myself and my four dogs enjoying the freedom to walking all over the streets without having to worry about traffic or anyone walking or jogging. The smell of clean air opens my nostril and travel to my lungs; I can feel the oxygen going through my body as I take deep breaths. I am taking my share of God's gift to all, which is clean air, before the island wakes-up with its cars, trucks, large tour busses and motorcycles and other elements that pollute it.

Freedom has been a rare commodity in my life, that is why I sap up every moment I get. I promised myself not long ago that for the rest of my life, I would enjoy every moment granted. I shall always be humble, thankful and forgiving for this freedom.

We entered what I call my 'Nature Garden' where every plant, of all shade and shape grows naturally; no one planted them, yet they are so beautiful. The night dew on the leaves looked like silver beads of pearl, the various fragrances from beautiful wild flower intoxicated me into a wild dance. I loosen the dogs, so that they too can join in the 'freedom dance' in the serene oasis, where my spirit is free. Through the silence I heard the music that I needed to dance, and dance, I did. There was no one to stop me; never again will I allow anyone to stop me from dancing. I will dance and dance and dance until there is no more wind inside my body. Dancing is freedom.

I took off my shoes; I needed to feel the cool, damped earth beneath my sole.

With my hands outstretched and my dogs waiting for me to make the first move. I begin to dance in silence, tai chi to start then a combination of waltz, cha cha cha, salsa and jitterbug. Twenty minutes later I closed with another calm Tai chi.

My dogs dance too; they run around, jump in the air, reaching for what I am feeling, and complete freedom from stress and fear. I am free to dance. I am high, high, high.

"We moved on, we needed to get to the beach before the sun comes up" As I walked through this path of the mangrove lined lagoon on one side and lush plants such as orchids, cherries, grapes and many more on the other side. I thought of how much I would have liked to share this experience with everyone in the world, so they too can see, feel and hear the peace that exits on this side of the Lagoon. A path that most of the inhabitants of the island don't even know exists.

The flowers opened to catch the morning dew; the butterflies of various colors began to come out with the first sign of light. The lagoon glistened with small ripples as the mother ducks and their ducklings came out from their nest under the mangrove.

The Pelicans, the island's national bird, are still asleep on electric poles that fell into the lagoon during a hurricane. A mongoose ran across the path, the dogs ran after it.

The gentle breeze caressed my face and tangled into my hair, water gathered into my eyes and caused everything to sparkle like little silver stars all around me.

Meditation is an important part in my life; I have been meditating since I was a child, long before I understood its meaning and benefits. It has become my way to start and end the day. I like to get to the beach early to avoid being disturbed in my quiet moment by tourist and local islanders walking with their dogs.

"Start your day with peace, love and forgiveness, meditate" Matar-Sanskrit-mother

Have you ever sat in an open area or by the sea early in the morning, and closed your eyes while the sun came up above the horizon? I bet you could never describe the color you see? Why? Because its for your eyes and your eyes alone to enjoy. If you have not, try it, you will see a color that no paint-mixer can produce or duplicate. But, I have to share with you what I see through my close eyes, '*a pomegranate red*'.

The sun was up, and so were the tourists, as they pass me sitting on the rock, some greeted my playful dogs and me. They made comments like "What a beautiful island"; "You are so lucky to be enjoying this beauty everyday"; "I wish we were living here, the blue sea and warm climate brings us back every year" "Thank you"

"Do you know how lucky you are?" ask a young lady. She waited for an answer. 'Should I sit this pretty young stranger on the sand and tell her how lucky I am?'

Nah, she wouldn't have the time to listen to my horrible, boring life.

The sand and water felt good under my foot. Walking in the water had been good therapy for my injured back. Still thinking of how 'lucky I am' or so it seems to many people, deep in my thoughts, not looking up, I walked strait into someone.

"Wow, don't knock me down" she said

"I am so sorry, I should be looking where I am going, did I hurt you?"

"No Wynette, you did not hurt me" with surprise and laughter in her voice.

"Linda, how are you? When did you arrive here?" Happily I ask my friend.

"Last night, you know I couldn't wait to be out here this morning looking for you"

We hugged each other and jumped around in circles on the sand, like Sabrina did.

I met Linda on this same beach. She and her husband Don have a timeshare at the Divi hotel along this same beach. She is a writer; we meet everyday when she is here. We sit under the Seaside-grape tree and chat for hours. I look forward to seeing her every year in the month of May. She is someone I like very much. Something about her makes me very comfortable. She is a good listener, I am always telling her stories told to me by my mother or folk stories of my homeland, Guyana.

"Who is this?" she asked as Sabrina comes running to me looking like a wet rat.

"This is Sabrina, the newest member of my family, she is in control, she is my boss"

"She is quite small, you have to be careful, anyone can put her in a pocket and go with her" The thought scared me; I picked her, put her in my pants pocket.

"So, do you have many stories for me? You know I can't wait to hear them"

"By just walking on the beach, folks think I am so lucky. I think if they hear my life story they may say "You're lucky to be alive""

"Come, let's go find our favorite spot and you can tell me all about it"

"OK, but I would think that after so many years and so many incidents in my life, I should be immune to little stuff, but I am still sensitive to some things. Let me give you an example, yesterday I went to a neighbor, two houses away from me, to take a gift for her newborn baby. She was happy, she asked what it was, and I told her it's a Susan Bee Anthony silver dollar. I told her that it is my tradition to give a newborn baby and a bride a silver coin, which will not tear of burn; it means that they will always have money-wealth. She accepted the gift and said she liked my tradition but the only bad thing was that her baby was born in this island. I asked her

"What is so bad about your child being born here? You live here, this island is a Dutch territory, why is it so terrible for your baby to born here?" she said

"It may affect him later to become a Dutch politician, because he was not born in Holland". I ask her "Why did you not go back to Holland and give birth, if you are so worried for the future of your baby? St Maarten is Holland's Paradise trophy. Why should you be ashamed of having a baby born here? He can be a politician right here. It's good enough for you to live here? In America, Alexander Hamilton who was born in Nevis, played an important part in its history, his picture is on the US $10 bill?"

Can you see why I am confused, Linda? Two days, two young ladies who can pass as twins, with two different views of this Paradise Island that is good for one thing but not for another? You see why I needed to sit that young lady down and tell her about my luck? Beginning with my grandparents, one half came from India, the other half was of African-Scottish decent in Guyana? How the outcaste daughter was cursed for marrying out of her race? The curse that affected so many lives, especially all her sons. That both my parents did not want me?

That one half of me tied me and left me to be eaten by giant red ants and the other half of me pushed me into the deep canal and one came close to taking off my foot when I was just a child? How I wanted one half to see whom my mother was but couldn't dear let the other half know that she was my mother? That my father hated me just because the curse didn't fall on me too? Or so he thought? Should I tell her that I was left to die of Malaria in Africa? Or that I went to America, homeless and penniless yet, single-handedly I raised three children by doing three fulltime jobs and many house/butt-cleanings to have three Valedictorians / Ivy leaguers? That I was called 'The Jewish Mother'. Should I tell her that this Jewish Mother was the only person from my apartment building who went to work seven days a week, from morning to night? That it was after an accident and after feeling useless and used up, like driftwood, I drifted and drifted and ended on these shores, beaten, battered and dried out? Should I tell her that someone found me and show me what true love is all about for the first time at age 54? Should I show her the dents and marks that will not leave even with love and tender care? She is on vacation, she don't have the time to hear how lucky I am. Now that I am thinking about it, yes, I am lucky."

Linda and I found our favorite spot under the Seaside grape tree. We sat on rocks in the shape of beach chairs, which we arranged ourselves for comfort.

"My mother told me long time ago, never envy others for anything they may have or how they live, especially if I do not know how they acquired their riches. She said: "Once upon a time, there was a beautiful Queen who had many servants, fine silks and jewelry. She lived in a large palace with plenty to eat and drink.

A very poor woman with a husband and five children lived in a small mud-hut was hired to wash and oil the Queen's feet three times per day for a meager wage. Though small, the money helped to make life much better for the servant and her family.

The poor woman loved her husband and children but liked being at the palace where she was in an environment she craved and dreamt of having. One day she told the Queen that she envied her for having so much, when she had so little. The Queen told her if she wished they could exchange places. She agreed happily and they did.

One day while the ex-queen washed the new Queens foot, the Queen began to cry, she said she no longer wanted to be the Queen; she was unhappy and wanted to go back to her family and her poor life. The former Queen asked her what made her unhappy, she said. She slept in a large palace with fine silks and sweet oils but nothing to do. No children, no husband, no laughter, she was unhappy and wanted to change places.

The now poor servant told the Queen that she was happy with her new found children and husband; she said, "There is no one for you to envy now, you are the Queen, you have everything. I will not be coming back here, I have my husband and children to love and they love me. I have true love and happiness. I don't envy you"

The lesson I learned from my mother was, never grudge others for any reason"

"I am a good listener if you want to tell me your story," said Linda, her arms on me.

"It will take a long time, very long time to tell you about my life and how I got here"

"That's O K, I am here for three weeks, if we meet every morning, I will listen while you talk, in that time you could tell me your story. Where do you want to start?"

I looked into my friend's kind eyes and I saw a warm smile and honesty that made me trusted her. I kept my past to myself for many years. "Linda, I really and truly need to tell someone my story before I forget. I will start with my grandparents"

Kasy and his wife Banchani went to the Ganges River in India on a pilgrimage to bathe and offer prayers. A regular event attended by thousands of Hindus.

Some Touts encouraged them to join a large number of Indians migrating to British Guiana. They were told that the British Colony in South America was in need of people to work in the sugar, cocoa and tobacco plantations. They were promised their own land, housing, good wages and a free trip by boat. They were told that Guiana had many rivers for them to bath and practice their religion. That it was the land of many waters.

That after ten years they will not be bound to work in the plantation anymore.

In August of 1901, Kasy left his mother and two brothers in their little village in India, promising them that if he did not like it, he will return home to Mother India.

He was nineteen years old, his young wife was seventeen, entered a large crowded ship bound for Colonial British Guiana.

One of the stipulation was no Brahmin should make the trip. In other words, Brahmins were not asked to leave India because of their high caste. All the other caste could.

It was said that in order for the poor Brahmin to join the other Indians, they had to deny who they were and claim to be of a lower caste.

But when they arrived in the colonies, they resumed their religion and high caste.

The sole reason for most of the Indians going to the British Colonies were economics and promises of a better life.

Kasy and Banchani had another reason for wanting to make a move to another place. Banchani had lost two babies in her five years of marriage. She was twelve years old when she got married. Infant mortality was very common in those days in India.

Even though her mother-in-law was kind to her, she knew that there were talks among the families and villagers that something was wrong with her for not being able to bring forth her babies.

The journey was long and horrible; many lives were lost due to bad hygiene, lack of clean water, food and medical supplies. Promises made to them were not kept.

Kasy, being a young Hindu Pundit was called upon many times to perform duties such as counseling, for people who had problems dealing with depression, seasickness, long confinement in a small area and the never-ending trip.

He preformed last rites to men, women and children who died by suicide and other causes. He had a watchful eye on his own wife whom he suspected was pregnant again.

He was given a small room on a range in the logy of Bound Yard in the sugar plantation at Port Maurant Estate, on the east coast of Berbice.

"Where is the house and land that they promised us? We could be living next to untouchables" asked his wife, as she stood on the dirt floor of the kitchen, shocked, surprised but still respectful and submissive to her husband.

Kasy himself, shocked at the broken promises, knew he had to be strong, he knew he could not walk back to India, he would have to start with whatever was given to him until he could save enough money to go back to India.

He had come of his own free will; he had trusted the White Sahib.

He was told that he came to Guiana from India as an Indentured 'Bound Coolie' Servant. For a meager payment, the Indians had to take the places of the now freed Negro slaves, who refused to work again in the sugar plantations, even though they too will be paid the same meager wage.

The sugar plantations were gold mines of the Colonies. Freedom to Negro slaves was a big blow to Colonials but it was not going to stop them from reaping all that the Colony had to offer. Yes, it had a lot to offer. Sugar being the most important but there were much more, rice, gold, diamond, timber, coffee, cocoa, cotton, bauxite, balata, cheap labor and most of all good warm climate where the Europeans lived like Kings.

Kasy tried his best to adjust to the life style. He found himself in the middle of every caste, from the highest to the lowest of Indians working and living together.

Five rooms with five families made up a range, each room had one door.

After six months of living in *Bound Yard*, (named for the newcomers who were bound to work for ten years before they are given a room in Free Yard) among the chicken, ducks and pigs that are eating from the latrine trench, which ran parallel to the dirt road that everyone used to their ranges. Like the ranges, the latrines were built to accommodate ten persons at one time. A zinc wall separated men and women latrines. They were built across a trench, the feces float and ferment in the still water. "It is unhygienic," complained Kasy to the Management.

"So what? The Negroes lived in it, and even worst, you lived in worst condition than this in India so what are you complaining about? Asked the Overseer.

But Kasy could not take it anymore; his wife was going to have a baby any day. He was desperate, he went to the Manager's office and said "I will kill myself and family if I have to live in this filth any longer" Management did not like to hear that because many Indians had already committed suicide because of the terrible conditions they were forced to work and live in on the Colonies.

Kasy was given a one-room house in Miss Weby.

With the help of the a Hindu *Nani* or *Old lady* who assisted in child delivery, Banchani gave birth to a frail little boy in 1902 whom the 'Book' named Kachan.

The baby was very sick at birth; his parents were worried that he too would not survive. Cries and prayers seemed not to be of any use.

As Banchani held her dying little child in her arms, she felt a sense of relief that her mother-in-law was not there to say that even though she was in another country, she still could not save her child. It would be worst if the boy do not survive.

Things were not looking good for the little boy, when the Nani went to bath him. She quickly called Kasy and Banchani. She asked them to sit flat on the floor, both of them holding the sick child. They obeyed. She untied a *phie*, a cloth purse, tied with a string around her waist. Took out one cent and gave it to the young couple and took the baby from their arms. She told them that she was 'buying' him from them, that from then on he belonged to her. She directed them to use the cent to buy some fruits and together they should eat all of what the cent bought.

She took the almost lifeless little boy, naked as when he was born, to the Sideline trench of running water. She ducked him three times and renamed him. A name only she would call him. She loaned him back to his parents. It was a common practice, and still is, that someone will buy a dying child from the parents and even though the parents still have the child, the person who bought the child becomes a Godparent.

Five other children were born in their little one room house at Miss

Weby, Manraji, a girl in 1905, Tatrani, another girl in1907, Lungbeharry, a boy in 1909, Bakraji, a girl in 1910 and Satarine another girl in 1913. Between the last two, they lost yet another child.

Nani, the old lady, had to repeat the buying of Tatrani in 1907 because she was so sick, no one expected her to live. Nani named her Dhero.

Kasy became Kasy Marage to the Hindu community. He stopped working in the fields and moved with his family to Whim Village after building a large wooden two-story house. He began teaching young Hindu men to become Pandits and religious leaders. He opened several Hindi night schools for men and boys, encouraging them to teach their wives, daughters and sisters Sanskrit/Hindi at home. He said, "Sanskrit/Hindi should be the only language spoken by Hindus. That way they will never forget their Motherland India.

For many years he sent money through the Post Office to his mother and brothers back in India. One day the Money Orders returned with a stamped message that read, "No one by this name lives at this address" He was deeply saddened. From the amount of returned Money Orders, he knew his mother may have died and his brothers moved away from his village. He knew he would never know what had happened to them.

Kasy Marage became one of the most respectful and demanded 'Holy leader' in the district. He built several Temples and schools for Hindustanis; his means of living were from donations and gifts-dachna, seethe- for his services. He lived very simple and religious. He demanded that his children uphold the same and maintained their high caste. Being a Brahmin was like being 'Chosen'. In Whim there were very few such, it made him even more important in the eye of the villagers, who were predamently Madrasis, a darker shade of Indians who were considered a much lower caste.

Arranged marriages of his children, boys at fifteen and girls at thirteen years old, one year older than when he and his wife got married, were done according to his wishes and will. They all married to Brahmin of course.

Tatri was thirteen years old when she married Ramdas. She never saw him before.

She slept with her mother-in-law until she got her first period, one year later.

Her mother and mother-in-law taught her how to tie a string around her waist.

"You have become a woman today, you have to wash your napkins every day and hang them at the back of the house, no one but you should see them. During the time while you are in this state, you are unclean; you do not go to the temple, bath in the trench or sleep with your husband" the scared little girl had no idea what her mother was saying, especially the part about 'sleep with your husband' but she listened.

"This will last of about a week, after that you will move into your own home with Ram. He is your husband, you have to obey him and do everything he says. No more crying for me, you are a big girl now, here is where you live now. I was married to your father when I was younger than you. I lived with him in my in- laws home, you are lucky, you have your own home to start and practice everything I taught you. We are just a little distant apart, you can come every day, but here is where you will live now"

Little Tatri sat in a fetal position in the corner of her new home and cried. Her mother and mother-in-law had to coax her several times after Ram went to fetch them.

That ended one night when Ram went home drunk after being teased by his friends of being soft. "Wah happen to you man? You ah man now, which is why you get married. You have to show you Dulahine (bride) that you ah the man. You have to take what is yours; you can't wait for her to come to you. She is young and bashful. You are strong and brave. Drink mo rum and go take what is rightfully yours"

Her young innocent life was changed forever. His rum breath and cruel, inexperience actions caused her terrible pain, blood all over the white sheet, made her even more afraid. She wondered if that was the life of all the young Indian girls, including her mother and sisters? Was that the life she had to live for the rest of her life? She cried herself to sleep every night, she became afraid of her husband.

"Mahy, he is not religious, he do not wash and pray in the morning"

Dhia, a bouncing baby boy was born to Tatri and Ram when Tatri was fifteen years old. Finally Tatri had someone to live for, her son. She became a wonderful mother and a better wife, just like her mother told her, that things would change. Her young baby became a shield from the nightly abuse, but that was short lived. Ram asked his friends how long he had to wait after the baby.

He resumed his husbandry duty in the same abusive manner. He would grab her by the hair and demand her service. Even if she was nursing her baby, she had to stop.

Her mother warned her that if she continue to resist her husband, worry, complain and stress herself, that she will nurse the baby 'bitter milk' "you have to bear it, you have to understand that he is your husband, he has the right to do what he wants" The obedient wife had no choice but to bear it, she had no one to turn to.

Her father reminded her that she was a Brahmin who had to uphold her high standing.

When the beating continued she did not tell, if anyone asked about the bruises, she said nothing. It did no good to complain. She realized that she has to 'bear it'. Her son had growing into a loving little boy. She nursed him as long as she could because she was told that the longer she nursed him, the longer it would take for her to become pregnant again. She stopped nursing him at age tree.

She became pregnant. Happy that she may have a girl and a companion for Dhia.

She sat by the door at nights and told her son stories of her childhood. She instilled in him the importance of religion, and to be proud of his Indian heritage. She would hold his head to her stomach and say "listen to the baby play in my belly, just like you did when you were in it. "What do you want, a brother of sister?" "A brother"

"When you grow up you will have to go to English school, it is the law, but you will never stop speaking Sanskrit. You will become a Pundit just like your Nana"

"No, I will become a policeman and lockup my Papa when he beat you"

Ram came home drunk one night and made his usual drunken demands, Tatri tried to explain to him that her belly was too big for his kind of rough demands. She told him that he could hurt her the baby, she begged him to leave her alone, not to wake little Dhia who was sleeping on the other side of the cloth blind between them.

Her plead fell on drunken ears, Ram beat and kicked her all over the room, she begged him not to hurt her baby. She tried to shield her stomach from his blows but he was too strong, he knocked her out with a punch to her head and took what was his. Some hours later, she came to and found herself lying in a pool of blood, she felt a lump of stillness between her legs, still connected to her as she tried to move. She called out for little Dhia who was screaming behind the blind that's separating them, she said, "Dhia, bhacha, (child) run go bring Agiee -grandmother" Dhia tried to lift the curtain to go to her, but she quickly said "No, no don't come to me, go bring your Agiee"

Her brothers and brother-in-law made a little white pine coffin wrapped in white cotton and took her dead baby girl to Babojohn burial ground.

Her mother took care of her for a few days until she was strong enough to resume her wifely duties.

Everyone knew what had happened, but no one said anything about it. As if it was part of everyday life, they told her to try again for another baby.

She had difficulty trying to explain to Dhia what had happened to his baby brother that was playing in her belly. "It was not a brother, it was a sister, she was too small, and so God took her to play with other small girls who do not have sisters to play with"

Tatri had no friends, as a child she had her sisters to play with, as a wife and mother; she had her husband and son to care for.

She went to the market everyday for fresh fruits and vegetable. Once per week she went with other women of the area to get firewood. That was the extent of her outings.

The Plantation needed the men to work in the fields, if they were to punish all the men who mistreated their wives, who will produce their crops?

"Never use one spoon in two pots, each pot must have its own wood spoon.

Never put a pot spoon to your mouth. There should be no need for you to taste your cooking if you follow everything I teach you. Always cook extra just incase" her ma.

She remembered how quiet her father was, she could not remember a time that she heard his voice raised, he hardly spoke to the female members of the family. If there were anything to be told to them, he had his wife relayed it to them. Only her mother was allowed into his room, she took his meals, made his bed, clean and tidy it. Whenever he went away on retreats out of the district, Tatri would go into his room and look at all the stocks and stocks of books and other religious items he imported from India. She saw how simple yet powerful her father was with his religion. He had bags and bags of starter kits to be given to young Pundits upon graduation. She found among his belongings, Rupees that he collected from Indians, with the hope that if he did not like it in Guiana, he would take his family and return to India. She would sit in her father's room for hours and enjoy the peace that existed in it, especially the smell of all the different incenses. She knew that her father was special and she loved him dearly.

He was proud to be one of the true sons of India; he lived in Guiana just as if he lived in India. His wife told her children that he brought India with him to Guiana.

Tatri needed firewood to cook dinner, she waited for a long time to see if any of the women were going, usually they went to the back-dam on that day and time for safety in numbers and helped each other to put large bundles of wood on their heads.

Several times on her long walk to the woods, she kept looking back, hoping that someone would join her, or she may be lucky to find some of the women already there. No one was there and everything seemed very quiet and lonely.

She quickly gathered some strait, dried wood, tied into a bundle and tried to lift to her head, but because of pain on her hands and arms, caused by trying to block blows from Ram, she was unable to lift the bundle of wood to her head. She became nervous being in the woods alone. She decided to make the bundle small enough for her to manage, but instantly she saw some cows passing on the dam, she knew there must be someone behind them. She ran out of the woods to ask for help, hopefully a woman.

She stood face to face with a big, tall Black man. She quickly covered her face with her hernee and ran back into the woods, shaking with fear.

She had seen Black people before, but never so close. She was trembling with fear. She heard all the bad things those Black men did to Indian women.

They said that Black men use some kind of magic on Indian women and put them into a trance. The Indians called it the 'Blackman Magic'. That's why women went in a group.

Sitting on the bundle of wood, shaking with fear, hoping that the Black man had gone. She looked up and he was standing in front of her. She almost fainted.

She wanted to scream but lost her voice, there was nowhere to run to, he was too close to her. She closed her eyes and thought of her son whom she will never see again.

She felt two strong arms pulled her up to her feet, her round head pad was placed on her head, held in place, then the bundle of wood lifted with the other hand, gently balanced on her head. When she opened her eyes the Black man had vanished.

The Sideling Trench was the Ganges River for most of the East Indians who lived in the Port Maurant sugar plantation. They wash everything and do their religious services.

Beside all the usefulness she had been enjoying from the canal, she found a new desire to go to the water. It happened just after her encounter with the Black man.

Even though she did not see much of his face of heard his voice, the thing that kept her thinking of him was his strength and gentleness, plus the fact that he did not hurt her like she was warned. She had no desire for the Black man. She wanted her husband Ram to have the strength and gentleness she felt in the midst the fear. She blocked the ugliness and fear told to her about 'that kind of people'. She dwelled only on the gentleness of the man who did not harm, but helped her.

The mixture of anger and tenderness displayed by the Black man made her long for her husband to be like him. He already possessed the anger half, if only he could be a little gentle with her and allow her to enjoy her still youthful life.

That evening while she washed in the canal, the moving water became her lover.

She had lost most of her teeth, two more babies, she was a young woman who looked old, her shoulders hunched, her hair had lots of bald spots and her light complexion highlighted all the dark dents and marks.

The only joy in her life is her son Dhia; she hugged and kissed him every moment she had. As he grew older, she had to do so in secret, not allowing anyone to see that she was hugging her son, especially Ram. If he saw them sitting together, he would cuss and call Dhia names and Tatri will surely get some blows

Backraji, Tatri's younger sister got sick and went to her parent's home at Whim.

She had a son name John who was younger than Dhia.

She was afraid to go back to her abusive husband. She was also pregnant.

Kasy always refused to harbor any of his daughters who wish to take refuge at him.

The two sisters decided to do the unthinkable. They decided to get themselves a little room at the Logy and Tatri would get a job as a grass weeder for the plantation.

The two sisters were enjoying their freedom, and the boys went to school and play.

Whenever Tatri went to fetch firewood, water or any need to leave the house, she would carry the two boys for safety. She often wondered who was she more afraid of, Ram or the Black man? She was good at hiding the evidence of Ram's encounters during the months of being away from him. He stacked her and whenever she was alone he attacked her. Many times strangers came to her rescue.

She did not have safety in numbers one day when she was returning from the market. As she turned into the crossroad that led to her logy, she saw Ram standing against the large tamarind tree. She looked around to see if there was anyone around to save her this time but there was no one in sight. She was too close to him; she could not run away, she knew there was nothing she could do to avoid him. As she reached the tree, shaking with fear, praying that Ram will not hurt her.

"You know how much shame you bring on me? Ram said to Tatri as she came face to face with him. " All me friends want fee know wah kind ah man ah me, that me wife and son a live wid her sister and not wid me. You ah sham me to everyone" He grabbed her by one arm and slammed her to the trunk of the tree. Her basket of fruits and vegetable was tossed aside as she dropped to her knees from the impact. He stood her up against the tree and said "Only when a man wife dead, he must live alone, me wife na dead but me live alone and in shame. You know me can kill you right now, right ya and live wid no more shame?" He then punched her in her stomach, knocking out the remaining wind in her, her knees gave out under her and she went down in a sitting position. It seemed even death was not around when she needed it. She wanted to die; there was nowhere she can hide from him anymore.

Ram slammed her head against the tree trunk and she felt the warm liquid seeping down her back. Suddenly she saw Ram being lifted high up in the air, and then dropped to the ground like a bag of rice. Ram cried out in pain as he was once again picked up and thrown against the same tree trunk. Through the blood in her eyes, she saw a hug dark shadow standing over Ram's slump body. "Thank you God," she said.

She felt two strong arms lifted her to her feed, placed the basked on her arms, making sure that she was steady on her feet and led her in the direction of her destination. As she staggered on her way, she felt blood from the back of her head seeping down her sari. Blood from her forehead mixed with tears ran into her open mouth. A mixture of salt and plasma tasted like death, she was sure that if one was to taste death that that was what it tasted like.

She was convinced that even 'Yama' the God of death did not want anything to do with her. As she stumbled on her way to the trench, the one place where she found peace. With all the strength she had left, she said "Sri Hanuman, the mighty God who removes problem and pain from all those who invoke you, I call upon you to remove me from this that I have been forced to live in". Over and over she chanted the same words. She became louder as she walked faster towards the Sideline trench.

Bystanders thought she had 'run mad' as they saw her drenched in blood, from her white hernee and sari down to her food. She was almost in a running stride as she chanted louder and louder "Om Hanuman, God of might, take me to the sea with all your might" She had to hurry because the blood in her throat was clotting.

No one tried to stop her as she set the basket down and walked into the running stream.

After what seemed too long for any human to survive under water for such a long time, two men who were watching her, dived into the water and found her some distant down the trench where the swift currant had taken her. As the men rolled her naked body to get the water our of her lungs, a woman who lived across from the trench, brought a sheet to cover her naked body and a small vial of smelling salt, which when placed to her nose, revived her.

Her mother had to nurse two daughters and take care of the two grandsons.

After all the blood was washed away, the deep gash on her head was exposing her skull. Her mother gathered some cobweb from under the house and stuffed the deep gash then tied her head tight with a piece of white cotton. She then made a large cup of strong sugar-water and gave her daughter to drink. - It was believed that drinking strong sugar-water dissolved clot blood from the body- She had been giving Tatri strong sugar-water for twelve years. Every time she saw the bruises she gave her daughter strong sugar-water and hot-glass suction treatment. She often wondered how much more could her daughter take before she dies like so many women. Even her own daughters, who were dying from their husband's abuse?

While her mother was caring for her, Ram was fighting for his life in the Port Mourant Hospital. His almost lifeless body was picked up by some factory workers and taken to the hospital. When he was asked to explain his condition, he said, "one damn mule cart ran over me" The doctor knew he was lying but did what he had to do.

Both of Ram's feet were shattered from the knees down. His head was cracked open and he lost sight from one eye. His cast feet dangled from slings high in the air. For three months he remained in the hospital, no one; not even his family went to see him.

Kasy hunger to keep connected to Hinduism, both spiritually and mentally, kept him in a higher realm. Even the physical pleasures he shared with his wife had ceased after his last child was conceived some twenty-six years ago.

His religious doctrine and belief earned him the respect of all. People refer to him as the 'High Priest' the 'Marage' the 'Spiritual Leader' the 'Swami' and 'Head Pandit'. He did his best to live up to the honors given to him. He was designated head Pandit for the whole region of Berbice, a hug responsibility that consumed his life and took him away from home for weeks at a time. His wife kept him up to date of events.

He realized his choice for his daughters were not good ones.

He had never hit his wife or ever spoke to her in a harsh manner because his wife had never given him reason to do so. She was an obedient and submissive wife.

"We cannot blame anyone or anything for things that goes wrong in our life. We have to take responsibility for our life and make the best with what we have. No one put me in chains and brought me here, like they did the Negro. I trusted the Colonials and believed in their promises. Unlike the Negro, I came here with my own free will.

Unlike the Negro, I was allowed to keep my name, my religion, my way of dressing, my food and culture and was paid, meager as it was, for my labor. I was angry for many years for being fooled and tricked into coming here, but when I learned what the Negro went through, their names, religion, food and culture taken from them. Even their families were torn apart and sent to different plantations all over the colony without ever seeing each other again. They worked all day without payment. They were flogged and killed for disobeying the masters of the plantations. Forced to eat animal meat, especially the parts that White man did not eat, like the skin, foot and tail and guts.

While the men and women slaves worked in the fields, the old women kept the little children. I heard the children were fed in a long wooden throve like hogs. I realized that at least I have an identity. I am a proud man from India. My name came out of the book, based on the day and time I was born, not out of the mouth of a man who owns me"

Tatri was getting stiff, sitting with her head down, listening to her father.

"I learn to take responsibility for everything I do in my life. If I go to the forest to meditate and an animal attack me, people may say the animal was bad but I say that I invaded his domain. If someone is drunk, he blames the rum and not himself. If a man beats his wife, he blames his wife but not himself. People have to blame someone or something else for their misbehavior. We are Brahmins, the high caste of India; we are the chosen people of God. We have the responsibility to behave in the manner for which we were born. Ram is a Brahmin, he may have slipped into the wrong side and disgraced his caste, but he is still a Brahmin and you must give him that respect at all times". She could feel that he was looking at her when he said, "You should not blame anyone for all that has been going on in your life. From the beginning you rejected your husband. No man wants to be rejected. Something is seriously wrong with you. You cannot keep a child in your belly anymore; they die before they are given a chance to see the sun. You need to do a puja and beg God for forgiveness.

You are welcome to visit your mother and help the same way you have been doing in the past, but you will never be permitted to spend another night in my house.

You are to follow, keep tied to him, your chosen husband, for as long as you are alive"

"Matar, look at me, I am supposed to be twenty-eight years old, but I look older than you, I have no teeth in my mouth, all knocked out by the husband you are sending me back to. I go to sleep shaking with fear of being raped in the worst form. I think of the amount of my blood that has been spilt by the husband whom you and my father choose for me, I wonder what have I done wrong, why are you sending me back to be killed?" She looked at her mother, whipped her eyes with her sari and say

"You should have left me to die when I was born"

She tried over and over in her mind to put a face of the dark shadow that saved her that day under the tamarind tree. Finally she decided that it was God, because she believed that God appears in different shades, sometimes dark, sometimes light.

Dhia seeing his father in the hospital, asked, "Mhy, I couldn't believe my eyes. What kind of cow did all that damage to him?" His mother listened to her son's report and felt sorry for her husband, she said "No, not a cow did that to him, not even a mule cart did that to him, it was the Almighty Hanuman, the Monkey God of Might"

Ram was discharged and Dhia brought him home from the hospital. He looked old and malnourished. His face was full of hair; no one shaved him after the cast was taken off his face. His head and feet were still in bandages. He did not see nor hear from his right side. He seemed so helpless that Tatri and Dhia held him and cried in the privacy of their home.

None of Ram's drinking friends went to see him during his six months in the hospital and recovery at home.

One day as Tatri returned from the market-then and now, people go to the market everyday for fresh stuff. There was no fridge to keep anything- she saw Ram drinking.

He demanded money from Tatri, when she had none to give him; he demanded that Dhia find a job to bring home some money since he can no longer work in the fields. He said, "I had to work in the fields from age of twelve, my son is fourteen years old".

I have been talking to you, Linda, nonstop for four hours. My dogs are restless.

"Why didn't someone help Tatri during the years of abuse? Why didn't she go to the police? Why didn't she just leave and go to another state with her son?" asked Linda.

"You are an American, you are thinking like an American at this present time. Remember I am talking about British Guiana, just after slavery but still ruled by the Colonials. I am talking about the time between 1900s and 1930s. As I told you before, no one got involved in others domestic affairs. There were no police in the sugar estates that would get involve in domestic affairs. There were no states for her to go to. She lived in a Colony divided into villages and sugar plantations. She had never left her village to go visit anyone except her parents. Her sisters lived in other estates but they never visit her. She never had any opportunity to leave there. She was a woman. Women in those days had no rights. Many were killed unnoticed. It was not uncommon for people to live and die in one village without once stepping out of it to another".

I felt good telling my story, most of which was told to me by Tatri. I felt as if I was emptying my brain that was so over cramped with stories just waiting to be oozed out.

The next morning I went through the same routine with Sabrina and my other animals. I reached my 'Fortress of Solitude', 'Oasis of Tranquility',

After I meditated and had a quiet moment for myself, Linda arrived.

She had the widest smile on her face and two bottles of cold water in her hands.

"I could not wait to get here this morning. I thought of Tatri and her dilemma.

Do you know that that kind of abuse is still occurring all over the world? When would abusive men know the value of women? When would they realize women are the keeper of the world, no woman no world. Who will continue the human existence if there were no women? Can you imagine what would become of women if those men could have had babies?"

"Yes, they would have gotten rid of us and all the baby girls they produce, just like so many countries where they are still killing baby girls, as we speak. Women are still struggling to be human beings. Bear in mind that not all men abused women in those days, but most did. Today most women are not being abused, but some are still living with it, even being killed or disabled by their male partner"

"Are you ready to tell me more of your story? I could not wait to get here"

Tatri was cooking dinner when she heard Dhia cried out "No Phy, no knock me no mo, no, no, Phy no knock me, me will go look for work tomorrow"

She ran out to find her son on the ground and Ram hitting him with a coconut branch. She mustered what little strength she had left in her body and pushed Ram so hard, he went sprawling on the ground.

She picked up her son and took him inside the house. She cleaned and dressed his wounds with homemade medicine. She forced him to drink the sugared water and did the hot glass suction. She covered her son with a sheet as he lay on the floor shaking.

She went by the fireside and picked up a cutlass-machete that she used for chipping kindling. Holding it high in the air with both hands, she went running outside to find Ram. She looked around the yard but he was nowhere to be seen. She went to the latrine and slapped the flat side of the cutlass on the door, shouting,

"Come out, come out of there, you no good longarra 'bum', come out and let me put an end to your miserable life. Come out right now, you disgraceful nimakaram-nogood"

Tatri went to the trench, washed and went to her Alter. She sang, prayed and cried in one tune. Her OM echoed like a large church bell. She tried to meditate but she could not, she was too occupied with pre-meditation, all her shackras shutdown.

She placed the cutlass under her sari and sat by the door waiting for her husband.

She said nothing to her mother when she went to wash and clean for her parents. She had been so useful to everyone around her, yet so useless to herself.

Three nights later, she slept on her right side so she could lift the sheet that divided her from her still ailing son, just incase he would need her.

The first blow sent her into darkness. She felt nothing else. Even though she was being beaten to a pulp with a piece of firewood. She felt nothing.

PART II

Two little girls, ages eight and ten sat in a swing on the porch of their home.

Sudith and Mary Jane were waiting for their father, Michael Archibald Hunter, a manager at the sugar plantation in Montserrat, a volcanic British Colony of the Leeward Islands. Every afternoon they waited because Daddy always brought something. Most times it would be sugarcane cut into little bite-size pieces, for his two daughters.

Clarabell stood in the kitchen, looking through the window for the same person whom her daughters are waiting for, Michael Archibald Hunter her 'husband'.

She thought of her mother Mary, a child slave who became free upon emancipation in 1833-38. She imagined her mother working in the plantation, then in the 'big house', where as a free young woman, obeyed Massa request to stayed with him, she did and had three children, Clarabell being the last and only girl, was born in 1858.

Its now 1884. Clarabell was twenty-six years old and had been the 'wife' of Archibald for eleven years. She lived in the Manager's Compound. She was called Ms Hunter. She had the life of luxury and was respected just like any other White Manager's wife. Her children played and attended school with only Whites.

Clarabell was tall, just like her father James. She had long black curly hair and a light shade of brown. From her mother, she inherited the wide cheekbone and slim stature and that African behind.

When her father died, a relative of his came from England, put her family out of their home and sold everything to another English family on the island.

They were left with nothing and nowhere to go. Her mother Mary found lodging in the logy and began to wash and iron cloths of the White Overseers of the sugar plantation.

Clarabell and her brothers were called 'Mulattos', a mixture of Black and White parents. There were Mulattos in all the colonies controlled by Whites. Mattered not if they were Spanish, French, Dutch, English or who ever, once they were White, they spread their sperm all over where there were Negro and Original Indian women.

Some colonies had more mulattos than others, but none were left untainted, thus producing the 'middle class or Colored or yellow-skin'.

There were not many single White women for them, so they quenched their desire with the Negro or Indian women. It was forbidden for a White man to marry such a woman but in some small colonies, blind eyes turned if he lived and had children.

In Archibald and Clarabell case, in Montserrat, it was accepted to live together.

The island was very small and it was more important to produce sugar and other crop for export than it was of whom the White men slept with.

Everyone knew each other in the small island. The locals and foreigners worked and lived together. The only monster they had to be afraid of was the mighty volcano.

Clarabell, a beautiful teenage Mulatto loved to walk by the seaport, especially when the large ship arrived from England. She looked at all the White people as they disembarked. She especially liked to watch the ladies in their pretty cloths, shoes and hats. Their stockings, gloves, ribbons, lace and lipstick were keenly admired.

She was fifteen years old and her job was to take the laundry to the Overseers quarters and collect the few pieces of silver paid to her mother for her hard work.

With the wooden tray balanced on her head, she enjoyed her chore after school, especially when she and her family sat around the fire and she reported to them whomever she saw leaving the island or how many newcomers arrived.

One day as she stood close to the gangway of the just-arrived ship. She saw a tall, very white, handsome young man walking towards her. She gasp for breath when he looked strait at her and said, "You are a very pretty young lady, Miss" as he looked at her with his topaz-blue eyes. No one had ever called her 'Miss' before and no White person had ever looked at her the way he did. She felt something growling in her belly.

She quickly held on to the tray on her head before it fell with all the laundry.

Her brothers worked in the fields and since they were older, they played the father role in her life. They did not think that she should get married so young, instead she should continue to help her mother with the washing and delivery of cloths and continue to go to school and become a school teacher.

She told her mother about the young 'Backra'-White who arrived in the island and what he said to her. Her mother discouraged her by saying, "Don't pay no mind to talk like that my choil. I see too many of them Backra come here, them say dat them love de island women, them live wid dem, have children wid them and when dee time come faa dem to go back to dem country, they lef dem gal and dem half-breed picknie. Do you think I gon allow you to go through wha me bin through?

Yes, them White man like Mulattos like you, over dem black skin gals, but always memba it tak one Black woman to make a Mulatto, you still Black in dem eye.

It had been eleven years since Mary made that long speech to her daughter. Clarabell moved in with Archibald. She oiled the wheels of opportunity with her good looks and charm. She had her mother retired and moved into the Overseer's compound with her. She made her mother comfortable by giving her own quarters on the ground floor of the 'big' White House that she shared with Archibald. She used her charm and womanpower to have Archibald helped her two brothers, "Take them out of the fields and get them better jobs. After all, they are 'Colored'. They have half White blood just like me. They are my educated brothers".

Archibald got William a job at the storage depot and Milton supervisor at the wharf.

Clarabell often wondered what her life would have been had she not defied her mother and accepted Archibald's love. She knew he loved her and she also knew that she loved him from the moment she saw him walked off the ship's ramp twelve years ago white as an egg. Now he was not much lighter than she was, with his tropical suntan and maybe his close association to her, rub off some of her color onto him.

She knew that he loved her, he told her that all the time. He took her everywhere, to church, social events and the way he looked at her as he walked behind her with his eyes full of desire, she knew that she loved him for loving her.

He sat on the wooden bench in her mother's one room logy, express his love for her.

Clarabell was a virgin when she moved into his home on the hill, where only Whites lived. She believed that Archibald too was a virgin.

She looked at her two daughters on the porch and said a prayer in silence.

She never stopped thanking God for her Archibald, the father of her two beautiful girls.

They have had a good life from the time they were born. Nannies to take care of them. They went to the English school and attended all occasions that only Whites attended.

She never forgot her roots; she had her mother as a constant reminder of who she was. She and Archibald encouraged the children to play with all races of the island.

Her brothers and servants brought their children to play in the large, manicure yard.

After dinner one evening, Clarabell knew something was wrong. She poured some brandy and handed it Archibald. They went out on the on the porch and sat in silence. She put her arm around his neck, played with his red hair then said, "What's the matter my darling? You seem to be worried about something.

Are you having one of those breathing attack? I will get the compress for your chest"

Archibald knew that he had to break the news to the woman he fell in love the first day he stepped onto the island, his love, his companion, and best friend, the woman who gave him his two beautiful daughters, but how?

"No, no, I do not have a headache. My breathing is fine, but I do have something to discuss with you. I was summoned to the Head Office this afternoon and was informed that I am being transferred to British Guiana, one of the largest British colonies, the only English speaking country in South America"

Clarabell sat quietly and waited to hear more from her Archie, as she alone called him. Her mind was racing, 'Am I being my mother's daughter? Am I going to be threading in my mother's footsteps? Would I be as strong as she was when my father died? What would I do? What could I do? [Archie insisted that she finish school while they lived together] I would never have another man even though I am still a young woman. I could never love anyone but my Archie" she looked into his teary blue eyes.

As if he was reading her thoughts, he quickly said, "You do not have to worry, you and the girls are going with me. That was the only reason I accepted the assignment. I will never leave you and my daughters. Never as long as I live"

"Who will tell the girls? How are we going to explain to them that they have to leave their family and friends here to go somewhere behind God's back where I never heard of before? What am I going to do with my mother?" She began to cry.

"I will tell the girls on Sunday. As for your mother, I will make arrangement for her to receive the compensation that she is entitled to for being a child slave and a pension for her services after slavery. She can either move in with one of your brothers or I will get her a little cottage of her own"

Archibald had never seen his Clara cried before. He saw that she and his children were well taken care of. He used every privilege given to him as an Overseer, A large house on the hill, servants to care for the children, horse-drawn carriage with driver, and supplies of food and clothes from England. She had no need to cry.

In his eyes Clarabell was the most beautiful woman in the island. He loved to watch the envied eyes of his fellow Overseers whenever they attended a ball or important occasions. She wore her hair with a strait part in the middle of her head and huge neat bun at the back. Only in the privacy of her home did she let her hair loose to fall down her back, or when her daughters wanted to practice their hairdressing skills.

He bought her beautiful pearls and jewelry from England. All her clothes and hats were specially ordered from the import stores. She looked elegant in whatever she wore. She was urbane to everyone. She carried her tall, slender body with pride and confidence. She had a well-defined heinie that moved in a rhythm as she walked.

"I was told that we would be given the same conditions that we have here. We can take some of our personal things but we have to leave most of the large furnishing for the person who will be replace me here"

"What will happen to all the people who work for us? They have been with us for as long as we have been together, what will become of them?"

"I will arrange for them to remain with the new Overseer, with good references"

"How soon do we leave?

"We have two months until the next ship pass through here. That should give us enough time to get accustom to the fact that we will be leaving"

"No time is enough for me to accept the fact that I will be leaving my home and family to go and live somewhere else. I have never left this island, not even in a fishing boat to the neighboring islands around here. I do not know what other people in other country look like. What language dem talk? Would daa be kind to us?"

"All British Colonies are the same, with the same races of people and they all speak English as the main language. I know it would be your first trip out of your homeland and my second. I felt the same way when I left Scotland to come here.

I found happiness here with you. We are just going to a bigger, and better Colony"

Mary, Clarabell's mother went berserk when she was told.

She placed the kroshae needle on the table. Placed her hands on her head and began to wale in a singsong manner. "My child, my child, my only daughter, how can you go way from here to Timbuktu where you no know noting bout? Me and you brothers go never see you and me grandpicknie dem ever again. Oh God, wah dis falling pun tap me head? Oh God, oh God, me picknie ah go way lef me"

"Never forget who you are, be kind to everyone and member everything wa me teach you. If you gon have more picknie, drink only milk, no coffee, chocolate or black tea, them will make the babies dark. Me never drink nothing dark when me was pregnant wid de three ayou and look at you now, wid nice golden skin color.

Once a Black gal come out of the field to enter Masa's bedroom, you should never go back to the field again, less he ded or you no kno how to mek em appy. You been doing very well so far, you got that Backra man all wrap up round you lil finger.

Keep doing wa you doing wid plenty love and kindness, me choil. No forget respect"

Montserrat seemed smaller and smaller as the large steamed ship sailed away from it. Clarabell kept her tear soaked eyes on her mother and brothers who were waving goodbye to them, until she could see them no more.

Archibald did his best to comfort her. He assured her that nothing will change, that he would always take care of her and their daughters.

"Have I ever given you any reason to be unhappy?"

"No Archie, I am not unhappy being with you, I just feel sad leaving me family"

"I had to leave mine too, but I found you and now I have my own family.

Can you find it in your heart to look at our two daughters and I as the family that you will now start a new life with? I am not asking you to forget your mother and brothers"

The journey seemed endless. Prejudice and seasickness introduced themselves.

The first evening of their trip, in the ship's dining room, Archibald and his two daughters were accepted but Clarabell was refused entry. She was told that she had to stay and eat in a cabin below deck with Chinese and Indians, or she could eat in the kitchen with the Negroes.

Archibald protested to the highest authority, the captain, who said,

"That is the rule Mr. Hunter, as the captain of this ship, I have to uphold the rules"

Archibald refused eat in the dining room without Clarabell, he arranged for their meals to be served in their cabin so that they can eat together as they always did.

The captain soon changed that. He said to Archibald

"When you boarded this ship I did not recognize that you brought a Negro winch

into my ship. Now that I am aware of this fact, I have no choice but to put her in the lower cabin below deck with her own kind"

"In that case, we will go below deck with her" Archie told the captain,

They slept on bunks among the non-White. Indians, Chinese and Negro.

Seasickness kept Clarabell and the children in bed most of the first week.

They came out whenever the ship stopped for two days to let off and take in passengers and cargo. They stopped in Dominica, then St Vincent, Granada and Trinidad.

Clarabell was already in a state of disbelief of the way she was treated coupled with the seasickness and the endless trip, she became very unhappy and asked Archibald, "Please Archie, could we just go back to Montserrat? We could come out at one of the ports and take another ship back to our home"

"It is not that simple, I am transferred to another position. My place in Montserrat is already filled. There is no job there for me to go back to"

She cried most of the way and he comforted her all the way, "Things will be different when we reach Guiana, you will see. All this will be like a bad dream"

In the wee hours of the morning the ship entered the mouth of the Demerara River, the entrance to British Guiana. As the ship cruised into the channel, the sun was raising. Archibald stepped out of his hole to enjoy the fresh land breeze and waved back to the fishermen in their small fishing boats.

"Clara my dear, we have to be getting ready, I can almost see the dock. You should join me on the deck to see your new home, it looks beautiful from here." Said Archibald, trying to coax her out of her depressing state.

As the ship moored at the Demerara Wharf, Archibald was surprised to see so many people so early in the morning busy in and out of the many ships that lined the wharf. In Montstraat only one ship can moor at the small wharf. He told himself that this is really a large country with lots of export, because of all the large ships that lined both side of the river.

He did not see when the short, stocky White man walked up to him and said,

"Hunter, Archibald Hunter?"

"Yes sir, I am Archibald Hunter"

"Welcome to British Guiana old-chap. How was the trip?"

"It was very unpleasant but I will not talk about that now. What did you say your name was?"

"R. Brown, I am the Chief of Affairs in Demerara. Its my duty to have you settled into your assigned plantation"

At that moment Sudith and Mary Jane came running to Archibald shouting, "Daddy, Daddy, there you are, we were looking for you everywhere."

"This is Mr. Brown, say hello then go get your Mommy to meet him, he is here to help us settle into our new home."

"You have two lovely daughters, any sons?"

"No, but I hope to have many more, in this vast country."

As the two men spoke, Clarabell appeared with her two daughters.

Mr. Brown looked at her and his whole demeanor changed. He was speechless. Archibald thought he was just like so many who are left spellbound with her beauty.

"Clara this is Mr. Brown, he is here to meet us"

"Howdy Sir" said Clarabell as she stretched her hand out to him but Mr. B. did not take it, instead he said in a firm manner, "Hunter,

I need to talk to you in private, lets go to the captain office, follow me, I will lead the way."

Clarabell took her two daughters and went back down into the hole. She sat on the edge of the bunk and began to tremble. She knew something wasn't right. She saw the same look on Mr. Brown's face as of the ship captain's when he refused her service.

"Have you gone mad Hunter?" asked Brown who had turned red as a cherry.

"Do you know what you have done bringing a Colored woman and children on your new assignment? The message I received said that you, your wife and two children were coming. I had no idea that you are coming here with a Colored woman.

Your daughters can pass as us, without any question, but not her. Do you know that this is not allowed in this part of the world and it is punishable by law? This is British Guiana old man. The King and members of the Royal family visit this colony

What are you going to do? Take your Colored concubine to the banquets and balls or official events, the Mess hall, the golf course and other places for Whites only?"

"I did it in Montserrat, Clarabell and I have been living together for over twelve years, no White man had never treated her the way you and the captain of this ship did. She is my companion and the mother of my children, if she is not welcome here then I will return to where it is alright to live in peace"

"Wakeup man, you lived too long among the Negroes, now you think you are one of them. You are a White man, start behaving like one and do not disgrace my race. I have no problem sleeping with them. I am guilty of that fact myself, but in their hut is where it begins and ends. I do not take them anywhere or own their children. You have to learn old chap" Archibald looked blank, trying to hold his composure, trying to breath.

"I will refuse this assignment and return to Montserrat, I am sorry for all the inconvenience I have caused you and all the White people but I cannot begin to think of what you are trying to do to us. If it is alright with you, I would like to ask you to please make all the arrangements for us to return to Montserrat"

"The only thing I can arrange for you is to have you thrown out of this ship, into the streets of Georgetown, where some of your kind are selling magazines and newspapers to people like me. Yes there are some just like you, who forget themselves and are now living like peasants, selling whatever they can on the street. One is a cleaner at my church. Another is selling vegetable in the market with his Amerindian woman"

"I will do anything as long as I am with my family"

"You are a fool man, the law here will not allow it because she and her children are foreigners. I will do everything in my power to see to it that you life becomes unbearable. There is enough of your kind disgracing the White race with their local Darkies. Be it Kaffaa – Negro, Collie – East Indian, Buck – Amerindian or whatever color, other than their own race.

They get away with it because the women are local. Your woman is a foreigner, thus will be sent her back to her place of birth. As for you, you could stay here and clean the streets, or take up your assigned position at the plantation"

Archie was giddy, he could not think straight. Everything was coming down on him like rocks falling from above. He had to think, think quickly. He asked

"Then what do you suggest I do for the sake of Clarabel and my two daughters?"

"I have to think for a while, I was not expecting to face this kind of calamity.

Now I have to work on something in a hurry"

Archibald had his first taste of reality, the reality of being different from his woman and children. He did not know what to do or say as his brain shifted from side to side like the waves of the Demerara River hitting against the ship.

"The best and only solution I can come up with right now is, I will send you to Ifluct Sugar Plantation on the West Bank of Demerara where we recently lost an Overseer. I am in the process of finding someone to replace him, you will fit in perfectly"

"At this Ifluct, Clarabell and the girls will come with me?" asked Archibald anxiously yet breathlessly.

"No man, there will not be anything like that here, when will you put it into that skull of yours that here and now is where it ends for you and your Colored family?"

"What will become of my family?" Archibald was becoming sick, his knees were hitting against each other and his hands were wet. He was having difficulty breathing.

"I will send her to Port Mourant, the plantation that you were originally assigned to.

They will be given a cottage and a weekly allowance. It is the best I could think of in such a short time. Or I can arrange for them to go back to where they come from"

Archibald placed his head into his hands and began to sob. It was at that moment little Sudith, who was listening to everything through the ajar door, ran back to their cabin and told her mother what was being told to her father.

(Years later Sudith said that Mr. Brown was the meanest, ugliest White man ever lived)

If Clarabell was upset or worried, she showed no emotion, as if she was prepared for whatever was dealt to her. After her first experience in the ship's dining room, she expected anything to happen. She got up and opened one of the trunks, she took out a large family portrait that they had had painted just before they left. She began to separate Archie's belongings, especially the compress made by her mother for Archie whenever he gets an attack of shortness of breath. He was Asthmatic.

She knew she would be strong for him, with whatever decision made for their future.

"How did my Archie age so much in a matter three hours?" Clarabell asked herself as she reached out her arms and took him into them. Archibald was shaking and she put him to sit on the bed and held his head against her stomach. She rubbed his back and chest with the homemade medicine of camphor and coconut oil.

Her main concern was his health. At times he suffered with shortness of breath. When that happened she had him sit up strait and rubbed his chest with the mixture.

"We are going to be separated for a short while" he managed to say before he grabbed her slender waist and pulled her closer to him.

Their two daughters joined them and the whole family cried without understanding what was happening to them.

"I will be sent to a place call Ifluct at one end of the country and you and the girls will be sent to Port Mourant on the Eastern end. It will be for a short while.

As soon as I can make contact with the higher authority, we will be together again"

"But Daddy, we have never been apart in my whole life, who will be my Daddy while we are separated?" Asked Sudith, crying and holding on to Mary Jane.

"Daddy will join us shortly, in his absence I will be both Mommy and Daddy.

You two will have to help me because I will miss him just like you will.

It will not be too long, Daddy shall be with us soon" Clarabell holding on to her family.

Archibald agreed to leave the ship in the night when his daughters were asleep.

"That's alright, I will arrange for you to be taken to the Guess House until arrangements are made for you to travel to Iflugt. I am glad that you have seen the sense in this terrible, unruly situation. There will be no life here for you otherwise"

"You promised that you would make all arrangements for my family comfort?"

"Yes, yes old chap, the Colored folks will stay on in this ship. In two days it will set sail for Berbice. I have enough time to send orders to the Port Mourant management for them to have accommodation ready for them.

Do not worry old chap, this is a promise I will keep" he looked at the two little girls who had joined their father crying, he said.

"You can take the girls with you, no one will know who their mother is and I will never tell. Their mother, on the other hand, is a young, beautiful woman, she will have no trouble finding a man her own kind and have more children of her kind"

When the horse and carriage arrived for Archibald, he was wrapped in the arms of his Clarabell, just like they did from the day she moved into his home.

He kissed his daughters goodnight earlier and they were asleep. He was doing with his lover what lovers do when they have to part. They were crying and hoping that they will see each other sooner than Mr. B thinks.

"I am a Colored, and as one, I am aware of whom I am. Even though I have never experienced any racism since my father died, does not mean that I do not know what it is. I accepted the fact that you could never marry me. That did not stop me from loving you. No one can stop us from loving each other, not even this Mr. B would"

"Keep all my things, I will join you as soon as I can. I want my daughters to know that I will be with them soon"

When the deck clerk knocked on the door, Clarabell's heart sank and she felt Archie's heart pounding against her chest. With tears in his eyes, he said

"Do not cry my darling, I will do everything I can to join you and the girls soon"

Minutes later, Clarabell had to push him out of the door. Walking arms in arms with him all the way out of the ship. Promising him that she will take good care of their daughters and will wait for him as long as she lives.

She remembered watching him walked towards her twelve years ago, her young eyes were full of sparkles. Now, after what seems like a lifetime of love and happiness, she was watching him walking away from her. Her eyes were swollen and clouded with tears. She wondered if another ship would bring him back to her once more.

She knew that her love for him exceeded her need of him at that moment.

'Unlike my mother who was left with nothing but her three half-breed children, I have his love no matter where they send him. I have five large trunks in this ship that Archie instructed them to give to me. He took nothing but a small grip with a few things to keep him until he comes to join us. I know he will be waiting for us when we get where we are going, I know he will be waiting for us' Clarabell's thoughts as the ship sailed along the coast of Demerara and then into Berbice river.

The ship's horn was so loud it woke everyone and everything in its surroundings. Clarabell gather her daughters and took them to the rails of the ship for them to see the port. "Will Daddy be there to meet us? It has been four days since we last saw him. I miss him very much Mommy". Cried Mary Jane.

Clarabell held her daughters and prayed silently for her Archie to be there to meet them.

She imagined his long red hair flying in the wind and his blue eyes telling them how much he missed them, and they would live happily ever after.

"You and the children come with me, the porter will get your trunks," said the White man who walked up to her through the crowd of people working their way out of the ship. *Mr. B did a good job describing her, or maybe because she was the only Colored woman in sight, this man knew who she was,* thought Clarabell as she obeyed the stranger's command, still hoping that Archie was at the port waiting for them.

The stranger took them to a horse and carriage with a Negro man standing next to it. "He will take you to Port Mourant Sugar Estate, he knows which cottage you will be occupying at Portuguese Quarter. Your belongings will follow in a mule cart".

He never told her his name or the name of the carriage driver, but in the eighteen miles trip from New Amsterdam to Port Mourant, she had an ear full of what to expect and how to survive, from Sam the driver, who became their lifelong friend.

Portuguese went to Guiana to trade. They settled in an area in the sugar plantation called Portuguese Quarter.

There were little cottages with latrine in a fenced yard. Palm trees adorn the cottages.

Clarebell was given one such cottage. It had two small bedrooms, a small living room/dinning room and a little kitchen with a wood burning stove. A far cry from Montstraat, but a high standard for some locals who live in logies and grass huts.

It was the children whom she had to explain the fall from one way of life to the other. She taught them to take care of what they had and try to understand that until their father came, they will have to be thankful for what they had.

She received her first brown envelope with five shillings from the sugar plantation office. An Overseer delivered it, he was young and much more polite to her. He asked for the names and date of birth of her daughters, made a note of it then he said,

"You are welcome to shop at the English Store for whatever supplies you need. Your children will be enrolled in the English School. You will have to provide their names and age when you take them. It's a short walk over the bridge.

They will be welcome at every occasion given for the Managers, Overseers and their family. The school will inform them of such events.

I wish you a pleasant stay in this Colony and if there is anything we can do for the children, just let us know. They are welcome to attend the English Church"

After Sam, he was the kindest of the men she had met so far.

Her days were long and her nights were endless.

The questions from the children about their father, of which she had no answer, made it harder. Every day she told herself 'He will be here today or tomorrow'.

She made the bed just like it used to be; his side table had his pipe and tobacco, his pajamas and robe on the cloth-horse, his slippers on the floor. A place was set on the head of the dinning table. His kilt and bagpipe was in display for all to see.

His shaving cup and brush were on the washstand as well as his silver head razor.

She waited and waited for the only love of her life to come to her.

She was twenty-six years old, how old she will be before she sees her love again?

Months turned in years, Clarabell tried in every way possible to find Archie.

She asked the managers if they would send a letter to him, which they refused.

She had the children ask their friends at school to ask their fathers to help them find their father. She tried to post letters to him but never knew if he got them.

She became a seamstress. She made dresses for everyone who wanted her service, especially the White women. She kroshaed beautiful collars, sleeves, gloves and hats. Her business grew and so were her daughters.

Remember Sam? He remained her friend and helped wherever a man was needed. He brought firewood and hard-to-find foodstuff. He always had an ear out for news of Archibald. He took the girls to the races and cricket games. He was a good friend and the only person Clarabell trusted in the strange land that was now her home.

She kept in touch with her family in Monstaarat through letters. Her brother William did most of the writing. He kept her up to date with the happenings of her mother and the other family. He wrote,

"How are the girls and Archiebald? You take and give them all our love.

Mama refused the cottage given to her on George Street. She preferred to move in with my family and me. Talking about family, mine has grown by one more".

She wrote back, "We are all doing well and getting older" She never told her family what had happened and forbid her daughters to do so. "It will kill your Nana if she knows that they took your Daddy away from us"

Sudith and Mary Jane grew into beautiful young ladies. They did very well at school. Sudith played the piano and Mary Jane blew the bagpipe. They were members of the school band and played at concerts. They were popular with the young people of all races. They were involved in Plantation Youth Program where Sudith taught other children the piano and Mary Jane taught the young English men the bagpipe. She was very proud of herself for learning all the Scottish tunes from her Daddy.

They were often asked of the whereabouts of their father. They made up stories that he was in England and would soon join them. One day Sudith got very angry and tired of making up stories of her father's absence, she screamed out to the whole class,

"Do not ask me where is my Daddy, go home and ask your Daddy where is Michael Archibald Hunter. Remember that name, Michael

Archibald Hunter, he is my Daddy and they took him away". She ran out of the classroom all the way home crying.

Clarabell altered her beautiful gowns, dresses, petticoats and shoals to fit her daughters; she had no need for them anymore.

She never accepted invitations to go out even though there were many.

Her daughters wore them to balls, banquets, church, concerts and social events.

She shared her jewelry and pearls between them. She saw what she once looked like.

She saw what Archie saw. She wished he could see his daughters now

She wondered if there are some young men who would look at them the way Archie looked at her? Would they love them the way he did her?

Many men of different races asked Clarabell for her hand in marriage or her companionship. The Chinese man at the 'foods shop' asked her to move in with him. The Portuguese called her 'ouro preto' Black Gold. Mr. DeSilver, a Portuguese 'rum shop' owner, sent her Meadera wine and she sent him fruitcake for Christmas.

The Englishman, who brought her allowance, lingered as long as she would allow him. He drank tea from her silver tea set and comment on how lucky she was to have such fine English things in her home.

That was when she would politely hand him his hat, cane and opened her door.

The aristocrats called her Miss Hunter. The locals refer to her as 'the Mulatto with the two Backra picknee'.

She carried herself in the manner for which she was respected.

With her tall, slender body, she moved with such poise that everyone on the street took notice. Some saw beyond her beauty, a sad, lonely beautiful woman who no one knew anything about. She was a sad stranger.

Sudith finished school at sixteen and began giving piano lessons to whomever could pay for her service. Most of her students were children of the Managers and Overseers of the Plantation. She also gave free lessons to children who were poor.

Mary-Jane, two years later, finished school and began working with her mother, who was well established in the business of making clothes, hats, gloves, even shirts and trousers for boys. There was a big demand for their elegant embroidery work.

In those days, there was no high school. After completing sixth standard in school, there were only trade schools for boys, such as carpentry, goldsmith, sugar boiling and so on. For the girls, dressmaking, cooking classes, housekeeping classes and so on. Teachers and nurses came from Europe. All law enforcement officials were from Europe.

Clarabell had students too. Her little living room had two sewing machines.

She teaches her young students to sew. She produced many good seamstresses.

Kroshae was more difficult. One had to be able to read to follow the patterns in the books. Mary-Jane became versed with it. She made beautiful centerpieces, tablecloths, socks, and gloves, alter cover for the church, collars for dresses and handkerchiefs.

The three women from Monstraart were growing older, still waiting for Archie/Daddy. The years did not change their hope and dreams for him.

Clarabell attended the Rose Hall Scotch Church and became very active in its affairs. The Congregation was mixed. Christians of all races attended and participated. Her daughters however, attended the English Church where only Whites attended.

In those days and even now, the church and school were of the same denomination and in the same property so, if one attended the school, he/she will attend the same church.

Clarabell realizing that her daughters may have a better chance of passing as White because of their light skin color and soft blond hair. She did her best to keep a distance from their public life. She did not want their White friends to see her low decent. Heartbreaking as it was, she knew that if she didn't, it would surely affect their lives and any chance of them marrying a White man from school or church.

Men at church admired and respected her. They often asked her out for a walk or to a cricket game, to the races or to a banquet, to a dance or vaudeville show but she was never interested in going out with anyone. She was waiting for her Archie.

Sam said to Clarabell one evening, "There is a gentleman wanting to make your acquaintance" Sam tried his best to speak proper English when speaking to her.

"He is a decan at your church. He said he been watching you for years but you never watch back. He ask me to ask if you will have tea with him after church?"

"Who is this person you are speaking of?" she asked, looking at Sam shyly.

"His name is Mr. Malcom Alexander. He is widower looking for a wife"

"So, he is looking for a wife? Or someone to take care of his children?"

"No, no, his mother and sisters take care of his children. He wants a wife"

"I already have a husband, his name is Archie, he will join us soon, you will see"

"I have been looking, along with you, for years for this Archie to come. Me wonder if there is really an Archie, or you jest make it up to keep men away?" Sam was pushing his luck, but he promised Mr. Alexander that he would do whatever he could to arrange a date for him. He continued with a softer tone.

"You are a young and beautiful woman. How long are you going to wait for the Backra to come to you? You are living in the wrong world lady, that kind ah ting na happen haa. You can wait til Jesus comes back, but dat Backra man not coming here to you in dis country. All me life, me never see one Backra man live wid one Colored woman, More so to marry her. Dat na happen in dis country. Not in British Guiana.

How long you go keep dis up?"

"As long as I have to," she answered angrily.

In 1891 Clarabell married Malcom Alexander.

After waiting for Archie for 7 years. She was 33 years old, still young and beautiful.

Malcolm was a 43 years old widower. A hug Negro man surely could be from the Mandingo tribe. He was very dark and very handsome. Lots of parents wanted him for their daughters. He was a hard workingman, devoted to his four young children.

The first time he saw Clarabell in church seven years before, he told his mother "You can stop telling me about getting married again, I found the lady that I will one day make my wife. She is some lady, Mama" it was a long wait, but he succeeded.

Clarabell moved to her husband's home at Rose Hall Village, Middle Dam.

In 1895 she gave birth to a son name Charles Wycliff Alexander.

Mary Jane was fifteen years old. No White knight came on his horse for her.

The moneyed class was the White who sent the young men to study in England.

If they ever returned to Guiana, they came with their English wives or they notified all the waiting maidens that they got married 'back home'.

She knew that she was not going to wait for one of them to come back for her. Unlike her sister, she was more adaptable. She had Negro and Indian friends. She made herself comfortable with whom ever was friendly with her.

It was one of her Negro friend, Hyacinth, who invited her to the Aklyne Scotch's Church Tea and Bazaar.

Her father was Scottish and she wanted to see a Scotch church and if there were Scottish people there, maybe someone would look like her Daddy.

She looked for him in every tall, handsome, Scottish gentleman she saw.

It was at that bazaar in 1891 she met Egbert Barnaby Alexander again.

He was the twenty- years old nephew of her stepfather whom she had met once before at her mother's wedding.

He was very much a Negro like his uncle Malcolm, tall, dark, gentle and handsome.

He was bubbling with excitement when she agreed to put her white-gloved hand on his arm as he proudly walked her around the festivity.

They sat next to each other for tea and cake. She made mental notes of his manners and etiquette. He never left her side and later, he offered to take her and her Hyacinth home in his donkey cart.

Egbert had asked his uncle Malcom to arrange a meeting with Clarabell for him to ask permission to court Mary-Jane. When he met her at the bazaar and saw that she did not reject him, he felt much hopeful that her mother would not object.

1892 Mary Jane Hunter married Egbert Barnaby Alexander.

She moved to his parent's two-room thatch house at Lancaster Village where she gave birth to ten children.

Sudith remained in the cottage with all her father's belongings. She never married nor had any children. She was Godmother for all of Mary Jane's children.

She earned her living from teaching music.

Egbert thought 'Mary-Jane' was too long a name for his wife. He called her Janey and everyone follow suit, even her mother and sister liked it.

When Janey became pregnant and complained on the length of time, Egbert warned her that there would be many such, because his mother had thirteen.

"I am not your mother, I can hardly wait to have this one come out. Don't you tell me about having any more after this one" holding her large stomach.

Mary-Jane Alexander was born in 1893, named after her grandmother, Nana.
William Benjamin Alexander was born in 1895, named after her uncle.
Milton Clarence Alexander was born in 1901, named after her other uncle.
Ulrick Wycliff Miller Alexander was born in 1904, named after his brother.
Michael Archibald Hunter Alexander was born in 1906, named after her father.
Clarabell Inez Viola Alexander was born in 1909, named after her mother.
James Nathaniel Alexander was born in 1911, named after her grandfather
Harriett Eldora Alexander was born in 1913, named after his mother
Winifred Anita Alexander was born in 1915, named after his Grandma.
Bertram Barnaby Alexander was born in 1921, named after his grandfather.

Egbert's parent names were Parnell Albert and Anita Harriett Alexander.
Mary Jane's parent names were Michael Archibald Hunter and Clarabell 'Hunter'

{No one seems to know or remember what was Clarabell's maiden name}
Egbert had twelve siblings. They were Noble, Albert, Panell, Ulrick, Beatrice, Mrs. Hawker, Mrs. Profit, Mrs. Barry, Mrs. Tendell, Mrs. Bennett, Mrs. Henry and May-May. Two died in infancy.
When the sisters got married, they were called 'Mistress.'
Egbert, being the youngest, had to address his older siblings as Brother/ Mistress…

Sudith visited her sister at Lancaster every Saturday afternoon, when her last student left. She never took students after midday on Saturday and never on Sunday. That time was for her sister and her Godchildren at Lancaster.

They would cook, bake and sit around reminiscing old times, how things turned out.

"Do you remember anything about Monstaarat? " asked Sudith.

"Yes, of course, I remember Nana Mary, Uncle Willy and Uncle Milton.

In order for me not to forget them through the years, I keep the picture in my heart of the three of them waving goodbye to us in the big boat. I look at the picture in my mind often enough that I will never forget them. I named my children after them.

"The people here in Guiana can't make sugar-cake like Nana Mary did"

"The people here can't cook anything like Nana Mary did, she was the best cook"

"Is that why your children think that you are the best cook?

"All children think their mother is the best cook. The first food they ever ate was from their mother. Why you think grown people still go to mama for her cooking?

I watch how Dada, his brother and sisters enjoy Nana Harriett's cooking.

I learn everyday from her how to be a good mother and a good cook".

"You are right, I do not think anyone can cook or bake or sow like our Mommy"

"Do you think of Daddy often?

"Every day of my life. More so now, that I have to be scolding my own Archie all the time. I wonder if Daddy was as mischievous as he is. Sometimes I tell Archie that my father was a good man and that he has to live up to his grandfather's name"

"What you think Daddy would have said about you marrying a Black man and having so many children?"

"I think he would have given me his blessing, love Egbert and everyone of his grandchildren. In my heart, after all these years, I still feel that I will see him again".

Egbert [Dada] was a good son to his mother, a good husband to his wife and a wonderful father to his ten children. His father Parnel Albert Alexander died soon after he got married. His mother lived with him and his wife in their two rooms. She was present at the delivery of all their children. Janey adopted most of her mother-in-law's strict tradition and passed it on to her own children and grandchildren.

He became a foreman of Port Mourant Sugar Plantation punt house. He was a welder

He earned enough money to build a large wooden two-story house to replace the two-room mud hut with thatch roof, the home of his parents and thirteen children. Since he was the last child, he stayed with his parents after the others got married and moved away from the home but not from the village.

The boys built their homes one behind the other on the same land at Lancaster..

The girls however, moved to their husband's family land or villages.

His wife never complained of the small hut that she was brought into. A far cry from the wooden cottage she shared with her mother and sister.

She humbled herself, respected his mother and adopted his culture. His mother Harriett, loved Janey from the start, her only reservation was 'if the Backra girl really love her son'. With keen eyes, she watched and saw two people truly in love. She became the second mother to her daughter-in-law.

She was in the chamber to receive every one of her grandchildren delivered by Janey. They called her Nana Harriett. Nana means Grandmother

The loving relationship between Harriett and Janey made Dada a very happy and thankful man, for the mother and wife God had blessed him with.

He told his sons to marry girls who respect their mother and their family. He said

"I am a happy man because my mother and my wife are happy with each other".

My friend Linda would not allow me to take a long breath.

Even when we go out to lunch or dinner, she sat next to me to ask questions from her notebook. Her husband would say "Can't it wait for the beach tomorrow?"

Melinda Jordan was Janey's childhood friend. They attended school together.

Melinda was Portuguese; of course she lived in Portuguese Quarter. She was White and was waiting for a White prince to come or even a Portuguese merchant.

In 1892, Janey asked her to be her bride's maid at her wedding.

After all she was her best friend for all the years she had been in the country.

Melinda said, "No, no, not atoll would I be a part of such a mistake. I told you before that you are making a fool of yourself and a fool of that poor Negro boy.

Why do you want to do that? Look at you and look at him, do you see a matching pair?

I see a miss-match. Change your mind while you still have one left"

After some years and some children later, Janey met her childhood friend again.

"Every time I see you, either you have a big belly or a lil picknee sitting on your hip. When do you sleep? In that little mud hut with his mother present, how the two of you manage to do what you do to be pregnant every time I see you?"

"Do you know that every time I see you, I try my best to avoid you because I do not wish to hear your low class remarks? I thought that after so many years, you might have changed your thinking and become a more understanding person"

"Change, what you mean change? You are the one who changed. You were just one step away from having pure White children. It takes three generations to change a race. You already have two, your mother half White and you, three quarter White. If you had marry a White man, or a Portuguese, your children would have been pure White".

"You mean that I should have been waiting like you and Sudith are?

Can't you see that while you are waiting, I am living? I am very happy. I love my husband. He never called me a bad name. I saw what the White man did to my mother and father. I would rather be loved than be scorned. You should take some time and do the 'eye to eye' thing with people who are different from you.

You would see that they are not so different after all. You might even find love"

When the 'big house' was finished building, Egbert saw to it that he furnished it with the finest furniture that he could buy. He bought a piano for his wife and children. He bought fine silver and crystal.

In the kitchen was a new wood burning stove and good quality iron pots.

In the hallway between the dining room and the kitchen, were the shower and 'dry latrine' meaning that one had to fetch up water to bath and fetch down the slap can to empty in the outhouse or latrine.

Egbert tried his best to give his wife some of the things that she was accustomed. His wife often told him that she was happy with him even if they live in a turtle shell. She told him that she enjoyed their old two-room house, especially when they sneaked out when everyone was asleep, to have romantic, moonlight rendezvous.

At the opening of the 'big house' Janey invited her old friend Melinda.

Hoping that she would see that her husband Egbert is as good as any man who works hard, live a respectable life and love his family.

Surprisingly, she accepted the invitation. She arrived in her horse-drawn carriage with its Negro driver. Her white gloves clutching her white pattern leather bag and her white hand key wiping the sweats.

"Why do you tie your head like a Cullie woman, hiding all that beautiful blond hair? Just look at this dress you are wearing? An African frock that don't suit you. Why are you deliberately pulling yourself down just to fit in with these people? Aren't you embarrassed to be around here with these people who are so different?"

Melinda said as she pulled at Janey's head tie and frock. She looked at the other people present, with scorn. She refused to eat or drink any thing offered to her.

She even refused to sit. She walked in every room with the same smirk on her face.

"Why did you accept our invitation? Do you feel good coming here to air your mouth out on me? Well let me tell you something, after all these years, I still wanted you to be my friend. I do not know why, but I did. As of now, I will no longer think of you as a friend. This is my life and my choice. I have dignity. You see, my old friend, when someone has dignity there is no room for embarrassment".

Janey knew that the end of her friendship with Miss Jordan had arrived.

Many moons from now I will tell you more of Miss Jordan.

It was very common for parents who had many children, to give one or two to other family who did not have any.

One of Dada's older sisters, May-May was married and had no children.

She asked Janey for one of her children, since they already had five at the time.

"Dada said he would never give away any of his sons. Mary-Jane is my only daughter; I cannot give her to you. Wait until we get some more girls, then, maybe he will agree to give you one. {Janey prayed that that never happen, giving away one of her children, that is}

Clarabell was furious, "What do they think, that you have a bunch of dog-puppy to give away, or a pack of kittens that you cannot feed?"

"Mommy, calm down, it is a custom being done here. Two of Dada's sisters went to live relatives who had no children and they still remain his sisters. They are very happy with their aunties and uncles. They know who their parents are, their sisters and brothers too. Their names remain the same and they visit their home as often as they wished. No matter whom they live with or where they live, on Sunday after church, they all come here at their mother's home for soup." Janey tried to comfort her mother.

"I still say that my grandchildren are not puppy-dogs to be given away as such"

Inez arrived in 1909 and May-May was right there to remind Janey and Dada of their promise.

Janey remembered how her mother blew up just at the thought of giving one of her children away. But she had to live with her mother-in-law who also asked that one of the children be given to May-May.

"Nana, I will keep this one, I waited for many years to give Mary-Jane a playmate. Please talk to May-May, she will understand if you explain how I feel".

Sudith was more furious than Clarabell. She said "Dada have eleven other brothers and sisters who have lots of children, how come May-May don't ask them for one of their children? You know why she wants yours? Is because they have nice brown skin and soft, curly hair"

Dada and Janey kept their promise. In 1913 when Harriett was born.

Three years later she was given her to Auntie May and her husband, Uncle Nattie. Two middle-aged people finally had a child of their own to love and care for.

They were parents at last. They were happy at last.

Two years after Harriett, Wini arrived. It made it somewhat easier for her to agree to let one of her girls go live with May-May.

Janey now had five boys and four girls. The boys were growing up fast. Willy was twenty. He was working as a sugar boiler at the estate and courting Clara.

Mary-Jane was married and moved out. Milton was working with his father at the punt factory and courting Dotty.

"Mother, Mother, come quick, a think Archie dead. He no moving and fraff coming out he mouth" It was Rick, drenched in mud and breathless.

"What is wrong with Archie? Where is he? Why are you in this condition?

"You have to come Mother, you have to come see how he dead".

"Shut up boy, no child of mine is going to die before me, where is he?"

Janey placed her nursing baby Wini into the arms Nana Harriett.

She grabbed her panama hat and hurried up the dirt road to Manchester, where Archie was lying in soft mud.

There was a large crowd gathered around him. A lump crept up her throat.

"Oh Dear God, please, just let his eye open wide enough to see me, the look that I will give him, he will be afraid to die. Please God. Please don't let my Archie die".

Archie was eight years old. It was rainy season. The road to the Manchester School, which he attended, was knee deep in mud. He decided to get a boat, charge his schoolmates one cent per trip. He pulled the boat with a long rope around his waist for a half of a mile. He did that for several trips in the morning, then from and to for lunch.

It was on his afternoon trip with the boat full of children, he fell to the ground.

Some villagers helped to put Archie in a donkey cart {it was the common transport} and took him and his mother to the hospital at Port Mourant.

A message sent to Dada, gathered Willy and Milton and rushed to the hospital.

"What happen Janey? I hear one of my boys is dead?

"They have him in the theater" whether it was fear of anger that kept her calm, no one could tell. She calmly said to her family, looking around the little building.

"I made ten children and did my best to raise them healthy. I never come to this hospital door-mouth until today. I am here today because your son, the businessman, the ship captain, the smart-ass, decided that he is going to start a transport business.

He charged each child one cent to carry them in a boat to school. He pulled that boat in that deep mud from this morning, carrying up to seven children at a time in it"

"Where did he get the boat from?

"How would I know? Where did he get this notion from, at eight years old?"

In one year Archie had eight different operations to remove the knots from his intestine. It seems like every month he was in the operating room.

The doctor finally told Janey "Mrs. Alexander, it would be against everything I learned in school, if I was to perform one more operation on this little boy. I am running out of chloroform. Take him home; feed him lots of soup and porridge made of lots of meat, fish, milk and eggs. Boil nuff sinew, chicken, fish and give him the broth".

The doctor looked at Janey, at Dada, and then back to Janey, he said,

"Your son's stomach is the size of a chicken craw. More than three quarter of his knotted guts had to be taken out. That is the way it will remain for as long as he lives. If he lives. I am not going to fool you, he may not live through this month"

Janey now had two babies to take care of. Archie and Wini.

Archie demanded his mother's full attention. Under no condition he should vomit. He was fed standing up. He had the best to eat and Mother had to stand with him to make sure that the food goes down slowly into his little pouch.

Nana helped with Wini and cooked all the good food for Archie.

Nana Tama, a cousin of the Alexander who lived next door, 'bought' Archie, making her his Godmother. She helped Janey and Nana Harriett caring for him.

When the others complained that Archie was getting the best food, Mother was quick to remind them that he cannot eat as much they do.

Archie did not attend school for about two years. He and his baby sister Wini became very close, a closeness that remained throughout their lives.

March 21st 1921, Bertram Barnaby Alexander arrived. Six years after Wini.

Janey never took so long between babies, but because she was centered on making sure that Archie survived, she did not allow Dada to be anywhere near to her.

Bertram was handsome from the time he was born, so said all those who were present at his birth. "The bottom of the jar is always the sweetest," said Sudith

Sudith took one look at her nephew and said to her sister Janey, "This one is mine"

Archie grew up to be as strong as a mule. "Is all dat beef sinew and cog dat you been feeding him. You spoil him Janey". Said Nana Harriett when Janey, worried that he would hurt himself, would complain every time he played ruff or fall down.

He and his brother Rick were close as friends because of the short age difference. He had to give respect to all his older siblings and demand it from the younger ones.

By age fifteen, he had several cows and other livestock, and was cultivating rice fields.

At sixteen, he knew that he was in love with Clara Bowel, a pretty fifteen years old girl from the same village.

They grew up together, met at school and church. He was friends with her older brothers and would use every opportunity to visit them just to see her.

"Mother, I would like to write a letter to Mr. Bowel for permission to courten Clara"

"Are you sure that you are ready to do that son?

"Yes Mother, I am old enough. I have many heads of cows, sheep and goats. I am planting six acres of rice. I am working hard, I want to stay here, I know the family will be moving to the estate where Dada and the boys can be close to work.

This house will be empty. I would like to stay here and start my family just like you and Dada did. Lancaster will always be my village, I don't want to live anywhere else"

Of course everyone was informed of Archie's intention. Mother did not make any major decision without informing her whole family.

"He is too young. He is still a child, a sickly one too. Who will be able to take care of him like you do? I do not agree, just the thought it makes me angry" said Sudith.

"Sudith, you cannot say that, if that is what Archie wants, we should give him our blessings. We could have lost him eight years ago. Look how much he has accomplished and how grown up he is. Let us all support him," said Clarabell.

The Letter

Lancaster Village
Berbice
September 23,1922

Dear Mister Bowel,

My name is Michael Archibald Hunter Alexander. They call me Archie for short. I live with my parents Egbert and Mary Jane Alexander and my Nana Harriett. I am 16 years and one month old. I have many heads of cows, 32 sheep and 21 goats. Many of my flocks are heavy to drop soon. My count will grow bigger. I am planting 7 acres of rice land hope to lease some more land to plant more rice.

My reason for telling you all of this is because I would like to ask your permission to courten your daughter Miss Clara Bowel. I saw her in school and church but never speek wid her because of respect.

Since me been little, me tell me that one day I will write home for her, then I will marry her because she is the only girl me will ever want to marry and take home to my home. I am sure of it from my head to my toes. Me can never love any other girl.

This is the day me hope you will grant me my lifelong boyhood wish.

With much respect
I remain yours truly
Michael Archibald Hunter Alexander

The letter was hand delivered personally by Archie to Mr. Bowel.

Some days later, an appointment letter was sent to Archie. A very short note but it was in a brown envelope. It read

"Thank you for your letter to me. I will see you this coming Saturday at 6pm"

Archie could not hold himself down when his mother gave him the letter from Mr. Bowel. He felt happy that he got an answer and an appointment.

Many young men write home for girls in the villages, some never get back an answer.

"Make sure to come home from the back-dam early enough to bath and get ready.

I do not want you to be late for such an important event.

Your sisters will starch and iron your good cloths. I will have Rick polish your good shoe. Yes you will wear a shoe and a tie. No son of mine ever went to meet his in-laws looking any kind a how. You will dress for the occasion" Mother's speech.

Archie was early. He brought back all the food his mother prepared for him.

'Nana Harriett was ailing and Mother forbid her from doing anymore cooking'.

"Mother, I am excited, I don't have space for food"

"Aright, getting excited, its only normal, but you should always remember that others live to eat, while you are the only member of this family who have to eat to live"

His sister Inez, who was a seamstress, made sure that everything was just right for her brother. His white shirt was stiff with starch. The seams on his pants can cut butter. She trimmed his soft curly hair and whatever little mouthstach he had.

The whole family gathered around to see Archie dressed-up. It was a rare occasion for him. He was most comfortable bare-footed. He did not like much cloths on him.

A triangle piece of brown cotton, two ends knotted around his slender waist and the third end pulled from his back, between his legs to his front and tucked into his waist. It was called a something that I do not remember, if I remember later I will tell you. That was his only clothing most of the time.

Inez tried to dab some sweet smells on him. He objected before she did. "I am not a girl to smell sweet, when I bring Clara home, you can dab her all you want"

Villagers on the street stopped and stared. " Ah Archie bay a you da? Wa you a go? Wa appen bay, somebody ah get married? We never see you dressup like this?"

Archie was most uncomfortable with the tight, shining black shoes. He walked lifting his foot high in the air. He prayed that it would be the only time that he would ever have to go through such torture for a woman.

"Remember your manners. Do not enter the people's yard unless someone opens the gate. Do not walk in front of the person who walks you into the house. Do not sit down unless they offer you a seat and they sit down first. Do not look around the house like if you left something there. Speak only when you are spoken to. If Clara is invited into the room, do not look at her or in her direction. Most importantly, if they offer you something to eat, refuse it, say you had dinner already. Nobody is going to give any son of mine 'catch food'. 'Catch food marriage don't work. Just be respectful and mannerly.

I will be waiting right here for you when you come back"

The dogs sounded the alarm as Archie waited at the gate of the Bowels.

After some time, which seemed to him as forever, Mr. Bowel came to the gate.

He was a tall, strapping, light colored man. He looked at Archie from head to toes then stepped away from the gate without opening it. He said,

"You want to courten my daughter? Do you think you could afford to support her? Do you think that by writing of all your flocks, crops and doings that I will be willing to have my daughter marry you?

Archie wanted to answer Mr. Bowel's first question but he never got a chance. As soon as one question was asked another one came and another. He knew he had to wait until Mr. Bowel gets off his pulpit before he could speak.

"I know you are from fine upbringing. You have a family of fine character.

You are a hard working young man. I know all about you but you do not know anything about me and what I want for my only daughter Clara"

Mr. Bowel stepped closer to make sure that his listener can hear him loud and clear.

"Look over there, that is the police station. That is where my daughter will find a husband. Yes she will marry a policeman who will give her servants and gardeners and nanny for her children. I will never agree for her to marry a cowcatcher that is always walking around with a piece a cloth wrap around him and rope around his shoulder.

I respect you for being so brave, but I will not think of such a thing. I refuse permission.

I now bid you goodnight" Mr. Bowel then handed Archie his letter.

Every one of Mr. Bowel's words was like sledge hammer on his head.

Archie watched as Mr. Bowel disappeared into the darkness. He could not move. He was stuck. That cement, I think, hardened his heart forever.

It was dark. Archie saw that most of the villagers, who had lined the road on his way earlier, were now indoors. If any of them saw him in the condition that he was in, they will surely think that someone had died.

By the time he reached home, his tie, coat and shirt were on his bare shoulder. His socks tucked into his shoes in his hand.

The whole family was eagerly waiting for him.

Upon seeing her son's face, Janey quickly quite the others and took her boy aside.

"Whatever it is that happened tonight should not affect you for the rest of your life. You will have to try and try again, until you succeed"

Archie stood and looked at his mother but did not hear a word she said.

"Just now, all your uncles and aunts will be coming here because Nana Harriett is not looking well. You will have to put out the white flag on the road, in the morning for the doctor to come in and see her. Do not let her see you in this comatose condition. \ She is calling for you all the time. Go in and see your Nana"

Archie became alert. He must go to his Nana. She told him more stories of her life as a child of slaves. He had her to himself for the years that he was sick and like you Linda, he was the sponge that sucked up all that she remembered of her childhood.

"Nana is me, Archie. I hear you not eating. Well I am here to feed you just like you feed me when I was sick. I want you to be well because I need you Nana"

In 1922, Nana Harriett died. She was 95 years old, which means that she was born in 1827, the height of slavery in British Guiana.

Archie cried his heart out for his Nana. At times Mother wondered if it was only for his grandmother that he mourned so badly or was there more that he was pouring out of his heart for. She became worried about him because after the funeral, he wrapped himself into his triangle cloth, throw some rope around his shoulder and bid his mother farewell.

"What do you mean when you say you are going away for a long time? You have never been away for a 'long time'. What are you trying to do to me at a time like this, when I just buried my second mother, and, best friend? What are you going to live on? Where are you going? Are you trying to be a Bush Negro? Are you trying to kill me?"

"No Mother, I am not trying to hurt anyone, I just need to be away for a while"

On weekends when Dada and the boys came home, they came to a home in mourning, a home full of sadness. He said, "Mother, I am going with the boys to look for Archie. We want to come home to our old home. I am going to look for your son". "No, no, no, you do not do such a thing. I am sorry I have not been myself lately but do not go looking for Archie. Leave him alone. If he is alive, he will come back home when he is ready. I will not be able to bear seeing you and the boys coming back without him. I shall try to do my duty at home. Please leave him where he is".

Two months later Archie returned home. Skin and bones was he. The corner of his mouth was raw with 'wapya' scurvy from malnourishment.

Janey had to nurse her son all over again. She did not have Nana to help her. She had two babies to take care of, Bertram, one year old and Archie, sixteen years old. She was determined not to loose Archie. She postponed her relocation to the plantation, to stay in Lancaster to nurse him back to good health. The beef sinew broth, the fish head soup, the eggs and milk cog and all the goodies she used eight years ago to keep him alive, she was pouring into him once again.

Willy, their first son went to Dutch Guiana with his wife Clara and two children Sunny and Asme, to work as a sugar-boiler at a plantation there.

He was the first of their sons to leave Lancaster.

The Alexander family moved to Port Mourant Sugar Plantation in time for Christmas.

Archie had planned to stay at the 'big house', get married and raise a family? Well his excuse for changing his plan was because "Nana is gone, she was the only one I was going to stay here for. She never left this village since she became free.

I know she did not want to go the Plantation. She said it has bad memory for her".

"Who will take care of your livestock and farm? Asked Mother.

"No worry Mother. Animals need grass and water to live. My cousins Percy, Askar and Collins will milk the cows and take care of the farm. I will come back on Sundays and open the house to air out and brand my baby animals"

Archie never mentioned the Bowel incident and Mother never asked. The brown envelope containing the letter sat in the souvenir draw for many, many years.

Archie became an apprentice for the cane lifter operator. He learned fast and by the age 18 he became the operator.

Port Mourant Sugar Plantation was predominantly Indian.

The Alexander's' was one of three Negro families to live in the plantation.

They had no problem blending in with the Indians. They lived in peace and harmony.

Every one called her Mother. Some also referred her as the 'White Lady'.

"Sudith, if you live in India, your friends will be Indians. We are living in Port Mourant. The only friends we are going to have are the Indians. Myself and my family will live with them in harmony".

"It shouldn't be hard for you, you already dress like them. You tie that Madras head tie - rumhal better than some Indian women"

Archie made friends too, only Indian friends, ofcourse. He had four very special ones. Joe, Bang, Secharan, and Tiger. {I am sure that Tiger had other names but everyone called him Tiger} Those five men remained friends throughout their lives. They did everything together. They drank, womanize, laughed and cried together.

At the races, cricket, weddings, rum shop or any goings on, you will never see one without the others. They were truly a team that never accepted anyone else into their club. It was a team of brotherly love and loyalty throughout their lives.

August 26,1926 an Indian lady brought a two-days old baby girl to Mother.

"Dis a you son picknee. Me husband go kill me, this a one Blackman picknee".

"Whose child is this? Why are you bringing this little baby to me"

"Me jes tell you, dis ah you son choil, she is two day old. Me can't let people see me come haa. Me a beg you. Tek de picknee and let me go befo daylight"

"What are you going to tell your husband and family when they ask for the baby?"

"Me go tell dem it dead"

Mother did not have to wonder which son of hers fathered the little baby girl in her arms. She knew who he was and she knew this was going to happen sooner or later.

She heard all the stories of the women, married and single, fighting each other for her stud. She said to Dada. " Don't be surprise if we hear that some woman husband hang your son from a tree or he break his legs escaping from some man's bedroom"

"Mother, what can we do? From the time that boy come here, the women follow him everywhere. They want to cook and take food for him. They want to cut grass for his cows. They want to move in with him. I don't know what to say about this, Mother.

The little baby girl was registered and christened Esther Elizabeth Alexander. She was born on the 24th August 1926, one day after her father 20th birthday.

Mother's internal furnace blew war smoke when Archie arrived home.

"All my children, when they come of age, we arrange a marriage with suitable, respectable mates. They get married and then they gave us grandchildren".

Mother needed to breath. "What makes you so different? I am sure without a doubt that you are Dada and me child. How can a child of mine be so different? You are doing everything that your brothers never think of doing. I am older than you and you are dragging me around. Ask Dada what you are doing to me"

Archie said nothing; he stood like a lantern post, looking at the infant in his mother's arm. Afraid to come back to the subject of the baby.

"Who is the woman who brought this child here?

"I don't know, Mother"

"What do you mean, you do not know?

"No Mother, I don't know which one of them came to you"

More smoke was escaping from her ears, now through her eyes.

"You mean that there are more than one Indian woman in the 'family way'?"

"I don't know Mother. I did not put them in the 'family way'"

Esther became Mother's youngest baby. She was loved and cared for, with her five years old uncle Bertram. She was the image of Archie, a head full of long curlets.

There are lots of beauty in mixed race children, but, without a doubt, it's the hair that is unmistakable the most distinguished beauty.

Archie's helper and friend Tiger, collected Archie's lunch everyday from Mother's careful hand-prepared kitchen. All the other food prepared by his many love interests were devoured by Tiger and the other workers on their team.

Everyday women would drop off food at the security gate for Archie. They had no clue that he did not even taste their delicious Indian food.

Mother complained to her husband about Archie's popularity with the women.

"Is the sinew Mother, the sinew. How come none of the ladies ever look at me?"

"Because they have to look through me first"

In 1936, Clarabell died. She was 78 years old. She had 25 grandchildren and ten great grandchildren from her two children, Janey and Charlie. Sudith had no children.

By 1937 all of Mother's children, except Archie, were happily married and started their families. They all heard her speeches before their wedding.

To her daughters she said, "Always remember that he has a mother. You could never be his mother. Don't try to take the place of his mother by trying to talk to him like if you are his mother. Not because he put his mouth to your breast, he becomes your son. He does it to you for the pleasure you will give him. He did it to his mother for his existence, for him to become a good and healthy man for you. When a man loves his mother, he will have no problem loving his wife. He is happiest when his mother and his wife, the two most important women in his life, are happy with each other. Like Nana Harriett and I. There are many other things you can be to your husband, but not trying to be his mother. A mother prepares a son for a wife from the time he comes out of her belly. She is careful to put a bellyband on to prevent bound-nable. She wrap-up his 'lolo' with several layers of bedding to prevent breast milk from falling on it, because they said if that happens, when he becomes a husband he will not be able to do his duties as a man. She nourishes him well and sends him to school, all in preparation for when he takes a wife. Not to divide his family, but to be a part of them, to join them.

If his mother lives to be a hundred years old, he will always be her son. He picked you to join his family, not to break them apart"

To her sons, she said. "You are taking a wife, not a mother. She doesn't have to cook like me. She will have her own style, the way her mother taught her. You are not her father. Don't talk to her as if she is your child. Wait until you get your own children. Always respect her family, especially her parents. They choose you to join their family, not to find faults. Whatever you do or however angry you may be, do not, under any cloud, dark or light, hit your wife. You are not her father."

To her future daughter-in-laws, her speech was similar to that of her daughters but she added, "Don't feel that you have to like me if you don't, but don't ever try to turn my son against me and his family. He will ask himself for all his unhappy years with you, "How come my mother and my family were not this bad until my wife came along? We were a family of twelve with lots of room for ten more and as many young branches to make our tree stronger and well rooted. I miss being a part of my family"

To her future son-in-laws, she said, "My daughter is your wife, not your mother. She knows all her family's faults; you don't have to point them out to her.

Her father never raised his voice or his hands on her. That is my duty. Whatever it may be, if you feel the urge, don't. Come to me, I will take care of her, but, do not, never, ever put your hands on my child. Her five brothers will be on you before your hands come down.

If I get to you before they do, you will not even have a hand to come down"

Mary married James Barkley. They had four Joseph, Cecil, Rupert and Vera.
William married Clara Emanuel. They had two children, Vernon and Esme.
Milton married Dotty Babb. They had four children, Erma, Paul, Melvin and Jean.
Ulric married Trude Naar. They had five children, Eddy, Ranny, Mavis, Archie And Wini. He lived in Dutch Guiana now Suriname.
Inez married George Katick. They raised Harriett's son Earnest.
James married Georgina Lewis. They had six children, Phyllis, Grace, Connie, Joyce, Elma and James.
Harriett married Moses Malay. Had three children, Doreen, Earnest and Stanley.
Wini married Winston Baxter. Had four children, Monyx, Alvin, Cheryl and Shirley.
Bertram married Eloise Brush. They had six children, Merle, Noreen, Barbara, Ulric, Milton and Bernadette.
Do you see that someone from Mother's ten children who is not married? I will not call any name but I will mention that there was Esther, her first granddaughter.

In 1937 Willy returned to Guiana from Suriname and went to Ifluctt Sugar Plantation. He was a senior Sugar Boiler. His mother was happy that he was back home.

"Willy, remember this name 'Michael Archibald Hunter' Your grandfather, my Daddy. Ifluct is the plantation those people sent him when we arrived here. Ask all the questions you could about him, somebody must know something about my Daddy"

The telegram read, "Mother come Saturday. Will meet Georgetown train station".

The whole family gathered to celebrate the anticipated excitement. Sudith, who was suffering with elephantitis, wished she were going with her sister to she her Daddy.

"Mother, if you find him, bring him home. Here will be his home" Sudith cried.

Bertram accompanied his mother on the journey. She had never left the area since she arrived as a child. Her thoughts throughout the trip were on her Daddy. She averaged that he would be about 82 years old. Would he remember her?

She had many, many questions to ask him, like why did he not try to find them? Why did he not fight for them? Did he know that her Mommy waited for years for him to come to her? Why, why, why.

Willy met Mother and Bertram at the Georgetown train station.

He hurried them to catch the ferry to cross the Demerara River, the same river that took her father from her when she was ten years old.

"Did you find him, Willy? Did you find him Son?" Mother asked anxiously.

"No, Mother"

"Why did you let me travel all this way, cross so many waters for nothing?"

"Mother, its because I want you to meet someone and hear what he has to say"

The next morning Willy took his mother into the estate logy to meet Thomas.

He was an old man. The hard life he had showed in his weak knees and trembling hands. His toothless mouth drooled, but his eyes were excited.

"You son say you wan fe know bout you papa? Now me see he eye in you".

Mother became excited. She was in the company of someone who knows her Daddy.

"Yes, I am looking for my father. His name is Michael Archibald Hunter"

"Yes, yes, me know im, me bin he house-boy when he come ha.

He bin one sad young fella, always sad. Me cook, he no eat. Me talk, he no talk back. Me try to make he laf, but he no laf. He bin one sad young Backra. Me was a lil houseboy, but me never forget dem sad blue, blue eyes of him"

"Where is he now? Mother could not control her anxiety any more"

"Me go carry you where he is"

With the help of Willy and Bertram, Mother followed Thomas to the Ifluct crematory. On a concrete slob written these words. 'Archibald Hunter-1886'.

Mary-Jane stood over her father's burial spot and wept for her Daddy.

Willy and Bertram saw their mother cried only twice before, it was when her mother Clarabell died and Nana Harriett.

She said to Thomas, "He did not live here a long time? He died soon after he came?"

"Yes mam, me tell you he bin a sad and sick young man. He jes dead in de bed when me go one manin to wake he up".

"Did anyone come from England or Scotland for his funeral? She asked, shaking.

"Wa you say? Notin like da. Me go to office to report him dead, two porters come to cary em to de burin gron. Ah one of de porter write he name an de year on de concrete"

"You mean he had no Overseer at his funeral?" Asked Mother, shaking with grief.

"Jes what me tell you, he ben yong and no have no fren. He was one lonely Backra"

"We were just miles away waiting for him? Oh God, this is too painful for me"

"Like me say Misee, He na live hare long, but he had some of the gardeners and bouseboys pay dem respect. Me wife go wid me because he ben good to me".

Mother reported her findings to her sister Sudith. They cried together and sat in silence for a long time, and then Sudith said, "Well is only me and you now. No more waiting and hoping. He pined away and died for us. We did not even know it"

Sudith distributed all her father's stuff that she kept with the hope that he was coming back, to her six nephews, mostly cufflinks and tiepins. His cloths and shoes were given to them on special occasion, such as when they got married. She would say

"It's your grandfather Archie's, take good care of it"

All of Clarabell's fine jewelry that were given to her two daughters, were later given to Mother's daughters, daughter-in-laws and their brother Charlie's daughters.

Rick saw that the rice farmers in Suriname were plowing their fields the old fashion way. Two men, one with the rope around his shoulder pulling the heavy plow while another push it into the ground to tilt the dirt. It was hard work for men.

Rick knew the easier way; the way the people in Guiana does it, with oxen.

He sent a letter to Archie.

"My dear Brother, I miss you more that I can write word on this paper. I have a job but I still miss home, my family and you. I spoke to some rice farmers here and I think we could start a good business, supplying cows. You should see how they plow the rice field? Two men pull and push the heavy plow. That's the way our grandfathers did it fee them Massa. Now we have cows to do dat".

Archie could not meet the demands. They were partners in a lucrative business.

When Archie was asked how did he manage to take those huge oxen in such a small boat across the torturous Corentyne River? He replied

"I drunk the cows with rum, tie their legs together, then, I get drunk and lie on top of them. All the captain do was pray that cows do not sober within the three hour trip"

Archie became famous and somewhat rich. He used the money to buy more cows.

His proud brother Rick was always quick to point out to the Dutch people that it was his brother Archie who was the first man to brave the danger of the sea to bring cows over here to help the farmers produce more rice without breaking their backs.

Archie was appointed constable by the estate management. It was a service to the plantation. He got no pay. He kept the peace and report any crime that he thought should be reported. He was given two kaki outfits, a police cap and a batten. His duties were mostly in the night if some drunks were fighting, he had to stop it. If neighbors were feuding, he had to make peace.

His Mother did not approve of it because all hours of the night he had to be out settling fights. She was afraid he would get killed by one of those machete-welding drunks.

Others said that he was the best person for such an assignment because he was respected by all of the estate residents. Being such a hard working young man.

He was also feared by most of the men who have seen how strong he was.

An Overseer went to Archie's place of work one afternoon and said

"Mr. Alexander, Dr. Koo came over to the office to report that a woman was brought to the hospital last night. He said she is in a bad way after being beaten by her husband. You know we do not pay much attention to these cases but when the doctor comes in person to report a case, we have to investigate".

Archie's report back to the Overseer "I saw an Indian woman with a hole in her head. I tried to lift her arms, they sounded like broken glass.

Because of the dried blood that is caked up all over her, I cannot tell or average her age. She seems like an old person because she has no teeth. But I don't think she is that old.

She did not say a word to my questions. I do not think she will live.

I think I know that lady, but, I am not too sure"

PART III

After a lifetime in the hospital, Tatri was discharged. Still broken, deformed and as incoherent as the day she was taken there. She lost track of time.

Before Dhia went to get his mother, he went to his grandparents at Whim to ask them to accept them at their home rather than they having to go back to Ram.

His Grandfather told him,

"We cannot take a man wife and child away from him"

"Nana, 'grandfather' she will die if she go back to him"

"If that will be God's will, there is nothing I can do to stop it"

On their way home from the hospital, they saw a herd of cows followed by a Negro man without shirt and some rope sling across his shoulder.

Upon seeing the man, his mother pulled him to the parapet and used him as a shield

'Why is she afraid of him?' he wondered

Archie stopped and looked keenly at the woman with the young boy.

'No, this couldn't be the same woman. She died. She had to have died. No one can live after what I saw some months ago'. He peeked under her hernee to see her face.

Archie and Dhia shared the same feeling at the moment. He knew that if this woman goes back to the same man, she would surely die. He had seen too many of those cases and many times he wished he had done something to stop the inevitable.

He looked at Dhia and said, "You are a big chap, you should get a job and take your mother away. Your father would surely kill her if he continues to beat her in the manner he has been doing. She has more lives that a cat"

"What can I do? I am fifteen years old. I go to school to become a policeman.

I do not know where to go to look for a job or what kind of job I can do?"

"You are fifteen years old and you don't know what to do? When I was thirteen, I knew what to do. I had my first pair of cows and watch two turned into four, then eight and more and more. I been working from then and I never stop.

Unless you are a little spoil boy, you too can find a job and take care of this woman.

Come to the main gate at the factory next week, I will arrange for you to get a room at the logy and a job for you" Archie spoke strait to Dhia, not looking at the covered headed Tatri, as if she was not there, or, what he was saying did not concern her.

Tatri had half of her upper body and left hand in a body suit of plasters paris.

She walked around in a daze and did not speak much to anyone.

The doctor told her that after six weeks, she should return to take the plaster off.

She saw the stares of all the people she came in contact with. The way she walked, like a robot, drew attention, especially from the children, who laugh, walk behind her pretending to be like her with her left hand bent into her hip and her elbow sticking out.

Ram heard that Overseer and Constable were involved in the assault case. He knew what would happen to him if his name goes to Manager. He kept clear of his wife.

After the plaster was taken off. Tatri put her long awaiting plan to motion.

One Friday she told Dhia, "When you leave school, meet me at the Manager's Gap"

Tatri gathered her son's clothes and books, her two saris and all her gold and silver jewelry that she had hidden in a milk can, in a hole under the house.

Her holy books and some of her alter items. She placed them neatly into her basket.

Without a cent to her name, she walked out of the 'house of death'.

She had outgrown fear. She was not afraid of anyone anymore. She graduated from pain and death, the two things that make people afraid. She had no fear.

Dhia did what he was told and met his mother at the Manager's Gap.

The four o'clock factory bell rang and mother and son stood outside the gate, waiting for the man, the only person who ever made a promise to help them.

Dhia was nervous and it showed. He was biting his nails and praying that his father, or anyone who knows his father don't see them there.

His mother stood as if she was a mechanical robot. Her tightly covered head had no room for worrying. 'The ship in the deep sea has to sail or sink'. She thought.

"Look Mhy, the Black man ah come"

"You talk with him, tell am you come for the room he promise you"

As Archie exit the factory compound with Tiger and other friends. He noticed Dhia and his mother. He asked, "What are you doing here?"

"We are waiting for you. You promise to give us a room, my mother will work and I will go to school. Once she left de house she can't go back. My father will kill her"

Archie looked at the two people standing in front of him and wondered to himself 'Why did you open your mouth? Why did you not just pass them and go about your business minding your cows? Why do you think that you could save everyone? What kind a mess you get yourself into now, Archie?'

"Your mother will work? With which hand? Take a look at your mother and tell me who will hire her, and for any kind of job? You come to me at this hour to get a room and job. I told you months ago to come for me to see what I could do for you.

Did I tell you that I own this sugar estate or that I can put a spell on the White man and get room and job right now, because now is when you are ready?"

Archie's friends ran out of patience waiting for him, they told him to meet them at Dhalwa's Rum shop, their regular meeting place after work, especially on Fridays.

He looked at the robotic sculpture standing as if her knees were going to buckle and she was about to fall. He knew she came prepared to sleep on the dirt by the gate until she gets somewhere to go. She was not going back from where she came. 'Of all the people, why did these people pick me?' Archie asked himself. He quickly answered himself, 'Because you were the one who made the offer to help, fool'. He had enough Indian women following him around. Many waited for him right at this gate, to bring him food or to ask when will they see him. This is one Indian woman he needed to stay miles away from. She is a Brahmin woman. He knew how they held themselves higher than everyone else.

Archie thought for a while, 'what the hell did my big Black mouth get me into?'

He paced the whole length of the factory fence, back and forth several times, shaking his head, wondering what is the quick fix to the problem that he was faced?

"Come, ayou follow me" he walked towards the Manager's Gap. He took a shilling from his pocket and gave it to Dhia and said, "Go across to the market and buy some food for you and your mother. Hurry back before we miss the last bus".

Archie took the strangers to the 'Big House' at Lancaster.

Dhia promised himself that whatever happened in the future, he would never let anyone hurt his mother again.

[Sometimes children make promises they cannot keep when they get older]

It was dark when they arrived at Lancaster. Archie said to the young boy,

"Hold your mother hand and I will hold your hand. We have to cross a very wide swamp on a narrow one-plank bridge. Be careful not to fall in the water"

Tatri and her son were in Lancaster Village, predominantly Negro village,

one village away from Whim, predominantly Indian, where her parents lived.

They have never climbed so many stairs to go into such a big house before.

In the house, everything was strange to them. There were glass window with fancy curtains, chairs, table, shouvenir with china and crystal that they have never seen. Archie lit the lantern that placed mother and son in a world they have never seen before.

'The house is too big, we are going to get lost from each other' Dhia's thought.

'Why do they need such a long table with twelve chairs? Is this a school or a church?

As if Archie knew what Dhia was thinking, he said,

"This is my family's home. You and your mother could stay here for only one week, that should give you time to find a place over at Whim or Little Kenny, where there are only Indian people living. In the mean time, make yourselves comfortable. There is a rainwater tank downstairs, a garden full of food and a kitchen to cook in.

I hope you buy enough food for you and your mother to eat now?"

Dhia watched as Archie disappeared in the dark. He thought

'This man do not even know our names, yet he shelter us in his family home?

They are not as bad as I was told'.

Dhia was fascinated with the large piano in the living room. When he struck the keys; his mother lifted her head and looked at him. She had never heard such a sound before. She told her son not to interfere with 'the people things'. He sat in the rocking chair by the window and began to rack. He went over to the easing chair and put his legs up on the leg-rest. He was like baby bear, trying everything in the house.

"Mhy, look what the man lef on de table; he lef two shilling in dis pay-pocket [envelope] Dis go mek three shilling he give us. He must be proper sorry for us or he get nuff money to gee way. Now we get two shilling and two bits. [A bit was eight cents, three bits was one shilling] We now get money to our name".

"Linda, I know you do not understand the broken English spoken in my country. From now on I will try to tell you my story in English that you could understand".

"That's ok Wynette, I am figuring it out. I like to listen to people who speak differently, once there are some English words between for me to understand the conversation.

Mother and son were up before the sun. They surveyed the surrounding.

Dhia had to explain the uses of everything to his mother. He learned about such things from his English schoolbooks, but she had never seen any of them in her life.

Tatri could not understand what she was seeing; she asked "You mean to tell me that people bath in the house and kaka in the same house where they eat and sleep? Oh God, what kind of people do things like that?

They cook, eat, bath, kaka and sleep in the same house?" In her world, those five duties are done in five different areas.

Dhia went into the garden and pulled some sweet potatoes. He lit the stove and was about to put the potatoes in a pot when his mother stopped him, she said, .

"Other people pot can never be clean for us to eat from. They cook what we never eat.

Our place of living may change, but our religion and culture will never change. Never"

"Alright Ma, I will roast them in the fire. Will you eat one if I roast it for you?

Mother and Esther boarded the bus the same time as they did every Saturday.

They go to the garden at Lancaster for fresh provision, vegetable and fruits.

The Leach brothers took good care of Archie's garden and animals. They harvest for themselves and there were always plenty for the Alexander family and neighbors.

The Alexander family was self-fed through the hard work that Archie started.

The whole family, sibling and all enjoyed the fruits of his labor and Archie enjoyed the fact that he could provide for his family.

"Gramother, look, somebody just dig out some sweet potatoes" Esther pointed

Tatri and Dhia heard voices in the garden and peeped through the kitchen window. They saw a White lady, dressed in a long sleeve frock with embroided collar and gold buttons down the front. She had a wide brim hat on her head, held in place with two golden hat pits. She wore black shoes and brown stockings.

They looked at the young girl and saw that she too was dressed in a cotton frock with a two wide sashes tied to her back. She too had a hat on her head with the sashes tied under her neck and she too wore shoes and socks.

"Who are these people?" whispered Tatri.

"I do not know, but I am sure that they are the people who own this place. Remember I told you that whoever own this house have to be very rich? Now you see. Only rich people dress like that, look like that and talk like that".

"Look, look up there, Gramother, smoke is coming out of the chimney"

Mother dropped what she was doing and hurried up the steps of her 'big house'.

"This is my kitchen. Who in God's name is in my home?" When Mother is angry, she changes from white to red. She said out loud,

"Who ever you are, with such big balls to come into my house, come out now".

Tatri and Dhia came out of the dry latrine where they were hiding.

Mother looked at the two strangers in her house. She was angry of what she saw, she was even angrier that her thoughts were wrong. They were not neighborhood children.

"Who are you? What are you doing in my house?"

"I am Dhia, this is my mother Tatrani. Her call name is Dhero"

"I hear your names, now, what are you doing in my house?"

"We have no where to live. When I took my mother out of the hospital after my father beat her and broke her shoulder, I saw a man with some cows walking on the Sideline dam. He offered to help us get a home and a job. He bring we to this house yesterday". Dhia answered in a very humble way. He knew that the man, who brought them to the house, has nothing to do with it. He was a Black man. 'This house belongs to this lady, she is rich and she is White'.

Upon hearing the young boy explanation, Mother did not have to wonder who the 'man' was that brought these people to her home.

She looked at the Indian woman. She saw a battered, frightened, deformed woman.

She wanted to ask so many questions about the woman, but she had much more important questions to ask when she gets back home.

Esther was fifteen years and so was Dhia. She was her Grandmother's baby.

She was a beautiful young lady with long, black, slightly curly hair and a smooth brown complexion. She was well mannered and respectful. She had Mother as her teacher.

"What you saw and heard this morning, is not your concern? Do not mention it to anyone. This is big people business, don't let me hear that you said a word about it"

Mother cautioned Esther as they ended the long, silent bus trip back to the estate.

Tatri counted their pieces of silver. The White lady gave Dhia two shillings for helping them with supplies to the bus. They had four shillings and two bits. They were rich. She never had that much money at any one time. She said to her son,

"Go look for a store. Buy two small pots, enamel cups and plates, two wood spoons, one-cup dhal, [yellow split peas] half gallon rice, one pound sugar and gill salt, [a gill was two cents]

"But Mahy, look how much pots and plates, spoons and cups we have here, why do you want to spend the money that we have to save to buy a house, to go buy things that we already have in this house?

"Me tell you before, these people are not Brahmin. They eat all kind of food that against our culture. They cook and eat in what is in here. We are not going use these things. They are unclean. See if the money can buy a small tawa for me to make roti".

"Mahy you have to stop talking like that, we are in a different world now. We are just like beggars, we have nothing, we are in somebody else house and you are talking like if we are better than these people who give us the only money we have. You should not stay in their house if you feel this way about them.

You people are so superior that you become the biggest snob". I doubt if she understood what he meant. He felt that he had to let her know that she has to change to survive.

"I was born a Brahmin, I will die a Brahmin, and so will you".

Dada saw that his wife was in an unapproachable state. He knew that whenever she was like that, he never question her. He was a patient man who will be by his wife side whenever she decides to blowup. Let her boil and simmer on her own.

That Saturday afternoon when the hot bread and cakes were sent to her children's home, a message was also sent. "Tell your parents that I need to see everyone here tomorrow. I will not be sending any soup to them. They have to come here"

Mother knew when to stop, when sending messages of importance.

She knew that if she didn't say what was so important, they would all show up.

She was thankful for the way she raised her children, they all remained tightly woven around each other. All their spouses did the same. They too were her children.

Saturday was the busiest day in the Alexander's' household. Besides going to Lancaster for produce, Mother oversees the baking. I mean baking in large quantity and variety. Most of the female did the preparation. They grate coconut, pound corn, kneed bread, cream butter and sugar and light the huge outdoor brick oven.

The smell of bread, buns, turnover, cornbread, cassava pone and lots of other cakes, bring the neighborhood children around the yard for their share. ' Depending on what products are in season or in abundance at that time. For example, if guava is in season, one can smell the guava jelly being boiled. If cassava were in abundance, cassava bread would be drying on the top of the water tank. Starch would be stocked for the laundry business. Cassava pone would be plentiful.

In the kitchen, meanwhile, the cowheel, oxtail, brisket and sinew were boiling since last night in the largest iron pot owned. It is for 'split peas' or 'cowheel' Sunday soup.

After church on Sunday, all Mother's children and their spouses come home for her soup, the soup they share with their parents every Sunday, all their lives, just like Nana Harriett did. They bring their children, who are fed first, then sent outside to play.

Her children often said "After eating Mother's cowheel-split peas soup with fufu [boiled green plantain pound in a mata and pestle until it is soft and lump less] on Sundays, you can go for the whole week, never feel hungry until the next Sunday"

Archie was at Dhalwa's rum shop with his four friends, boys Saturday night out.

His brother James was with his friends at another table.

He went to Archie's table and greeted the men. He looked at his brother and said, "What's going on tomorrow? Mother sent a message that we are all summoned home after church. Do you know what's happening?"

"I don't know. Maybe she just wants to see all of us at the same time. You know some Sundays some of you do not show up for dinner. That upsets her. I suppose she just wants to see all her children at least once per week. I really do not know why".

Archie was raised as a Christian, going to Sunday school and church every Sunday. Now he is too busy with work, cows, farming, and of course, his freedom as a bachelor.

He went to church if there was a funeral, on Good Friday and Old Years Night.

Dada, the quite husband, father and grandfather, sat in his easing chair, reading his Sunday's newspaper, smoking his pipe. Anything happening, his wife will inform him.

He watched his wife in church, she prayed long after the prayer was finished.

She did not mentioned what was worrying her, he was patient enough to wait.

He held her hands, in the privacy of their bedroom as they changed their church clothes. He looked into her blue eyes, the same blue eyes he has been looking at for years.

"Mother, whatever is bothering you, I want you to know that I am here with your". s

"Don't worry, my love, you will hear soon enough. I did not want to upset you".

The whole clan descended at Bound Yard, in Mother's house.

The men sat in the gallery with Dada, catching up with the news of and cricket scores.

The ladies joined Mother in the 'extra' large dinning room to feed the children.

Every one knew that something big is happening. They wondered among themselves.

Willy and Rick were missing from the family. Willy, a chief pan boiler at Ifluct plantation, and Rick, now married, with a son, lived in Suriname.

The remaining eight children, seven spouses and several children, lived in and around the Port Mourant sugar plantation where Mother and Dada lived.

Their Baby son Bertram was now married and lived with his parents in Bound Yard.

Saturdays and Sundays were happy days for Mother and Dada. They watch all their offspring gather around them. They share and receive love and respect, just like their parents and grandparents did before them.

Whenever Mother prayed, she always in silence says to God. "Pease, Dear God, don't let anyone, man or woman, come into this, my close family, and break us up"

Mother looked around the crowd and noticed that one of her children was missing.

"Esther" she called out "go and tell your father that I am waiting on his presents"

"Knock, knock, Daddy, Gramother is waiting for you. Everybody is there waiting"

"Go tell her I am coming"

Archie stumbled out of bed. His room on the range was the next building from his parents home. His back window was big enough for him to enter and exited his parents yard. It was covenant for Esther to take his meals or clean his room and for him to visit his parents without walking all around the long range to his parent's gate.

Under normal circumstances, he was allowed to sleep out his Saturday night hangover. Esther would take his soup to him, but this was no normal circumstance.

"Is someone sitting at my table without a shirt on?" Asked Mother.

Archie left the room. He soon returned proper dressed and sat with his family. Just as anxious as they are as to what is the big happening today?

Mother said the prayer as everyone clasped their hands and bowed their heads.

"Dear Father, thank You for granting us the privilege to be together and glorify Your name. Thank You for this family you bless Dada and I with. Thank You for taking care of my two boys, Willy and Rick and their family. Thanks Father for this meal that we are about to partake. Father, give me strength that I need at this moment. Amen"

Everyone remained seated after the meal. Questioning eyes, looking at each other.

"I ask you all to be present here today because what I have to say, concerns the whole family" Mother said. "I went to Lancaster yesterday and found a woman and a boy living in my home. No one asked my permission or told me about it"

'Oh my God, now I know what this is all about. She saw the people I took up there' Opened-eye, opened-mouth Archie was in shock. 'That's no big deal, I will explain that I was only helping two people who needed a place to stay for a week'

"Mother, I can explain. I do not know those people. I just wanted to help them"

"You don't know them but you want to help them? What part of the cow ass you think that I came out of? Are you making a fool out of this family and me?"

"No no Mother, I am telling you the truth. I do not even know their names"

"Well, I know their names, its not Alexander. They are two high class Indians"

If a pin fell, one would hear it, that's how quite it was in the room.

"Mother, you know I never tell a lie. I do not know those people". Archie had everyone's attention. He only had to convince his mother that he is telling the truth.

"The first time I saw that lady was about two or three years ago. She had no one to help her put the bundle of wood on her head, I saw that she needed help and I helped.

The second time, I was coming home and I saw a man beating a woman so bad, I know he was going to kill her. I stopped the man.

The third time I met this same lady, was when the manager sent me to the hospital to take a statement from a woman who was badly beaten by her husband.

The fourth time, I was coming with my cows again when I saw the woman and her son leaving the hospital. I swear, I thought she had died. I knew it was she because of the young boy who was with her. I saw that boy with her when I went to take a statement from her at the hospital". Archie was thankful that no one interrupted him. He looked at his father. His father was a good, respectable man who had to defend himself many times for being overly kind to some estate residence, especially Indian women.

"Yes, I opened my big mouth and offered to help. Its what any of you would have done. I told the boy to come meet me at the estate, that I would arrange a room and a job for him. He is old enough to work and share a room with his mother. I did not see the boy come to me so I forget about it until Friday afternoon when I saw mother and son waiting for me at the factory gate. I took them to the 'big house'. What else could I have done? According to Mother's training, what any of you would have done?"

"You should have brought them to your room. You have a room of your own. You bring all kinds of women there. Why didn't you bring them here to your room?

Why did you take them to my house?" Mother's voice echoed throughout the room.

"Mother, it all happened so late in the afternoon, it was the only place I could think of. I was going to tell you about it today when the whole family are together".

"You mean to tell me that you took it upon yourself to take people to my home on Friday and planned to tell me about it on Sunday? Is that what you are telling me?"

It's Mother's speech time.

"Look around this table. Look around you; Archie, all your brothers and sisters are married and living respectable lives. You are thirty-two years old. Your mother still cook your food, your mother still wash your cloths. Your mother still has to wonder if you came home last night or if some one of those women's husbands put an end to escapade. I do not send Esther to your room early in the morning because I don't know whom you have in there. A child can be confused with many different faces.

You were not old enough to button your crouch when a married woman brought your two days old baby to my doorsteps.

Your lifestyle has to change. It has to change now. I will see to it that it change now".

The silence was deafening. Every eye was on the defendant and his eyes were on his mother, wondering, 'what is she talking about? What does she have up her sleeves?

"Its time for you to become a man. Take up your responsibility as such".

"A man? A man you said, Mother? I have been a man while I was still a child.

When all my brothers and sisters were going in school, to become respectable, I was in the fields trying to prove to everyone that I am not a 'mother's-boy', that I am a man.

I do not mean to be rude if I sound so. I just want you to know that I am a man.

I work hard, Mother. Every grain of rice this family eats, comes from my hard work. All the coconut, all the meat, all the fruits and vegetable that you all enjoy, come from my hard work. Yes I drink my rum and see some women. You all know that I wanted to be just as respectful as you are. I wanted to do nothing but make Mother and you all proud of me. I wanted to get married and have a family just like you. What happened? I was rejected and insulted. I took that insult like a man. I also took that freedom to pursue whatever whims and fancy that I wish.

I am not doing what everyone else is doing to make you happy, Mother, but I am a man and I am truthful man" Archie had the floor. Everyone was listening.

"You cook for me because you don't think anyone else could keep me alive.

You wash for me because you want to. I have people who want to do those things.

You have every right to be angry. This whole family has every right to be angry.

I will take whatever words you have for me, but, don't say that I am not a man.

I am not thirty-two years. I am thirty-one and a half years old" The room was dead quiet. Dada had a slight smile on his face. He was proud of the way Archie stood up to his mother without being disrespectful to her. It takes a man to do that to his wife.

After that long speech, Mother lost her momentum. She searched for words.

"In my book you are a man. Because you are a man, you are going to do what is right. You are going to do what a man would do when he met a woman four times.

You are going to marry that lady"

Everyone looked at Mother. 'Has she gone mad? The man just told us that he does not know the woman. How can she want him to marry someone he does not know?'

"Mother"

"Yes Egbert" she hadn't called him by his name in years, but this is serious times.

"You heard Archie said that he do not know the people. That he was just helping them? Why would you want him to marry someone he does not even know?"

"You heard your son said that he met this lady four times? You don't meet someone four times and not know her. You don't take someone you don't know to your family home. I met you two times before we got married. How long do I have to wait for him to get married?" She shifted her eyes from her husband and stared the question to everyone around the table except Archie. The room was calm as a millpond. No one wanted to agitate Mother at that stage. Everyone wanted to be neutral. They all knew that whenever it comes to Mother and Archie, they don't say much, because she would quickly turn on them if they agreed with her, against him.

"Married? Married, Mother are you saying that I have to marry someone I do not even know because you so badly want me to get married. I tried that once, remember? I was not good enough then, I am too old now. Most of all if I want to get married, I will pick the person I will marry. I have a whole lot to pick from. I haven't seen anyone yet"

"I do not want to think that you are being rude to me?"

"No Mother, I am not being rude to you. I am just speaking to you as a man would speak to his mother when she is dragging him to the slather house"

"Oh, that's what it is? When a man gets married, he goes to the slather house? Look around you, you see anyone here look like if they are about to be slathered? Where do you get this hatred for marriage from?"

Archie looked strait into his mother's eyes and said,

"You know where, Mother? You know where and why I hate marriage"

Mother was the matriarch of her family, did not acquire that position with an iron fist. Far from that, she held herself with the highest standard. She gave respect to everyone, no matter how old or young. She was very firm but gentle. She loved her family and held them together with her strong, loving arms.

She told her ten children, "This family is a tree. Its roots are your grandparents.

Its trunk is Dada and I. You are our branches; we made you strong and healthy to keep this tree looking good and full of new branches.

There are plenty of room on each one of my branches for additional growth, meaning spouses, children and grandchildren.

This tree is strong and beautiful; don't let anyone break you off. It will loose its strength and beauty. It will leave an ugly knot. Only God should take a branch off our tree"

I forgot to mention that in all the todos with Mother's family, her sister Sudith was always present. She knew it would be no use trying to talk to her sister at times like this.

"Yes son, I know what happened. That was then, a long time ago. You wanted to marry someone you loved but her family did not want you. Even though it was a selfish decision on their part, we had to respect it. It was not the end of the world. You are still alive I pray you bring one of your lady-friends and say 'Mother I want to marry her'.

The woman in my house at Lancaster is the only woman you have taken home. I mean home, not your logy room but our home. You must have realized that she was special and that you could not bring her to your room here". She was getting there.

"You see son, sometimes when you don't get who you want, you take who wants you. Obviously this lady wants you. She came to you, she went with you. Who knows? There may be a spiral connection why you keep bumping into her life".

Archie realized that his mother has made up her mind and her case. With her perfect English and her convincing theory, he had no one who will disagree with her. He knew that when his mother made up her mind on something, there was nothing anyone could do. Her intentions were always for the good of her family.

Everyone present wanted Archie to get married. After all, everyone gets married and raise a family. Nine out of ten of them are already married and have children. They all agreed with Mother. They didn't have to say so, she knew from the way they were avoiding Archie's pleading steers.

After a long silence, Mother continued. "You said that the lady will stay in my home of one week while they find a place to live. If this is so and she leaves in one week, I will forget this whole meeting. You can go on living the way you see fit; after all, you are a 'man'. But, if I hear that you still have anything to do with this particular woman. You will marry her. On the other hand, if she does not leave in one week, we will have a wedding, with, or without you. Have I made myself clear?"

The meeting was over.

Tatri and Dhia went to Whim to see their parents/grandparents.

They entered the house that gave them the feeling that someone is dead.

Her mother and only remaining sister, Satrani were huddled in one corner on the floor. Her father and her two brothers Kachan and Lunjbeharry were sitting on the other side of the room.

I do not remember telling you that her sister Backriji, whom they lived together for a while, the mother of John and Mybee? Well she died not long after going back home.

Tatri rushed to 'fall' at her father's feet but her eldest brother Kachan, quickly stop her. He opened his arms wide, shielding his father from her, without touching her.

"Do not touch him. Do not touch anyone in this family ever, ever again"

Tatri stood close to her son. She was thankful for him beside her, her knees get so weak.

She looked at her mother and sister but they had their heads down.

She looked at her father and brother sitting on the floor. Praying that one of them would stop Kachan from being so cruel to her.

She knew that she was in trouble and she was prepared to take whatever punishment handed down on her, as long as she was forgiven and allowed to stay home.

Kasy stood up, but Kachan stood between him and his daughter.

"Why did you leave your home?" asked Kasy, his eyes were red from crying.

"Bhapoo [father] I could not live there anymore. The pain is too much. I cannot even die. I tried so hard to die. I pray to die during my meditation, but it will not come"

"So you broke the laws of God and moved out of your home and left your husband?"

"No Bhapoo, even God refused to help me. I read the good book, chant mantras, meditate for hours, fast for weeks and do puja all the time. Where is God? Bhapoo"

Still humble with her head down, Tatri was fighting with everything she had left.

"Whom is this man you runaway with? Asked Kachan who couldn't wait to speak?

"I do not know him. I did not runaway with him, he just help abee [us]"

"You mean to tell me that you don't know this man but you move to his house?"

"No, he helps abee because none of my own family would help me"

"When did you meet this man?"

"Long time ago, he put a bundle of wood on my head at the back dam" the gasp from everyone fills the room.

"Go on, tell me more of this man who did more for you than your family"

"The next time I see him was when me and my son was leaving the hospital. He tell Dhia, not me, up to now he never talk to me, that he can help abee"

"How did you get to his house?" asked the executioner Kachan who did all the questioning. The eldest son usually play the part of the father and sometimes more harsh and feelingless than that of the father, most times to show their superiority.

"How did you get to his house?"

She did not answer.

"What did this man do to you to make you follow him to his house?" It was commonly said that when a Brahmin person runaway with anyone out of his/her caste, the person must have done something evil to lore the pure Brahmin away.

"He did nothing to me. He na even talk to me," said Tatri

"Wa kind a man is this? Is he a Brahmin or is he a low class Madras or Chamar?"

"No, he is a Cafree [Black] man". She had to be truthful even though she knew that it would shock them all but she never thought how much.

Her mother and sister began to wail as if someone just drop dead. It's the end.

Kasy, dressed in full ceremonial outfit, spoke.

"When I hear of your disappearance of Friday, I prayed that they find you dead.

That way, I would cremate your body, preside over your thirteen days schraad, morn for my loss, just like I did with the others, and go on with respect and dignity."

"I never wanted to disrespect you and my family, Bhapoo, but look at me, I am a cripple. I cannot use one side of my body. I have been beaten so many times. I have no teeth in my mouth. I buried three bacha, kick out of me belly, not counting the ones that fall in the latrine pit" Tatri was fighting with all she had.

"You are a disgrace to me. You are a disgrace to my caste, a disgrace to all Hindus and a disgrace to my Mother India".

Dhia realized that he had to say something on behalf of his mother

"But Nana, my mother did not commit any sin. She did nothing bad.

It's just she and I living in the house. Nobody else live wid abee"

"Quiet child. The only thing I will say to you is if you ever want to remain who you are, a Brahmin, stay here with us. Do not go back with this woman. If you do, you will be an outcaste just like her. You will never be welcome here again. This is your chance to free yourself from the sins of your mother." Kasy had the floor.

"How can I ever walk with my head high or expect people to respect me, when my own daughter left her husband and runaway with a Black man?" he said it with such scorn that Dhia had to take note because he did not see anything bad about the man.

Kasy continued "How will I ever be able to teach young men the value of being a proud Hindu when I am so ashamed of myself for what you have done to me?

You have shamed me in the worst kind of way. I will never forgive you."

Tatri held on to her son for support. She was hungry, tired and weak.

Every time she tried to speak, Kachan put up his hands to stop her.

"You must never enter this house or any of God's house ever again."

"But Bhapoo, you can't mean that. She was just running for her life. Do you know how many times I wanted to go and chop Ram in little pieces for what he was doing to my sister. How many times must she die?" asked Lunjbeharry, her baby brother.

Kachan quickly shut him up by saying "You're the least to condemn Ram about his drinking. You drink the rum and beat your wife, but she doesn't leave you for a low class. You are not worthy of being a Brahmin yourself. Just don't open your mouth"

"You can die only one time. In this family she is dead" Answered Kasy.

"Please, my husband, do not call death upon my daughter whilst she still live.

Punish her in whatever way you choose, but please, in the name of all my Gods; I beg of you, oh great one, do not bury my child. Let her stay here and be a slave to all her family as a punishment. Take her son from her but don't send her away, I beg of you"

But Kasy did not hear his wife.

Looking at Dhia, he said, "You could stay here with us but you have to promise that you will never see nor speak to this person ever again".

Tatri squeezed her son hand so tight; she could feel his fingers getting cold in her hand. She was afraid that they were going to take the only person she has.

All the women were crying and praying at the same time while Kachan waited to throw Tatri out of the house. Like the faithful sheepdog making sure the stray leave the flock.

Kasy lifted his hands, gesturing that everyone be quiet and listen only to him.

"If anyone of you, your children, your grand children and any of my unborn blood line ever disobey my order and ever speak to her, all of you too will be outcasted."

The crying got louder but he did not hear again.

He looked once more at his daughter, who was standing with the support of her son, head down and tears washing her cheeks. He said in a much softer voice.

"Go now. Never come back to this house. Do not tell anyone that I am your father. Never utter my name in your mouth. Never use the given Hindi name or my name. Tatrine belongs to me now. She is dead. As long as you walk this earth, don't ever let your shadow, long or short, fall on another Hindu" He took the wooden beads from around his neck and began to smooth them thought his fingers. He was warbling.

He looked at his daughter for the very last time and said.

"I wish I could capture your sprit, I already have your soul. I can put them together and burn them. This way you will go with nothing. But I do not have that power.

I cannot strip you of your sprit, but I have your soul to burn" almost in a whisper, with his bloodshot eyes staring strait at his daughter, he said.

"In the presence of God and my family, I place this curse on you, if you should have more children, none of your boy children will ever 'hear or call' my name"

Neither Mother nor son could sleep. The words of Kasy rang in their ears. The next morning, Dhia said, "Ma, tomorrow the tide is late. I will take you back to your parent's house. I am sure that Nana will not be there. We can beg Nany to help us. She may be able to talk to Nana now that he may be less angry"

"Son that is exactly what I was thinking all night. If anyone can help, it would be she."

Tatri fell to her mother's feet. She began to cry, she told her that she and her son had moved away from Ram, and that she was there to beg her father to allow them to stay with them. As if yesterday did not happened.

She noticed that her mother did not show any surprise in seeing them. As if she was expecting them. They noticed that she was crying. Her eyes were puffed and red.

"Mahy, I come here to beg your pardon. I could not live with Ram anymore.

The next time he will kill me"

"Betty, [daughter] it would be better if he kill you than you do what you did".

"Nanny, it is me who took my mother there. We have no one to help us. My father will surely kill her one of these days. I will be the one without a mother

I am a big boy now. I will never be disrespectful to you. I watch for years as my father beat my mother. She ran to the only family she had, and what did you do? You sent her back to get some more, again and again. Well the way I see it now, I am the only family she has. She is my mother and I will take care of her. She came here to see if you would take us in just until I get a job and a place to stay. We have one week.

"Batha, [son] take your mother and go from here before your Nana come home.

He has been so disgraced of this happening; he went away since yesterday, after the burial puja. The three men had their head shaved and left. I do not know where. Maybe he is at the seaside, maybe he is in the forest. Wherever he is I know that when he returns, he will be a different man. I do not want him to see you here".

"Do you mean me too, Nanny?"

"Yes, you are living in the Blackman house too. We told you to stay here with us".

"Did you say that there was a burial service here? For my mother who is sitting here in front of you? Are you saying that they went through with that ritual yesterday?

"Yes, your Nana would not change his mind. Your uncles shaved their heads in your place. You, her son, should have shaved off your hair in mourning for her."

Tatri and her son walked out of her parent's home and saw the black 'death' flag on a long bamboo stake in front of the house, at Whim.

Dhia was hungry and thirsty from their fasting and praying for the meeting.

He looked down at his almost lifeless mother sitting on the ground.

He wondered 'what will become of her now that she is an outcaste? An untouchable? What is she thinking?'

He slid himself beside her and began to throw pebbles into the trench. He had to take his mind off the black flag flying in his grandparents yard.

He helped his mother up after a long rest. He continued to throw stones, but not in the trench. He threw them behind his back on the road. He was throwing the stones to chase back any evil that might be following them to their new life.

"Well Ma, is me and you now. We will have to live with our disgraceful self.

We will have to live like everyone else, low class, according to your high-class family.

I would rather be a low class and alive than die from hands of a drunken high class"

"Son no talk like that. When we get to the house, we will make a alter.

. You cannot stop being who you are. You are a Brahmin and never forget that".

"Yes Ma, I will never forget that. Tomorrow I will go to the rice mill and shops to look for a job. We have four days to move out of the people's home. Don't try to stop me with that 'school and policeman' talk. That has changed. You are looking at the man who will set you free from your bondage. You will have to accept some changes.

Yes, we are Brahmin, two very, very poor and homeless Brahmin.

I am not going back to that house of your family. They have a dead flag symbolizing your death and you still want to go back there? You go alone". Dhia had his say.

Archie thought, 'That was close, for a while back there, I was sure that my mother had made up her mind and I was heading strait to the abattoir'.

He was on his way to Dalwha's rum shop. His four 'already married' friends were waiting for him for their Sunday afternoon relaxation.

"Yes me brother, I believe, but you pick the wrong kind to help this time" said Joe.

"Those people look down at all of us because we are not Hindu. Even though we are Indians and our folks came from the same place as theirs. We are not the same," said Tiger, the youngest of the group.

"They look at you with scorn, as if you get shit all over you". Said Secharn.

"If we invite them to our home for a wedding or any other occasion, some may come but they will never eat or drink anything. That's an insult to me". Said Bang.

"That woman is taboo. Get rid of her, and stop being so kind to the wrong people"

Mother could not get the deformed woman off her mind. She said to Dada.

"I think this is a good opportunity for your son to settle down."

"But he said he don't even know the people."

"Most Indian women get married without knowing their husbands"

"That's when the husbands are Indians. My son is a Negro man".

"You know I don't see difference in people. I only see people. Two of our own daughters are married to Indian boys. I never look at them as different. Now I see a young woman, badly beaten and broken up. I see my own young son who needs to be married. I see two people who we can bring together in marriage.

Who knows? They might love each other and have a family. Both these young people already have one child each. They are still young and can have more children. I just want Archie to settle down."

"He will do that in his own time, Mother. Our two daughters married Christians"

"You did that when you were young, he is thirty-two. Double what I was."

"Mother, I just think that you should leave it alone

"Yes, I will, for one week

Mother and Esther made their usual Saturday morning visit to Lancaster.

Mother hoping that the people in her home didn't move out. That would spoil her plan. 'Oh God, please let them still be there, otherwise, my son may never get married, and, like every good mother, I want him to get married. As You know Dear God, all my children are already married? This is my only chance to make this happen to Archie'

Esther hoping the same, she liked the young boy and she think he liked her too.

Mother was surprised to see how well kept the yard and garden was.

The rubbish heap was smothering to ashes. No one ever burned the rubbish before.

A clothesline was tied on two posts and laundry was swaying in the breeze. She went up to her house and found a squeaky clean home. She wondered

'How could a crippled woman such as she, do all of this?'

Tatri was much more opened with the 'White lady'. Her English was bad but she tried to answer some of the questions. She verified that she had never spoken to Archie and remembered seeing him only twice. She said it was his offer to her son that brought them to this house. Mother was proud of her son, he told her the truth.

Mother's motherly womanly instinct took hold of her. She began to think of all the Indian women in the plantation that she saw and heard got killed or mane by their husbands. How many times she herself had to intervene into those brutal abuses. How many times she asked her husband and sons to speak to those abusive husbands. How many times she sent Archie, the constable to save some woman from a sure death?

Linda, in those days' men answered to no one when they brutalize their wives.

Not that the Negro man did not hit their wives, but not to the extent as the Indians.

You see, when a Black man hit his wife, she fought back, or her whole family ascends upon him. If he could stand after that, he never lifts his hand on her again.

On the other hand, when the Indian man hit his wife, no family member gets involved. If he goes to church, the Pundit would try to change him.

It is forbidden for an Indian woman to fight back or defend herself.

Mother knew of many cases where Indian women lighting themselves ablaze.

Many hang themselves. Many throw themselves in the sideline canal and very few managed to escape with their lives. She was looking at one such few.

Years later, there were stories of Indian women got even with their abusive husbands. They ground glass and put into their husband food.

There was a much later story of an abusive wife who took out all the diamonds from

her ring, mixed them into tapioca-sago portage and gives her husband to drink.

Her children saw her saving his entire poop as he lay dying from bleeding stomach.

They asked, "Ma, why are you saving Papa shit?"

She answered, "I have to save something to remind me of him"

Black women got even with their abusive husbands too. They left the home and take their children back to their parent's home/village and soon hookup with another man.

I heard of stories where they light their husband afire while they sleep. Not themselves.

The most common was that the black woman, after being beaten, would boil some coconut oil, and while he sleeps, she would pour it into his ears to fry his brains.

"Where is your son?" asked Esther, who search for Dhia and did not see him.

"He went to work on a fishing boat. He should be home soon with some fish.

If you want some to take home, I will clean them for you". Said Tatri, looking at Mother. "My son brings fish. I learn to clean and cook it for him and his friends".

Mother liked what she was hearing. 'A Brahmin woman who never touch anything rank, is cleaning and cooking fish for her son? She can change. I think she will change. Her humbleness is plucking at my heart. I want her for my daughter.'

Archie took a bus ride to Lancaster on Sunday, hoping to find the house empty and his burden disappeared. He walked through the house, it was empty, "Thank you dear God, they left. I can go meet the boys feeling as free as the stallion in the pasture"

He found Tatri sitting at her alter, under the house, next to the rainwater tank, meditating, unaware that there was someone looking at her.

He stood quietly and watched her and wondered what she was praying for?

He quietly walked away to get the bus back to his friends.

She was having a conversation with God "Ohm Hanuman, Son of Pavan, the wind God. Oh Lord, bestore upon me strength, wisdom and knowledge, taking away all my miseries and blemishes.

Ohm Mahaveer, bring the companion of wisdom into me and dispel dark and evil thoughts out of me. Sri Ram Chandra said you are as dear as his brother. He praised you highly for saving Laxman. With your compassion all the impediments and difficulties in the world can be overcome easily.

No one can enter Rama's adobe without your consent, Oh sentinel of the Lord. I beg for your consent Ohm Hanuman. I will chant your name constantly so that I will be cured of all pains".

She did not know that there had been a visitor standing behind her.

It was nine days since she left her home at Miss Weby for Lancaster.

While she prayed at her new alter at Lancaster, her family were sitting in a circle, under the mango tree at Whim, performing a 'nine-day' puja for her death.

Kasy Mirage was reading from his 'good book' as he performs the ritual.

"Lord Mahaveer, evil sprits cannot come near your devotee who chants your name.

Ohm Hanuman, in your colossal manifestation, you killed the demons, fulfilling your Lord's mission"

The service or ritual, continued despite the loud crying from the female.

The fire fed with incant and doop, an aromatic wood used to burn at religious ritual.

In the duration of the service, only once did the name Tatrani mentioned. That was at the end when Kasy threw everything he used for the puja, into the fire and poured the 'oil of death', causing everyone to be covered with scented smoke.

Just imagine, the same day, same time, both father and daughter, sitting in different areas, are praying to the same God, Shri Hanuman, the all mighty Monkey God?

After church, Mother whispered to Reverent Byar,

"Reverent, I need your help. I will send Brother – Milton - to meet with you one afternoon this week. He will explain everything. I know you do not have the time now and Dada is waiting for me."

"No, no, Mrs. Alexander, I have time, I can hear your problem right now"

Rev. Byar was a person who believed that he had to know everything about every one of his parishioners. He knew everything that went on in the district. The women who clean the church and his home 'The Mann's'. The men who work in the church yard and take care of the graveyard. Even the people he met on the road or market. Every one kept him up to the moment with whatever was going on.

He performed most of the marriages. Baptized all the young children in church. Gave last rites to many, for as many years as he was the Rev. at Aklyne Scotch's Church. That was more than forty years.

He felt that if Mother had something to tell him, he should have known about it before she even mentioned it. 'It must be something, if she sending her son to see me. I will know what it is before he gets here' thought the confident Rev.

"No Rev., my son will come to see you. He will tell you why I need your help.

Sunday Dinner, everyone was present. They knew that Mother was going to make an announcement. None of them wanted to miss it.

They knew their mother, and they also knew that the people in the 'big house' were still there. 'They asked Esther who conformed it'.

Mother doesn't make treats that she can't execute.

They were disappointed when Mother said nothing. They began to talk.

"I think Mother gone soft'

"You know that when it comes to Archie, Mother is always soft"

"Well, I was hoping that we would have a wedding. I would really like to see this boy get married and settle down"

Even Archie was surprised that the iron lady didn't say anything. For a moment there he held his breath when she took her seat next to Dada and looked strait at him.

The rest did not hear when Mother asked Inez and Milton [Brother] to remain.

Milton was called Milton before he had younger brothers and sisters. As soon as they came along, he became Brother and even his parents and others follow.

Children called him Uncle Brother, the name he was known by for the rest of his life.

"Brother, I want you to go and meet with Rev. Byer tomorrow afternoon"

"Why Mother?" asked Dada

"Because I want the Rev. to announce Banns on Sunday"

"Banns? Banns for whom?"

"Banns for your son Archie. I know it has to be announced three Sundays before the wedding. I do not have three weeks to wait. I want it announced next Sunday."

"But Mother, I thought we had forgotten all about that. You heard the boy said he did not know the people. Why can't you just leave things alone?"

"When it comes to your son Archie, I left things alone for too long"

"He is my son now? All the other times he is your son?"

Inez and Brother sat and listened to their parents go back and forth until their father succumbed to their mother, as usual.

"As I was saying, Brother I want you to ride up to Aklyne tomorrow afternoon and ask the Rev. to please announce in church on Sunday, the wedding of Michael Archibald Hunter Alexander" Mother knew that there would be no turning back now. She turned her attention to her daughter Inez.

Inez was the sixth of her ten children, a very good seamstress who credited her expert craft to her grandmother Clarabell. She had a successful business. Most of her customers were Overseer wives and children. She had about four to six young ladies working for her. She also made the clothes that her entire female family wore and the young boys had their shirt, pants and book bags done by her establishment.

She followed into her grandmother Clarabell's footstep and the sewing machines in her shop, once belonged to her grandmother. This made Mother very proud of her daughter.

"Inez, I want you to go up to Lancaster and measure the lady in the house.

She is one of them high caste Indians. She only wears sari, but you know they will not have anyone getting married in an English church, dressed in a sari.

Measure her and make a nice white dress. She can wear her hernee as the veil.

Measure her foot on paper. I will go to Bata and get a pair of white shoes for her".

"Good afternoon Rev.Byer"

"Come on in me boy. Your mother told me that you were going to come up to see me. Come inside and make yourself comfortable" said Reverent Byer, he was not able to find out from his sources, what was going on in the Alexander's' household?

The Rev. was a short, bulky man in his sixties. He wore thick glasses and mouthstach twisted and turned up like cow horns. He was very nosey, as it was in those days, how else would he be able to pray for his parishioners? He baptized and married everyone of the Alexander's' children. He felt it was his duty to know everything about them.

The Rev. ordered the cook to bring some ginger beer and cassava pone to the study.

"Well me boy, what is the big favor that Mother want from me?" waiting eagerly

"Well Rev. Mother would like to ask you if you could please announce banns starting this coming Sunday"

"Announce banns? Who fa?" The Rev. eyes almost came out of their sockets.

"Its for Archie, his full name is Michael Archibald Hunter Alexander"

"I know what Archie name is. I christened him just like I did with all of you"

"I know Rev., it's for the record that I mentioned his full name to you"

"Oh, that's it, Archie, who do not attend church anymore, may have gotten some girl from the village pregnant and now they want me to prepare the shotgun?"

"Yes Rev. Mother wants this done as soon as banns are published according to the church. You know that she will have no one else but you to perform the ceremony"

The Reverend was writing into his ledger. He asked

"Who is the bride to be and how far is she in the family way? I don't want to have a midwife on stand-by in church"

At that moment it hit Brother that he did not even know the name of the woman his brother is supposed to be marrying. 'Pregnant? I don't know if she is. I don't know her name, I do not know anything about this person whom my brother is marrying'

Brother was dizzy. The minister was waiting to write the information in his ledger, and Brother was wondering 'Jesus Christ, son of Mary, what kind of wild goose chase my mother sent me to without all the information required for an announcement?'

His brain was searching for a name that wouldn't let the minister know the true situation. Only Baptized Christians get married in the church. Brother knew that he did not dear tell the Rev. that the person in question was a Hindu Indian.

"The girl's name is Jane. I do not remember her title, when I come to church on Sunday, I will give it to you. Her first name is Jane"

"If you don't know her title, that would mean that she is not from around here? Where is she from?

"You are right, she is not from around here. She just moved in the area"

"And Archie had to be the first to hit on her and get her in trouble?

"Something like that, Rev."

"I now see why Mother could not tell me what was troubling her.

This is too shameful for a family such as the Alexander. I feel sorry for your mother.

Because of your family good standing in church, and, even though Archie is a backslider and a sinner, he still donates large quantity of produce and rice for our Harvest every year. For those reasons and only these two reasons, I will grant your Mother this favor". He mopped his face several times, and then he stared at Brother. "I thrust that this girl in question was baptized in a proper Christian church?"

Inez joined the bus at Manager-Gap, going up the coast to Lancaster.

As she passed the villages, she remembered the miles she walked from Lancaster to Port Mourant and back to take her father and brothers hot meals.

She enjoyed the bus ride; she reminded herself that not so long ago she walked this same distance barefooted. Reminding herself from where she came.

Walking on the long, slender bridge, which she and her siblings ran blindfolded then, now, she is careful not to fall into the water. 'How soon things change' she thought

She almost smelt the cleanliness as she entered her childhood home.

Everything was neat and clean. The curtains moved with the wind through the window. The furniture well polished and the white pine floor as white as the day it was sliced.

Inez entered her mother's bedroom. She noticed that everything was just the way they were left except that there was no dust or cobweb from lack of use.

"Hello, hello, anyone here? Called out Inez as she walked through the house.

"Yes, me here in the kitchen" answered Tatri as she walked to meet the visitor.

Inez looked at the humble, crippled woman standing before her and wondered if her mother and brother had gone mad?

She couldn't believe this person that she is looking at is the person her mother is so determined to have her brother married.

Her first impression was that she was looking at a very, very old woman who was battered and bruised, who had no teeth in her mouth, who had lots of bald, hairless patches on her head and a left arm that was almost connected to her hip, could not be the person she came to measure for a wedding dress?

Still in shock, she sat on the bench in the kitchen and blinks her eyes several times.

After sitting for a long time without seeing, feeling or thinking, she felt a warm hand on hers, she looked up to a toothless mouth and two eyes so full of pain, yet, smiling gentle at her and offering a cup of water to her. She needed it.

Inez searched Tatri from head to toes to find a single reason for a wedding.

Every time she looked at the lady, she saw two sad eyes smiling back at her.

'How old is this woman? She is not droopy like old people, yet she looks so old. Whatever little hair she has on her head is jet black, not one gray hair on her head'

"How old are you?" Were the first words out of Inez mouth.

"Me a thirty year old"

'Did she say thirty or two times thirty?'

"How many years you get?"

"Me get thirty years now" Tatri answered,

Inez searched her heart and soul to find a reason why a woman who is just two years older than her could look so old? After a long, silent examination of her conscience, she went and sat on the floor next to Tatri. Placed her hands on Tatri's shoulders and looked into those sad eyes and said

"Who did this to you?"

She began to count her blessings. Her thoughts drifted to one

Sunday in 1926. She was eighteen years old. She was in church with her family when she noticed a stranger across the isle. He was a tall, dark and very handsome young Indian man.

Throughout the service, Inez heard very little of the service. She was decreatingly surveying the stranger, and, he was doing likewise.

Reverend Byer got their attention when he said

"Today, join me in welcoming a new member to our congregation.

He is a Scotch Church member from Skeldon who was transferred to Port Mourant Estate. Ladies and Gentlemen, join me in welcoming Mr. George Kattick to our church". The young man stood and acknowledged the Reverend and the congregation. His smile was to everyone but for Inez he added a wink.

Next Sundays at church, George asked Inez,

"Has anyone written to your father asking permission to courten you?"

"Yes, why are you asking?"

"From the first time I saw you I have not stopped thinking of you. I was wondering, if you were not spoken for, then I would write home for you"

"Why" She asked as she twisted her lace hand key.

"Because all I have been doing since I got here was thinking of you.

I asked around the estate about you and your family. I know enough about you"

"Why are you asking about me?" She was enjoying it.

"I just told you, I couldn't stop thinking of you. Do you like him?"

"Him? Who him?"

"The boy who wrote home for you?"

"Oh him? No" she forgot about her lie to his question. "No I did not like him, so my father did not give him permission to visit".

The following Sunday, George presented to Dada Alexander a letter, requesting permission to court his daughter Inez. Permission was granted.

George brought his family to meet the Alexander family. Three months later he and Inez were engaged.

"Mother, George wants to take me to Skeldon to see where he is from".

"Oh yes; when is he planning to do this?"

"Next week Saturday, Mother".

"Did he discuss this with Dada? Dada did not discuss this with me"

"No Mother, we are engaged, he don't have to ask permission to take me anywhere?" Inez was sure to make her answer a question rather than a statement.

"Well, young lady, let me tell you something, yes, you are engaged.

The reason a boy engage a girl, is to prevent other boy from looking at his girl. You see how quick he was". Mother looked around for an audience but there was none. Inez knew better never to approach her mother with a subject as such with any one around.

"Let me tell you something else, young lady, the only time you go anywhere alone with George or any other man is after your wedding, never before.

What do you think people would say if my young daughter went someplace alone with a young man? Engagement gets broken" after a moment to think, Mother, said

"Tell George that you and I would be happy to go to Skeldon with him on Saturday"

One year later they were married. She was nineteen and he was twenty-two.

The estate gave them a large two-story house with a large fenced yard in Free Yard.

He was a Sugar Boiler and his job entitled him to fringes such as a gardener and a maid.

After what seemed like more hours than they counted, the two women held each other on the floor of the 'big house' and cried for a long time. They wiped each other's eyes with their garments and cried again and again.

Inez cried out of pity for Tatri.

Tatri cried because, finally, she found someone who cared enough to pity her.

Tatri told her son about the visitor, "She is beautiful, I can't tell if she is Black or Indian? I just know that she has a good mind.

The nice lady make me stand up pan one piece a paper, then she draw me foot"

"Well I do not know what is her intention but I think that the owner of this house do not want someone living here wearing sari and hernee all the time. These are English people and they want you to dress like them if you go live in dem house"

"No, no, notatall, nobody go mek me change the way me a dress and me na wear no shoes pan me foot. This foot never ben pan nothing but God ground"

"Then you better start packing you lil basket to move out of the people house"

Knock, knock "Daddy, daddy, is me Esther, Grandmother send me to wake you up. Breakfast is ready and everyone is waiting to eat"

"Go tell her that I will eat later" Many Sundays the family ate without him.

His mother carefully put away his soup until he is ready for it. Not this Sunday.

Knock, knock, bang, bang "Archie, get your drunken ass up and find yourself at my dinning table right now"

Archie walked into the dinning room full of all his siblings and their spouses.

He was carrying a huge hangover and thought that he was seeing things.

His brother Rick walked over to him planted a kiss on his unshaved cheek and a bear hug that lifted him off the floor.

He sobered up quickly when he saw his eldest brother, Willy and his wife Clara and Rick wife, Trude in the room. 'Something big must be happening. Could it be they are here for Easter? Mother always said that Easter is the most important holiday'

After all the hugs and kisses, Archie placed himself on the bench next to his brother and pal, Rick. Still holding on to him.

Mother, sitting at the head of the long table, still dressed in her Sunday best, gloves and all, holding her husband's hand, looked slowly around the table.

All ten of her children and nine of their spouses were looking at her. She was on high cloud. She was happy because she knew that they are here to support her.

"Is there someone at my table who is not properly attired?"

Archie sprang up and left the room. Returned a few minutes later wearing his shirt, pants and hat. He did not wear shoes. Even his mother could not change that.

With all the excitement he sat at the table with his Wilson felt hat on his head.

"I think somebody needs to go to the looking glass and see if he is disrespecting my table? First he comes here without a shirt on, then he sit at my table with a hat on"

Archie wondered 'why is she picking on me like this today? Even though she is right, I still have a feeling that she is out to get me for some reason or the other. I know my mother more than anyone else around this table'.

"Let us pray. Dear God, thank You for your everlasting love and guidance.

I need them more than ever at this time. I know that I could always call upon You, because I know that only You, and through You I will find the right answers.

Thank You for bringing my boys and their family from so far across the waters.

Thank You for bringing everyone here today, even the ones who seldom come.

Thank You for this dear husband whom you have chosen for me.

Thank You for this food that You have provided and we are about to partake.

Once more, Dear God, give me strength to do what You want me to do. Amen".

Dada took his wife hand in his and said, "Mother, please think carefully before a mistake is made. One that none of us can correct. Think before you act"

"I am thinking my dearest husband. I am doing what I should have done a long time" she looked at the table, making sure that everything was in place and the food was steaming. She slowly took off her hat and gloves while all eyes were on her.

"Willy and Rick, I want to thank you for coming and bringing your wives and children at such a short notice. Dada and I are so happy to see all our children in this room once again"

Everyone enjoyed his/her soup. Archie was uncomfortable serving himself.

His mother always did it for him to make sure that he gets the sinew and the best cuts.

Several times she attempted to go to his aid but Dada pulled her back to her seat.

"Loose the apron string, Mother. Starting right now" said Dada, in his soft voice.

"Some of you do not know it yet, but we are gathered here today to make arrangements for a wedding this coming Saturday"

Archie was so busy with himself planning what he and Rick are going to do while he is visiting, that he did not pay any attention to his mother's announcement.

Words got around and everyone else except Archie knew who was getting married. "James, George and Barkley, your job is to start building tents around the house. Borrow Mr. McKay mule cart and go to the Lodge house and bring benches, tables and dishes and whatever else we will need from there.

Bertram, sun and brush one of Dada's suit for him to wear, it's a waste of money to make a new one that will be worn only once. The man does not wear proper clothes.

Make him a white shirt. At least that should be new, if we get lucky, he may wear it again He has to wear shoes, but you know that after the wedding, they will be thrown under his bed to dryrat. Polish one of Dada's and let him wear it for the day".

Like a school boy asking for permission to speak, Dada raised his hand and said

"Bertram, make the man a new suit. A man must wear his own suit to his wedding"

"Waaittt a minute. Whoooo the hellll are you people talking about?" Archie was on his feet about to jump on top of the table. Upon hearing about the shoes, he realized that he is the only one in the family who do not wear shoes. Who is getting married?

"Sit down. Don't you ever be disrespectful in my home? Set your ass down"

"A man getting married? Everyone knows about it but him? What is this?

Archie got no response from anyone, not even a sympatric glance from Rick.

"As I was saying before the rude disruption, Inez and Wini will be busy with the sewing. Inez will be the maid-of-honor and Esther the flower girl.

The nights before the wedding, if you have to tie him to the Sancoka tree, do.

We will get him to church and get him married. We can do it. Make him a man"

The silence around the table was defining, bringing smoke out of Archie's ears.

With no interruption T-Janie on center stage, continued to deliver her instructions.

"I already spoke to Bhalo about cooking and feeding the Hindu people in his yard.

I asked Mustafa to cook for the Muslim and everyone else in this yard.

Archie will bring one of his young bulls on Friday and have it inspected by the sanitary inspector before Mustafa pray and do what he has to do.

I am trying to make this occasion the grandest; afterall my son is getting married.

I want everyone to come and have a good time. They must eat, drink and be merry.

Because I know that the Hindu will come but will not eat. I arranged for Bhalo, who cook at all the Hindu occasions, to do everything in his yard, which is just across from ours. This way, we make our Hindu friends comfortable. They will eat.

With Mustafa doing the Hal al, our Muslim friends will be happy, they too will eat.

All our other family and friends are going to eat no matter who cook the food".

Mother was feeling good. She did not see any sign of disapproval from any one.

She looked strait at stunned Archie and said,

"I waited for years for you to bring someone home, anyone, and say to me that you are ready to get married. I would have done what I am doing now, years ago.

Even if you had dressed a crapro [frog] and said 'Mother this is what I want for a wife', I would have called a meeting just like I am doing now, and get you married.

But, what did you do? The only child of mine to get another man's wife in the family way, and, I have to raise that child. That was fifteen years ago.

That same woman continue to make children for you, all of them looking like you and Esther. Oh yes, every time when another child born, the saying, 'It's Archie's alright'.

Every night I have to wonder which woman husband is going to chop you into pieces?

It would seem as if you were born to disgrace this family. You wear a piece of loincloth and walk the streets like a sahado [Indian priest].

You refused to eat with a spoon. You refused to wear shoes. You refuse to speak proper English. You have only Indian friends, not that I have anything against that, but you have made yourself more of an Indian than the Indians themselves. I do not recall making you for an Indian man. Your father is a Black man. You are a Black man.

What made you so different from all of my other children? Answer me, Archie"

Archie was sober and was fully aware of what's happening around him.

He knew that if he used the only weapon he had left, his mother may think twice before going through with her crazy plan. 'This is my last chance to get out of this'

"Mother, please let me tell you how sorry I am for being so rude to the family.

Everything you said today, I heard many times before and you are right, as always.

I am who I am. I cannot change now". He paused, looked at his mother for her reaction.

"Mother, the reason I never bring home a girl to you or think of getting married is because no one can cook for me. All my life, you have been cooking my food.

I never ate from anyone else. Only you know how to prepare my meals"

He saw that what he said did not move anyone. He heard some giggles around the table, but his mother was not impressed.

"Dada, I beg of you, don't allow this madness to go on. Say something,"

"Madness? Is that what you call what I am trying to do? Madness?

All your brothers around this table wrote letters and got permission to courten their wives. Dada and I received four letters for your sisters"

"I once wrote a letter too, Mother" Archie's voice trembled with emotion.

Inez cried out loud as she remembered the event as if it was yesterday.

"Yes you did. You certainly did. That was what, sixteen or seventeen years ago?

It certainly did not stop you form being the stallion of the plantation.

Everywhere I turn, I see little Dugla children [Indian and Black mixed] looking just like Esther. I know an Alexander child when I see him/her.

I know it's not my husband because he is home five minutes after the factory bell rings. When he goes to lodge, he goes with his sons.

I know they are not your brothers' because they are all respectfully married.

They know that if any of their wives come to me complaining, we will join forces.

That leaves only you to mix the two races in this estate". She needed to breath.

"If, what happened with your letter so many years ago, affected you so badly, you should have gone to Dr. Sharples and ask him to ah, ah, what's the word Dada?"

"Castrate or kapoon or altar, Mother"

"Yes, that's it. Cut it off"

Archie thought 'I have to win this fight. I will fight with all I have'

"Mother, don't do this married thing now. I know you have made lots of plans and I will still bring the bull for Mustafa to cook. We can still do everything as you wish.

We can put the wedding off for a later date. We can have a family celebration for having Brother Willy and Rick coming with their family from so far to be with us.

It could be an Easter celebration. We could have an Alexander family reunion"

Some around the table nodded their heads in agreement. Even Dada looked at his wife and nodded his head and took her cold, shaking hands into his.

Linda, what do you think? In 1938, a thirty-two years old man pleading to his family not to make him marry someone he hardly knew. What do you think?

I think it should be left up to Archie to decide if he wants to marry or not.

I think so too.

"I waited for years for you to bring a girl home. I have two homes. This is one and Lancaster is the other. You finally brought a girl home and I approve". Mother said as she stood up and looked at the ones who nodded their heads. Her lips pouted.

She walked away from the table, secured her hat on her head with golden pins.

Her white gloves in place and handbag in hand, she said

"This meeting is over. You all know what you have to do.

I have to go and invite the whole estate to my son's wedding next Saturday". She shouted for Esther and said,

"Esther, get your shoes and hat, lets go invite the whole plantation to your father's wedding. You will now have one and only one legal step-mother"

Every household in Port Mourant Sugar Estate got the same invitation.

"My son Archie is getting married on Saturday coming, you are invited from 2pm"

Esther got so accustomed to the same announcement that she began to repeat the words as she walked along with her grandmother.

Rick joined Archie at the Chinese Bridge, where, as children, they sat the edge of the bridge with their legs dangling over the Sideline canal, daring gravity.

He sat next to his brother, put his arm around his shoulder and said.

"Mike, I did not know why Mother needed me to be here. I got a telegram from George saying 'Mother needs you, come Sunday for ten days. No health emergency'

I think the same telegram was sent to Brother Willy. What can we do if Mother calls?"

"But Rick, I know if no one else believe me, you will. I am telling you the truth; I do not know the people. I said it so many times that I feel that my tongue is going to fall off. Why is this family going along with my mother to do this to me?"

"I do not know my brother, all I can say is that Mother has a point when she said that you must have some feeling for this woman. You took her to the 'big house' Mike. You don't take a woman you don't know, to live in your family home?

And I think the rest of the family wants you to join the club of married people"

After a long silence, Rick said

"Lets go meet the boys a Dhalwa, I have to task of telling them about the wedding"

"You don't tell them. Let me be the one to tell my friends, in my own time"

"No Mike, I am sorry but Mother ordered me to do this task, with or without you"

Greetings to Rick, congratulations to Archie and questions like, 'is it true Mike?'

Joe, Bang, Secharan and Tigar at their usual table. They were so surprised to see Rick. When he told them the reason for the visit, the party was no more.

"Mike, the five of us have been friends long before we were old enough to wear long pants. Is that right? Asked Joe. [Boys wore long pants when they get their first job]

"Right" answered confused Archie.

"Then why would you keep such an important event from us? We have to hear it from your brother who come from across the sea to tell us that our best friend is getting married, when our best friend sat right here with us last night?'

"He did not think that we were good enough to share in such an important event"

"That's not true"

"Then why would you keep something as important as this from us till now?"

"I don't know"

"What you mean? 'You don't know?' What you don't know?"

"Nothing"

"Lef de man alone. Can't you see de man change? Dis is not de man who drink with us last night. Dis is not the man who we know for all dem years. Dis a one different man"

Dhalwa, who knew the men all their adult lives, felt it was time for him to speak.

"Alright boys, listen to me for a minute. You are friends. You have been friends for too many years. I admire the five of you more than anyone else who comes in here. I never have to ask any one of you to pay your bill on payday. Each one of you knows whose turn it is to pay". Putting his hand on Archie's back, he continued,

"This man has not changed. He attended every one of you weddings, he attended your entire grand parents funeral. He shared in the joy of all your children arrival.

I do not recall a time when he was not in the midst of you. Why are you so quick to judge him? Give the man a chance to explain what is happening, or why the hurry?

Archie sat motionless, cradling his head in his hands to prevent it from exploding.

The rum was not working fast enough, so, he had to hear what his friends were saying.

"Now, just one minute" Archie's hands were up. The rum will help him now.

"I listened to all of your lowdown talk. Questioning my loyalty to this gang.

I don't blame you for being surprised at what Rick told you. But, to question my position among you, makes me wonder about your loyalty to me"

Four Indian and one Negro shared a rare love and closeness that was the envy of many. After many years, that friendship came to question. It was especially hard for Archie whose love for his friends had never ever quivered.

"Remember two Fridays ago I was late coming here?" Archie reminded himself that men do not cry among men.

"Remember I told you that I was helping a lady and her son to find a place to stay?

Archie was shivering. He did not tremble when his mother put his neck on a noose this morning. Why is he so troubled because his friends are questioning his friendship?

His mother had been his main squeeze all his life. Without a doubt, he knew that had it not been for his mother and his grandma Harriet, he would have been absent long ago.

Beside his mother and family, his four friends were the closest to his heart.

His heart was breaking because they were doubting his love and trust for them.

"Don't ever accuse me of keeping secrets from you. What I told you is the truth"

Archie was speaking and everyone was listening.

"Mike, if you wanted to help these people? You could have brought them to us and we would have taken them to our home. We have done that before.

We are married people with families. If we help a battered woman and her children, our wives and children look up to us as heroes.

You, on the other hand, my brother, is a bachelor. When a bachelor takes a woman to his home, that's a different story. Especially when he knows this person for more than a year and met her more than four different times.

You must admit that there is something more than what you are telling us?"

Rick knew that when it comes to these five men, everyone else should do what he had been doing since he delivered his mother's message, sit quietly and listen.

"Look on the bright side Mike" said Bang, placing his arm around Archie's neck,

"You can look at this whole matter in a happy way. Getting married is not such life-threatening ordeal. You will be joining us and we wouldn't have to worry about you brucking you foot from jumping out of somebody window.

I do not care what class this lady is. All I can gather is that if she did not trust you, she would not come to you for help, and, if you did not feel something for her, you would have left her alone the first time you saw her in the woods.

You would not have taken her to your home when she to you for help. Give it a shot"

Archie got up, straighten his Wilson felt hat he had been using as a stress squeeze.

He walked to the door, leaving his friends and brother still laughing. He said

"Everyone is incorrectly presuming to know what's right for me"

Archie walked through the entire sugar estate. Just walked and walked. He had no place in particular to go but he was walking to clear his head.

It was after midnight when he decided where he was going.

Ivoreen heard the whistle that she had been answering to for some years.

Leaving her husband asleep, she went out of her room, down the stairs and under the range where the whistler was lying in the hammock.

Ivoreen was a young, beautiful Indian woman who was forced to married a much older man when she was fourteen years old.

She had five children but neither her husband nor children knew that she quietly sneaked out to meet Archie in a hammock under the house in Free Yard where the logy were some steps off the ground, unlike Bound Yard where it was on the ground.

"So, me hear you ah go married next Saturday? Wa go happen wid me afta da?"

"Please, not tonight. I just want to sleep tonight. I will leave early in the morning"

Forty-two years later, Archie told me that Sunday February 27th 1938 was the worst day in his life. Too many lives were affected, to this day, based on that decision.

After slavery, most of the coastal land was divided into villages.

There were Negro villages, like Lancaster, Liverpool, Manchester, Ulverston, Ulnas.

Then there were Indian villages, like Whim, Little Kenny, Bloomfield and so on.

By just hearing the name of the village, one knew if it was an Indian or Negro village.

By the 1930s many Indians and Muslims moved into the Negro villages and lived in harmony with the Negroes. But, not one Negro felt comfortable enough or was allowed to move into an Indian village.

Katy Gunraj and her husband Bull, a young Madrass couple moved to Lancaster in the mid 30s with four children and a fishing boat. They made their living selling fish.

Their little one-room, mud-wall, grass-roof hut was two lots away from the Alexander.

When Katy saw the Indian woman and son at the "big house', she and her neighbors began to wonder who the strangers were?

The thing about a village was that nothing happened or no one moved in without everyone knowing about it. Whether they move to Waterside, Middledam or Backdam. Everyone had to know who they were? Who gave or sold the land to them? Why did they move here? Where they come from? Are they prepared to live in peace with the villagers or they are here to separate and discriminate? to change their peacefulness?

Villagers gathered anywhere where there are more than one person standing.

They discuss current happenings. They had a very good support and communicating system. Everyone looked out for everyone. The elderly and children belonged to every villager. They cared for them as their own, for no monetary rewards from anyone.

Tatri and Dhia were happy with their new life.

Dhia already had a job and friends. Tatri yarned to meet other women, just to speak with. Even though she was at peace, she was alone. She never had any such before.

She stepped out of the yard and walked over to Katy's fence. She said

"Me and me son a live in the big house. Me see you and want to come meet wid you"

"Me know you and you son a live there. Where ayou come from? How come ayou a live in dem Black people house?" Katy got the chance to ask the question that so many villagers were asking among themselves.

"Aby a stay here for a lil time, til me son can mak nuff money to mek a house"

Katy had many questions to ask the Bramhin woman standing by her fence.

She took one closer look at Tatri and decided not to ask her any question.

She saw what she needed to know. 'One hell-of-a battered woman looking for a friend'

Katy became Tatri's best friend. Every evening they sat on the steps and talk.

Tatri told Katy everything about herself and what she went through with Ram.

But when she told her that her parents live at Whim, the next village, and who they were, Katy's reaction was the same as others who knew that it was a bad mix.

When Tatri told her about Inez measuring her, Katy said

"Dem a English people, if you a go live in dem house, you go ave to dress like dem. They no want people walking around in sari and hernee.

You na expect to wear dem sari and hernee and live in dem people house?"

The women folk were busy baking, sewing and cleaning.

A wedding in those days was a two weeks affair. One week before, one after.

The festivity includes singing folk songs, beating drum by using an old saucepan with a spoon or stick, eating and drinking until the wee hours of the morning.

Some go strait to work after such a night, others slept on benches, floor or wherever, but woke up in time to continue the preparation and be ready for the night fun.

The night before the wedding was when everything broke loose.

Its called the 'Kwa kwa' night. The older folk sang old African songs in a broken English, telling the bride or groom what they have to do on their wedding night.

Children were not allowed in the area where the singing and dancing were done, because the actions of the folk singers and dancers were not appropriate for children.

It was the highlight of a Negro wedding, and no one wanted to miss that night.

Saturday March 5th 1938

This day changed the lives of many people for the rest of their lives, especially the ones who were not even born yet. The unborn paid a greater price.

In Bound Yard, everyone was busy from four o'clock in the morning.

"What time did you tell Chundon to come with his car?" [Chundon was a Syrian and only businessman in the area who had a car. He rented it for special occasion, especially weddings. He enjoyed watching the envious spectators lined the road as he drive slowly with a bride and groom in his shining Chrysler] Mother asked Bertram.

"Eight thirty, Mother"

"That's good, he will have to make two trips. He will first take me, Dada, Esther and Inez. He will drop us off and take Inez to Lancaster to dress the bride.

He will then come back here to pick up Rick, Archie, Wini and Harriett, drop them at the church then go pick up Inez and the bride".

Other family members gathered around to listen to Mother's instructions. She said.

"Rick, make sure you make him looking good, I am depending on you to make sure that he is present in church. Everyone else, make sure that all goes well here.

We should be back with the bride and groom about twelve o'clock, enough time for you to meet your new sister and to welcome our guess at two o'clock".

Mother went into her bedroom where her husband was getting dressed.

He was known by all as the 'quiet one'. He never raised his voice on anyone.

He very seldom had to scold any of his children. His wife did it for both of them.

"Egbert, do you have the ring?" on serious matters, she called him by his given names. He did likewise.

"What? What ring? Janey"

"The ring Dada, the ring. Your son is getting married today. Did you get a ring?"

"Why do I have to get the ring? I am not the one who is getting married". His disapproval of the whole affair came out in his voice.

"You know Archie was not going to buy a ring. I am busy getting everything done"

"That's the problem Janey, you are the one who made all the decisions. You are the one who knows what is best for everyone. You are so busy making sure that everything goes your way, you forget that for a wedding you would need a ring".

"How could you say something like that, at a time like this?"

"Yes Janey, I need to say that and much more" he was looking at his wife who had never seen him so angry. He continued "Ever since you came home from up the coast three Saturdays ago, you have been striking the whip. You have made up your mind and some how, you have made up everyone else's mind. I wonder if you realize what you are doing?" his wife tried to say something, but he stopped her.

"No Janey, you hear me out. Archie told you the truth. He is so much like me. He is always willing to help. Does that mean that one has to marry everyone he helps?

If that's the case, I too should be marrying every Indian woman who comes to me for help. They ask for jobs for their husband, they ask for money to feed their children, and yes, I too help Indian women whenever I can but I do not marry them"

He looked down at his wife who was sitting on the bed, looking up to him. She had never seen him so blunt. He always did his best to please her but this time he is angry and he knew in his heart that something wrong is happening and he has to be a part of the wrong. He has to find a ring to seal the wrong.

She was the 'iron lady' but whenever she entered their bedroom with her husband, she left her iron fist outside the door.

Her husband gently pulled her to her feet and put his large arms around her slender shoulders and said, "The only ring I ever had to get is the one you are wearing"

After he allowed her to display her tender side, he wiped her eyes with his lips.

"Where is that cigar box that you keep the jewelry?"

She reached under the bed and pulled out a brown grip, opened it and handed her husband the old red cigar box that one of the Manager of the plantation had given to Dada, full of cigar of course, when their first child was born.

The empty box was too beautiful to throw out. It became their jewel box.

Dada took a ring out of the box and placed it in his wife's hand, he said.

"Your son has a ring"

"No, no, Dada, we can't use this, this is Nana Harriett's ring".

"Don't I know that it's my mother's ring? This is the ring my Dada

124

placed on my Mama's finger on their wedding day. It came off her finger the day she died"

"This ring belongs to your whole family. It should remain in this box. We will find another ring from somewhere"

"My mother would be dancing in her grave when the ants take the message to her that her grandson Archie got married and he used her ring at the ceremony"

"Thank you, thank you my dearest husband. You know I want only what's best"

Linda, we will talk about the ring again, a long time from now.

Husband and wife helped each other get dress. She straightened his tie and mouthstach and he pinned her hat to her hair allowing her golden curls to fall on her back. He took the powder puff and patted her face to cover the lines left by her tears.

He looked at his wife from head to toes. Then from stockings to garters and said,

"How many years have we been married? How did you remain as beautiful?"

"We've been married over forty years. You're the one who keep me happy and gay"

As Mother and Dada were about to exit their bedroom, Mother tuned to him and said,

"I get my strength from you" she reached up and kissed him.

He replied, "I get everything from you" he reached down and kissed her.

The ride to Aklyne Scotch Church was wordless. Everyone was in his or her own thoughts. Even Chundon, the driver felt the need to oblige.

Mother, Dada and Esther were dropped off at the church. They were shocked to see the church and its yard were already full of people.

Mother walked up to the alter where the Reverent Byer was standing, draped in his long white robe and white scarf around his neck, holding the bible of course.

He was surprised at the crowd of people who squeezed themselves into the benches. Women sitting and men standing against the walls of the beautiful, old wooden church with stain glass windows. Many were standing in the churchyard.

The Reverent knew that after announcing that Michael Archibald Hunter Alexander will be getting married to Jane on Saturday, March 5th, most of the villagers would be there to see if its true, but, he never expected everyone to be there.

It was not unusual for many onlookers to go in a churchyard to critic at a wedding. On this day there were more villagers who went, because they heard that Archie was getting married and they wanted to see who was the girl who finally trapped him.

Some of the women had hoped that they could have been the one he would have married some ten, fifteen years ago, when they were young and available.

The church was so full that Mr. Corte, the deacon, had to plea with the crowd to leave four front pews empty for the wedding party.

"Reverent, I want to thank you for granting me this favor in such short notice"

"Mrs. Alexander, it is a privilege and an honor to serve your family.

I stood right here and married most of your children and christened all your grands"

"Yes Reverent, but with the time being so short, you could have refused us"

"No, I could not do that to your family, not after what has happened. Like I told Milton, I know that no matter how short notice I get, once my people are in trouble, especially someone from a family like yours, I will bend the rules.

Milton told me everything. I know that Archie has been, what should I say? Different from the rest of your children. I hope that this mischief that he get himself into will open his eyes and bring him back to church"

"Reverent, thanks again" Mother thought 'What the hell is he talking about?'

Chundon drove Inez two villages away from the church, to Lancaster.

She balanced herself on the long slender bridge, carrying the bridal attire.

Inez entered the 'big house' and smell the clean. She wondered how could a crippled woman do all of this?

She entered the large bedroom and laid the white brocade dress, a satin petticoat and bloomers on the large lace canapé bed that was her parents.

She placed the white shoes on the floor, stepped back and examined everything.

Mother sent a lace mantilla for the bride's head. It was something old.

She was pleased with her work. She left the room to go find the bride.

'Eleven years ago I got dressed in this same room, with my Grandma, Mother and Aunt Sudith fussing over me. Putting a shilling in my shoe so I will always have money. Tying blue ribbon on my hair, wearing Mother's old gloves and borrowing Grandma's pearls. I was a perfect bride. What kind of a bride is she going to be?'

Inez spoke to herself as she looked back into the empty room.

She found Tatri in the garden.

Tatri stood up wearing the widest, toothless smile. Her friend is back to visit.

"We have to make haste, the car will be coming back for us in short time"

Tatri reminded herself to do anything, go anywhere, once it is not back to Ram.

"Alright, let me wash up, I will soon come upstairs to meet you" she remembered her friend Katy's words, "They may want you to change to a Christian. If you go live in dem house, you go have to wear frock, not sari ".

They entered the bedroom and Tatri looked at everything lying on the bed.

Inez saw the question in her eyes, her heart sank. She didn't know what to say.

She started by putting her arms around Tatri and began to cry.

Tatri dried Inez tears. Still smiling, she nodded her head, making

Inez feel more at ease. In other words, she gave her permission to do whatever she wants with her.

"We have to make haste, the car will be here to take us to church"

'Just like Katy said, I am going to church to become a Christian' Tatri's thoughts

Inez could not stop the tears streaming down her face as she helped to undress Tatri. She wondered how does she get dress without help?

She gasped for air when she saw Tatri's nicked body. Her light complexion exposed all the dark marks on her body. Very little of her body was speared.

Inez later described Tatri's back, "It looked like someone glued some dry twigs or branches on her bare back. Its no wonder that she still cover herself from hear to toe"

The tears flowed as Inez tried to dress a Hindu into 'Christian' 'English' clothe.

For the first time in thirty years of life, she was getting dress but it was not a sari.

Tatri was getting dress with all the items of an English lady. The kind of clothing that her father always condemned and forbid.

Inez saw the discomfort in Tatri's action of not wanting to expose her woman's part. She put on the petticoat first, then the bloomers. Then she struggled with the dress, which she had to use hook en eyes to accommodate Tatri's deformed left arm.

Inez stepped back, with pride and admiration in her teary eyes.

She looked at Tatri, standing like a manikin, a toothless, smiling manikin.

She looked as if she was poured into the white dress. Like you see in the showcase.

Her slender waist and wide hips made the dress looked as if it was sewed on her.

Tatri combed her long, black hair, making sure to cover all the bald spots. She put a strait path in the center of her head then made a bun at the back of her head. She then placed a red dot in the center of her forehead and the same red sandoor on the path on her head. [An indication that she is a Hindu woman who is married]

With all her gold and silver jewelry, including her heavy foot-ring and nose-ring, Tatri had Inez in a state of amazement. She was shocked to see how this shy, helpless, battered person turned herself into a statement for all to take notice of.

Inez looked out of the window and saw that Chundon was parked on the road.

"We have to hurry, the car is waiting for us. Put these shoes on and let's go"

Tatri, still smiling, shook her head from side to side and said

"I never wear a shoe before and I am not going to wear one now. If you are in a hurry, we better go"

Inez picked up the pair of white shoes from the floor and followed Tatri out of the house, down the stairs, on to the long slender bridge and into the waiting car.

Chundon looked at Inez with shock in his eyes. Inez looked at the bride with amazement. She wondered how can someone with no lipstick, rooch or anything that makes a woman looks beautiful on her wedding day, be so pretty without even looking at herself in the looking glass?

"The bridal car is here, the bridal car is here. Everyone please take your seats. Those of you who do not have seats, please stand against the wall and be quiet" Mr. Cort said.

The organist played 'here comes the bride' and everyone stood up and looked at Inez holding Tatri with one hand and a pair of white shoes in her other hand.

The church was so quiet, if a bird had dropped a feather, one would've heard it.

Archie and Rick stood up and faced the alter.[In those days, the groom did not look back at his bride-to-be until the priest give him permission to face her]

Tatri's head and face was covered with the lace mantilla that Mother sent.

Her long hair fell down her back, down to her butt when she came out of the car.

Bear footed with heavy silver foot rings, she walked up the isle, holding on to Inez.

The congregation was still. Some had their hands on their heads, some had their hands on their open mouths and others had their hands on their stomach.

Everyone had dry eyes from lack of blinking.

Reverent Byer took one look at the woman holding Inez hand and he appeared to be in a cardiac distress. His neck and face swell like a bullfrog.

After sucking in some oxygen, the priest looked at Dada, using his index finger like a caterpillar, he said "Mr. Alexander, I would like to speak to you in the Vestry, now"

Reverent Byer was standing by the window sucking the fresh air he needed so badly.

Dada entered the room not knowing how he was going to clam the priest.

"How could your family do this to me?"

"What Reverent?"

"Bringing an Indian women to be married in my church?"

"You have married Indian people in our church here before?"

"Yes, but they were Christian Indians, not Hindu Indians"

"Who cares Reverent, whether they are Christian, Hindu, Muslim, Bhudas or Amerindian, aren't they all God's children?"

"Yes, but rules are rules. If they are baptized into Christianity, there will be no objection marrying them or presiding over their funeral.

I am sorry but one has to be a Christian in order to be married by me in this church.

I took one look at that woman walking into my church and see Hindu all over her.

Dada knew that he had to be softer in his tone, he said.

"Reverent, I promise you, I will see to it that she gets converted to Christianity"

The priest mopped his face and around his neck then asked Dada

"Can this girl speak and understand English? To understand the marriage vows?"

"Yes Reverent" answered Dada. He knew very well that he knew nothing about the lady in question. Like the Reverent, it was the first time he too had seen her.

"Alright Dada, I will do this for you and your family. I do not want to bring anymore shame and disgrace to ayou today"

"Thank you, thank you Reverent. You are truly chosen by God to do His service"

"Yes, well someone has to do it. Let me go out there and do my duty"

Tatri stood next to Archie but closer to Inez, whose hand she never let go.

She did not hear a word or understood a word that the priest was saying.

She knew the moment she walked away from Miss Weeby she moved into a new world.

She promised herself that she would accept whatever that new world had to offer.

She knew that she was getting married when she saw the clothes on the bed.

Katy had told her "If the dress is lil below your knee, you are getting baptized.

If the dress is long to your ankle, then you are getting married"

Once again she was getting married but did not know to whom.

'If I am getting married to this man standing next to me, then at least I know him'.

Tatri's thoughts as she absorb her surroundings through the lace.

"Linda, you very seldom asked question while I speak" I asked my friend.

With her blue eyes wide open, She asked,

"How could Tatri get married to Archie if she was still married to Ram?"

"You see, in those days Hindus get married traditionally. The parents make the match. Sometimes from the time the children were born.

The wedding was done according to Hindu rites. Combining religion, culture and tradition but not registered to make it legal"

"The Colonials, after slavery, did not get involved in people's tradition anymore The only requirement was that they record the birth of every child born in the Colony.

All eyes were on Tatri. Some craning their necks to see her face, some looking at the outline of her body and how well the dress caressed it, others, including all the Alexander family members, wondered 'Who is this bare-footed bride?'

"Michael Archibald Hunter Alexander, do you take this woman Jane to be your lawful wedded wife, to protect and love through sickness and health till death do you part?"

"Yes"

"No, you do not say yes, you say 'I do' "

"I do"

The Reverent turned his attention to Inez, whom he saw as the only one who will help him through this strange and buzzard ceremony.

"Jane, do you take this man, Michael Archibald Hunter Alexander as your lawful wedded husband, to love, honor and obey til death do you part?"

Everyone was still. They needed to assure themselves that it was not a manikin but a real walking, talking somebody standing with Inez.

But Tatri was still in her dreaming state until Inez tugged at her arm and indicated that she should pay attention to the priest, whose eyes were halfway out their sockets.

Tatri obeyed Inez and nodded her hear.

"No, no, I need to hear her say the words" The Reverent demanded

"Reverent, she can't speak or understand English" whispered Inez.

"My God, what have I gotten myself into"

"Nothing bad, Reverent, you are joining together two people of different race and language. In the sight of God, you are doing what He wants you to do, putting these children together, regardless of any shortcomings". Said Inez to the nervous priest.

"I know that she has to say those two words. I will make her say them to you"

Inez lifted the mantilla off Tatri's face and said

"Look up to the Reverent and say 'Iiiii doooo' "

Weather he heard her or not, the Reverent knew that the ceremony was coming to an end and he must restrain his discomfort. He knew he was doing a big favor for the Alexander family, he also knew that this family was one of the largest and staunch supporters of the church. He knew that he and the church would benefit handsomely in the future for this big favor he is doing for them.

"The ring please"

Dada took the ring out of his pants pocket, held it in his hand for a while, as if he was deciding whether to pass it to Rick, the Best man or put it back into his pocket.

A hunch from Mother made the decision for him.

After the Reverent blessed the ring and instructed Archie to repeat after him

"With this ring, I thee wed" the Reverent watched very keenly as Archie struggled to place the ring onto Tatri's married-finger. He had to go on his knees to be able to praise her left hand far enough for him to slip his Nana ring on his wife's finger.

It was the first time that everyone saw the softer side of the Reverent. He actually stepped down from his pulpit to help Archie place the ring on the deformed bride.

"I now pronounce you man and wife. Lets go to the vestry to sign the register" he led the way to the small adjacent office. Inez and Tatri who did not let go of Inez hand throughout the whole confusion, still held on to her, followed by Archie and Rick.

The reverent opened a large ledger and pointed where the bride, groom and witnesses have to sign.

He brought out an inkpad, roll Tatri's right thumb into it and pressed it at the part where the bride was supposed to sign.

He then instructed Inez to hold the bride's hand, using the pen, make an X under her thumbprint. [That's the way it was done if one could not read or write]

The organist played 'Thank God the bride got married' as they exit the vestry.

There was no bride and broom holding hands. No bouquet of flowers for the bride. No rice throwing on the wedding couple.

Tatri held on to Inez and walked out of the church just like they walked into it two hours ago, with Inez still carrying a pair of white shoes in her hand.

"Brother, make sure get the real name of the bride for me, because I can't get the married certificate without the right information"

133

"Reverent Byer, on behalf of my family, I thank you so very much. Another priest would have thrown us out of his church from the beginning, but you are a very understanding man of God"

"Yes, yes my boy. I sure don't understand all of what happened here today though.

Maybe one Sunday after the dust settled, you will join Mrs. Byer and I for tea. Then you can explain what really happened here today"

Mother clasped her hands on Tatri's face and kissed her cheeks. She said

"You are my daughter now, no one will ever hurt you again"

Dada took Tatri's hand and said "I welcome you into my family my dear"

Understanding a little of what were being said to her, Tatri nodded her head to everyone. She knew that nodding her head meant yes and that there were not many yeses in her life. Now that she was given another chance to live in another world, she will make 'yes' her password into her new world.

Archie was on the other side of the churchyard, surrounded by curious information seekers/ mostly men, including his four best friends, needed a drink.

"Well me boy, we thought you will never do this. Who is this lady that bring you to the alter?" he wanted to say "My mother"

"Now that you are a married man, you have to stop running around wid dem gals"

"Archie, why you never like Black gals?"

"Me notice you pick one real high class Indian. How you do that?"

The questions were coming from all around him but he did not hear any of them.

His thoughts were on the poor, twisted, toothless barefooted person who is now legally his wife. His responsibility.

His thoughts drifted back into the church, standing so close to her. He did not hear a word spoken by the priest. He was looking at the woman standing next to him.

Through the laced mantilla, he saw the dark circle around her eyes. The brown marks on her face that stood out against her light complication. But the thing that drew his attention most of all was how calm and serine she was. She had a sense of quietness that he could not help but respect. For a moment he forget the madness.

Archie looked over the shoulders of the men gathered around him and saw Tatri holding on to Inez who was speaking to Mother and Dada. He thought 'She is my bride, she should be holding on to me, not my sister'. He whispered only for the wind to hear and take it to her "I will take care of you. No one will ever hurt you again".

He remember the electrical jolt he felt when he was on his knees, holding her hand and trying to put the ring on her finger. He knew it was something he felt in his heart.

"Mother, I am going to take 'her' back to the 'big house' " said Inez, with her Siamese glued to her side.

"What? Why? How are you going to do that?"

"I am going to get Chundon to take us to Lancaster. I will help to undress her then I will come back here for you"

"Have you gone mad? What about the reception?"

"No Mother, I have not gone mad. With all due respect, Mother, I allowed myself to be a part of this madness. I listened to you and like always, I believed that you know best". She placed her arm around Tatri's shoulder, pulled her close to her and said

"Well Mother, you get your wish. Your last single child is single no more. You had a wedding. Your son, Archie is married now. Lets all go back home and have a wonderful reception, without her. I will not subject her to anymore of this masquerade.

Do you know she did this just so she would be allowed to stay in peace in your house?"

"What are people going to say if there is no bride at a wedding reception?

"Let them say what they want to. Do you think that the wild bunch that ran out of the church, heading for our home are going to see the bride? Oh no, they are going for the food and drinks". Said Dada.

"Thank you for understanding, Mother. I know you will find an answer for them"

Inez walked with Tatri on the long, narrow bridge to the 'big house'. In silence they climbed the stairs and entered the house.

Inez looked around and said to Tatri. "This is your home now. No one will put you and your son out of it. You are now legally Mistress Jane Alexander".

Tatri nodded her head as if she understood every word. She took the pair of white shoes from Inez's hand, placed them down on the floor and took Inez two hands to her lips and kissed them. She then went down on her knees and kissed Inez's feet.

[An Indian way of giving respect]

Inez quickly pulled her to her feet and said "No, no you do not have to do that to me, I am your sister now. I am just like you. I am married too, to an Indian man name George. Your name is Mistress Alexander and my name is Mistress Katick"

Tatri still nodding and showing her gums, Inez said as she undressed the bride.

"From now on, you sleep in this bed" patting the mattress on the large canapé bed.

"This is where you and your husband will sleep. No more sleeping on the floor in that small room. Your son will sleep there alone and you will sleep here. Do you understand what I am saying to you?"

"Yes, me understand"

Car can get to Port Mourant much faster than the caravan of bicycles, donkey carts, mule carts, cow carts followed by walkers and runners who could not fit in any of the carts. Chundon car was full to the seams as he passed the excited crowd.

"But were they all invited to the wedding'? Asked Linda.

"No, but they were all village people. You see, all village people are considered family. It's an insult to 'invite' a family to any occasion. You only invite friends, not family. Family atomically knows that he/she has to be there. If for some reason someone did not attend, people will inquire and someone will have the answer. Could be sickness, a new baby or in the midst of harvesting rice.

One just had to belong to the same village and atomically he/she is family.

You only had to tell one person of an occasion, whether it is a wedding, death, birth, sickness or anything that's news and the whole village will be informed before your tongue gets wet again. An invitation is an 'option' we do not give family an option".

The bride-less wedding party arrived back at Bound Yard. As the car pulled up to the gate of the house, Mother picked up her imaginary whip.

"Dada, go and take off that jacket, you look like you frying eggs under it.

Sap your head and face with some lime rum. Get some cool ginger beer and come back to the gate to start welcoming our guests"

"Yes Mother"

"Mary, the whole village of Lancaster and other villages are on their way here. See to it that they get some cool maby or ginger beer. This heat call for plenty to drinking"

"Yes Mother"

Mother looked around to make sure that everything was up to her approval.

She saw the just married Archie standing under the Sankoka tree, jacket, tie and shoes in hand. Still trying to figure out what is happening, his mother's voice brought back.

"Archie, what are you doing? Standing there like a wild cow getting ready to bus rope and run away?" she placed her hand on his shoulder and continued

"Go to your room and get yourself together, then come back and join your father to welcome your friends". With her hand still on his shoulder she said

"Son, whatever you do today, will be excused because you got married, but only one thing I will ask of you, please come back out here wearing your pants and shirt"

"Yes Mother" Archie knew that once his mother starts talking, she was like a car that has to run out of gas before it stops. But she refuels quicker than any car.

As he entered the room, he was shocked to see how his unkept living space was transformed into to a room fit for human, or should I say for a bride and groom?

He was accustomed having his things thrown or hanged where he wanted. Now he wondered 'where is the towel that I covered my mirror with in the night? I have used that same towel to cover my mirror for as many years as I live in this room. Where is it?' [It was a custom to cover mirrors in a home. There were many explanations, such as, protection from lighten. It is claimed that lighten can shatter a mirror.

Protection from Jumbee, they said if one woke up in the middle of the night and looked into a mirror, he/she would see a spirit or a jumbee instead of his/her face.

If a funeral is passing on the street, the mirror had to be covered along with the windows and doors closed to prevent the passing spirit from entering the home]

Once per week Esther would change his bed and collect his dirty clothes. That was the extent of his housekeeping. He loved it that way.

On the white bedspread, laid a pair of blue pajamas and a pink satin nightgown. 'This is Mother doing. She thinks of everything, just to make things right.

Archie threw the socks and shoes under the bed, knowing that the cobweb would make better use of them.

Jacket and tie thrown over the wooden partition of the room. 'Who ever want that, they can have it' he spoke to himself.

He attempted to take his pants off but quickly remembered his mother's warning.

He sat on his bed and came face to face with himself through the mirror on his dresser. It seemed brighter after all the smoke smug had been cleaned off.

The mirror that he shared a very close relationship with. Closer than anyone else.

It saw him in his birth suit, in his drunken state and worst handovers.

He rehearsed his speeches in his mirror before he faced his mother.

In times of fear, or of joy, his mirror saw it, even if no one else did.

He told his mirror everything, and in turn it was very honest and truthful to him.

As they looked at each other, Archie said. "I got married today. You are looking at a married man. Do I look different? I made two women very happy"

Archie exited his room, cigarette in his mouth and a bottle of rum in his hand.

He was young, tall and crudely handsome. His white shirt opened, exposing a mat of soft curly hair on his chest. His flat stomach and muscular body caused some of the male guess to envy him and some of the female to envy the bride,

He walked through the crowd of well wishers, accepting their good wishes and whatever else they said to him, just like he told his mirror.

The most asked question was "Where is the bride? Who is the bride?

He politely smiled his way through the festive crowd to the back of the yard, next to the cow pen where his four friends were sitting at the usual spot under the jamoon tree.

They sat close to each other and ate, drank then danced to different music.

The five married men had so much fun that Mother had to wake them up on Sunday morning by splashing a bucket of cold water on them.

Tatri displayed tremendous strength, courage, respectability and restraint.

She knew that she had plunged out of the abyss into a new world. She will live everyday of the remainder of her life with gratitude to God for the freedom.

Three weeks without being beaten was a lifetime of freedom.

She realized that no dialogue would end the standoff in Whim. She just had to move on. She thought it would be as easy as it seemed. How wrong, how wrong she was.

She looked at the wedding dress and everything else that was placed on her by Inez. She left them on the bed to show her son when he returned from the sea.

She knew that she would fold them neatly and place them into the bag that they were brought into along with the unused white shoes, either for Inez to take back or for her to keep. She knew that she would never wear them again.

Tatri sat on the steps, waiting for her son. They both have things to tell each other.

"Tell me all about your day at sea, son"

"It was good Ma"

"What did you do? Did you work hard today?" she was stalling with small talk.

Tatri led her son into the large bedroom and pointed to the things on the bed.

Dhia stood stead fast and gazed on the items on the bed then he looked on the floor at the pair of white shoes. He looked at his mother with questioning eyes, opened mouth.

"What is all of dis? Where did you get all ah dis?"

"Member me tell you about the lady who come and measure me and me foot? Well that same lady come dis morning and put all dem thing dis pun me. Me na wear shoe"

"Wa she dress you with all of these English clothes for? Dhia asked, still in shock.

"She take me in a caar to the church near to de school wa you go go"

"You mean she tek you to the church fe get married?" he ask coldly.

"How you know da?"

"I am a big boy, I know what some people wear when they get married"

She told her son everything, from beginning to end. Just like when she used to sit on the step of their hut in Miss Webby and she told him stories of her childhood and India. This time she still sits on a step and tells her son everything on her day-to-day activity.

Dhia listened to his mother, he saw the innocents in her as she seek his understanding. a

"Now, you are legally married"

"Wa da mean? The nice lady told me the same words"

"Da means that you now have legal rights to stay in this house. If you not legal, you can't stay in somebody house. Now you are a legal resident".

"Who is the man dem married you to, Ma?" Dhia was not happy.

"De Black man" Tatri said, trying to see a sign in her son's eyes, any kind of sigh.

"De Black man? Which Black man dem married you to?" still no sign.

"De same one who bring aby here and give aby de money" Tatri was shaking.

Dhia saw that his mother was in distress and he was not going to make things worst.

He reached down and placed his hand on her shoulder and said

"Well, like I said, you are now a legal resident of this big house. That is if this house belongs to him? I do not think he would bring us here if he did not own it?

We are here, we are happy, no one to beat you up, we are happy. Who care wa kind a man you married as long as we are safe and happy"

Tatri whipped her tears with her hernee, she felt a little lighter, her son understands.

His support and understanding was all she lived for. She said

"The lady wa dress me and carry me to de church, when she bring me back, she tell me dat me must sleep pan dis bed from today" she patted the large canapé bed.

Katy went to Sahardat store and bought three yards of flowered cotton and a square of Madras Rhumal or headtie. She took the cloth to her dressmaker and told her to make a two-piece outfit, the kind the Indian women wore in those days. She asked that it be make to fit her but with the skirt being a little longer for a taller person.

She took the finished outfit and the rhimal to Tatri one evening. She said

"I bring you a wedding present. I think you should stop wearing those high class sari and hernee and start dressing like ordinary village people, this way the villagers will start looking at you as one of us, not the big-shot that you are" Katy was her first true friend. She got several other outfits made for her friend and watched her change from a high caste Brahmin to a local Indian woman from the village

Tatri and Katy sat on the steps of the 'big house' one evening, enjoying the full moon. Katy looked at her friend in a childish way and said

"You know, when its full moon like this, is when a man and woman hugup and do de thing. Me always enjoy a full-moon thing" she smiled wickedly and said.

"Wa happening? It been over three weeks since you get married, but Archie na come fe see you? He na come fe do his husbandly duty to his wife?

They put their arms around each other's shoulder and giggled like five years old.

Every Friday afternoon Archie gave Mother a small brown envelope to take to Lancaster on her Saturday's visit.

Saturday, following the wedding, Mother and Esther made their trip to Lancaster.

"Esther, you go and pick the vegetables and wait for me here, I am going to have a private talk with your step-mother"

"Alright Gramother, but she can't even speak English"

"Hush child, don't be rude. Do as I say, don't get into big-people business"

"I am not being rude Gramother, it's just that she can't speak English properly, and, you do not know how to speak her language"

"Who said I couldn't?"

Mother and Tatri went upstairs. Mother sat on the bench and Tatri sat on the floor.

Mother looked around the kitchen and could not remember a time when she ever had her kitchen so neat and clean.

Mother intended to be patient, to pick her words and combine them with signs to make Tatri understand her questions.

She has had lots of experience in that area. Having lived so many years among Indians, some of whom did not speak a word of English, she yet understood them.

Dada once told her that the Hindu despised the Englishman so much, that they refused to speak one English word.

"Where did you come from, my child?"

"Miss Weby"

"How did you know my son?

"Me no no you son"

Mother looked down at Tatri, she was looking at a battered yet beautiful young woman. A broken, yet honest young woman. Her heart quivered. She moved to the floor and reached out and grabbed her daughter-in-law into her arms.

The two women held each other and cried. They felt love of a mother and a daughter.

'Oh God, I hope I did the right thing. Please God, for the two young people's sake, let it be the right thing' Mother's prayer as she held on to Tatri

'Ohm Bhagwan, thank you for this mother and the sister you have given me' Tatri's prayer as she held on to Mother. She remembered that Inez had done the same with her. She wished the same or similar was done to her by her own mother and sisters.

Baldio, the quack dentist, arrived at Lancaster expecting that Archie's wife would be a Black woman. He was shocked to see Tatri dressed in her full Indian attire.

He spoke Hindi with her and asked for Archie's wife?

"Me ah his wife"

Baldio was speechless. He had to catch his breath before speaking.

"You are a high class Indian woman, what are you doing here? Are you telling me that you are the wife of a Black man?"

"Did you come here to ask me that?" Tatri was getting brave.

"No, Archie send me to measure his wife's mouth for false teeth. I did not know that his wife is you. I went to the wedding but no one saw the bride. I was expecting a Black girl. Not a Marageen as his wife"

"Do you use the same tools on everyone mouth?"

"Yes, but the Hindu people go to Albion to a Hindu quack. They don't use me"

"Good, then do what you come to do with the same tools you use on everyone else. If that is too hard for you, just close your eyes and imagine that I am a Black or Madrassee woman" Tatri knew she had to build her own path to life. She had to look forward because there was nothing for her to look back to.

She knew that it will take time, but she must start somewhere. This is a good time.

Archie told Baldio to put a gold cap on the top eyeteeth. He said he wanted her to have a golden, spackling smile.

"Mother, here is the envelope to take to Lancaster tomorrow"

"Why don't you go and take it yourself? You have been married now close to a month and you have not gone to see your wife. I am not taking it this time. You go and take it to your wife yourself" Mother handed the envelope back to her son.

She got her way. She had a wedding, now the marriage must be consummated.

She had been watching his every move. Checking whether he slept in his room.

It would be the only time she would be happy if he did not sleep in his room. She knew she did not have to worry where he was. After all he was now a married man.

The only worry she had now is when will he go to his wife at Lancaster? Until this happened she thinks that he is still rebelling against her.

Mother was contented with herself. All her ten children were married.

It was a nice wedding and everyone did s/he best to make the guess happy.

Her sons Willy and Rick left with their families, they went back home.

She sent all the wedding gifts to Lancaster. She told Tatri that they belonged to her because wedding gifts always belong to the bride.

When she went to Lall, the Hindu grocer and Zen, the Muslim grocer to settle the grocery bill for the wedding, she was told that she owed them nothing. They told her that Joe, Bang, Seecheran and Tiger paid all the bills.

They all knew their mother to be strict but kind, strong but fair. She held her family together with iron claws and pour love all over them.

"Alright, now that all of you are here" Mother holding Dada's hand and looking over her speck tickle at each of family around the table, she continued.

"First of all, Dada and I would like to thank each and everyone of you for the good job done for making the wedding and reception a grand affair" she looked at Archie.

"There are no more bachelor in this family. Everyone has to live up to his marriage responsibility, including your husbandly duties. Dishing out your own food is now part of that responsibility too."

Archie was relieved when Brother asked permission to speak.

"Mother, Reverend Byer needs the name of the bride for the married certificate?"

"The bride has a husband, direct your question to him. Its his responsibility"

"None of you believed me when I said that I did not know her name. It is the God's truth, I do not know her name" Archie said, his voice hoarse and eyes half-opened.

"Well, you will begin to know her and her name as soon as you can get your donkey-cart ready and take all the wedding gifts to Lancaster to your wife" Mother looked at her son more closely and said

"From what I am seeing, you are in no condition to do that today, but find the time to do that before the week is over. When Esther and I go next Saturday for provision, I will have a good long talk with your wife and find out who she really is"

Inez was the only one who knew Tatri in a personal way, after their emotional bond.

"I will go up to Lancaster this afternoon. I need to see how she is doing. I will get it"

"Her name is Babe" burst out as if he just remembered, Archie said.

"What? Whose name is Babe?" it sounded like everyone asked the question.

"The lady all of you are talking about. My wife"

"I thought you did not know her name?" asked Mother

"That is the God's truth, I do not know her name, but, now that she is my wife, I would like to call her Babe" Archie seized the moment to speak.

"From the very first time I saw her in the woods waiting for someone to help with the bundle of wood, I saw a pitiful, frightened young girl.

"Mother, Dada, you taught me to have compassion for other people. She came to me for help. I took them to Lancaster for a short while. But Mother made her own plans" looking at his mother he said

"This is the very last time I will tell anyone this truth"

It was the first time the family had heard so many words at one time from Archie.

Dada knew his son was just like him, many words didn't find their way out of them.

The first time he spoke, he said to his son in his gentle tone.

"Son, there is no need to lament over what is done, you have to move on. Everything will fall into place and you will find happiness in being a married man"

Everyone had his and her soup in silence.

Archie got the donkey-cart ready, packed all the wedding gifts in it and send them to Lancaster by Collins, his young cousin.

Archie went to the Port Mourant hospital to meet with Dr. Koo. He was a Chinese doctor, about the same age as Archie, a short, little man who was known and respected by everyone in the district. He was the only certified medical doctor of the district. He trained the nurses and dispensers. He trained young apprentices to become lifesavers, so they can take charge and run the hospital whenever he had to go beyond the plantation

"Archie, what brings you here? Don't tell me that married life is taking it toll on you already?" Dr Koo.

"No Doc, I am here it ask you if there is anything you could do to straighten my wife's left hand? It needs your attention".

Tatri unpacked the wedding gifts. She placed them amongst the other pots, pans, dishes, glasses and bed linen that were already in the home.

There was one item that caught her attention. It was a little teapot.

It was gold trim with white and blue. It had ships and birds in the ocean and a lighthouse with trees around it.

She took the teapot as her only wedding gift. She placed it on the bedroom dresser.

That teapot became her bank. Whenever Archie sent money and Dhia brought money home, she put them into the little gold and white teapot.

"Dada, it's been almost a month since the wedding. I tell Archie to take the gifts to Lancaster to his wife, but he sent them with Collins. He has not gone there"

"Janie, you don't think that I know that my son has not gone to his wife?

"What am I to do about it, Dada?

"You are to do nothing about it. You have done too much already"

"What do you mean by that?"

"You know what I mean? Leave him alone, he is a married man now"

After Mother refused to take the brown envelope to Lancaster, Archie went to his sister Inez and asked her to take it.

"Please take this to Lancaster for me"

"Take it to whom at Lancaster?" Inez asked angrily.

"You know who? The lady up there, Babe"

"The lady up there, Babe? She is you wife. Her name is Tatriani Kasy.

Your wife's name is Tatriani Kasy. We can all call her Babe. It depicts her personality. She is like a baby now learning to speak. But her given name is Tatriani Kasy, now Jane Kasi Alexander Don't you forget it. Take yourself, your wife is waiting for you"

Saturday night, Archie met his friends as usual. He went to the bar and ordered a bottle of lemonade and brought it back to the table.

"Wa happen Mike? You sick?"

"No me na sick, me just no want to drink rum tonight"

"You no want fe drink rum tonight and you no sick?

"Yes, me na want to drink rum tonight and me na sick, wa wrong with dat?"

Archie was scared and it showed as he waited for the midnight bus.

He sat on the wooden bench of the almost empty bus and realized that he was shaking and his palms were wet. His mouth was dry. He wished he were back at the bar with his friends drinking some of that Demerara rum.

He tried to shake off the feelings. Reminding him that he is a man. A strong man, A man who have had lots of women but none of them ever given him the shakes.

The bus stopped in front of the Alexander estate, the shakes returned.

It was a bright night thanks to the full moon.

The shakes made it difficult for him to walk on the long slender bridge that he could have walked on with his eyes closed in the darkest night.

Calmness came over him as he entered the house. He walked softly on the floor.

He entered the master bedroom and sat in his father's 'big chair' next to the bed.

He looked at the outline of his wife. She slept on one side as if the other side was his.

Her long black hair shun with the moonlight. The shape of her body with wide hips and flat stomach caused him to have a different kind of shake.

It was the first time that he had seen her face without it being covered with hernee.

He stared at his sleeping wife for a long time. Looking at every dent and mark.

Tatri lay on the lace covered canapé bed and stared at the full moon peeking at her.

She was at peace. As if she was dreaming, she often reminded herself that it is real and that Ram would not come in to brutalize her anymore.

Between sleep and awake, she saw a tall, dark shadow.

She felt a movement in the bed. She felt a necked, warm body next to her. She knew that her husband was home.

Not knowing what form the encounter it will take. She braced herself for whatever happened.

She knew that it was time for her to submit to her husband. She was taught from the tender age of thirteen that it was her duty as a wife to accept her husband. Katy reminded her of that too.

Tatri found herself on the flipside of what she was accustomed to. Instead of her being afraid, or shaking with fear as she did when Ram throw himself on her, it was Archie who was shaking like a fevered child.

She had to wrap her arms around his slender waist to assure him that it was all right.

The ecstasy she endured during his tender introduction gave her a high, just like what she felt in the running water of the Sideline trench.

She felt his arms around her waist, she closed her eyes as tight as possible, afraid to breath. She did not want it stop.

His gentle caress and soft touches caused her to cuddle his head in the valley of her breast as he murmured words she did not understand.

She heard his sobbing and felt his warm tears on her body.

She patted his head in a comforting way. Feeling the softness of his curly hair. She wondered why Black people cry so easily?

She was told that Black people had no feelings, they do not cry. Yet she comforted Inez as she cried with her. She comforted Mother as she cried with her and now she had to comfort her husband as he cried on her chest.

Tatri lay awake and listen to her husband heavy breathing. She never thought that a wife's duty would be so full of pleasure and tenderness.

She looked at his sleeping face and felt a jolt in her heart. She knew that she had 'feelings' she was not dead and buried. She is alive. Very much alive.

He slept with his mouth open and she saw that he had a mouth full of white, strong teeth. She envied him for having all of his teeth when she had none.

She quietly slid out of the bed, went to the dresser and took out her dentures from the glass of water, placed them into her mouth, smile in the mirror and slid back into the bed and watch her husband sleep.

Tatri washed her body from head to toes, like she did every morning at 5am.

She sat at her alter and prayed.

"Oh God, with my body, mind and intelligence, with all my senses, my action was of myself"

"Your Uncle came last night, he is sleeping in the big room" Tatri whispered to Dhia as she gave him tea and roti.

Dhia looked at his mother in a strange way and bowed his head.

"What is the matter"

"Nothing Ma"

"Yes, something is wrong, I can tell from the way you are not looking at me"

"Ma, nothing is wrong. He is your husband. This is his house. He has every right to sleep here with you. At least he did not beat you"

"Then you are not angry with me?"

"No Ma, I am not mad with you. I thank you for being here and I thank him for giving me a home to live in. Why should I be angry with you? I know that when a man and a woman get married, they do things together in their bedroom. I am a big boy now, Ma. I know things like that and I accept it"

"He is your Uncle now, you know that?"

"Yes, he is my step-father, I will call him Uncle Archie" Dhia said halfheartedly.

Archie woke up in a state of confusion. He became aware that he was not in his bed. He did not have a rum-breath or hangover. His naked body covered with her sari.

He fell asleep with the moonlight coming through the window and woke up with the sun on his face.

He lay on the bed that used to be his parents. He thought of how many children were conceived on this bed.

The smell of Indian spices reminded him that he was not in his mother's home.

In his mother's home, he would smell coffee, homemade bread, home cured ham, homemade butter and pepper pot. In a Negro's home, that is.

In an Indian home, there will be dhal, roti, curry and most drank tea with milk.

Tatri watched her husband from the kitchen window as he walk towards the latrine.

He was shirtless. His strong muscular body shivered her body. She looked at him as he walked around the yard. He broke a piece of black sage to brush his teeth.

As she peek at the young, strong man who was so gentle with her last night, her heart told her to go out in the yard and take her husband hand and lead him back to her bed. Dhia was gone, they were alone and her heart knew it and yearned for more.

She told her heart and whatever else was aking for him, that 'women did not do such things'. That a woman's place is to be there, and, to be ready whenever her man needed her services. That was what she was told.

She hoped that he liked the way she had been taking care of the home and yard.

'

Neighbors were out hailing 'howdy' to him.

"Archie bay, God bless dis ol eye ah me one dis Sunday manin"

"Yes Nana Tama, good morning to you" as he opened the gate and embraced his 77 years old Godmother.

She wrapped her wrinkled arms around his waist, her white head on his bare chest.

Archie bend down and held her close to him. He knew she was at the church the day he got married, but so was everyone else. He could never forget her.

"Bay, me cant tank you enough for the allowance you sen fe me wid Collins.

"You know you don't have to thank me for anything Nana, I am the one who have to thank you for helping to keep me alive" his arms around her shoulder.

"No son, me only buy you, God keep you alive"

Archie put his shirt on and left. Not a word whispered by his wife of him.

Inez felt sorry for her brother, but she felt a deep compassion for Babe

Inez knew what lay ahead for her. She wondered if her sister-in-law would be strong enough to handle all that will be thrown on her?

Inez knew how it was to be married to an Indian. She knew what mix marriages could do to families and communities. She was thankful that both sides blessed theirs.

She and her sister Harriett are married to Indian men, but they are Christian Indians.

George Katick and Moses Malay were Christian and everyone was equal in the eyes of the Christians, but that was not the way with Hindus. It is forbidden for a Hindu to marry anyone but a Hindu. Not even another Indian of a different caste.

Inez and George had no problem with their union. They met in church and they believed that God has His hands on them.

Sunday after church, Inez asked her husband to accompany her to Lancaster to visit Babe. "Alright, let's go, I too want to meet the bride. I want to see if she is build strong enough to handle your brother, the plantation stallion" George teased his wife.

"Good morning to you, this is my husband George" Inez wanted Babe to see that she, a Black woman, is married to an Indian man. She hoped that by knowing that, Babe would feel more comfortable in her own situation.

Inez was surprised to see that her sister-in-law was on cloud nine. She was different.

She was smiling and hugging Inez. She fluffed up the chair cushions and offered the rocking chair to George and moved another chair close to him for Inez to sit.

Inez heard Babe humming as she brought them cool water from the clay goblet. Still in shock, she looked at her husband, he looked at her, they both looked at Babe, who was sitting on the floor, her folded legs covered with her skirt, talking and smiling, showing off the twenty-four karat gold cap.

'What did she do with the sari and hernee?' wondered Inez.

"That is not the same person you described to me a month ago? You said she was a battered, broken, toothless Hindu woman. That woman we just saw is not the same? Is it?" George asked Inez as they waited for the bus.

"One can make lots of changes within a short time when one has to"

When Mother was about to send Esther to get Archie for the dinner, Inez said

"Mother, leave him alone. Before all this to-dos, Archie was the only one allowed to be absent from this table. You leave his soup, or should I say 'all the meat from the soup', by the fireside to keep warm until he is willing and ready to eat.

I know what your reason is for him to be present. Don't worry anymore Mother.

The marriage has been consummated"

Katy couldn't help noticing the overjoyfulness of her friend when she came over for them to sit on the steps to chat that night.

"Wa happen? You catch something good?"

"Yes, yesterday night" Babe was beaming; her laughter sparkled in the moonlight.

"He come?"

"Yes"

"He really been ya"

"Yyeess"

"How was it?"

"Niiccee. Me never know dat me can feel so gooood when a man do it wid me"

Mother became Archie's messenger. She delivered money, jewelry groceries and whatever goodies he bought at the estate for his wife and stepson.

She spent more time getting to know her newfound daughter, Babe.

"Your husband said that you should go to the hospital to see Dr. Koo.

Archie already spoke to him about straitening out your arm" Mother looked at Babe for a reaction from her next statement.

"Your husband wants us all to call you Babe. He thinks that it is a beautiful name"

Babe smiled and nodded her head in agreement. She then said

"My sister Inez tell me dat me husband want all ayou fe call me Babe. Me like dat. Me family call me Dhero, no body call me Tatrani, that is my book name, me house name is Dhero" Babe tried her best to explain.

"I understand, everyone has a book name and a house name. My book name is

Mary Jane, then my husband changed it to Janie, then, my children changed it to Mother. Now everybody calls me Mother, even my husband"

"Your husband call you, Mother?"

"Yes, and so are all the people, old and young. They all call me Mother but my grandchildren call me Gramother"

"Alright, Dhero or Babe, when me hear dem me know is me"

Katy, felt compassion mixed with anger whenever she saw the dents and dark bruise marks on her face and face. She wondered what her body must look like?

Katy accompanied Dhero to the hospital whenever she had to go to get her arm straightened. On one such visit, as Dhero stepped out of the bus, she came face to face with her eldest brother Kachan. She fell on her knees, bow to his feet to pay respect.

When Katy came out of the bus she found her friend on her knees, crying.

Dhero pointed out her brother who was entering the same bus.

"Me bow to pay homage to him, but he move he foot to kick me"

"Listen to me girl, you have to ride the waves of changes in stride. Stop falling on people's foot. You live in a different world now. We don't fall on nobody foot"

"Me have to do that. It is asking for blessings, forgiveness from elders".

"Now is the time for you to choose. Do you want to live in hell or high water?

You cannot live in both and expect everyone to accept your double standard"

Babe had a full mouth of teeth, top and bottom dentures with a shining gold cap. Her left arm was being worked on. They had to break it several times to straighten it.

Her son Dhia was adjusting well too. He worked at sea and attended private tutoring from Mrs. George, a schoolteacher who lived next-door to them in the village.

He insisted that he would one day become a policeman, his big dream.

Her best friend Katy was her only friend and she treasured her.

She made a paste of ground charcoal and mud clay to help clear out the dark areas of her face and arms. There was nothing she could have done about the holes, dents and baldness. Those were her life long reminders of her survival.

She became beautiful, especially when dressed in skirt and top that Katy kept taking to her and the expensive jewelry that Archie and Mother got for her and peace of mind.

"Ma why you took only the teapot out of all the presents you got?"

"Because it has water, boat and birds, they all mean freedom"

Babe walked with Katy to the Whim market whenever she needed supplies.

She waited until her friend finish selling the fishes that her husband caught.

She needed Katy by her side to go to and from the market.

She wondered who was doing her mother's market errands now that she was dead?

She used her friend as a shield when she passed her parents home.

She always saw the flag that symbolized her death. The pain never eased.

The Hindus treated her as if she had leprosy. They became the hostile tribe. They would spit on her path and kick the dirt. Some spat on her and cursed her in Hindi.

Lots of times Katy spat back at them and curse them in Madrassi.

She reprimanded Dhero for not retaliating to their insults. She said

"You have to spit back at them. You have to kuss them back. You have to kick the dust back at them. You have to disrespect them because they have no respect for you. You have to stop thinking that they are high caste and you have to bow to their shit. Kuss dem back. You hear me? Kuss dem back.

Me sell fish, dem not buy fish, so dem and me not have to be friends.

You na have to be friends wid no Hindustani who ah spit on you and kuss you"

The Madrasis, Muslims and Christians who were also treated in demeaning ways by Hindus, had no problem accepting and being friends with Dhero.

They knew that she was now part of their community. The untouchables.

Katy was happy with the transformation of her neighbor and friend, Dhero.

Her children and Dhia were getting along very well. What else could she wish for?

"Mike, you behaving like a jackass. You been married over two months but you are still behaving like a bachelor" said Seecharan at the rum shop,

"Yes man, fixing her teeth and hand is not being a husband. You have to bring her here to live with you in your logy room" said Bang

"Do you think we feel good that every night we go home to our wives and family and you go home to an empty room far away from your wife?" said Joe.

"I know for sure that you are not wilding about anymore. Me been checking you out and all your lady friends are asking me about you" said Tiger.

Archie looked at his four friends and said

"That lady frightens the shit out of me"

"What the hell you mean by that?"

"I mean I get the shakes when I go close to her. She frighten the shit out of me"

Two close friends sitting on the steps enjoying their evening chat.

They have been doing this for months now. They discuss the day's activity.

"I am worried about Dhia"

"Why?

"He change, he forgets who he is. He got friends who a mine hag and he a go in dem yard. Who know if he a eat meat wid dem?"

"What's wrong with that?"

"He is a Bramhim, he should not enter a yard or a house that have hag"

"My yard have hag, we mine hag and catch fish for a living.

Your son comes to my yard and home. Are you talking about us?" Katy was angry at Dhero's remarks. She felt insulted and stood up to leave.

"No Katy, not you, not you house, is the other kind of people I am talking about"

"Any other kind a people you are talking about include me because me na Hindu. Me ah one ah de other kind ah people.

Me leave me husband and children every night to come sit here wid you.

Me think you ah me friend, yet you still have dis thing about you high caste.

Me always ah come visit you, you never come ah me house. Now me know why, me ah mine hag" Katy left her crying friend and went home.

After two weeks, Dhia knew something was wrong. He saw his mother sitting on the steps alone at nights. He saw that she was sad.

She was not happy lately. She did not go to the market and she hardly talked to him when he came home from work.

"Ma, what's wrong? I know that something is wrong with you. What did I do?"

It's been months since Katy walked away from the steps of the 'big house'.

Every night she sat on the steps and waited for her friend. But Katy never came.

One day when Babe could not take the absence of her only friend in her life anymore, she got dress into one of the frocks that Katy had gotten made for her.

Bare headed, she walked out of the yard and went to Katy's fence. She sat on the ground next to the gate.

Katy saw her approaching but pretended not to have seen her as she swept her yard.

You see, during their absence, they played peek a boo. Pretending not to be looking.

"How long are you going to sit on the damp ground? You want to get pile?" asked Katy after a long time of ignoring Babe and worried for her health.

"As long as it takes for you to come out to me. I want to talk to you" said Babe, praying that Katy did not ask her to enter her yard. She knew what the answer would be. She was prepared to make changes. Her son's anger opened her eyes. But there were some things that she was not prepared to change. One was that she would never enter an 'unclean' yard or home. Her friend yard and home were unclean.

Both women suffered during the weeks of separation but Katy was not going to let her friend off the hook. She hurt her feelings and she was going to teach her a lesson.

"Why me have to come out to you? Me gate have no lock. You can come in me yard just like me go in you yard all de time".

Babe, until that moment, did not know how much she had hurt her best friend.

"Look, I am wearing the frock you get make fa me. It feel strange with the breeze blowing up in me …." Babe hoping that her friend would come closer to look at her, thus forgetting her last question. But Katy pretended not to hear her.

She went into her little grass hut, leaving Babe sitting outside on the damp ground.

"Me will never say anything bad about anyone anymore.

Katy looked around and saw Babe standing at the entrance of her home.

She quickly hurried to catch her friend before she dropped on the floor.

Babe was weak and shaking. The thought of loosing her friend Katy, took a lot out of her. She did not eat, and lack of sleep and other things, took its toll on her.

"Katy, me come here to beg your forgiveness" through the tears, shaking and running nose, she said "Katy, you ah me best friend. Me need you. Me need you to be my best friend. Me need you more now. Me never been insulted before me come here. Me never know how it feel when people low grade others because no one ever did that to me" still crying in a sing-song manner, holding on tight to Katy, Babe continued.

"Now when those people insult me and kuss me, I know how much it hurt.

Remember the day when that woman spit on and kuss me in Hindi? Well me see how mad you was, I did not tell you wa she said. She calls me a ' black dog whore'

Both women were crying when Babe said

"Me want to tell you something" she waited for a while, whipped her eyes and nose, took some air into her lungs and said

"Me not get dem 'thing' for two months now"

"Did you tell Archie?

"No, he never come back since me tell you that he ben here"

"Did you tell Dhia that he is going to have a brother or sister?"

"No, I cannot discuss things like that wid my son. I can only talk wid you"

"I am your friend, not the father. You should have come to me before.

Now I see why you are so maga and week. Are you having badfeelings and vomiting? When last you eat something?

Don't worry, I am here for you. I will take care of you" Katy held Dhero like a baby in her arms and rocked her side to side as they cried.

Mother took one look at Babe and knew what was happening.

Afterall, she was a pro at it. She had ten of her own.

Without a word spoken, Mother embraced her daughter-in-law and walked down the steps with a wide smile on her face.

"Since you came home from Lancaster you have this grin on your face.

What is happening with you? I am your husband. I should know what is happening with you, good or bad. I am not here for only the bad things. What are you so happy about?"

"You are going to be officiating a Christening soon"

Whispered Mother, into Reverent Byer's ears as he stood by the church door.

Smiling from ear to ear, Mother hurried away towards her waiting cart, before the priest could catch up with her.

'He like gossip, now he got something to wonder about' thought smiling Mother.

The reverent could not ignore the long line waiting to shake his hand and tell him 'what a nice service. 'Wonder who is in the family way in the Alexander's family?

It could be anyone of the young folks or even one of Mother's grandchildren'.

He knew it could not be Archie because his grape vine runners told him that since Archie got married, he never lived with his wife, that he still live in a room at Port Mourant estate, while his wife lives with her son at the 'big house' at Lancaster.

He was told that the marriage was an arrangement so that the lady and her son could live at the Alexander's home at Lancaster.

Sunday, with everyone except Archie present in the dinning room, Mother said

"We are going to have a baby"

Everyone around the table looked at each other. They were all in childbearing age.

Mother allowed the buzzing around the table to go on for a while, she said

"The one responsible for it is not here for us to congratulate him" she squeezed her husband's hand, reached up and closed his mouth and said

"Yes, Archie and Babe are going to have a baby"

By this time most of the family members had met Babe.

One Sunday Inez gathered all the women folks of the family and took them to meet their sister-in-law.

Babe was so excited to see so many women in the house. She ran over to Katy to get some fishes. There was plenty of rice in Mrs. Alexander's kitchen. Archie supplied it Bertram delivered it.

By the time the ladies finished their greetings and settled down to reminisce in their old home. Looking at pictures on the wall and fooling around on the piano,

Babe brought out hot Dhal, rice, fried fish, a hand of yellow bananas and a goblet of cool rainwater.

The women were shocked to see how fast Babe prepared all that food.

"How did she do all of this so fast?"

"Inez, did you tell her that we were coming?"

"No, I did not tell her anything. She is like that. I never came here and leave without eating something or drinking something from her. That was when she had only one hand to use. She is just like all Guiana people. We must offer visitors something to eat"

"I don't know how she did all the cooking in such a short time but I am enjoying it.

The men folks also met her. Mother brought Dada one Sunday after church.

Bertram was a regular visitor. He had lots of compassion for her. He sat and chats often with her and her son. The others came to see her and Dhia too.

Even Reverent Byer walked across the narrow bridge to see the person who had caused so much gossip in his district. He encouraged her to attend church but she quickly reminded him that she was a Hindu.

Mother's statement took the doubt out of some of the family members who still did not know if Archie had gone to his wife.

It is a known tradition for both Blacks and Indians, that when a baby is expected, very few items are prepared before the birth. A baby blanket, baby towel, some napkins–diapers and pins and some nightgowns for the mother-to-be, to wear while she is in lying room.

After the birth, you can put needle and thread to clothe and wool to make shimmies, bonnet, booty, as many as you can afford, in pink or blue.

Powder and sweet smelling soap will come with visitors.

"Inez, go to Talim store, get whatever is necessary to start preparing for the baby".

"Mother, leave things alone. My God, a baby takes nine months before it's born.

You just found out yesterday that Babe is pregnant.

By the way, I bet you that Babe did not tell you that she is pregnant, but, you who know everything, knows that she is going to have a baby?.

Soon you are going to tell us the sex and name of the baby.

Next Sunday you will be informing the Reverent Byer about a Christening"

"I already informed him"

With the help of Katy and the watchful eyes of Mother, Babe pregnancy was going smoothly. She did not tell her son about the expected baby. Such discussion did not accrue between a mother and a son.

When Babe was seven months pregnant, Katy accompanied her to the Port Mourant hospital for her finial visit where they will take out the plaster that she had been accustomed to. They broke and straighten, broke and straighten her arms several times. She was happy when Dr.

Koo told her "Come back in three weeks and I will set your arm free for you to hold your baby"

Katy walked ahead because her big belly friend was slow in getting out of the bus.

She turned around to see her friend flat on her back on the ground. She screamed out and ran back to her and tried to sit her up.

"What happened? Did you trip and fall? Katy asked anxiously.

"No, I saw my big brother Kachan, waiting for the bus when I came out.

I try to fall to his foot and he kick me in my head" she was holding her head, afraid that he might have kicked out the metal plate that is in her head.

"When are you going to stop falling to people's foot? When are you going understand that you have to stop doing this 'respect' thing to people who do not even look at you as a human being?" Katy looked around the crowd that gathered around them. She asked two men to help her friend to her feet.

"You have to put it in your cracked head that those people are not related to you anymore, and, that you are not related to them.

Do you know that you hurt the people who are helping you? The people love and care for you? Like your son? Like Me?" Katy was crying,

"What kind of an animal would kick a woman with such a big belly?

Why is he always at this spot when we come to the hospital?"

"Because he come to the Seawala Temple, where he is the pandit-priest, for the early morning prayer. Then he catches this same bus to go to Albion estate to work"

"What kind a priest is he? Kicking a pregnant woman in her head?"

News spread like wind in the estate and villages that Archie is having a baby.

Everyone was anxiously waiting to see if s/he would be invited to the big sware-party.

Others knew that they did not have be invited, they were villagers, they ah family.

163

Archie too, who did not visit his wife or Lancaster since his last 'shakes' encounter, was being kept informed of all the goings on.

His mother took the brown envelope to Babe every week.

He was beside himself with happiness when he heard that he was going to have a baby.

Like every man in those days, he hoped and prayed that he was going to get a son.

His friends and Mr. Dhalwa were planning their own party too.

Mother and Esther went to Lancaster on Saturday, January seventh for their usual gathering of produce. Visit with Babe and sometimes Dhia, if he was home.

Mother saw Katy leaving the 'big house' in a hurry.

She asked her if everything was OK. "I think the time is close. I went to rub her back with some limerum" answered Katy.

"Thank you Katy, you are truly her best friend"

Mother stood in the yard, looked around for a spot to put the navel cord and plant a tree. She said to Esther.

"Can you take the bus by yourself back home?"

"Yes Gramother, I am a big girl. I can come out at Manager's Gap and walk home to Bound Yard" Said Esther, excited to make her first solo bus trip.

"Alright, lets pick only what you can carry. Go home and tell Aunt Elo to put some things in a bag for me. She will know what I need.

Take the bag to Aunt Inez and tell her to bring it and Aunt Mary up here right now"

Mother looked at Esther in a stern manner and continued. "Don't go telling anyone anything that you know nothing about. Don't get into big people's business"

"Yes Gramother"

Mother placed her hand on Babe's hard, pointing belly and smiled. She said

"Its time, whoever is in here is ready to see the sun"

She played with the belly as if she was a midwife. Trying to determine the position of the baby. She is very experience in this department. With ten of her own and twenty grandchildren by this time.

She was present at the birth of every one of her grandchildren, just like Nana Harriett.

Even Rick who lived in Suriname, brought his wife Trude to his mother's home to give birth, Reverent Byer Christen the baby, partied, then, they return home with a British Guiana birth certificate for the baby. Rick was very proud of his birth land.

Linda, I think I told you before that in those days, a pregnant woman went to her mother's home to give birth. There was no maternity ward in the hospital. However there were Midwives assigned to various district. One midwife could be responsible for more than seven or eight villages. Black and Indian villages.

Many times if the midwife was too busy with other cases, she would instruct female members what to do until she could get there.

Sometimes things went so well that she was not needed, but there were times when she is needed to get the 'afterbirth-placenta' out of the mother. Many times that caused the demise of the mothers.

Many babies died from complication that inexperience helpers could not fix.

Many mothers died from hemridge or fever caused by septic.

Dhia came home to a house buzzing with women. He knew it was time.

Katy placed her arm around his shoulder and said

"Get some of your things and go over to our house. You will stay there until everything is quiet around here. Don't worry about your mother. Everything is going to be all right. We do not need any man around here at this time"

Datson Egbert Alexander arrived in the wee hours of the morning of Monday January ninth 1939. He shared the same birth date as his mother Babe.

He was a bouncing baby, full of energy, strong lungs, head covered with strait hair.

The women present were surprised to see how Babe went through the delivery so calm and restraint. She did not make a sound.

Even the most experienced of them could not believe that for two days this woman went through labor without a sound of discomfort.

After mother and baby were cleaned up and put to sleep, Mother took the ladies out.

They sat and enjoyed hot roti and fried fish, compliments of Katy's husband Bull.

Mother braced her head on her hand and began to cry. Something that she seldom does.

"What is the matter Mother?" asked Mary

"Nothing my child, nothing"

"It must be something, you don't cry for nothing at a happy time like this?"

"Did you all see how that girl endured her pain for two days without showing any discomfort? Not even once?" she wiped her eyes with her handkey and said

"Inez, only you have not yet experienced the pain of giving birth.

I know about that kind of pain. Many times my mother had to stuff a piece of clothe into my mouth to prevent me from screaming the roof off or cussing Dada"

"Maybe she did not want to embarrass herself in our presence"

"Embarrass? When it comes to giving birth, no embarrassment can stop the pain"

"Mother, who do you think the baby looks like?"

"We have to wait for daylight to determine that, but from what little I saw and felt, he reminds me of one that I had myself"

"Linda, my question is, can a woman give birth naturally without feeling any pain?"

"I guess it depends on the woman. Maybe she was immune to pain"

Babe woke up and looked at her little baby boy next to her, wrapped in white blanket. She felt an electrical jolt in her heart. She felt love for him and his Daddy.

What she did not know then, and did not know for many years to come, was that her son arrived on her thirty-second birthday. Yes, she was born January 9th, 1907.

"Girls, you can go back to Port Mourant this afternoon. Katy and I can take care of mother and baby. Tell Archie that he has a son. Tell him that he has to go to the hospital and register the birth of his son. I know that the wind must have carried the news already. Catch him while he is still sober"

Mother was involved in everything that had to do with her family, except choosing her grandchildren's name. That privilege belongs to their parents.

She knew that Babe was going to open her holy book and give her son a Hindi name.

She did, his book name is Baldio.

Datson Egbert was a handsome baby.

He was the stamp of Archie. He was dark in complexion and had a head full of soft curly hair. The kind only mixed people can have. Not too strait, not too curly.

He was the long awaited son the family wanted for Archie. 'A man must have a son'.

As soon as the baby was weaned, everyone of the family wanted him.

They took him away from Babe and Lancaster for days at a time.

Mother and Mary agreed to share his visit. Mary emptied a draw from her dresser, while Mother ordered a rocking bed for him to be on display.

Archie was never so happy. He wanted to take Datson to the rumshop.

Mother jumped all over him by saying

"How dear you think of taking this little baby into a rumshop?

Because all your spare time is spent in one does not make it right for a baby to go there. If you want to showoff your son to the whole estate, bring them here to see him"

Inez and George stood as Godparents for Datson. Reverent Dyer did the service.

The Christening party was held in Bound Yard. It resembled a wedding party.

Archie was so happy for having his son; he would go up to Lancaster just to walk through the village, carrying his son on his neck.

Everyone was posing with the baby for picture. They took him to Mooto Photo studio for professional photos to be given to family members and sent to Rick and Willie.

After a year and some months of Datson's arrival, Archie paid Babe another 'shakes' visit, as if it was time for him to thank her for his son.

When Datson was one year and six months old, Babe noticed that whenever she called or tried to get his attention, he would not respond.

She mentioned her findings to Katy and Mother. The two women did everything to prove Babe's finding wrong.

They walked behind him and clapped their hands. Nothing happened.

Mother took a pot and spoon and made lots of noise, nothing happened. She began to stomp her feet on the floor in frustration. Only then did she get his attention.

He looked around to see who was hitting the floor. He felt the vibration.

Babe was divested. She knew something that none of them knew. She was in shock.

They took Datson to Dr, Koo who informed them that the baby was mute.

Archie was beyond devastation. He was loosing his mind.

He took his son to every doctor, every church of every denomination, every obeah house and every 'see far' psychic to see if any of them could make his son hear.

Babe was afraid to tell anyone that she was pregnant again, not even Katy.

She hid all symptoms form everyone. But a baby grows in the belly.

Mother's keen eyes saw that she was pregnant. She asked Katy if she knew that Babe was in the family-way, she said no.

They confronted Babe, who broke down and admitted that she was six months pregnant but was afraid to tell anyone.

The people, who were present for Datson's delivery, also surrounded and supported her throughout this pregnancy and delivery.

On December 6th 1940 Babe gave birth to another baby boy.

Archie registered him David Emanuel Alexander. His book name is Davandra.

His light complication, strait nose and strait hair and face was that of a Hindu Sadhu.

Harriett and Mose stood as Godparents for David.

David did not get as much attention as his older brother did.

No one took him to Port Mourant, or to draw picture with him, or to Motoo's Studio.

Their excuse was that he had his older brother to play with.

Archie took his boys on slow donkey cart rides to the estate and around the village. He loved both his boys but everyone knew that Datson was the main artery to his heart.

Once again he showed his application by another 'shakes' visit.

Dhia was eighteen years old and was ready to write the police exam.

He asked his Uncle Archie if he could speak to his cousin George Alexander who was a police officer, to quiz him before he takes the test?

Dhia passed the written test but failed the required height by two inches.

There were not many Indians applying to be policemen. They were more rice farmers and cane cutters. They were shorter in height.

Blacks however, once they pass the written exam, had no problem with the required height of five foot, nine inches and taller.

I am proud to tell you that in the 1940's the Alexander family had many police officers serving all over the country.

Remember Malcome who married Clarabell after his wife died?

He had four grandsons serving in the police force at the same time.

It was a record to have four brothers serving in law enforcement at the same time.

George still lives in Rose Hall. He is ninety + years old.

That record was never broken to this day.

They had a sister, Oliva who was a renowned pianist. She was known through out the country. She had a music school. Sudith was her music teacher many moons before.

During that same period, Dada and Mother had three grandsons in the police force.

They also had two great-nephews, Dada's sister grandsons, at the same time.

Babe confided to Katy about the curse her father placed on her the last time he spoke to her. Her reason for telling her friend was because she was seeing the same signs with David that she saw with Datson.

"Why did you keep something like that to yourself? Why didn't you tell your husband or your mother-in-law?"

"I don't think I should even tell you, but I am so afraid, I have to tell someone"

"You will have to tell Mother when she comes. We will go to check him out"

Dr. Koo, once again conformed Babe's nightmare. David was also mute.

All that Babe was seeing and hearing was her father and his words.

"I place a curse on you. None of your boy children will ever speak nor hear my name. They will never hear or speak my name. They will never speak or hear my name. I put a curse on you. I have your soul. I have the power to place this curse on you. They will never hear about me, they will never speak about me, they will have your spirit but not your soul, I will possesses their souls too"

The Alexander's world was spinning around in different direction and opinions. Babe was dying from inside out.

Dhia was looking at her like a stranger whom he had never seen before.

He rarely spent time with his mother and his two brothers.

His life was also turned up side down. He no longer work at sea. He was a carpenter and a cane cutter at the plantation.

His friends told him that his mother was a witch and that they were afraid to work with him because she could put a curse on them. They said that they could fall off scaffoldings while working on a building. They did not want to work with him.

People called her the 'cursed witch'

Even some of Archie's family believed that she was cursed and that there should never have been a marriage.

They felt that she had brought shame and curse to the family.

Bertram, Inez and Mother were the only ones who visited her. They did their best to console her and to assure her that its "God's work, none of us can change that"

Mother too, was suffering. With the haunting question on her mind, she tried to find support from anyone besides Inez and Bertram. She got none, not even from Dada.

Many Sundays her soup was ran cold and uneaten.

It was a very low, low period in the Alexander family life.

Mother was loosing her strength to hold her family together.

She won the battle but was loosing the fight.

Archie was missing. No one knew where he was. He did not sleep in his room.

His friends could not find him. He did not go to work, a place that he had never been absent throughout his whole working life.

His friends enquired at the office and were told that Archie was on two weeks leave.

"But where is he? Where could he be? We looked everywhere. Under every house and shed in the estate. Where could he be?"

The Alexander's banded together to find Archie.

Mother sent the three brothers from Lancaster who are always working in the fields and taking care of the animals, to go to Archie's cow pen in the savanna. She remembered that the time when he took refuge there.

"Look everywhere for him, if you do not find him, look up in the sky for 'carrying crow' – vouchers - If you see them circulating an area, go see what they are eying"

As quietly as Archie left, he returned. He was never the same again.

Dhia saw the pain and shame in everyone around him. He heard all the mean things being said about his mother. He could not take it anymore.

One Saturday he went to the estate to see Archie. He said.

"Uncle Archie, I am in deep distress. Everything that is happening with my mother and two brothers is driving me crazy. I cannot bear to see what is happening to my mother. She is moving around like a zombie. She has the two boys sitting at her alter for hours at a time. They are my brothers, but I cannot stand to be with them. I do not know how to play with them. What do I say to someone who cannot hear me? I don't know what to do, Uncle" Dhia was choking with emotion, he continued.

"I have to tell you what I came here to tell you.

When me and me mother moved into the 'big house', we went to see my grandparents at Whim. There was a funeral ceremony going on. I asked who died? They said "Your mother"

My mother pleaded with the family. She tried to explain the truth to them, but the puja went on as if we were not there.

As my grandfather was about to push my mother out of the house, he said

"I place a curse on you, if you have more children, none of your boy children will ever be able to call my name"

As soon as I heard about Betose not being able to hear or speak, I knew right away that it is my grandfather course. Now we have to go through the same thing with Davo?

Do you know that Davo looks just like my grandfather, Kasy?" Dhia was crying. He was on his knees, holding his head between his legs and rocking.

Archie tried to comfort his stepson. He said

"Let me tell you something son, from the time we found out about Datson, I have been going to every place where I think that he could get help.

Every man wants a son. He wants to teach him how to rope a steer, how to saddle a donkey cart, how to return my whistle, how to say Dada. I want my son to hear my voice and say, "My name is Datson Egbert Alexander, son of Archie Alexander" Archie was sitting on the ground next to Dhia. Dhia was surprised to see how calm he was.

"Those two boys are my sons. I do not know what else to do, but to love them"

The Sunday after Dhia's visit, Archie got in his donkey cart and went to Lancaster.

Without saying a word, he picked up his two sons under his arms, like two bunches of banana. He hurried across the narrow bridge.

Babe began to scream with all the strength that she had left in her lungs.

"Kaaatee, Kaaaateee, Kaaaaateeee, come quick, come quick.

Katy and many neighbors came running upon hearing Babe's screams.

"What happened? Where did Archie take the boys?"

"Archie gone wid me picknee. I don't know where he gone wid dem. He left his donkey cart and gone running down the road.

Please run down the road and bring back my babies to me"

"Why didn't you run behind him to see where he is taking the boys?"

"I can't move, me foot is broke" said Babe.

Katy and some villagers ran down the road to find Archie and the boys.

She saw a large crowd following Archie. He entered Whim and the crowd followed.

News flew across the pasture, to the cricket field. Dhia dropped his bat and ran to the road just as Archie was entering Kasy Marage yard.

Kasy and his wife came out on the porch after hearing the commotion outside.

Archie looked at them and said

"You are a holy man? What kind a holy man are you?

If you are so holy and have so much power to put a curse on my sons, I beg of you, please fix them, take away your curse or, you keep them, they are your grandsons"

Archie stormed out of the yard and through the large crowd. Leaving his two little screaming sons, Datson and David sitting on the ground in their grandparents yard.

Years later, onlookers remembered the day Archie was mad. He had rabbis.

Kasy looked at the two frightened little boys. His wife attempted to go to them, but he pulled her back, looked at the crowd that included his other grandson Dhia.

He went into his house and slammed the door shut.

Some people curse, some throw rocks on the house, some booed and some cried.

Dhia and Katy picked up the two frightened little boys and took them to their mother.

They found Archie sitting on the front step, cradling his head in his hands.

They went to the back and found Babe in a trance state, chanting an arti-hymn.

Aum jai jagadesh haray, as loud as her hoarse voice would allow her.

The first and last verses of the hymn go like this in English.

"Oh Glory, praise the Lord of the World. Dear Lord quickly dispel the anguish and agony of Thy dear devotee. Merciful Lord who art the remover of sorrows, Thou are my King. Please open Thy arms. I am at Thy door. O Lord, dispel confusion from my mind and destroy my sins. Infuse me with faith and devotion. I am Thy child in worship".

Katy and Dhia let the boys go. They ran/creep to their mother crying, "Moo, moo.

Babe grabbed her two boys in her arms, held them tightly and kissed their tears away.

"Ma, Uncle Archie is sitting on the front steps. You need to go offer him something to eat or some water" said Dhia

"I think you should go talk to him. You never talk to the man. Everytime you want something said to him, it's always through his mother, your son or me.

For the first time, Dhero, go talk to your husband" plead Katy.

As Babe got up from her alter, Katy noticed that her right ankle was swollen and twisted out of shape.

"Wa happen to you foot Ma?" asked Dhia

"Me fall down son"

"How you fall down and twist you foot like that?" asked Katy

"Me gon tell you later" said Babe

Dhia helped his mother up and became her brace as she walked to the front steps to talk to Archie.

She was relived to see that he was still holding his head down. She did not have to look into his face when she said.

"Me go have another baby" her voice was poly

"What did you say? What did you just say?" Archie's bloodshot eyes were wide opened. His lips were trembling and his fists were ready to break something hard.

"You are sinful. You are the devil. You are cursed.

I should have left that man to kill you under the tamarind tree. That way you would not have brought so much shame and curse to my two sons and me.

Three times I came close to you, three times I got the shakes. I should have known that you are the devil. Only the devil give a man shakes like that" Archie was on fire. He had an audience of concern and curious neighbors and villagers around the yard but he did not see them. He was wild. He was blinded by fury and pain.

"No mooor, no moooor. Dear God, no moooooooore. Jesus Christ. God Almighty, no moooore. I do not want to see you for the rest of my life. You are cursed"

Archie began to run. He ran so fast on the narrow bridge, everyone looking expected him to fall into the water. He continued to chant at the top of his voice

"No mooore, no moooore, no mooooore" until he could not be heard anymore.

The donkey never stopped galloping until it reached Bound Yard.

"How did you broke you foot?" asked Katy
"I jump from the top of the stairs to the ground" answered Babe
"Why did you do something like that?"
"Me no want this baby"
"So, jumping form the top of the stairs to the ground would stop you from having this baby? You are more foolish than I thought.

Do you know that you could break your neck and every bone in your body, yet a baby will survive in your womb if it is to live?

How come you did not tell me that you are expecting again?"
"Me no want dis baby. Me no want dis thing inside me belly. Me no want ammm"

Many lives changed within four years, but that Sunday was remembered for many, many years. Some never forgot.

Archie never returned to Lancaster until many years later.
Esther never returned to Lancaster.
Dhia was drifting away from the 'house of silence'
Mother came on Saturdays with the brown envelope.
Katy, the friend, sister, neighbor and humankind never left Babe alone.

When I hear of the unconditional love and friendship that Auntie Katy had for Babe-Dhero. I wondered if it was possible for one stranger to be that kind to another?

I found many strangers who were just as passionate in giving me unconditional love.

"Katy, I have to move out of this house. I have to move away from here"
"Where are you going? Where are you thinking of moving to? How are you planning to take care of your two little boys and another on the way?" asked Katy.
"I do not know where, I only know that I do not want this baby and if I am to live, it will not be in this house" said Babe.

"You must think of somewhere? You can't just want to move without knowing where you want to go. My house and yard is unclean, remember.

Maybe you are planning on going to your parents home or back to Ram?" Katy was angry. She knew that her friend had nowhere to go and at the moment she was more alone with her two mute sons than ever before.

With Dhia spending more time with her sons, other friends and working at the estate.

He was away most of the time

"No, I am not going to anyone of them. I just have to go away from here.

Can you help me?"

1942, Katy found a Madrassi family who was willing to lease a house-lot to Babe. The lease was for ten years at eighty shillings-$18 per year.

The land was in Whim Village.

Even though it was breaking her heart to watch her friend move away form her. She could not bare to see how her friend was pining away everyday.

When Katy told Babe and Dhia about her find. They refused to move to the same village where Kasy lived. Their wounds were raw. Whim was not the place to heal.

"The land is far away from your parents. It is closer to the waterside.

You are the one who asked me to help you. That's all I am trying to do.

Do you think we want you to leave here? Do you know how many villages and people I begged for a piece of land for you? Many of them do not want you anywhere near them. Many do not want you in the same villager with them.

This lady who is willing to lease this land to you, is from my church. She does not care what others say about you. She is a brave and religious lady. We Madras people know how it feels to be outcaste and treated badly by your kind of people.

Dhia got some friends to help him build a little grass-roof mud-wall one room house.

The house was about three feet off the ground. It had two doors and three wooden windows. It stood on stilts. It had two steps with four traders each. The back step had a little landing.

The grass, wattle, posts and mud were free. They were collected from the forest, savanna and trench.

The lumber and nails had to be bought. That's when the little teapot became useful.

Dhia, the carpenter, made a table, two benches and some shelves in the kitchen.

He built a wall, dividing the one room into two.

He built a wooden bed, mattress stuffed with grass, for his pregnant mother.

Close neighbors gathered in the yard of the 'big house' to try to persuade Babe from leaving. "With ah big belly, broken foot and two little boys to care for, don't leave"

"This is your matrimonial home. You should never leave it.

Archie may be mad at the moment, but he is a lamb. I know him from a baby.

He is a good and kind boy. Stay in your home, my child" said Nana Tama.

"Where are you taking these two little boys? This is their home. They can live in this surrounding without being teased and taunted.

Do you know what will happen to them and you in another village where you and them are strangers?" Asked Mrs. George, the schoolteacher who tutored Dhia for his exam.

During my research for this story, Mrs. George told me that watching Babe and her three sons leaving Lancaster, was the most heartbreaking scene that stayed with her.

"The neighbors around the 'big house' were kind and understanding to her plight.

We did not want her to leave here. Especially taking those two little boys.

I personally felt hurt that she took them to a place where they were a different race. There were not many mixed race children at that time. I knew that they were going to have a difficult time in a village where people did not care for their kind.

I watched as Dhia carried Datson across the narrow bridge and sat him on the edge of the road. He came back and got David and did the same. Then he came back, took the teapot from his mother's hand and led her across the bridge. Her foot was wrapped with a white cloth. She had a crouch under her arm to support her weight. She was about six months pregnant.

Katy followed with some of their belongings in a large fish basket on her head.

It was a sad day for me to watch them walked down the road, Dhia carry little David.

One behind the other, they left Lancaster"

There is a tradition that I follow up to now. When someone is moving into another home, old/new, there are some items that must be placed into the home before other things and people move in. They are a table, a bed, a fireside and in a basket, some silver coins, matches, small parcels of foodstuff such as flour, sugar, salt, peas, rice, soap, water and fresh fruits and vegetable. There would be lots of garlic around the house, especially over the doors and windows to keep out any unwanted spirit.

The occupants and friends would eat the fresh fruits on the table when they enter the new home. The vegetable would be cooked on the new fireside for their first meal.

The other small parcels would remain in the basket hanging from the ceiling for years.

You never use anything from that basket, regardless of your urgent need to do so.

The belief is that the home would never be out of money, food and friends.

Katy and Dhia did the above, the day before Babe and her two boys moved in.

Babe thanked them for making it possible for her to have her own home.

She sat on the floor, holding her Betose and Davo in her arms. Through her tears, she tried to tell them "This is your home, we are going to sleep here from now on".

She was learning to communicate with her two mute sons. There was no book or school where one goes to learn dumb signs. She had to make up her own signs.

Mother went to Lancaster on her usual Saturday visit and spend some time with the boys and Babe.

It was a sad period for all involved in this miserable situation. Especially Mother, who was the one who was the 'brainchild' for the maddening situation.

She listened to the silence. Then she looked around for some movement.

She walked through the quiet house. The only sound she heard was floor creaking under her weight. She sat heavily on her canapé bed and began to cry.

'Did she cry for loosing them or relief that they are gone? What do you thing?'

After church that Sunday, Inez and George went to Whim to find Babe.

Katy told Mother where to find Babe. She still hoped that her friend would return.

"Babe you have to go back to your home" pleads Inez.

"This is my home now"

"No, your home is at Lancaster. It's your sons' birthright. Do not deny them that."

"This is my sons home now. Here is where I will take good care of them"

"Do you know that Archie can take them away from here and you?"

"No, he didn't want them. He took them to my parents home and left them there"

The following Sunday Inez returned, taking some clothes for the boys and Babe's wedding clothes and shoe. She said

"I am still hoping that you would take the boys back where they belong.

What kind of life are they going to have here?

At Lancaster they were surrounded by family and friends, here, you have bars on the door to keep them in. What kind of life is this?" Inez was angry.

Babe's mother Banchani died in 1942.

Dhia refused to go with his mother to pay their respect. Babe asked Katy to accompany her. Katy asked her husband Bull to go with them.

Because Kasy Mirage was the equivalent to an archbishop of the district, lots of pandits from all over came to the funeral.

Babe and Katy sat on the side of the road. Bull stood close to them.

Babe saw her eldest brother coming towards her. She said

"Katy, lets go, my brother is coming. He may want to kick me again"

"You sit right here. You come to mourn the death of your mother. Do not move. This is the government road. Nobody can chase you from here"

Katy told Bull that the man coming towards them is the man who kicked Dhero when she was pregnant with Datson.

As Kachan got close to them, Bull stood like a shield in front of Babe and his wife.

"You come one foot closer to her and there will be two cremation today"

Katy visited her friend regularly. She brought supplies, as Babe could not move around well, plus she could not leave the two boys alone to venture out.

Katy noticed that Dhia was doing work around the house to make them comfortable. He made a shelf for his mother's teapot. He made a shed and his mother made an alter.

The bars on the doors were low enough for adults to hop over but high enough to prevent the boys from coming out.

They were afraid the trench so close to the house, the boys could fall in and drowned.

In those days, drainage and irrigation was of great importance for the whole colony.

Every district had permanent 'shovel men' whose job were to dig all trenches and drains in the distinct. Guyana is below sea level. Floods are annual events.

"Dhero, I spoke to my priest at church and he and other members want you to take the boys there for them to pray for them," said Katy.

"My husband took them everywhere. No one can help them. They are my curse"

"Give it a try, you never know. God is more powerful than man's curse"

"Are you asking me, a Hindu, to go to a Kali Mai temple?"

"Yes. You and this Hindu shit is driving me crazy, and, is driving me away from you. Do you want these two boys get help or not?" Katy too was angry with Babe.

Babe realized that the only person she has in the whole world, is angry with her.

She decided to attend one of the Kali Mai Puja.

Holding the hands of four years old Datson and almost two years old David, she walked through the crowd of Madras people praying, dancing and singing for them.

Babe took the boys regularly to the Kali Mai Church.

The Alexander family was furious about it but there was nothing they can do. Mother forbids them from interfering with Babe and her children.

The Madras people began to accept her as a member of their church.

She was still cursed and spit upon; Katy was quick to report them to the church elders.

"We will have to take this one, one dotty at a time. Soon we would have a road.

You do not have the wealth or the strength to build a road one time, but one, one brick will eventually become a road for you. Win them over one by one" with her arm on her friend shoulder, Katy continued.

"You are going to have a baby any day now. I don't see you making any preparation for it. Where are the things that the church gave to you? The napkins, blanket and towels should be on the table for when the time comes"

"I will not need them"

Babe worked in the rice-field all day. The contraction started but she worked on.

She had a private plan to birth the baby in the water and leave it there.

Other field workers saw that she was in distress, insisted on taking her home.

Dhia came home shortly after his mother. She said to him

"Take the boys over to Sani Mother. Let them sit at her bottom-house until you go back for them. Come back as soon as possible, I have something to tell you"

Dhia knew from the looks of his mother that it was time. She looked strange.

"Son, you are a man now. I need your help. I think this baby is going to come soon"

"Let me run and get someone to help you. Ma I am a man, I can't deliver baby"

"No, no, no, I don't want anyone here. I want only you here to help me do what I have to do. When the baby comes out, take the knife from the table and cut the nablecord. Don't look at it, just wrap it in the cloth on the table and take it to the Button Wood Walk. Its getting dark, no one will see you".

"Ma, you gone mad? Talking like a crazy person. Why would you want me to do something like that? Do you know that what you are asking me to do is a crime?

Do you know that I will be hang if I do what you are asking me to do? Dhia was shaking with shock and anger from his mother's request.

If anyone knows of his mother suffering, it would be him. He watched her suffered in so many different ways. This past four years had been especially hard on her.

He saw the pain and frustration whenever she tried to communicate with the boys.

But, he was sure that his mother had not gone mad. He said

"I am the one who studied to become a policeman. I learned the laws and what the punishments are. I refuse to be a part of your madness" Dhia walked away from her.

He looked back and saw his mother lying on the back landing. He rushed to her side.

With her knees up and legs opened, she had her skirt pulled down like a tent.

"The baby is out, get the knife and cut the cord" Babe ordered her son.

"No, I will not do that. I will run and get help. If you do anything while I am gone, they will hang you. You hear me Ma? Don't do anything foolish. Lie still until help comes. I am going for Sani Mother first then I will run and get Nurse Reed and Auntie Katy. Do not move. Ma, I will see to it that they hang you if you do anything wrong"

Nurse Reed arrived shortly after followed by Katy and Dhia.

Babe was still lying on her back on the landing.

Dhia removed the bars from the door.

Katy took the baby from between her friend's leg after the nurse cut the cord.

Nurse Reed worked on Babe to get the afterbirth-placenta out while Sani Mother held up a lantern.

Katy brought the little cleaned, wrapped baby into the room for Babe to hold.

"I do not want it"

"What you do not want? The injection? It is my duty to give you this to prevent infection or tetanus"

"I do not want that baby"

Nurse Reed who had been a midwife for many years and who had delivered most of the youngsters in the area, was not surprised to hear a new mother saying such things. But because Dhia had told them what his mother had asked him to do,

The nurse said to Babe

"I brought so many babies into this world, but none of my own. If you do not want this baby, I will take her. I always wanted a little girl. I have too many boys"

"Her? You mean it is a girl? Its not another boy with the curse?"

"Yes it's a girl. You are not going to put her at the Button Wood Walk for crabdog to eat feast on her. I will take her" said Nurse Reed angrily reaching for the baby.

Babe realized that Dhia must have told them what she requested of him.

She took her little girl, lay her on her chest and circle her two arms around her baby.

.

BOOK II

AM I MY MOTHER'S DAUGHTER?

My very first memory as a child was when I was maybe about three or four years old. I was standing at the open door, holding on to the bars. I saw my mother and three brothers coming down the road. I became so excited that I peed on the floor.

'I still pee in my pants if I am excited'

There was a young woman in the house with me. I remembered that she was so angry that I peed on the floor. She pulled me down and rolled me like a mop on my urine.

Later I learned that when I was a little girl, my brother Dhia got married.

He and his wife slept in the bedroom and my mother and her children slept in the gallery. I was told that she babysat me while my brother and mother went to work.

She got pregnant and when it was time for her to give birth, she went to her parents home,. She had a baby girl. She never returned to Whim with her baby to her husband.

I was told that my brother and mother went several times to bring her back, but her family said they did not want her to take the baby to a house of 'gunga' Dummies.

My mother sent money for the baby for years. My brother never spoke about them.

My earliest recollection of my family.

My Mommy Dhero was tall with long, black hair. She had a light complexion,

A beautiful smile and arms full of tenderness. She held the three of us like an octopus.

My Buddy Dhia was and still is in my mind, the most handsome Indian man that I have ever seen. He was as light as my mother. He had split chin, a strait nose, a round face and strength enough to carry all three of us on his back on our Sunday morning piggyback treat.

Baldeo-Betose-Datson was dark like me. He established authority over us youngon at an early age. He was quiet and he was very handsome.

Davindra-Davo-David was like Dhia, light complexion. He was a Hindu Sadu.

He was the nosy one. He knew everyone and everything that was happening at Whim.

He and I got into trouble doing things that we shouldn't. Datson was always there to scold us and confine us in the house, behind the bars.

Finally, there was me, Basmati-Babzy-Wynette. I was born on a landing, outside the door. I do not know how to describe me for that era. There was no picture of me. There was no looking glass for me to see what I looked like.

As a child growing up in Whim, I knew from a very early age that my two brothers and I were different. We did not look that much different from most of the villagers. The only difference that I could think of was that we had some curls on our heads.

But some of them had more curls and blacker than us. So what's the difference?

I knew that we were different because of the way some of the people treated us.

The same people who tolerated us in the presence of my mother and brother Dhia.

Would treat us like animals when they were not around.

My mother sold fish and seasonal supplies to the Black villagers because Indians would not buy anything from her.

My brother Dhia went to Skeldon sugar estate to cut cane. He went on Sunday afternoon and came back home on Saturday afternoon.

I was little. I was left in my brothers' charge. I had to go wherever they go.

The people used us to clean their animal pens, fetch water, cut wood, dig mud from the trench for them to dab their fireside and yard. They gave us buckets to go to the cow pasture to collect fresh cow down for them to dab their yard.

I saw big men stood by the donkey cart full of large heavy bags of stuff, loading them on the backs of my little brothers. Most times they had to cross narrow bridges with that weight on their backs.

Some humankind passerby would say, "Big man like you would have little boys fetching heavy bags like that? What kind ah animal are you?"

Me, being the ears and mouth for my brothers, sometimes disliked the people who objected to the abuse. Why? Because I will not get the little reward that came with the abuse, I get to use my ears and mouth with others. Assuring myself that I am not mute.

We had some truly good and kind people amongst the mean ones.

They were Auntie Katy, Uncle Bull and their children.

Auntie Chunu, Uncle Naga and their children.

Auntie Amoy and her sister Auntie Pandu and their family.

And Auntie Dull and her family.

They protected us. We could go to their homes and feel accepted.

We were not allowed to go to Auntie Katy's home at Lancaster. My mother said that she lived too far away and they had plenty biting dogs. She came to visit us regularly.

Later I learned that Lancaster was my mother's forbidden village.

My mother cooked every morning. Roti, curry fish, vegetable, dhal, and rice.

Every day, same food. She left the food by the fireside to keep warm.

Hungry time, Datson would share the food and I would wash the enamel dishes.

There were lots of fresh fruits on the table. So why? You would ask, did we go to people's yard to do all kinds of laborious jobs? For them to hear me when I speak.

I remembered when I was about five years old. It had rained heavily for days.

The whole of Whim was flooded. Now you know why the houses were built on stilts.

My mother warned the boys not to go out of the house. She told me to look after them.

"Find things to do with them. Play with them in the house. No mek dem go out. There is too much water in de yard. Me can't see the bridge or the dam"

The boys stayed indoor until they got board. They warned me to stay inside.

They went outside to play in the water. I watched them from the open door with the bars. I wanted to be a part of the fun. I have always been a part of whatever they did.

I scaled the bars and sat on the top step. Worked my way down to the step where my feet submerged into the murky water. It felt good. Now I know why they are happy.

My brothers saw me playing with the water. They hurried over to me and Datson gave me a wiping. He put me back over the bars and warned me with his finger.

I did the same thing again. If they could have so much fun, why shouldn't I?

They saw me again. They were not about to let me spoil their fun. They took a long piece of rope, tied the middle of it to my waist which was under the water.

Then they tied each end to their own waists. This way I was safe and they could go on having fun. They raced to see who could stay under longer.

Fun they had. When they plunged into the water, I went down. They plunged everywhere. I went down every time.

I was screaming whenever my head was above the water, but my screams fell on deft ears. They saw that I could stay under even longer than they could.

My mother returned home early. With the flood she could not do much business.

She saw the boys playing in the water. She saw them pulling some thing. She thought it was a piece of wood.

Upon a closer look, she saw that it was her lifeless little daughter. Me, her Babzy.

Her screams brought out neighbors through the water to see what happened.

They rolled my little body on the high dam. Two men held me upside down to get the water out of me.

It was finally decided that I was dead. There was nothing else anyone could do.

My mother held her limp child in her arms and wailed as loud as she could.

I was told that the two sisters, Auntie Amoy and Auntie Pandu took me form my mother's arms. One said "if she is dead already, we can't kill her again. Let us try something. Running water does pull water out"

They held me upside down in the trench. They kept my head under the water.

Everyone watched in harrow and surprised as my little body wiggled and when they lifted my head out of the water, my floodgate opened and the piece of rag that was blocking my windpipe came out.

Brain damage or not, those two Aunties were the second of many to save my life.

While the bystanders, helpers, and a very thankful mother gather around to see the speared child, a man name John, who was a village ranger, came with a shotgun in his hand. He said to my mother.

"Why don't you let me take you out of this shame and curse. Just say yes and I will use three led into these three Kaffree animals who bring shame to this village"

Some people laughed but some looked at him in shock and disgusted.

My mother was afraid of him. She warned me to never let my brothers go anywhere near his home or yard.

Most of the people I mentioned are now gone, but I learned a lot from them.

Datson and David were very creative. They made slinging shot with the strongest wood-guava wood and old bicycle tube.

My mother warned me to make sure that do not shoot birds. So I had to find old milk cans for their target. Then I had to find the right size stones and keep out of the range of fire. They made yoyo with old cotton reel. They made kites that stayed in the air long after everyone else had long dropped.

My brothers were good at whatever they were allowed to do.

Villagers came to get my brothers to do laborious and dirty jobs. Of course I had to go along with them.

I remember, one day my mother came home and saw that the boys did not complete their chores. They had to pen the sheep under the house and fill the drum with water from the well at the main road. She said to me.

"What happened here today? Why you didn't make the boys do what they had to do? Where did you go with them today?"

"Mommy, you should see how strong Betose and Davo is. They empty a whole cow cart full of dhan-rice paddy on their bare backs.

Everybody stand and watch them carry big bags across the bridge and pack them up"

My mother sat on the ground and cried. I wondered why she wasn't as proud as I was?

"Did any of the men carry bags on their backs too?" My teary mother asked.

"No, because my brothers are stronger than them" I said proudly.

"What kind of people would use two little boys to empty a cow cart full of big bags of dhan while they stand and watch?" she cried out loud.

If that question were asked of me today, my answer would be,

"Some mean and heartless people from Whim Village. My birth land"

My mother asked Sani Mother, who lived at the back lot of our house, if the three of us could stay under her two-story house while she went to work?

We did the same things for her. The only difference was that we did not go all over the village doing other people dirty jobs.

My brothers had to cut the firewood and fetch water to full two drums plus ours.

We grated piles of coconut for her to make oil. We had to clean and feed the pigs.

I had to scrub the floors upstairs, the only time I was allowed in her house.

My mother cooked our food everyday. She would pack a saucepan full of curry and rice with dhal in a cup. She would put lots of fruits in a basket for us to eat.

We had no need to go anywhere or beg anyone for anything. I guess it's venturing out.

I remember, sometimes when my mother was late on coming home, Sani Mother would give us some food in an enamel bowl. I had to wash the dishes, wipe the kitchen floor and fetch up firewood.

I was happy when my mother came before their dinnertime. That way they do not have to give us food in the bowl and I do not have to do those extra duties for it.

One day, Datson shared out the food that my mother left, earlier than lunchtime.

I became so hungry by afternoon, I reached into the hag-washing barrel and took out some pieces of coconut and shared them with my two brothers.

One evening when my mother was late in coming home, I saw Sani Mother's grandson coming down the stairs with the enamel bowl. I heard someone telling him to give it to us instead. I heard him saying

"Every time I have to give them my dog food? What is my dog going to eat?"

My brothers and I were eating the dog food from Sani Mother's dog bowl.

I do not remember what kind of cloth we wore. I would imagine that they would be made of brown cotton and flour bags.

The boys wore long shirts reaching them to the knees. A single piece of garment made of flour bag. Flour bags were the cheapest and strongest cotton around. Flour was the most consumed foreign product. It came from England and India.

The flour bag was used for almost every use. Clothes, bed linen, towel, baby napkins and every which way when a strong piece of cloth is needed.

Some people were proud to display on the back of their shirt 'Product of India'.

Four bags for four bits, a bit was eight cents, made a king size bed sheet. One bag made two billow cases.

My brothers used the twine that sewed the bag together, for their kits and yoyos.

Everyone used flour bags in those days. At the salt-goods stores, one had to put in an order and wait her tern or go to a bakery and get some in a hurry.

A flour bag, when bleached in the sun for some days, can be as white as any cotton.

Buddy's working clothes were made from flour bags. His traveling clothes however were made of kike. He played cricket in all white long trousers and long sleeves shirt.

I remembered that on Saturdays, Buddy brought his dirty clothes including his flour-bag sheets and pillowcases for Mommy to wash.

In Guyana, regardless of the weather, the sun never fails to show its hot golden face.

Shoe was not an item in the village. Most people walked bare footed.

Only policemen, postmen, and schoolteachers wore shoes. Buddy, however was given a pair of white kleeks because he was a member of the Berbice cricket team.

On Sundays my Buddy looked like an Overseers in his stiff white cricket outfit.

With the leased land came two acres of rice field.

Rice was the staple diet and a moneymaking product. Most people cultivated rice.

My mother and brother were planting the rice land before I was born.

They bought two steers and a heifer. Datson and David took turn milking the cow.

We had more milk than we needed. We shared with Sani Mother and other neighbors who would accept it from us. My mother made gee-butter with the cream of the milk. She used it at the alter, and to make pershad-sweetmeat for religious services.

There were many seasons. Cane cutting and sugar boiling seasons were in February to May, recess then start again in August through November.

Rice planting and harvesting season was July they plant, October they harvest.

The rain seasons were May to June and December to January.

I must tell you this Linda. Though I was a little child I still remember it as if it happened yesterday. 1947 India got its independence. It was the first time I saw that my mother had another side in her; A happy side.

In my young mind, she was the happiest Indian in the world at that time.

She was singing and dancing on the street. "Dancing is freedom. Dance when you free" Some people wondered why she so happy about another country's independence?

"India is my mother-land. We are free. We are free. God bless my Mother India"

She told the people who laughed at her. Most of them thought she was mad anyhow.

She went to Sahardat store and bought some yards of gold satin.

She made sari for her and me. She ordered dhoti and phagri for Datson and David.

My Buddy refused to have any part of the celebration. He called it a masquerade.

The day of the grand ceremony that was held in the cricket field, my mother wanted us to be early to have front seats.

I remember as we walked out to the place of India independence celebration, people were laughing at us, as though we were on a freak show.

My mother ignored the jarring and laughter. She hurried us along.

At the entrance they gave each person a flag of India. We were waving ours.

It was my first time seeing so many people, all wearing bright yellow, gold, green white and red outfits.

There was a large tent and lots of benches. We got front seats because we were early

There were lots of activities, boots with food and drinks. Men were singing and dancing to music from drum beating.

My mother kept the three of us close to her. She was waiting anxiously to hear the India's representative deliver the message from India to all Indians.

I remember a man came to my mother and said something in Hindi.

I saw her protest, shaking her head saying "nahee, nahee" no, no.

The man kept on saying whatever he was saying to her. He looked up in the crowd. She followed his eyes and saw her eldest brother pointing to her and nodding his head.

My mother got up, took us by the hand and began to lead us out of the ground.

The man took the Indian flag from each of our hands as we left.

My mother did not go away as they expected. She was not going to let anyone stop her from being present at her India Independence Celebration.

She took us outside the fence, stood there in the mud and watch the whole ceremony, and when they sang the Indian National Anthem, she sang with every wind in her lungs. She urged me to sing along. She urged her two dummy sons to dance.

Four people dressed in gold satin, standing outside the fence, celebrating India's Independence Day.

I was told that when the Alexander's heard of 'the masquerade that Babe put the three little Black children through and the mockery from the Indians'.

Some suggested that they go to Whim immediately, take the children to Port Mourant.

"I will take Datson, he is our Godchild" said Inez

"I will take David, he is our Godchild" said Harriett.

I don't remember being told of anyone wanting me.

"Stop, stop. All of you stop. You sound like you are talking about choosing a puppydog. Those children belong to Babe. No one is going to take them from her.

Even though she refused to accept help from this family and shield her children from us, they are still her children. Leave her and her children alone" Mother said

Between the sugar and rice breaks, people found other things to do.

They fixed their leaking roofs. Dig their trenches, stock up with firewood.

Men gather at one's yard, under a tree, to get a descent haircut and shave.

They caught lots of fishes, salted and dry in the sun. There were plenty to do.

Whenever it rained, the one main road that runs along the coastal side of the County of Berbice in which we lived, was always knee deep in mud.

The government was working on making a better road, because many times Officials cars or carts had to be pulled out from the deep mud by helpful villagers.

They began to 'burn dirt' to produce red bricks. It was done by clearing an area in different districts along the main road, always on the seaside because closer to the sea had better clay.

They packed hard kurda wood in a square fashion about twenty by two feet high. Then they packed hard clay-mud on top of the wood. Then more wood, then more clay, then more wood and so on until a high, square hill is built.

They then light the wood at the bottom and start a fire. That fire would burn for weeks. The finish product would be rock-hard red brick for building our roads.

They paid villagers to fetch wood and clay to build the small mountains.

My mother heard that villagers were making lots of money by fetching clay from the waterside to the heap, which was about a mile away.

She quickly joined the line. She had the three of us with her.

The man who handed out the baskets, the kind you saw in old Chinese movies, gave one to each of us.

My mother told the man that it was only she who would be working, that her children would only walk along with her.

The man told her "They pay by the shovel not by the basket. You can carry four shovels. The boys can carry two each and this little one can carry one shovel. At a bit per shovel, the four of you could get nine bits per trip. That's a good lot of bits".

I had my first job. We walked as fast as we could in the deep mud to make nine bits-seventy-two cents per trip.

We made four trips per day. The way to and from was treacherous. People were slipping and sliding in the deep mud. There were no way that we could have made more trips. Some people were digging dirt closer to the heap. My mother called it cheating.

We fetched dirt in a basket on our heads for six days. Me holding on to my mother's shirttail like a lamb following its mother

My mother was no mathematician but she knew exactly what we should receive..

When he gave her twenty-four bits less than what she had calculated, she question the man dressed in white with a khorkhat on his head.

"Listen to me, woman, we do not pay for little children's labor.

The King would have our heads if news get out of here that we used little children.

"Why did they take the shovel full of clay from her head and throw it on the heap if they know that they were not going to pay for it?" Asked my mother.

"I have to follow the rules. I will pay you for what is written down in the book.

Eight shovels per trip, four trip per day for six days. Take your sixty-four shillings and move out of the line. You have never made this much money at one time in your life.

We do not pay for one shovel load. It has to be two and more"

"You owe my little daughter eight shillings, Saa"

"You have not heard a word I said, have you? We cannot pay a child this young, for labor. It is against the law"

"You still owe my Babzy eight shillings". My mother walked away crying.

That was the first of many such 'work for no pay' in my life.

It was mandatory that children from the age of six must attend school.

My school was Akline Scotch School.

My uniform was a green kimono and white shirt, and green ribbon on my hair.

The seamstress made some white bloomers, my first, and a book bag from flour bag.

The day before my first day at school, my mothers cut my nails, clean my ears, rub me down from head to toes with fresh coconut oil, and scrubbed my neck with alcohol. She told me "You will be wearing a white shirt, you do not want a brown collar"

My first day to school was memorable. Except for the India Independence Day, I do not remember ever being dressed up like that.

My mother divided my hair in two and made two long plats that fell down to my waist. She tied two green ribbons at the beginning of the plats and curled the ends.

She could not avoid the obvious curls that were too short to be pulled into the pigtails. They peeked out all around my head.

I wanted everyone along our dam to see how nice I looked going to school.

In school, I saw more Black people in one place that I never saw before.

In the one large wooden school hall with four long wooden windows that were opened by using a long pole to push it open. There were two doors, one at the front and one at the back. There were lots of long desk and benches, and there were four Black teachers, teaching all Indian children, that was until I got there.

There were no walls or partitions separating the classes.

Each teacher sat at a desk against one of the four walls of the building.

Each class faced their teacher and the blackboard against the wall.

It was so organized. I often wondered how was that done with such an orderly fashion?

Teachers played a very important role in a child's life in those days.

A teacher knew you more than you knew yourself. They were free to discipline children. They were trusted by parents and pupils alike and were respected by all.

It is amazing to me now, as to how they did that? Keeping hundreds of children quiet and orderly in a big, big one-room school?

At Christmas time, the teachers' gifts from parents would be some eggs, rice, a chicken and a 'wild cane'.

It was used when needed. Most time it was a part of the teacher's items on the table or hang from its hook at the blackboard. The wild cane was always in sight. It was a silent reminder that the school is a place to learn or feel.

In my one-room ABC school that stood on stilts, were four ladies whom I never forget, they were Mrs. Moore, Mrs. King, Mrs. Ben and Miss Rose. All Black

They had their own class but they knew every child in the whole school by name.

My teacher was Mrs. Moore. She was plump with a serious but gentle touch.

My first day at school, my mother packed my school bag with a slate, some slate pencil and a green lemonade bottle with a rubber nipple, full of tea with milk.

Oh, I forget to tell you, I was not whined from my mother's breast.

When she was absent, my two middle fingers of my right hand comforted me in the house of silence. My green lemonade bottle, however, was just a buffer until I can grab the real thing from under my mother's blouse.

When the bell rang, I joined the line one behind the other and followed up the five steps. I was directed to my class. There were many long desks and benches.

We stood, clasped our hands and said a prayer then we sang the national anthem.

'God save our gracious King, long live our gracious King, God save the King. Make him victorious, happy and glorious. God save our gracious King, God save our King'.

When Mrs. Moore called out names from a book on her desk, each child stood up and said 'present'.

I waited to hear mine, Babzy, but she never called it. She looked at me as she kept repeating 'Wynette Alexander' over and over. She picked up the ruler from her desk pointed it to me and said "Child, are you deft? Can't you hear me calling your name?"

"No Miss, you no call me name. Me name is Babzy. Me no hear Babzy"

"No, your name is Wynette Alexander. When I call that name, you answer."

"Ms Moore me Mommy call me Babzy, short for Basmati. Me Buddy call me Win and me two other brothers can't call me anything because them can't talk" I said.

"Your name is Wynette Alexander. Its time for you know that" she said angrily

I told my mother what Mrs. Moore told me. She was furious for a while. Then she said "When I went to register you at the school, I had to take a paper from the church to them. The Natos stood as your Godparents. I gave your name Wynette and the minister of the church, knowing that you don't have a father gave you the name Alexander.

Alexander is your school name. No one has to know about it. Answer to it at school.

I think the Reverent gave that name to children who don't have a father"

My mother spent all her spare time telling me whatever she wanted me to know.

She told me that she have five sisters, Aunties Katy, Chunu, Amoy, Pandu and Dull.

She told me that the house Auntie Chunu lives in once belonged to her parents.

She never told me about the 'dead flag' that was planted for her demise. Later she did.

She never told me about Archie taking my two brothers and leaving them in that yard.

After I started school, my mother asked Auntie Chunu if Datson and David could stay at her house? She said

"You have a big long porch and yard. They can play and help do things for you rather than going all over the village where advantage is taken on them. Babzy is going to school now. She is not there to watch them anymore. Would you please help me?"

My mother cooked our food as usual and left it with Sister Mari. Auntie Chunu said.

"Dhero, no badda cook food and bring for the children. My house is always full of food. Look at the size of my family. 'They were she, Uncle Naga, Sister Mari, the eldest and only girl at that time, and five boys' then look at the size of our pots. Feeding three extra mouths is nothing for me. They eat Mari food and leave yours. Yours get cold by the time they are ready to eat. Sister Mari curry fish and rice is always hot.

If you ate our kind of food, you too could have a nice hot meal before going home"

The Naga family became our family.

Uncle Naga was tall, handsome Madras man. He had fishing boats and racehorses.

He became the father I longed for. He was a very, very nice father to my brothers.

Auntie Chunu was truly my mother sister. Just like Auntie Katy.

She loved us with no reservations. When people came to take the boys to do their hard work, she would curse and chase them away.

Sister Mari was the big sister for all of us. She loved to comb my hair and make little dresses for me. She had no sister at that time. I became her little sister.

The Naga family nor any of the other four 'sisters' and their family never treated us any different than their own children. They were the safe goal for us in an environment of cruel heartless people. They were all Madras's with the kindest hearts,

The teachers in my school had a special interest in me, maybe because I was the only different child in the school.

Mrs. Moore allowed me to sit at her table during classes after I was beaten, had my cloths torn and my crushed slate and book bag thrown into the trench.

At break time the others teachers gathered around Mrs. Moore's table to play with my hair and talked things that I had no clue about.

"That is not right. The child needs to know her family"

"Would you believe it? She doesn't even know her own name?"

"Did you know that Archie had to take her mother to court a few years ago?"

"For what?"

"For the magistrate to order her to take money from him to support his children"

"You must be lying. No man takes a woman to court for wanting to pay support"

"Believe me, he did. I am told that he deposited more than what the court ordered"

"Why is she keeping the children from their family? They are such a nice and respectful family. I heard sometime back they wanted to take the children from her"

"I don't agree that anybody, no matter who, should take children from a mother"

"I think somebody should talk to that woman. After all, this child is one of us"

"I would talk to her"

One day after four children busted my lips tore my uniform and called me names such as Kaffree baby, Black gal and dummy boy sister. Mrs. Moore punished them and gave them a long speech of how "God made everyone the same way"

Mrs. Moore said to me "Wynette, do you say prayers before you go to sleep?"

"I sing with my Mommy. I pray with her at the alter and I pray at the Kali"

"Have you ever gone to the church across the road?" Akline Scotch Church.

"No, Mis Moore"

"Do you know that you were christened in that church, not in a Kali church?

I am going to teach you two prayers. You must say them every morning and night"

She looked at me as if to say 'I am trying to get you out of your Whim cocoon'

"We will start with the morning prayer first. It goes like this;

'Now I wake and see the light, God has kept me through the night.

Make me good Oh Lord I pray, keep and guide me through this day, amen'.

"When you learn those four lines and know them well, then you will learn the night prayer that goes like this"

"Now I lay me down to sleep, I pray the Lord this child to keep.

If I should die before I wake, I pray the Lord this child to take, amen".

"I know that it's a lot to learn since you do not know how to speak proper English. We will work on it, line by line, alright?"

"Yes Mis. Moore"

I learned and say Mrs. Moore's prayers every morning and night in silence.

I could not let my mother hear that I was praying in any language but Hindi.

She disliked the fact that I was told things at school that she never wanted me to know.

She was afraid that I was learning who I was. Things she shielded me from, all my life.

I knew that some things that I was learning at school, made my mother unhappy.

I tried very hard not to tell her everything that I learned, especially if it was about Christian praying or English stories of God.

I could not tell her that I learned that there was a man name Jesus, who loved us all.

Morning and nights I made my two brothers kneeled with me as I say my prayers.

I started loud 'Ohm jai jagadesh haray, then my morning or evening English prayer.

My brothers agreed to kneel and clasp their hands because I told them that I was praying to God for them to hear and talk. I truly did that too, everyday of my life.

"That Mis. Moore is trying to take you away from me" my furious mother said.

After every one of her children was born, my mother opened her book and found names for us. Baldio was Betose, Davendra was Davo and Basmati was Babzy.

Only in private did she call us by our Hindu names for fear from the Indians.

She knew that even though we were her children, we couldn't use her book names.

Every day at school, about mid-morning, I would lift my right hand, showing my two fingers. Today we call it a 'peace' sign. Back then it was used for asking teacher permission to go to the latrine.

Mrs. Moore knew why I needed to go out of class the same time everyday? Afterall I sat at her table, she looked into my bag and saw the green lemonade bottle of tea.

I was the only child who took my school bag when I got permission to use the latrine.

Like I said before, I think she had a soft spot in her heart for me.

She allowed me to enjoy my bottle of tea under the school. That was until one of the children saw me sucking from my rubber nipple.

The whole school teased me. After they throw my bag, bottle and me into the trench.

My brothers fished my school bag out of the trench and my mother gave me my

Bottle the next day, she said

"Go into the latrine and drink your tea. The children can't see you in there"

One day I did the routine signal, hurried to the latrine and found a banana instead.

I ran out of the latrine and up the road, baling with all my might.

I looked up the road and saw my Mommy running to me with my bottle of tea.

I later found out that Mrs. Moore told my mother

"Wynette is a big girl, she should not be sucking from a bottle til now. If you need to give her something, give her a banana instead. [She didn't know I still wasn't weaned.]

She will be going over to the big school soon. What is she going to do then? Still suck from a bottle? Babe, I think you are trying so hard to keep her as a baby and out of the reach of others, that you don't know what you are doing to her.

You are going to have to face the fact that she is growing and that there is another side to her and one day she would want to know her 'other side'.

She is not like you and me, we know who we are. She only knows half of who she is. She needs to know the whole of who she is. She is growing. Only pot don't grow"

My mother was fit to be tied. She told Mrs. Moore

"My Babzy do not have anyone else but me and her brothers.

Stop poisoning her head about Alexander and those kinds of people.

We pray to my God. That's enough. She does not need to know about your God"

Mrs. Moore attended the church across the road. The same church the Alexander family attended. They asked her about me and she told them the truth about me.

I waited every afternoon after school under the Sweetie tree for Mrs. Moore. She was my shield from the children who always found something nasty to say or do to me.

She told me many stories. Most of them were about a fine family from Lancaster.

The only nice family from Lancaster that I was told about was Auntie Katy and family. I was told that it was not a good village for me and the boys to go to.

I knew Mrs. Moore was not talking about Auntie Katy.

We walked together until I reached Auntie Chunu's house. She continued on to Manchester Village where she lived with her husband, who was also a schoolteacher at another school and their children

I stay in the safety of the Naga family, with my brothers, until my mother for us.

When the children trampled on my Abacus – Chinese counter – Mrs. Moore told me to "Get forty small rocks, smooth them round, and then flatten one side so it would not roll off the table. Give them to me tomorrow" I did, with the help of David.

She colored the little marble like rocks in groups of ten, yellow, green, red and blue just as the ones on an abacus.

I was allowed to use her table to arrange my stones and do my addition, subtraction, division and multiplication. The stones went with me all the way to big school.

Today, I am my own financial planner. I can count better than I can read.

Since we began to stay at Auntie Chunu's. We were never hungry.

Her home was always blessed with plenty of food and bunches of banana hanging on the porch. We didn't then and still do not know about or believe in sandwich or bread.

Sister Mari fed us hot food and made sure that we wash our bodies at the standpipe in the yard with sweet smelling Lifebuoy soap. Then combed my hair in different styles.

People in Whim still used my two brothers when Auntie Chunu was busy.

Jack the barber, used them to clean his barbershop. In return they got a haircut.

Mr. Chundon used them to clean his movie theater. They get to sit in pit and watch pictureshow free. They clean his rumshop and wash his car.

My brothers felt proud to be working for Mr. Chundon because he was the richest Syrian in Whim. He was the only person who owned a car and my brothers were the only ones who could touch his car. Free labor has its privileges.

People were still treating my brothers like slaves. It was a common thing to do.

Whenever any of my five Aunties and their families saw it, they would stop it.

They had their own busy lives and could not watch them all the time.

On Saturdays I would follow them. Sometimes they would chase me back or even give me a wapping if they were going somewhere that they did not want me to know. They knew that I was telling Mommy and Buddy everything they did.

One time after Buddy scolded them for doing something, they knew I told him. David held me down and Datson came with a knife in his hand. They told me that the next time I rattle on them, they would cut off my tongue.

I was shaking with fear and they were hugging each other, laughing and dancing.

As to say 'We scared her good, bet you she don't tell on us anymore'.

Sundays were the happiest days in my household.

Early in the morning, while Mommy cooked roti and curry, Buddy would romp with us. He took turn giving us piggyback rides and would have all three of us walked on his back. We would massage his hands and feet with coconut oil.

After tea, Mommy would clean and wash. Buddy would cut firewood for the week. David and Datson would attend to the sheep, clean their pen and milk the cow.

I had to collect eggs, feed the ducks and fouls and clean their pens.

After breakfast, Buddy gets dress in all over white and go to play cricked.

Mommy would take the three of us to the trench and give us a good scrub.

My two brothers swam like fishes. My mother did not have to worry about them in the water. It was me whom she was protected of, maybe because of the bad experience.

My mother would oil us down, from hair to toes with fresh coconut oil.

She love saying to me "how many curls you want today?"

"One hundred curls please"

She would part my hair in four and make twenty-five curls in each corner of my head.

I used to love shaking my head and feeling the hundred curls falling all over my head. They moved up and down like yoyos.

I really enjoyed Sundays. I enjoyed my family. I enjoyed being able to speak.

When my mother sat down, I would dive for what lay under her blouse.

Buddy would say "Win, aren't you too big for that now? You have to stop"

I enjoyed myself when Mommy and Buddy asked me to explain what the boys were trying to say, or, for me to explain to the boys whatever they may want them to know. I felt useful. I knew that I was the only one in the whole world who could communicate with my brothers. Not even their mother could do that as good as I did.

It was a good feeling, understanding my two brothers, when no one else did.

Me, the baby of the family, was my brothers' interpreter and keeper. I loved it.

Loving Datson and David came naturally. I just love them with all my being.

After my ABC years with Mrs. Moore, her love, her protection, her lifelong teachings, I was promoted to the 'big school'. −Not because I was smarter, but because I was older - A much larger two-story wooden building, painted in green and yellow. It had many glass windows and two long stairwells.

My teacher in first standard was Mr. Clas. He was a tall, slender man.

Some of the children from my ABC class began to pull and pushed me around.

They said "Wa you do about daa now? You na get Mis. Moore fe beat aby now"

They did not play with me. Recess time I would stay in the class. I had the security of Mr. Clas and I was not pulled and pushed around in the teachers' presence.

They had an obsession with my hair. They would grab my hair and tossed me around from one to the other until I become giddy and fall to the ground.

I still waited for Mrs. Moore every afternoon to walk up the road.

One day I asked her "Mis. Moore, why de picknee dem na like me?"

"Wynette, they are children, not picknee. It is not that the children do not like you.

It's their parents who are responsible for them not liking you"

"But their parents do not come to school. How could they make dem children treat me so bad when they don't even know me?"

"Because parents say bad things in the presence of their children. You see, children love and respect their parents. They lookup to them, if their parents say something mean or hateful in the presence of the children, the children adopt the hate.

My school was having an excursion to #63 Beach, about 25 miles away.

My mother was more excited than I was, she said,

"Babzy, this is a good chance for you to make friends and have fun at the beach"

My mother prepared a basket with dhal-puri, duck curry, a large bottle of cream soda and some yellow bananas. She said, "I am packing plenty of food so that you could share with others, and if any of them offer something to you, you accept and say thanks. Small actions like that can change people's mind, and make them friendlier"

I was dressed in my one and best frock. My mother made my curls and loaned me some of my gold jewels. {I wore silver Jewelry everyday but on special occasion, she brought out the gold}. Children, especially Indian children wore lots of jewelry.

I was feeling beautiful because my Mommy told me that I was beautiful.

I was happy. It was my first time going away from Whim and Akline.

First time going in a bus, first time going away from my mother and brothers.

I got to my school, got on the long slender bridge to cross over. Out of nowhere came a group of children, they got on the bridge and began to jump up and down.

Me, my pretty frock and my mother nicely packed basket were in the trench.

Children laughter was not a nice sound in my head. It was a scary sound.

I picked up my basket from under the bridge and walked out, drenched in mud.

A teacher came running. "Come back. Come back and show me who did this to you"

"Mis. I can't show you who throw me in the trench. They all look the same when they laugh" my first of many to come.

My mother held on to me on the dirt dam of Whim, like a baby in her arms, she rocked me back and forth, my mud all over her, she cried and prayed in Hindi

"Ohm Begawan, is my father curse on my Babzy too?"

I looked at Buddy's little square looking glass, which he used for shaving.

I saw that I have two eyes, a nose, two lips, a chin and the same dark color as them.

So what makes me different from them? Why are they treating me so differently?

I even have a mother and brother who looked just like their mother and brother.

This confused child said to her Mommy.

"Mommy, come to my school just when it's over. I will come out running and shouting 'Mommy, Mommy' so that the children can see that my mother looks like them. Maybe they will want to be friends with me and not beat me anymore?"

We did that several times, it made no difference

When they trampled on my school bag and broke my slate into pieces, my brothers would climb to the top of Mr. Chundon's garage and take out a thick, heavy slate.

They would grind down the edges on the red brick road.

My slate was thicker and stronger. Now they teased me that I was a poor 'church rat' who have to use shingle from a rooftop to write on.

I atomically knew that after school, I should sit under the sweetie tree and wait for Ms. Moore to walk me to the safety of Auntie Chunu's home.

One day a group of girls grabbed me at the back of the school.

"Come on Wynette, let's play this game call 'More weight'. You lie face down on the ground, we will climb on top of you to see how much weight you can take"

I was afraid, yet happy at the same time. It was the first time I was asked to play.

I wanted so much for someone to play with me, now I have a whole group of them.

I was afraid that I would miss my walk home with Ms. Moore.

In weighing my options, I realized I had none. They were holding my two arms and pushing me face down on the grassless, sandy ground.

One by one the girls climbed on my back, stocking themselves criss-cross into a hill, each one yelling 'More weight', 'More weight'.

According to the rules of the game, the person on the ground should be the one to say 'More weight', to see how much weight she can take.

I never said it one time. I was struggling to breath.

Every time I breathe in, I was clogging my lungs with dust of red sand.

'This is not a nice game. I am choking. My bones are rubbing against the dirt'

Someone head was right over my face. My young, strong teeth found her ear and it put a 'dead lock' on it. It never let go.

It was her scream that took the weight off my back.

When they saw the blood running from my mouth and saw me spit out their friend's ear, they began to run in different directions.

I told my mother that I bit off Savitri's ear. My mother held her head and cried.

"You must never trust them. They are revengeful and would try to hurt you worst"

My mother waited for me after school. When she could not come, Datson and David escorted me safely to Auntie Chunu's.

Ms. Moore was always at one side, no matter who was on the other side of me.

"Gungaboy, gungaboy, gungaboy sister. God cursed you wid two gunga-mute brothers. 'Gungaboy sister' I answered to that name for years, I still do.

Despite everything that the children were doing and saying to me, if any one of them tried to befriend me, I would forget everything and follow her like a puppy dog.

I had only one friend in Whim. Her name was Bashone. She lived next door to us.

Whenever she was alone, she would invite me to play in her yard.

We played dolly-house in the hot sun. If I get trusty and ask her for some water, she would bring a cup of water and say to me "Hold you hand to you mouth, I will throw the water in you hand. Me mother say you can't drink from our cup, you're unclean"

She never let me go into her home and she never went into my little mud hut.

We would walk to the main road together on our way to school.

We walked together to the end of Whim. As soon as we entered Akline, my friend would run ahead of me so that the other children do not see her with me.

She did the same in the afternoon. She would join Ms. Moore and I from Whim on.

I was thankful for her partial friendship. It was better than none atall.

Like I told you, school children went home for breakfast at noontime.

Even though I ate mine at Sister Marie, I meet Bashone for us to walk to school.

One such day as I stood on her landing, I braced on the banister, it broke and I went tumbling two story down.

When she came out and saw me lying on the ground, she said

"Did I tell you not to come up our steps? You see what would happen to you when you do what you are not supposed to do? Come on, let's go"

"Me can't move. It hut tomuch"

"If you want fe skulk from school, you stan right wa you da. Me a go to school"

My left collarbone was broken. I was out of school for many weeks, wearing a hard plaster casing around my shoulder.

Auntie Chunu told my mother that it was time for the boys to stop wearing those long shirts and start wearing short pants. She said

"Dem boys 'dingaling' ah too big under dem long shirt. Dem need short pants"

My mother got some flour bags, wash them clean and took them and the boys to Elick the tailor to have pants made for them.

Short pants became my brother's only piece of garment. Most boys and men wore pants alone. It was too hot for more than that as casual dress.

My brother's long shirts became my 'night gowns'. The ones that were too ragged and had no buttons were used for 'floor cloth' and stripped for bandages.

Everything in my household was used until it was not useful anymore.

My mother cried in relief when the doctor took the plaster off my shoulder and told her that I healed well. She had feared that I might be deformed just like she was.

As I grew older, I had more responsibilities.

I had to full the lantern with kerosene oil, clean the class shade and light it before the sun goes down everyday. I had to make sure that the bucket in the latrine was full with clean trench water, and the old enamel cup hanging on the nail over the bucket. We knew nothing about paper in those days. We wash ourselves, using our left hand.

We had no need for a bathroom. We bathe with clean, warm water in the trench.

Our basic mealtimes were morning, noon and night for tea, breakfast and dinner.

Morning was roti, a large pot of dhal made for the day and green tea with milk

Noon was rice, dhal, curry fish or vegetable.

Night was rice, dhal, curry fish or vegetable, all except the dhal cook fresh each meal.

On holidays or special occasions we may have some meat like chicken or duck curry.

Mommy was true to her vegetarian diet. She never failed or got tempted, even though she prepared other dishes for us. She did not force her strict vegetarian diet on us.

She fasted many times per year but still fed us three meals every day.

I still remember how happy we were when my mother fed us with her fingers from her enamel plate. Her food was always tastier and even better from her hand to our mouths.

Her vegetable dish was very simple. She fried onion, garlic, tomatoes and lots of very hot pepper, vegetable and a pinch of salt to taste. Sometimes she used chana-chick peas or black eye peas. Our home always had a fresh pot of dhal every day.

The picture of my mother sitting on the floor feeding her three children from her plate has been stamped into my heart. I felt loved every time her fingers touched my mouth.

Some of the Indians in Whim invited my mother to religious services and weddings. They curry-favor her for her knowledge on Hinduism.

They knew that she was Kasy Marage, the famous pandit's daughter. They needed her guidance in many rituals, especially at weddings.

They needed her to help them make it appear as if they knew what they were doing.

My mother willingly obliged. She took every opportunity to practice her religion.

She always took me with her. I watch with pride as my poured out her knowledge.

Sometimes, however, the messenger-a man from the village, who is usually used as a messenger to go from house to house to invite villagers to a wedding.

He would carry a large sack around his shoulder and a smaller sack with some yellow rice in his hand. He usually ran this errand on Sundays when most of the people are at home. He would say something like this.

"Rampaul invite you to dem daughter wedding three Sunday from today"

He would then give the invitee a handful of yellow rice-the invitation-nawnta.

The invitee will then give him a cup of rice in his large sack on his back or a bit-eight cent. That was their form of RSVP. Accepting the invitation.

There were times however, when the messenger would come to invite my mother to a wedding. He would say the same words, but add.

"Dem ask that you don't bring dem Kaffar picknee wid you"

My Mommy would take the yellow rice in her hand, call the chickens and ducks and throw the invitation-yellow rice for them to eat.

That was her RSVP. A refusal and an insult. The messenger gets his gift of a cup of rice, but has to take her answer back to the inviter.

Whenever Chundon Theater had Indian movies, women would gather close to my mother to hear her intrepid the Hindi language, even if they spit on her the next day.

My two brothers delivered newspaper for Mr. Reed, the district postmaster and

Newspaper agent. He would tell me who were his customers, I would then tell my brothers where to take the papers. If he had a new customer he would tell me and I would tell Datson and David where else to deliver papers.

I will tell you more about Mr. Reed. Remember his wife the midwife when I came?

My brothers would leave home while it was still dark. Deliver their newspapers and be back home in time for my mother hot roti, curry and tea.

Some people suggested my mother commit my brothers to the 'madhouse'.

Every time I heard things like such, I held on to my brothers tighter and tighter.

I became their keeper at a very young age. From the time I could walk.

I often wonder how could I ease the pain that I saw in my mother's eyes?

I remember asking my mother "Mommy, how come we do not have a father?

Everybody has father. How come me, Datson and David na have one?"

"Not everyone get a father. Buddy doesn't get a father.

You, Betose and Davo no get a father. Me no get a father.

We ah one house full ah fatherless people, but we are happy, yes?

The four of you have a mother. Me no have mother or father"

Inez came after church a few times during those early days. I asked my mother who she was? My mother told me that the nice lady was a school inspector.

I believed her because most of the school officials were Negroes.

I realized later, that in order for my mother to avoid Inez visit, she would complete her chores and have me do the same very early on Sundays. Then she would take me with her to collect money from the villagers whom she had credited fish and produce.

It broke my heart to hear how some of those people insulted my Mommy.

"Why you come to me doormouth dis early Sunday morning fe money?"

"Can't you see that I am on my way to church?"

"Don't come to me fe no money, the dam fish was stink. me trow dem away."

Some of them never paid her but she continued to 'trust' credit them because she said that they had children to feed.

My mother was never resentful to the people who treated her badly. Not Indians, not Blacks. When they cursed and insulted her, she let it slide like water on duck back. She said, "When curse and insult comes out of ones mouth, there is nothing I can do to make them take that back. No 'beg pardon' can change bad words spoken. Harsh words can choke or cut your tongue. Always think before you say something you'll regret"

One Sunday, my mother and I were on our way to collect money in the villages.

Datson and David came out with us to the main road to fetch water.

They began to play by throwing water on each other.

A police constable was passing on his cycle from church. Some water got on his shirt.

He got off his bicycle, took off his belt and began to beat my two brothers.

They clasp their hands in prayer fashion, begging pardon; the belt came down on them.

We heard their cries and ran back to see what was happening?

I saw the police holding David, beating him with the broad, heavy leather belt.

My brother was screaming, my mother was screaming, I was screaming, Datson was sitting on the ground, already beaten with the belt, and bystanders were laughing.

With her hands clasp, on her knees, my mother begged the policeman to stop.

Their backs and faces were wale and bloody from the lashes of the heavy leather belt.

"Please PC, no beat dem no mo, me beg you, no beat me picknee no mo"

She tried to shield her son by going between the policeman and David.

"You need to get these animals into an institution where they would be locked away and not be a newsence to people" said the breathless policeman.

"Tank you Sa, I will take them home rightaway" said my weeping mother.

"You have to buy me a new shirt. Look at the condition of my good shirt"

"Please Sa, give me the shirt, I will wash with clean rain water and give it back to you as if it is brand-new" my mother was ready to go back to Lancaster

a place she had not gone in seven years, to get rainwater to wash this policeman shirt.

"Are you as deaf as they are? I said that you have to buy me a new shirt"

"But Sa, me no have no money to buy a new shirt" her pleas were not heard.

"I will hold them and wait right here until you find money, go to Sahardat store and buy me a new shirt. They know my size and quality"

"But Sa"

"If you do not come back in a hurry, I will take these two animals of yours to the jail house and lock them in the pound where they belong, with the other animals"

I sat with my brothers to make sure that he did not beat them anymore, while my mother hurried to Sahardat store. It was Sunday and the store was closed.

She ran to the back and bang on the owner's door.

"Please, me beg you, please 'trust' me a white shirt for the PC. You know his size"

My mother ran back to a larger crowd gathered around the PC and my brothers.

A scene that my young eyes were growing accustomed to.

My mother handed the policeman the shirt wrapped in plastic. She said

"PC can I come to get wet shirt? My son Dhia will wear it to play cricket"

"Don't you come anywhere near my home. The next time I see these animals running around wild, I will surely put them in the pound where they belong"

He tucked the new shirt under his arm and rode off to Lancaster where he lived.

In that period of my young life, that policeman was the meanest person that I have seen. Later I identified with Sudith and her feelings towards Mr. B.

I later learned that because of Babe's refusal to accept maintenance from Archie, he took her to court and had the magistrate ordered her to accept money from her husband.

Archie placed the money at the Post Office every month and the office placed it into a savings account in Babe's name. She refused to even touch his money.

Auntie Katy was a regular visitor to our home.

After she heard of the incident at school, she told my mother that she would go to the school to find out who were the children who are doing mean things to me.

"No, don't do that. If we do not pay attention to them, they will soon forget"

She kept my mother up to date with what was going on at Lancaster.

Even though my mother would pretend that she was not concerned with what goes on at the 'big house' she never stopped her friend from talking, and, she never stop listening.

I had no idea what they were talking about. Most times they sent me out to play.

"Who does the gardening?"

"The Leach brothers"

"Does Mother still come on Saturdays with Esther?"

"Yes, Mother comes alone. Esther is a big girl now, she don't come anymore.

The boys help Mother with the garden"

"Anybody living in the 'big house'"

"Yes, Archie eldest brother Willy and his wife and two children" Katy looked at her friend and continued. "Me hear how you refuse to let the children know their family. You refuse to take the man money to mine his children.

What is the matter with you? There are women who are taking men to court for support for their children. I never hear of a man taking a woman to court to force her to take his money. You are one crazyass proud jackass"

"And you are my best friend"

Things were quiet at school. I was weaned off my bottle, but I still seek the comfort of my mother's breast in the privacy of our home.

Mrs. Moore asked Mr. Clas to have an eye out for me. She feared that something more serious would happen to me after the incident with Savitri.

I kept to myself. Even if the other girls ask me to play, I refused.

I sat under the sweetie tree and play by myself at recess and walk with Mrs. Moore.

I did not care very much for Bashone anymore either.

She told me how sorry she was for leaving me on the ground.

"How am I to know that you broke your shoulder? I thought you wanted to skulk"

It was not only her leaving me on the ground with a broken shoulder. It was her behavior towards me when we were in public. I knew that it was not nice.

I learned that it is ok to forgive, the only way one can truly forgive, one has to **move** on. If you remain in the same situation, you never forget so you never forgive.

Mommy and Buddy were working hard. They were saving hard too.

They knew that in three years they would have to move off the leased land.

They both put their earnings into the little teapot.

Every month they would count their savings and tie them in bundles of hundred dollars.

They would discuss where they could buy a piece of land, and how much?

They would discuss the size of the house and the cost for it.

Even though I did not understand everything that they were saying, I knew that one day we would move out of this little mud hut into a wooden house with glass windows.

My mother was always telling me stories. I guess I was the only one she could speak to on our Sunday's family time. She said.

"Babzy we don't want more than we need. The smaller our house, the more we touch each other. We know when one has a fever because we touch him/her.

Once upon a time the government was sharing land to the villagers.

The rules were every man stand in a circle backing each other. Then the white flag comes down, each man would run, walk or creep as far as he could. Wherever he sticks his little flag, that's how much land he will get.

There was however one man who would not stop running. He ran and ran until he dropped dead. The government granted his family the spot where he dropped to cremate him. They told them "A dead man don't need land"

ANTS DO NOT LIKE LOLOBYES

One afternoon after school, I took my usual seat under the sweetie tree, waiting for Mrs. Moore. Two girls, who were playing skip rope close to me, asked if I would like to play? They said that they needed a third child to hold the rope.

'How quickly children forget? Especially when a child yearn to be a child'

I put my book bag down and join the two girls in the game.

We played a while, then one said "Me have to go ah latrine. Ayou come follow me"

I looked and did not see Mrs. Moore, so I followed them to the back of the school where there were two long narrow latrines, one for the boys and one for the girls.

The latrines can accommodate about six children each at one time.

The girl who said she needed to go, banged on the latrine door and about five or six girls came rushing out, laughing and some holding rope in their hands.

They rushed on me, grabbed me and pulled me to the back of the latrine.

They used the skipping ropes to tie my hands and feet behind my back.

I heard someone said "the ness is over there, drag her over there"

They dragged and lay me face down on a mound of giant red ants.

At first, I thought it was a big joke; the children would come back and untie me.

I listened anxiously for their laughter, but I heard none. It was quiet, dead quiet.

I lay still, believing that if I did not move, the ants may not know I was on their ness.

A child my age did not know any better.

I began to scream, I screamed as loud as I could.

I knew I was in trouble when I could hear myself no more.

I felt the ant's adobe crumbled under my moving body.

'I still remember that sound whenever I crumble dry leaves or hear corn popping'.

I felt the ants covering my face, biting on my eyelids, my ears, my nose, and my lips.

They went into my clothes, trapped and became more vicious.

Angry perhaps, because they did not get as much freedom to dance as they bite.

I began to smell fresh blood and raw flesh, but not for long.

The ants were crawling up into my brains, thus blocking my thinking machine.

I could not keep my mouth close anymore. As soon as I opened it to put some oxygen into my lungs, they took residence and found softer, moister meat to eat.

I could not smell or breath anymore, but I could still hear their satisfying sound and feel their giant legs and stings.

The giant red ants were devouring my entire body.

The ones caught in my mouth, were chewed and swallowed.

I could not keep my mouth close too long because my nose was blocked.

I was suffocating.

I lost all control of my bladder, my bowel, and my will to move.

They have eaten all my senses. I needed to sleep.

Maybe when I wakeup, the shackle will be loose and this will be a bad dream.

So I did what I always did. What Mrs. Moore thought me to do before I go to sleep with my face between my Mommy's breasts. I prayed.

"Gentle Jesus, meek and mild, look upon this little child"

The ants had their own lullaby. It put me into a deep, deep sleep.

Mrs. Moore saw my mother on the road and told her that I was not sitting under the tree when she came out of a meeting with the other teachers.

"But where could she be? She is not at Chunu; she is not at the house.

Babzy never go anywhere else. She don't have any friends to go at"

My mother hurried to the school, walked all over the schoolyard, looking for her little girl. She found my schoolbag under the sweetie tree.

She ran and got Datson, David, and everyone who would join her to search for me.

She was running and looking into all the trenches and mud holes.

It was becoming dark and everyone was becoming worried.

Auntie Chunu and Auntie Katy went to some of the children's home to get information of my disappearance. No one knew anything.

The minister of Akline Scotch church, Reverent Alley, who lived in the Manse across from the school, was getting ready for dinner.

As he washed his hand, he looked through the window, like he did every evening, to make sure that all was well in the schoolyard.

All seemed OK, about to move, his attention be drawn to the back of the latrine.

He squinted his eyes to focus on what he was looking at. Could he be seeing right?

It that someone in green and white uniform lying so still? He called his son.

"Look through this window, at the back of the latrine and tell me what you see"

Dr. Koo was furious. He looked at my mother with anger in his eyes, he said

"This child has no race, no belonging, no place in this backward country"

He continued through my mother's wailing, as if he was speaking to himself'

"I have never seen anything like this done to a child by children.

What kind of animals those parents are breading in this country?

I will have to make a report to the authority. This is a crime to be investigated"

"I do not know where to start. For the second time in my practice, I do not know what to do or where to start. You and now your daughter"

Am I my mother's daughter?

"She has a pulse, her heart still beats and she still has some blood. She is alive.

I will give her an injection. It's an antidote for deadly snakebite. That's how much venom in this child. No part of her body was speared from those venomous ants bite.

There is not much I could for her here. I do not have the staff to care for her.

I will give you some M&B pills. Grind them into powder and after you wash her well in the sea, get some young banana leaves, grease them well with coconut oil.

Lay her on the leaves, put the powder all over her and cover her with more greased leaves. Whatever you do, do not put any clothe on her or near her body, it will stick to the wounds and she will never heal.

Build a tent around her and cover it with a mosquito net to prevent the flies from eating her raw flesh" Dr. Koo looked around, then, whispered to my mother.

"Clean her badly eaten tongue with glycerin. Feed her rice mar, one spoon at a time. Nothing hot or rough must go down her throat. You will see blood in her stool.

Her eyelids are almost gone; keep a dark cloth over her eyes to protect them.

Look out for ants that will still be crawling out of her nose and ears.

Pray that she have the strength to come out of this alive and sane"

Reverent Alley announced in church what he found behind the latrine.

The congregation was rattledup; everyone had his/her own form of revenge.

"Now, now, listen to me before you start beating your warrior drums.

We will do nothing to disrupt the peace and harmony of this district.

Nothing like this has ever happened before. I too am angry and disgusted.

There will be an investigation. The culprits will be brought the authorities"

Through the mosquito net I saw Mrs. Moore, Mrs. King, Mr. Clas and some other teachers, among them was a young teacher name George Tendell, standing over me.

Our little grass hut had never had so many people in it, especially Black people.

Whim had never seen so many Black people at one time, walking on their dam.

I saw Inez before. Remember when my mother told me that she was an official?

But I never laid eyes on the White lady who accompanied Inez.

She was tall and beautiful, just like how my schoolbook described beautiful women. 'White with blond hair and blue eyes'.

Through the netting and without eyelids, I saw her eyes. I never saw a woman with blue eyes before, only in my schoolbooks. I wondered if everything she sees is blue?

Sometime ago, I saw the man who did not pay me for fetching dirt. He had blue eyes.

The Alexander family took my mother to court to get custody of her three children.

Someone said that she was an unfit mother who endangered her children before they were born. Knowing from where she came and who she was, she should have never gotten involved with their kind.

I was told that my mother stood in court, held on to my two brothers.

She said nothing. She did nothing. She just stood there holding tightly to her two boys.

I was told that the Magistrate read and heard all of their claims of her being unfit.

"She has the children running around half-naked. Some of the people in Whim have them like slaves. Doing all their dirty and heavy work.

The Indian children at school are always beating the little girl. Now she is fighting for her life due to the carelessness of her mother. These children needs to be protected by their own kind"

He asked her "What do you want to say for yourself?" she answered, "Noting"

The magistrate told the family that they have not proven that my mother was unfit.

"Like an animal in the wild, she is protecting her children from the animal of this community. She has done nothing wrong to her children. Working hard to mine her children is not wrong. It's the society she lives in, has wronged her and her children.

Who are you to say that she endangered her children before they were born?

Someone of you please explain that to me"

I was told that it was not Archie or his immediate family who brought the case against my mother. It was a distant Alexander family from the village who did it unknowing to Archie's family. But according to my mother, they were all the same.

Both parties had the same lawyer. The Alexander hired him. The court appointed him to represent my mother. His name was Sas Nari.

When the M&B pills ran out I could have moved out from under my tent and bed of leaves, my mother carried me to the edge of the trench and covered my whole body in clay-mud and leave me in the sun until the clay became dried and cracked.

Nurse Reed gave my mother a pair of sunshades for me to protect my eyes.

My mother became even more protective of us, and afraid of the Black people.

She began to tell me that I should never trust any Black person. That they were all bad people and that they want to take me away from her and my brothers.

"But Mommy, my teachers at school are good to me"

"Yes, they are the only good ones, all the other are bad"

Buddy told my mother to stop telling me things like that, he said

"Ma, you cannot tell her things like that. You are doing the same thing that the parents of those girls who did this to her, said to them, poison their young minds against other people. I have many Black friends. Stop telling her those wrong lies.

Some school officials walked me from classroom to classroom asking me to point out the girls who tied me up and left me to die on the ant nest.

I looked at almost every girl at the school and could not pick one of the eight girls who harmed me in such a bad way.

They mane me. They left me with scars that will go with me to my grave.

Not ever the clay by the trench or the juice of the 'money bush' could never take the marks off my young body.

I could not pick out one of the culprits. The ants had eaten that part of my brains.

They all looked as if they had the same mother and father. As if they were all sisters.

Life was going on around me.

My mother and Buddy were working harder after buying a 'house lot' at Liverpool.

Mostly Black people lived there but Indians from Whim were rapidly moving there and the Blacks welcome them.

Our little grass hut was beginning to deterate. The grass roof began to leak and the mud on the walls was falling off leaving peepholes all around. Whenever it rained, we had to move our little belongings to a dry spot and huddle together to stay dry.

When I told Buddy that he needed to fix the damage, he said

"No worry Win, I am too busy to fix this old house.

Do you know that this house is as old as you? Yes, it is almost eight years old.

Soon I am going to build us a nice big house made of wood, with zinc roof and glass windows and long steps and landings.

I could not read, write or learn anything. The ants had eaten all my learning senses.

Mr. Tendell took me to his home at Lancaster to do extra schoolwork.

One Saturday while I was at the Tendell's home, a tall gentleman came to the house. Mrs. Tendell embraced him and called him Brother Willy. She told me.

"Wynette, this is your uncle Willy, your father's oldest brother"

"I do not have any uncle, I do not have any father. I do not have Black family"

"Yes, you do. This is your uncle and my cousin Brother Willy

"I came here to see you. I am your Uncle Willy. I would like to take you to my home to meet my wife. We have lots of fruit trees and you can pick as much as you want. - To this day, you can have me follow you to the end of the earth for fresh fruits - You can even bring your brothers. I will show you where I live"

'If I can take my brothers, then maybe, he is not a bad Black man' I thought.

My visit to Brother Willy and Sis Clara was my first secret from my mother.

One Sunday, going with my mother to collect money, I saw lots of people crossing the long narrow bridge that led to Brother Willy's house.

My mother asked what was happening? And someone said that Brother Willy had died. It was 1950. He was fifty-five years old, I was eight years old.

I began to cry so hard, my mother looked at me and asked me why was I crying for someone who is Black, whom I did not even know?

I confessed to her that I was a visitor at the "big house' and I even brought the boys.

My mother almost fainted, when she came through, she said
"He was one of the good Black people"

Mrs. Moore suggested that my mother take me out of Akline School and enroll me in Manchester Government School. She said
"Babe, this child cannot learn, so the teachers cannot promote her to higher classes. I think that all that she has gone through over the years have traumatized in such a way that she cannot comprehend or concentrate on anything" Mrs. Moore tried very hard to convince my mother that moving me would be the best thing.
"Manchester is different. My husband teaches there. He will have an eye on her.
They do not have this kind of problem there. There are only Black children there.
Wynette will fit in well, you will see, she will begin to learn and make us proud of her"
"My Babzy is not Black. She is a Hindu. She is my child I am a Hindu.
"You are wrong Babe, Wynette is mixed. Her birth paper said she is of 'Mixed race'.
"Aright Ms., we go move to Liverpool, she will be closer to Manchester School"
"Mrs. Moore, why the Indian children who are blacker than me, beat and call Blackman-Kafa?" this confused child asked her teacher for the last time.
"Its not the color of your skin. It's the curls on your head. Curly hair belongs to Black people, even if you are lighter or whiter than them; your curly hair makes you a Black person. In their teaching, Black people are unclean. They dehumanize them"

During that summer, I asked my mother if I could go play with some girls my age who lived out by the main road.
My mother was so protective of me that she would not allow me to go to anyone's home, but the people I mentioned before. She told me the story of Lilawati, she said
"There was this pretty little girl name Lilawati. Her mother left her

with neighbors and went to the market. When she got back, the little girl was nowhere to be found.

People began looking all over. Someone found her tied in a rice bag in the latrine pit.

When the police questioned the couple, the husband told the police his wife had a dream the night before that for her to have a child of her own, she will have to sacrifice another child. He said his wife asked him to help her tie the little girl and throw her head first into the latrine pit" the story scared me, which is what my mother wanted.

It was a true story; the husband and wife were hanged for the crime.

My mother told me that if someone tried to lore me into any place where I should not go, that I should run away and go tell one of my aunties.

She became more and more protective as I got older.

When I asked her to go play with those girls, she gave me the speech and story.

"Yes, you could go play with them, but you play outside in the yard.

You don't go into their house. When you get hungry, go to Sister Mari.

Do not eat from anyone else. Do you hear me?"

"Yes Mommy"

I was happy to spend some of my August holiday with those three sisters.

I did not have to follow the boys all over the village anymore.

Datson was working at the rice mill and David worked with Buddy at the rice field.

One day as I played with the girls, I looked towards their house and saw their father at the window, making a hand signal for me to go to him.

When I told the girls their father is calling us, they looked, but he was not there.

We continued to play hopscotch. Every time I looked towards the window, he was standing there, shirtless, pointing to me, using his index finger to call me to him.

I became afraid and told my mother what the girls' father was doing. I said,

"Mommy, I think he had a bad dream and wanted to throw me into the latrine pit"

One Sunday my mother and I returning home to find lots of Buddy's friends and our neighbors in our yard.

My mother dropped everything and began to run towards the house, I followed.

We entered the house and found my Buddy lying on the table, covered with a white sheet. He was not moving. He did not answer when I called "Buddy, Buddy is me, Win. Open you eye and look at me Buddy. Is me Win"

Buddy and David were working in the rice field when a deadly snake bit my Buddy.

David ran and got other rice field workers and then went and got Buddy's friends from Lancaster, who brought charcoal and other antidote for snakebites.

My brother had to lie still for days while the charcoal and cyman teeth pull all the poison out from between his toes.

That was when I saw that my Buddy's best friends were Blacks from Lancaster.

He had no Indian friends from Whim.

Datson was working at the rice mill where there was a robbery. Many hundred-pound bags of rice were stolen. The suspect was charged and taken to court.

Datson, who told the owner of the mill that he saw the person who took the rice, was summon to court to point out to the magistrate who he saw stole the rice.

They took me to be my brother's interpreter since I was the only one who knew how.

The magistrate said to me "Don't be afraid child, you nor your brother did nothing wrong. I ordered for you to come here because I was told that you are the only person who can speak for your brother" He looked at some papers at his desk, then said to me

"Ask Mr. Alexander if the person who stole the rice is in this courtroom?"

'My brother is Mr. Alexander? I knew that teachers and police and important people were called Sir/Madam, Mr. and Miss/ Mrs., but not my brother who is the dummy?'

"My brother said yes, Sir"

"Ask Mr. Alexander to point out that person he was stole the rice from the mill?"

My brother pointed to the owner's son, not the man who stood accused.

After he beat his gabble and shouted "Quiet, quiet in the court room".

He looked at the owner of the rice mill, who was holding his chest with both hands.

He said, "Don't blame Mr. Alexander for pointing out your shame. He is the only believable person in this courthouse. He cannot gossip, he can only tell us what he saw.

He did not hear when you and your son told him to point out the wrong man"

Around this stage of my life, age eight, my mother was softening up about 'all Black people are bad'. I think it began to change after I told her that Brother Willy and Sis Clara were nice Black people, that I liked them very much.

She did however, very sternly warned me about one Black man who I should never trust. She told me, "He is a very tall Black man. He rides in a donkey cart. He hardly wears shirt and pants, only a piece of clothe wrapped around his waist. He always coils of rope around his shoulder. He parts his hair on the right side and has a small mouthstatch the width of his nose.

If you should ever see this man and he try to call you or try to hold you, run for your life. He is the Black man who will put you in the bags that has in his cart, tie the bag with the rope and take you to the 'backdam' and eat you. We will never see you again.

He is the Black man who does eat children" my mother repeated the above several times, making sure that I remember every detail of this 'child eating Black man'.

I don't want anyone to take my Babzy away from me. I don't know what will happen to me if dat Black man take my baby away"

I thought of all the things my mother told me. I wondered why she told me not to tell Buddy about this particular Black man. If he is so bad, why shouldn't my brother know about him? I asked my mother "Mommy, does people eat children?"

"No, not everyone eat people children, but this man, I know for sure that this Blackman eats little girls. He like them with long curly hair, like yours. There are not many like you, so he will be coming for you"

Summer of 1950 I was told that come September, I will be going to Manchester Scotch School, arranged my Mrs. Moore.

Despite her hard work and help from other teachers, I was not learning anything.

During the past year and a half, I was more absent than present at Akline School.

My wounds were not healing despite my mother trying everything and using every suggested remedy. I had difficulty being in the sun even with the dark glasses. I could not hear like before. It felt like things were fighting in my inner ears. It made me dizzy. I vomited every time they fought.

Children did not want to sit near to me, so I sat at the back of the class on a long bench.

That summer, one day I was playing at the back of Auntie Chunu's back yard. There was a girl who lived at the back street. She sometimes played with me when there was no one else for her to play with. She joined me by the pigpen where I was poking at a pig lying in the mud. Suddenly a gush of rain escaped the sky and came down on us.

The girl ran into her dirt floor home and I followed. I stood by the door.

She pulled the cloth curtain open. On the bed, my healing eyes saw two naked women, one on top of the other. I am sure I was not seeing double because they both jumped off the bed and chased after us.

That summer, there was a big county cricket tournament at the Whim Ballfield.

Cricketers were coming from all over the Country –Guyana is divided into three Counties, Essequibo, Demerara and Berbice. I am a Berbician and proud of it.

Many Guyanese cricketers played for and lived in England from those early days.

Buddy had several sets of outfit for the seven days event. My mother made sure that all were stiff and well seamed, with lots of white socks and handkerchiefs for each day.

My brother looked like a gladiator walking towards the arena, with his bat in hand, dressed in lily white from head to toes.

I had to run to keep up with his longer steps. Keeping close to his side, holding his hand and being so proud of my Buddy, followed him all the way to the main road. Sometimes I was allowed to carry his bat.

People along the dam shouted, "Good luck Dhia. Bring the cup home".

I just wanted all to see that he is my Buddy. I love him and I am so very proud of him.

When we reached the main road, my brother held my two hands and bend forward to look into my eyes. He said, "Win, do me a big favor, and keep Betose and Davo away from the Ballfield this whole week. I will give you something nice"

"What Buddy? Why Buddy? How Buddy? But Buddy why?" I was so confused by my brother's request that I forgot that children do not ask adults questions.

"Do whatever you can, however you can, just keep them away from the game"

He looked at me, still my gladiator, squeezed my two hands and said,

"Don't tell Ma what ah ask you to do"

I never told my mother, but that was the first time I knew how different my brothers and I were from our Buddy, prince, hero, father and the only man we ever love.

He was ashamed of them. He did not want the visiting teams to know that he had two half-breed dummy brothers.

You see, whenever Buddy hit a 'six' or' bold a wicket' or caught a ball- because he was an allrounder, he played in every position of the game. He was also the captain- the boys would shout with their wordless voices. They would dance and point to my brother and to their chest and twist two fingers to make one. Their way of saying, "He and I are one". They would draw attention because of their weird shouts.

Most of the surrounding villagers knew that they were Dhia's brothers. The visiting teams did not know and my brother wanted to keep his shame away from them.

The first day of the game, I told my brothers that Mr. Reed wanted to see them.

When we get to Mr. Reed's house, I quickly explained to him that I have to keep them away from the cricket field and that if he could think of anything to keep them busy.

The next day I told my two brothers that we are going to build a large wooden house with upstairs and downstairs, glass windows and furniture. I told them that we would have to help by working with Mommy while Buddy is busy at the cricket field,

They asked me what could they do to help? My young eaten brain was on high gar.

We went to cut and fetch firewood one day. Went to the rice field one day. Went to catch crab and sold in the village one day. Went to pick coconut to make oil one day.

The six day, Saturday, I could not think of anything else to do. My mother wondered why they were so helpful especially at a time when everyone was heading to the game? I took them back to Mr. Reed. He always found things for them to do and Nurse Reed always fed us with 'different' English foods.

Come Sunday, the final day of the tournament. There was nothing I could have done to keep them away from the game. They knew it was the best day of the week. They contributed to their new home for six days, today they are going to the game to watch their brother, their hero, win the cup. Datson and David were mute and deft but they knew everyone and everything going on in the village. They knew that this day was an important one for their brother.

Buddy team won the tournament. Datson and David join the crowd that ran out to the ball field to congratulate the winners. My brothers were in the midst of the men who lifted Buddy high in the air. My brothers used their voice box to get everyone's attention, they began to hug and kiss their brother, captain of the team. Telling everyone who could understand their signs that the captain was their brother.

My Buddy came home walking like my gladiator. Bat in one hand and the trophy in the other. Datson and David dancing around him.

I greeted my Buddy on the bridge, he was red with fury, he looked at me with such anger and called my brothers and I names that I never heard before, never heard again.

I never told my mother any of this but from time to time I would ask her what the names that Buddy called us meant? She would look at me crossly and asked

"Where did you hear such words? I do not want to hear such words out your mouth"

Do you hear me? Those are not words to say to anyone".

I never told her "But those are the words our Buddy Dhia called us"

That summer, everyone was talking about the picture that was showing at Chundon's theater. Even my brothers, who think that they are part owners of the cinema, would come home and reenact everything they saw in the first English-talking picture. A cowboy picture.

One afternoon, I decided that I too wanted to see this picture show. I ran home to get a penny-two cents- from the teapot in our bedroom.

I ran strait into our bedroom and found my brother on top of the seamstress's daughter. They were both naked on the bed that my mother and I slept on.

I had trouble understanding what was happening around me.

The seamstress's daughter was married. My whole family attended her wedding.

I sat on the bridge, shaking my feet in the water when my Buddy appeared.

"If you tell anyone about this, I will do to you what Betose and Davo only threatened to do to you. I will cut off your tongue and make you like your dumbass brothers"

Shame and fear caused my love and respect for my hero to thin off rapidly.

I kept away from him. I obeyed his orders because he was my elder.

When my mother was around I tried to be normal, I did not want her to ask me any questions where I would have to lie to her. I did not want to see my mother in any more pain. Her life, all my life, was full of pain and shame.

I did everything I could to shield her from pain and heartache whenever I could.

Lots of wedding happened on Sundays in August. Sometimes when my mother was invited. She and I would have our eyes on my brothers so that drunken men do not abuse them. But like I said before, my brothers knew everything that goes on in the village and no one could stop them from going there.

Many times I had to track them down to wedding houses where we were not invited.

I would find grown men giving my brothers rum and cigarettes. They would get them so drunk that they could get them to do anything to each other.

They form a human ring and have my two brothers fight each other. If one of them should try to leave the human circle, they will push him so hard back into the ring.

My brothers would be bleeding, but no one would stop them.

Before, when I saw things like that, I would run to the cricket field to get Buddy.

Now, I go into the ring and try to stop my brothers from killing each other for the fun of others. Many times I get the blows, but sometimes with the help of some kind-hearted bystander, I get them home and into the trench to wash off and get sober.

It must have been quiet a scene, an eight years old sister pulling two drunken ten and twelve year old brothers. My whole life was a 'scene'.

August of 1950 was a learning month in my life. I never saw the picture show.

Oh God, what freaks we were in Whim?

Come September, it was arranged that Mr. George Tendell would take me on his bicycle Manchester Scotch School. They agreed that it would cause problem if my mother, an Indian woman, took me to an all Black school. They did not want what happened to me at Akline to follow to Manchester.

They, all the Black teachers of Akline School were very sure of themselves.

They assured my mother that Black children are not as bad as Indian children.

Did I tell you that they were very sure of themselves? Did I tell you that none of them were 'half breed' like me?

Dressed in my brand-new blue and white uniform with blue ribbons holding my long, curly mane, I felt different. Just by not wearing that green and white uniform anymore, made me feel different. Made me feel safer.

"Mommy, I will have to tell Nennen that my uniform color is changed"

Mr. and Mrs. Nato were my Godparents. Mr. Nato, my Godfather, was the headmaster of Akline Scotch School, the one that I am now leaving with blood in my mouth and sores all over my young body.

Mrs. Nato was my Nennen – Godmother. She ran the grocery store in Whim.

Every Christmas season, as her 'Godchild' I get a brown paper package containing my school uniform material, one Christmas apple, five grapes and five walnuts.

Apple, grapes and walnut were scarce items, imported at Christmas time. Even the poor people would try to give their children a little smell and taste of England.

Mr. Tendell walked me to my new school and into my classroom.

I was the oldest and tallest in first standard.

"What is the matter with her? Why is she so soary? Why is she wearing those big dark shades? Why ah big girl like this have to be in 1st standard? She should be in 3rd standard at her age".

As if all the teachers had the same mindset. This teacher too, ordered me to sit at the back of the class. Once again, I had a whole long bench and desk all to myself.

I could not read, I could not write. Arithmetic I comprehended a little.

My long hair became the children's weapon against me. To the Black children at Manchester Scotch School, I was different because I had long hair. To the Indian children at Akline Scotch School, I was different because I had curly hair.

To this day, I believe that it was my hair that was my stamp of disapproval.

It couldn't be anything else. All the children from both schools had the same dark shade or color as me. In some cases I was lighter. Yes, it was my hair. It was neither, nor.

Although the children scorn sitting close to me or touching me, it did not stop them from pulling my hair as they ran pass me in the schoolyard.

They would tie my breads at the back of the desk and the teacher would say

"Alexander, standup" The whole class along with the young teacher would have a hearty laugh from my break-neck position.

My mother took my two brothers and I to Liverpool to show us where we are going to build our 'big house'.

It was a wooded area with only two houses far away from our lot. The lot was wide and very long. "Mommy, we could build ten houses on all dis land" I said

"Yes, we could, but we are building only one house at the front, the back will be my garden for vegetable and fruit trees"

Datson and David were so excited; they were working their hardest clearing to areas where the house will be built. We couldn't get them to stop to eat or drink.

"It makes no sense to fix our hut when we are going to break it down soon" my mother said. Any question that I used to ask Buddy or things that I told him, I now ask and tell my mother. I could not bring myself to look at him anymore.

It's not only the guilty that cannot look into the eyes of people they hurt. I was not guilty of anything, but I could no longer look into those eyes that I once worshipped,

One afternoon after returning from Liverpool, tired and hungry, my mother wanted to cook a nice dinner for her hard working children. We knew nothing about fridge or freezer, and with the climate of eighty-ninety degree, everything had to be fresh.

"Babzy, how about some nice fish curry with dhal and rice for dinner?"

Four of us went towards the sea, the boys carrying the hand-sane and me carrying the quake around my shoulder

We passed the Kali Mia Church and the Button Wood Walk. We cross the deep canal on a narrow plank. We were on the dam that led to the sea. I looked into the 'burn dutty hole'- remember I told you about me fetching dirt in a basket without being paid? Well after they dug the clay out, it left large, deep craters, when it rains, it gets full of water.

"Mommy, Mommy, look, I see fishes playing in the burn dutty hole"

"Oh, comeon child, how fishes gon be playing in dat hole. Where de fish come from to get into dat hole? Fish come from the sea; it is nowhere near here. Walk on lets go"

I grabbed David and pointed to the hole, he dropped the sane and ran towards it.

He picked up a mullet as long as my hand. The afternoon sun made the mullet shine like a silver sword.

We began to full the quake. My mother and Datson join us with their mouths wide open. "See, I told you, I told you that I saw fishes in here"

We didn't have to use the sane, we just reached into the hole and picked out the most beautiful mullets I have ever seen. Our quake was full and the hole was still full of mullets. "Mommy, let me run home and bring another quake"

"No, we have more than enough for us and all our neighbors. Tomorrow other people can come and get some"

My mother took what she need for dinner and some to fry and keep for a few days. She said, "You and Davo go and give two mullet each to all the neighbors.

Two would be enough for any size family. They are so big and fresh. Betose will stay and help cleaning the fishes while I start dinner"

Every neighbor we went to asked "waa ayou catch dis nice fish from?"

I had to repeat over and over where and that "Yes there is plenty left in the hole"

The most amazing thing happened that stayed with me throughout my life.

Some of the people went with lantern and flashlight that same night to get more fishes. But the Bun Dutty Hole was empty. No water, no fish.

The next morning, many people came to get my brothers and I to take them to the hole. When we got there, the hole was empty, almost dry. Not even our footprints.

In our shock state, we were cursed, beaten and thrown into the mud hole.

The same hole that I fetched dirt to build red brick road, gave me a miracle.

Back to Manchester School, I was a dunce. Ms. Bent put a dunce cap on my head.

I did not care about that because I was called a 'dunce' all my school life.

What would it matter if I dress accordingly?

We had to take a cup to school to get milk and biscuit. The Colonial government did a study and found that lots of children of the Colony were malnourished. So they brought in milk powder and biscuits from our motherland, England, to nourish us. We stood in line. I get a ladle of milk and three biscuits and go sit on the steps. Someone always accidentally hit my milk down or grab my biscuits from my hand.

When the school bell rang. Everyone had to stand in one strait line and march up to our classes. I always go to the back because if I am anywhere in front, I will eventually be pushed to the back. Let say 'I knew my place'.

The month of May is Maypole dancing time. Every young girl wants to be dressed in nice colorful dresses, holding the ribbon that matched her dress and hop and dance around a pole, to an audience of officials and parents.

I gather enough courage to go up to my teacher, who was in charge of choosing the girls who will dance the Maypole.

I whispered to her, not wanting others to hear because of their laughter and tease.

"Miss, can I be one of the Maypole dancers?" she looked up at me and said aloud.

"You ever see a Cullie dance Maypole?" she and the class went on overdrive.

I thought, 'this is not as bad as Akline. I could live with this kind of abuse.

They are not hurting me in a way to kill me like the Indians. Maybe I can even learn to read and write here. If my sores heal, maybe they might be friends with me'.

This child had nothing but hope.

As I was beginning to feel comfortable in my new school, I did not wait for my teacher to place the dunce cap on my head, I did it myself.

I began to be active in my classroom. I fill all the inkwells and wipe the desks and benches. I cleaned the classroom and blackboard every afternoon after school, so I would be the last to walk out of the schoolyard. I was a loner and I did not mind because I felt safer being alone.

One afternoon, as I walked up the dam to the main road, I saw a group of girls standing at the side of the dam as if they were looking at something in the trench.

As I passed, one of the girls said, "Come ha cully gal. Come see wah in de water"

As I walked over to look into the trench, I felt someone push me into the deep trench.

I remember trying to climb out, but the shoulder was too steep. Every time I came up for some air, I went down back to the dept of death. I did not remember anymore.

Old Mr. Thomas was passing, when he saw a group of girls laughing and dancing and pointing into the water. He jumped off his bicycle and asked what was in the water? One of them said, "We just push de cully gal in de water. We looking at the bubble"

Mr. Thomas jumped into the water and took me out. Once again I was rolled on a dam to get muddy water out of my lungs.

Other passerby stopped to see what was happening, and to lend a hand.

Mr. Thomas looked at the girls-funny, it was always girls who abused me- and said

"Ayou ah bad children. Me ah go strait to Mr. Frazer and tell him wah ayou do"

One week later, I went back to Manchester Scotch School- I had to go to school. It was the law-Mr. Frazer, the headmaster, greeted me at the door and led me to the stage. The stage was used for shows or whenever the headmaster had to make announcements.

All the blackboards were placed to the sides, leaving the whole school into an open hall. All the teachers stood by their classes and children sat quietly at their seats.

'What is happening?' I wondered. 'Did I do something wrong?'

Mr. Frazer began to call some names and some girls walked up to the stage.

He said, "I want all of you to look at these girls who I just called up here.

Take a good look at them. They nearly kill this girl last week. Well, after today, nothing like that will ever happen in this school".

Each girl received twelve lashes on their hands with the wild cane.

Not all at once. He called them one by one, gave them four lashes, and sent them to stand against the wall, and did the same over and over until all the girls get twelve lashes. Some were brave and took their lashes without a sound. Others screamed out with every lash with the wild-cane.

The whole school was quiet except the sound of the wild cane connecting to flesh and the cries of some of the girls.

"For those of you who reported these culprits, I thank you. Always speak the truth when you see wrong things being done.

Thanks to Mr. Thomas, this child is alive today" he looked at me and continued.

"If anyone from this school do anything or say anything to hurt you again, I want you to walk strait into my office and let me know. I will repeat this performance as many times as I have to if it happens again"

He looked at my teacher and said. "Miss Bent, I do not want to see that thing on her head anymore. You are being paid to teach her not to humiliate her. Do your job. This is my school, nothing like this ever happened before, and, nothing like this will ever happen again"

It never happened again. I still sat on the backbench, but no dunce cap.

Some children became my friends. At recess, they took turns to see who could better style my hair. They would ask me how could they get hair like mine? I said,

"You have to mix oil and water to get my kind of hair" I know that I was looking for some good blows when they use the oil and water and their hair don't turn like mine.

I got the 'oil and water' thing from a woman who was cursing my mother for marrying a Black man. She said, "Don't you know that oil and water don't mix?"

I wondered, to this day, why didn't the headmaster of Akline School, my Godfather, didn't do what Mr. Frazer did? Why couldn't he stop the horror from the first time when the children shook the bridge, threw me into the trench?

Why did I have to leave one school that was one village away from home, to go to another school two villages away? It was a much longer distance. I could not go for breakfast at Sister Marie. I had to take my meal to school. When all the children went home for their meals I sat on the steps of the school and ate mine out of my saucepan.

I was the only child to walk from Whim to Manchester to attend school. Why?

The big lorry dropped off material for our new house.

Mommy, Buddy, Datson, David and I fetched the pile of wood to the building site.

Buddy built a shed and stayed at the site to keep an eye of the material. During the day he laid out the timber and made agar holes and wooden pins. With the help of a professional carpenter, they measure and prepare the frame, sides, steps and roof.

Come Sunday, Buddy asked his friends for help to 'raise' the house-On Sundays people in the villages raise their new house because most of the men are home and would be willing to give a friend or neighbor a hand to build a new house.

There would be lots to eat and drink during the day-All of Buddy's friends and his cricket team came to help. Everyone in a village owns his own home, with pride.

Mommy and some neighbors did the big cooking and drink such as rum and lime wash by the bucket full with big blocks of hard ice from the icehouse.

That Sunday in August of 1951, from sun up to sun down, my brother and his friends and neighbors almost completed our new 'big house' that stood on stilts eight foot high with zinc roof and wood all around it.

By nightfall, when the helpers left, I walked around the house in amazement. With my mouth open, I had to bend my neck back to look at the height of our new wood house.

It took quiet some time for it to sink in that it is really our own new home.

I will be living in this house from now on, no more grass/mud hut.

Buddy and the carpenter did the final touches like putting in the glass windows.

Yes we had glass windows. The house had two bedrooms and a living room upstairs, a kitchen and a dinning –sitting area downstairs.

Mommy secured a perfect spot under the house, to build an alter.

Buddy made beds for him and the boys. It was the first time they slept off the floor.

Mommy and I had our old bed from our old house. She bought a chesterdraw from the village joiner. The dresser had two half draws and three long draws. It had one square mirror and two small draws on each side of it.

She placed her wedding dress and shoes-which I peeked at and asked her whose they were? She said they were for me when I get married-still wrapped in the blue stain, into the righthand side of the bottom draw.

On the lefthand side of the same draw, she packed all her old sari and hernee. That draw was not frequently opened.

Buddy built shelves all around the house, two in the living room, one for his trophy and the other for my mother's teapot-bank. Our old table and two long benches were the only furniture we had and needed.

I remember the day we finally moved out of our mud hut at Whim. Buddy and two friends began to dismantle the old house. My brothers and I piled all the useless material, such as the wattle, grass and small pieces of wood that would be of no use. My mother piled up all the useful material on to the donkey cart. When all was done, my home for over ten years was on a donkey cart and the rest was being burnt to ashes.

As we crossed the bridge and stood on the dam, Buddy and his friends dismantled our bridge and placed the planks on the cart.

As we walked away, I looked back several times at the white smoke reaching for the sky. I looked back at the spot where I was born nine years ago. It was now empty.

The wood from the old house was used to build a latrine, a bathroom and a kutila-storeroom. The plank from the old bridge was used as our new bridge-remember I told you that every home had a bridge. Everyone had to cross a bridge into his yard.

"What is the matter Babzy? You not run to meet you Buddy no mo. You na massage he when he come from cricked, no mo. Wha happen Babzy?" My mother.

"Noting Mommy, I am just so happy in this big house that I feget everything else"

The smell from the newness of the lumber in our new home lasted for years.

As I said before, Guyana has the strongest and sweetest smelling timber in the

World. It could be debatable, but it's still my opinion.

The yard was fenced and fruit trees and vegetable were planted. A part of the front yard was fenced to for my mother's flowers and tulsie-bazel for prayers.

My brothers dug a deep pond so that my mother could get water to wet her plants.

Liverpool was a long way from Whim. I miss Sister Mari and my Aunties and Uncles who loved and protected us from some of the shame and harms of Whim.

Datson continued to work at the rice mill. Every day he brought home his saucepan full of rice given to him by people who ground rice that day.

We had two buckets, one for brown, and another for parboil rice that he brought home.

"When beggars come to our gate, give them the best rice". said my mother.

David worked with my mother, who was contracting rice fields from owners to either sow or reap their rice. She had lots of young ladies working with her.

One such young lady, she liked very much and told Buddy about her,

"She is a nice girl, hard working and very respectful. I think she would make you a good wife. It's time for you to get yourself a wife. We have a big house, there is plenty of space for you and your wife to live here, that would make me very happy"

"Ma, listen to yourself; because some young girl is hard working and likes you, does not mean that I have to marry her. Do you know that her family mine hags? They make their living selling hag meat?"

"You are the one who told me to change. I am changing. I like her because she like us"

"Why would you, of all people, pick someone like that for me?"

"Because I am changing. I do not see things like that anymore. I like her for you"

Everyday my mother spoke of this nice young lady whom she loved and wants Buddy to marry. If she was telling me because she wanted me to talk to him, I was not interested. I lost all interest in my brother.

On Sundays, the girl my mother loved so much would visit our home.

She would help my mother in the garden. Grind masala and help with dinner.

She would stay until dark. When Buddy came home from the cricket game, Mommy would ask him to take her home.

That happened every Sunday until one Sunday Buddy did not come back home.

My mother was happy for his absence, for a while, that is.

After many days of her son did not come back home, she went to the girl's home to find out about his ware abouts? She was met at the door by a happy, smiling woman.

"Do you know where Dhia is? He did not come back home for over a week.

Where could he be? I have been asking all his friends for him. Have you seen him?" "Yes, he is here. We got married three days ago" she was a complete stranger.

My mother said she got so weak from the shock of the words and the smirk,

The transformation from the meek lamb to the wolf that was about to scratch her eyes out, in just one week. What has she done to that nice girl to turn on her with scorn?

For the remainder of her life, she never got over that shock of the hastened change.

She did not want to go back to that house or look at person she choused for her son.

She went to his place of work one day. He did not look at her but she looked at him.

"Son, what happened? How could you do this to me? I was the one who choose her for you. I want to have a nice Hindu wedding in our new house. What happened son?"

"Yes, you choose her for me. You are the one who told me that she was the best girl for me to marry. Well I did what you wanted. I married her. She didn't want you there"

"Yes, I did. I wanted you to get married to her because it seemed as if she liked us as a family. You know how I longed for people to like us. I really thought she did.

I was hearing talks around of how Galo-the seamstress's daughter-husband is threatening to chop you up if you don't stop fooling around with his wife.

Why did you get married without your family present? Without even telling me?"

"What family?" he looked at her in rage, as if she was a stranger bothering him.

"Me, Betose, Davo and Babzy. We are your family. What happened son?"

"Ma, it just happened. I am a big man and it just happened. You get married without me, remember?"

My mother said that she saw two people whom she never knew before.

They were throwing nails at her heart. She said to her son.

"OK son, you are right. Please bring your wife and come back home.

Build a small hut at the back yard for my children and me, and you and your wife could live in the new house. You worked hard for that house. Come back and live in it.

Please Son, come home. Bring your wife whom I choose for you"

Dhia and his wife moved in our new home. My joy of living in a big house was short lived. My mother and her three half-breeds had to move downstairs to the kitchen which now became our dwelling. We cooked, ate and slept it that small area.

It did not bother us because we were accustomed to small spaces.

My Buddy converted the boy's bedroom into a kitchen for his wife.

The newly weds had the whole upstairs to themselves. Even the bed that I shared with my mother all my life was now theirs. Our chestadraw became theirs.

Mommy took the contents of the bottom draw and placed them into a flour bag sack.

At nights my mother would role out the straw mats on the floor for the four of us to sleep on. I enjoyed it. We kept each other warm. We kept each other close.

Dhia's wife hardly spoke to us. She stayed upstairs all day until he comes home.

I tried to talk to her, remembering how nice and kind she was to us before.

She would not open the door. "You and dem gunga bay keep away from me"

My mother began to bend. Her body was leaning forward like a dying tree.

Around Christmas time of that year, I was comfortable in school. Not that I was learning. But I was at ease. I had friends who would walk with me on the road.

One such day, I was on the main road with two friends. I looked up the road and saw my mother coming down with her basket on her head. I looked at my two Black friends. I had to make a decision quickly. I committed the biggest sin that I will live with for the rest of my life. I ran into Cousin Nety's shop and hid until my mother pass by.

My friends never knew that the Indian woman, who just passed, was my Mommy.

Funny isn't it? At Aklyne, I wanted everyone to see that my mother is an Indian. At Manchester, I did not want anyone to see that my mother is an Indian.

This is one of the hardest parts of my story. What kind of world was I born in?

One of my choirs every afternoon after school was to fetch water from the main road standpipe and fill a punchin-drum for the two-family household use.

One such day, every time I fill my bucket with water, a boy kicked it down.

He did it several times. Cousin Nety came out and saw what he was doing. She said.

"Vincent, what is the matter with you? If you want to play with water, go into the trench. Stop kicking down the child bucket. Don't do that again. You hear me?"

"Yes, Cousin Nety. But me nah want no Cullie fulin water ha" he whispered

"What did you just say?" asked angry Cousin Nety

"Nutin, Cousin Nety. Me nah sa nutin"

I was able to full my bucket, with the watchful eyes of Cousin Nety.

I was halfway down the dam that divided Liverpool and Manchester when I felt a sharp pain on my right knee. I thought it was just someone throw a stone at me.

I tried to walk but could not lift my right foot. I looked at my knee and saw the green lemonade bottle head sticking out of my knee.

My bucket fell off my head and I smashed to the ground.

I sat on the dirt dam, not knowing what to do, I was in shock, I looked around and saw Vincent Frazer standing feet away with another bottle head, just incase he had missed.

I looked at him with shock and open mouth. He looked at me and smile.

Villagers gather around me, some try to pull the bottle head out of my knee but it was stuck to my bone.

"Someone with a bicycle go to Whim and bring a police," said Cousin Nety.

"No police. Someone with a donkey cart take us to the hospital" said Buddy.

I remembered the ride on the donkey cart to the Port Mourant Hospital.

Buddy holding me close to his chest, to prevent my body from rolling around in the speeding cart. The bottle head still sticking out on my knee.

There was blood dripping through the floor of the cart down to the redbrick road. My brother held me so close I could hear his heartbeat. I felt his breath on my face. I smell his sweat and remembered how I used to love smelling him, because they say

'If you smell someone, take long, deep smell of someone, especially under his arm, you will always love him and follow his cent wherever he goes' just like animals do.

I wanted to always love and follow my brother. That changed a while ago.

Now I am in his arms, he is smoothing my hair, wiping my face with his handkerchief.

I smell my Buddy once again.

Dr. Koo. It was always Dr. Koo. He asked, "Wah happen haa?" as he nug at the bottle head sticking out of my knee.

"Ah boy shi it on her foot" said Buddy

"Wa kind ah children ayou get up the coast? What mek dem so hateful and violent?

I will need some manual help to hold her down while I try to get that bottle from her bone" Dr. Koo said to my brother. "Pray that it comes out in one piece. If not, we will have big problem. It will mean sawing some bones to get pieces of glass out"

Buddy held my head, while other men held my hands and feet.

I felt my brother sweat and tears falling onto my face. I forgot the pain for a while.

When the doctor pulled out the green bottle head from my knee, my brother took one look at the deep hole left by the bottle, he fainted.

"Push that man aside and get someone else to hold this child head. I need her to be still while I probe into the hole for splinters of glass, before I can sow her up"

I was screaming with every thing I had left in me. It was not from the pain that I was going through with the long needle poking through my flesh. It was for my Buddy who was out cold on the floor of the hospital.

The doctor had to stitch deep inside the wound and then stitch outside to close it.

Everything was done without any numbing medicine.

When we returned home, there were some people in our yard. I saw Vincent and his parents. His father was holding his hand like a prisoner in handcuff.

When Buddy realized that he was the boy who had done this to me, he ran and got a cutlass. My mother grabbed him and said "No, my son. He is a child. He did something wrong to my Babzy but he is still a child and you are a man.

His parents brought him to beg pardon and to promise that he will do all of Babzy's chores and when she gets better, he will walk her to and from school everyday"

Vincent Frazer did everything that I did, down to going on his knees and scrubbing the floor. He had to fetch firewood, clean the shade and fill the lantern with kerosene oil, fill the bucket with water in the latrine, feed the ducks and fouls and collect eggs, cut Blacksage-chew sticks- in three-inch length, placed in a cup of water for us to brush our teeth. He had to sweep the yard and wash dishes, which he hated because his friends would laugh at him if they see him doing such girly things.

He had to keep far away from my three brothers hand reach.

Children are such forgiving people, even with scars that will stay for a lifetime. Vincent became my friend. I saw that he was genuinely sorry for what he did to me.

He never got to walk me to and from Manchester School.

Here again, I was absent from school. I was in bed on the floor of our kitchen.

Buddy would stop to see how I was doing before he went upstairs to his wife.

She never came down to see me. My mother had to place everything at my hand-reach for me to eat and drink. She prayed that I did not have to use the latrine while she was gone to work. My brothers took me in the morning and evening. During the day I had to control myself.

After getting married to Dhia, his wife never went back to work. She lived upstairs in our big, new house. She never came down to see us or ever spoke to us.

Auntie Katy and Uncle Bull came to visit one day, they found me on the kitchen floor. They did not like the condition that I was in, all alone with my knee bandaged.

Uncle Bull picked me up and took me out to his handcart. The one that Auntie Katy took fish to the market. They took me to Auntie Chunu"s, for Sister Mari to take care of me while my mother and brothers worked.

It was during that time that I saw one of the nicest Blackman that ever walk this earth. My opinion. I saw Mr. Bertram Alexander. He looked just like Brother Willy.

I was lying on the porch when I saw Auntie Chunu talking to this Black man.

He was not like the man my mother described who ate little girls with curly hair.

The man walked to me and said, "Hello, I am your uncle. Don't be afraid, your auntie knows me, I will not hurt you" he saw that I was comfortable with his presence. He added, "How would you like to go and meet some of your family?"

I looked at Auntie Chunu, she smile and nodded.

Auntie Betsy told me so much about my family. I was ready to meet them.

The Alexander's were being informed of all the attacks that I was having.

Since they lost their first attempt to take us away from our mother. They had no choice. Dr. Koo mentioned my last ordeal to Inez, who went to see him about her own illness.

The ride to Port Maurant was exciting. I went this far before to the hospital.

I was robbed of my first chance four years ago. I did not attend the school excursion.

I kept looking at the man who is taking me to the unknown. He had a gentle smile that would make any child comfortable.

We got to Port Mourant and my whole world changed. I never knew there was a part of my world that had so many different looking people. They were-in order of their existence in this land of many waters and six people- Amerindians, Whites, Blacks, East Indian, Chinese and Portuguese. There were many Mulattos-Black and White mix- and Duglas-Black and Indian mix- all living or visiting this one place.

I saw no White, Black or Indian people. I saw only shades of brown. From the lightest brown to the darkest brown people living together in a sugar plantation.

'Port Mourant Sugar Plantation is a nice place for me and my brothers'. I thought.

It was strange for me not to see any division by trenches, or separation by race.

I met the Alexander family in January of 1952.

They were so many. They were so different in shades of brown and texture of hair.

I was in a whole different world and my head was spinning around, looking at the crowd that gathered around me as if I was on show.

"This is your Gramother" I was looking at the matriarch of the family.

She was a tall, light brown woman with blue eyes and strait, long hair.

She held me close and asked if I was in a lot of pain from my wound? I remembered her. I saw those eyes through the mosquito net.

"This is your sister Esther" She was beautiful, medium brown with long strait hair. She looked at me, I remembered, as if someone just dragged me out of the latrine trench. She was in her mid twenties and had no time for strays.

"This is your Aunt Elo, my wife and mother of all our children" I loved Aunt Elo from the first time I saw her. She became my second mother.

My Uncle Bertram took me to all the other family members from Bound Yard to Free Yard. I met Aunt Mary and her daughter Vera who lived down the dam.

We crossed over to Free Yard and I met Aunt Inez, Uncle George and Earnest.

"I know that lady, she is a school officer. She came to our house at Whim"

"No, she is my sister. She is your Daddy's sister. She is your Auntie"

"I do not have a daddy"

"Yes, you do have a Daddy. Every child has a daddy, unless he is dead.

Your Daddy is very much alive. You do not know him, but you do have a Daddy"

"Uncle, that lady, your sister, the school officer, is she an Indian? She is married to an Indian man. Indian man only married Indian woman"

"In this part of the country, any man could marry any woman if they are in love.

You have two aunts who are married to Indian men. Your Daddy is married to your mother, she is an Indian" I was one confused child that day. Learning new things fast.

We moved on to meet Aunt Ilene and her children, then on to meet Uncle James, Aunt Georgie and their children.

Uncle Bertram was hurrying his tour. Every home I went to, gave me black cake and ginger beer. By the time we got back to Bound Yard, I had several pieces of black-fruit cake, wrapped in brown paper in a brown bag.

You can say that it was still the Christmas season. It was still festive all around and there were plenty black cake and homemade drinks such as ginger beer, mabee, sorrel, rice wine, cane wine and other fruit wines. Some things I never had before.

I sat on the back steps. On one side was a large clay oven; on the other side was a large rainwater tank. [My grandfather was a punt builder. All his homes had water tank]

Many young cousins and adults relatives surrounded me. Many neighbors, upon hearing that 'Archie's other daughter is here' came to see me.

I remember the only time I was surrender by a group of people was when they were about to harm me in the worst kind of way, or rescuing me from the harms.

Now I am looking at a group of people surrounded me, they were smiling at me and according to Uncle Bertram, and they were all my family. Many were Indians.

All my life I had a family of five, now I cannot count them and I cannot remember their names. The only name that never left my dumb head was

'Uncle Bertram'
.

I looked up and saw him. I saw the man who eats children like me. I saw the Black man that my Mommy warned me about. He looks the same way she described him.

He was dressed in pants and shirt. He had a bundle of grass on his head.

He just stood there looking at me, while I kicked and screamed and tried to run.

This is your Daddy. Don't be afraid, he will **not hurt you.** Said Gramother.

Uncle Bertram, with his arms tight around me, repeated his mother guaranty.

The man came and sat on the step next to me. He took me into his arms and began to hug and kiss me. To this day, I remember that day. It was the first time he was that close to me. It was the first and only time he held me in his arms.

I remember him rubbing his face on mine, hair stub from his face scratching my face. I remember the smell of cigarettes, the softness of his hair and the tears from his eyes.

The donkey galloped as fast as he could to get us back to Whim.

Uncle Bertram had promised Auntie Chunu that he would bring me back before dark.

I lie on the porch and try to digest what a day I have had. Can all those people really be my family? Could that White lady really be my Agee-Grandmother?

Could that man, the one with the small mouthstatch, really be my father?

Do I really have a father? When my mother said that I do not have one?

Maybe those people are having bad dreams. Maybe they want to sacrifice me.

I kept rubbing my face from the scratches of that man's hair on his face.

"Was he trying to kiss me or was he trying to eat me?"

For the remainder of my life, I yearned for that Black man to hug and kiss me again.

The brown bag with many slices of black-fruit cake let the cat out of the bag.

"Where did you get all this cake from? Asked my mother.

"Some people gave them to me, I will share them with my brothers"

"Who people? Ms. Tendell?"

"No Mommy. Some other nice people I met today" I could not bare to see the pain in my mother's face when she discovered that I was taken to Port Mourant.

She held her head into her hands and wail in a mournful way.

She looked at Auntie Chunu and said, "Why would you do that to me Chunu?

Why would you let them take my child away from me?" she was crying so loud.

"No one took your child away from you Dhero. Your child is right here with you. She needs to know the truth. This is the time for all of them to know the truth"

You cannot shelter them forever. I have done all that I could to help you.

I know that family too. There is nothing wrong with them"

On the crotch that my Buddy made out of a branch from a guava tree, and my mother padded it with some old cloth, I hopped my way to Port Mourant everyday.

Yes its true, I hopped five and a half miles every day to see the Alexander's.

Every night my mother came five and a half miles on a neighbor's donkey cart to take me back home.

She never beat me or said anything mean to me. We would just have a silent ride back home. I would do the same the next day.

Port Mourant held a magnet. That magnet was the Alexander family. I gravitated to them. That magnet was also the six races that lived in harmony in one sugar plantation five miles away from Liverpool. I just love them. I just wanted to be with them. I just wanted to be close to my newfound family, especially Uncle Bertram, Aunt Elo, Gramother and the children. There were plenty children, children from all over the estate, playing with each, regardless of their race. Adults stopped and talked to each other without cursing or spitting on each other. 'Am I visiting a fairyland? Like in my schoolbook?'

I am learning to speak proper English. My grandmother would

not hear it any other way. I was constantly told how to speak 'proper English'.

I did not care very much for the man who was my Daddy. I saw him looking at me from a distance, but seldom spoke to me. I did not speak to him.

I knew that my Mommy did not like him, so, I should not like him too.

Every morning, as soon as the coast was clear, I grab my brace and hopped my way to the fairyland. The place where I was allowed to go into homes, sit on chairs, eat from their tables and play with their children. The place of my beginning, the place where I speak and people spoke back to me. Like auntie Chunu home, only much more people.

I was lonely growing up in Whim, now Liverpool, because besides Mommy and Buddy, my words were silent, thus leaving me in a silent existence till now.

My young cousins would laugh at my broken dialect. They would say, "What language are you speaking? We do not understand a word you are saying"

Instead of pulling back into my shell like I did before. I was determining to learn to speak like them. I was going to learn everything to fit in with this family.

I love them. They claimed me as one of their own.

It was a long and dangerous trip for a ten years old girl.

I knew that I was hurting my Mommy by running away from her to the very people who she shielded me from all my life.

I saw the hurt in her eyes. The look of lost, the look of defeat, the look of helplessness. I wanted to stop her pain and hurt, but I could not stop myself from running away. I did not want to stop running away to Port Mourant.

At Port Mourant, I was a normal child. I found myself trusting everyone there.

"You should not have brought her here. Now she does not want to go back"

"It is dangerous for a little girl child to be on a desolate road every day"

"It is dangerous for her to live up-the-coast. Just take one good look at her then ask her where she got all those marks. Ask her why she is hopping on a brace to come here? Could it be that she is looking for us to shelter from the dangers that her mother can't do anything about? Because of the uncivilized people she lives amongst?"

"We seriously have to do something. She just can't come here everyday"

"Are you suggesting that we tell our own flesh and blood not to come here?"

"No I will never turn away anyone who comes here, more so my own.

We all know that there is a problem. We have to put our heads together and find a solution that would be good for the child without hurting the mother in anymore"

"What do you mean Mother? Anything we do will hurt Babe. We hurt her when you force her to marry your son. Now her daughter, the only person she has to speak with, is running away from her because she likes it here better" said Inez.

"While you gone gallivanting to Port Mourant everyday, I have to do all your work. If you are strong enough to go so far, you should be able to do your chores.

I din't cut you foot fa you to runaway" said Vincent.

I think he missed me watching him doing all my chores.

"Babe, I want to talk to you" Gramother said to my mother one night as she waited for me to get into the cart. - Many nights when she could not get the cart, and Uncle Bertram away, we would walk the distance back to Liverpool, in the dark, in silence.

To me, the distance to Port Mourant was much shorter than the same to Liverpool-.

"I know what you are going through at this time. All we wanted was for your children to know us. We are their family. It is wrong for them not to know us.

We do not like this outcome any more than you do.

It is dangerous for her to be coming this far every day, especially in her condition"

My mother was as mute as her two sons.

"We discussed this matter and come to the agreement that we keep Wynette here from Monday to Friday and she goes home to you on weekends.

What do you think of that?" she was speaking to the donkey, but she knew that Babe was hearing her. She continued to make her point.

"Look at her, look what the children at Whim and Manchester have done to her.

Here, nothing like that happens. We live in peace among each other here.

Do you know that your daughter cannot read nor write? She is ten years old and cannot read nor write" my mother kept her head down, listening.

"We can arrange for her to go to Rose Hall Scotch School where some of her cousins are attending. She may begin to learn if she don't have to look over shoulder all the time to see who will attack her next" all Gramother heard from her long speech, was braying of the donkey and slapping of mosquitoes.

"Babe, think about what I said. I will arrange to bring her down every Monday morning and take her back to you and her brothers every Friday afternoon by bus"

I felt sorry for my mother. I knew that I was hurting her. I knew I was being selfish, thinking of what makes me happy without thinking of the sacrifices, pain and sorrows that she has been going through for my brothers and me all our lives.

"Babzy, don't runaway no mo. Stay home till you fut get better.

I will take you to Port Mourant myself and hand you over to your grandmother"

My mother sat on the floor, legs folded, holding my hands, her tears flowing.

"A mother is supposed to protect her child. I could not protect you from all the bad things that happened to you. I could not stop them from hurting you because I could not find even one of them to say who tied you on the ants ness.

When I did catch one who hurt you, I protected him from your brother's punishment.

You are going to be safe with those people"

"You mean my family?"

"Yes, I mean your family. Even though they live not far from here, they live in a different world, a world where people are different from some of these bad people here. You will not be different there because there are lots people who are mixed like you.

Your sister Esther is mixed like you, no one did to her there what these bad people did to you here" I was consoling her now. I was crying on her chest. She continued

"I wish there was somewhere I could have gone with the three of you.

The only family I have here are you and my friends.

They did their best to protect you and your brothers, but they couldn't be everywhere.

I did not want you to go to those people, your family, because of my own feelings.

Now, I know that it is the right thing to do. I am ready to share you with them.

You should go and stay with your grandmother. Go to school and learn your lesson.

Don't feel bad for your brothers and me. We will always be here when you come home on weekends. I want you to go. I want you to be safe. Just wait til you are better. OK Babzy? Til you can walk to school without the stick"

I did what my mother asked. I never ran away again.

My heart was bleeding inside. I was hurting so bad for hurting my mother so bad.

Why didn't she take a stick and beat me for running away from her?

Why didn't she call me the names that I deserved to be called?

Why is she so accepting and so calm, why is she so willing to give me up?

"Mommy, I know that God is punishing me for something I did to you"

"You did not do any thing Bacha-Child, I am glad that you are going there"

"No, it is not for me running away to be with my family, its something else"

"What do you think that God is punishing you for? What did you do?"

"Mommy, one afternoon, the day before Vincent cut me foot, I was on the road with two girls from Manchester School.

Me look up the road and see you ah com toward us. I did not want them to know that you are my mother, so, me run into Cousin Nety shop and hide til you pass.

Mommy, my heart trembled all night. It trembled even faster every time you put your arms around me or kiss me or hug me to your chest when we sleep" I was crying uncontrollably. "Mommy, me think God use Vincent to punish me for what me did.

I want to be friends with the girls. If they know that you ah me mother?"

I could not finish that last sentence.

"No Babzy, you are a child, a child who has been battling two races of bigots.

If I were in your position, I would have done the same thing.

The day you are talking about, I saw you before you saw me. I knew you went into the shop to hide from me. I want so much for you to be a normal child and to have friends.

I just passed on. I was happy for you, not upset for what you did.

God will not punish a child for seeking a little happiness here, there and wherever"

I hopped to my friend and mentor, Mr. Reed.

"My Mommy agreed for me to go to my family at Port Mourant.

Since Uncle Bertram took me to meet them, I have been running away everyday"

"I know. Do you like them?"

"Yes, very much. I never know that one family can be so big. They are so many.

My head was spinning around from meeting all dem aunties and uncles. There are so many cousins. They can makeup a village by themselves"

"So, you really like them? Mr. Reed showed no excitement. I wondered why?

"What happen? You don't want me to go to them? You gonna miss me ha?

"Listen to me, my child. My wife and I do not have any children. Everyone's children became our children. Especially the ones she helped bring into this world.

If a mother dies in childbirth and no one wants the baby, my wife brought that child home and we raised him/her. Yes, we have many such children, grown and gone now. They are our children and their children are our grandchildren.

My wife did not bring you out, you found your way out before she arrived. She has a special place in her heart for you. She foresaw your problems from the time you entered this world. Not she, your mother, all the kind people around you, nor me could have prevented any of the bad things happening to you" Mr. Reed rocked in his chair by the window, looked across to me sitting in Mrs. Reed's rocking chair, my arm resting on the window ceil. He said.

After the Dutch, French and British played their game, it was agreed that the Dutch take New Amsterdam, which is now New York, America. The three Guiana's in South America were shared thus making Dutch Guiana, French Guiana and our British Guiana. Separated by rivers and languages. No Spanish because Christopher Columbus

Didn't like the dark, murky water surrounding the land. He liked blue waters.

Blacks were brought to their Colonies as slaves. They lived and died in the most inhuman fashion. It hurts for me to explain what I know. You will learn about it later.

The Indians were not snatched from their home. They did not witness the bad treatment of the Blacks, but were told, thus making them feel superior to the Blacks. Besides, in India where they came from, they had the caste system. From the highest caste to the lowest or the untouchables.

The Blacks too have their prejudice amongst each other. If one is blessed or cursed-whichever way one wants to look at it-with light complexion was called 'Colored'. He/she automatically feels that he is better than the 'darkie'. They get the better jobs with the government. They live in the big house with special privileges and many black servants. They look down at them and call them 'peasants'

Some even used their own 'darkie' mothers and grandmothers as servants and babysitters and have them stay at the back, never to be seen by visitors, or even to let people know that their mother is Black. Some Black people with light complication are the biggest bigot to their own Black people than the White or Indian is.

Nowadays, I see little Black girls with White, blonde hair, blue eyes dolly. What would happen when that little girl grows up? She will see that only White is beautiful.

I lived with my Mama. Then my Mama lived with me til she died. I was all she had and she was all I had. When I brought Anna to meet her and told her that I will one day marry her-that's the first time I knew that Nurse Reed had another name, Anna- she loved her despite others saying that Anna was too black for me.

My reason for bringing history to you is not for you to dislike anyone but for you to understand that there are good and bad people of all races and color.

I was a young Postman in this district. I got the job because I was a Mulatto.

My mother encouraged me to learn everything around me. I did, and after some years I new everything. I was better than my boss, at sending telegrams and reading codes.

In those days all the postmasters, police commissioners, headmasters and priests were Whites. I had a White postmaster, he told me that he thinks that am ready and qualify for his position when he retires. He said he has already recommended me to the General Post Master; I will go to New Amsterdam to write the Postmaster exam.

The day before my trip to New Amsterdam, my White boss came to my home.

He gave me a plain sheet of white paper and a sheet of carbon paper. He said

"Reed, when you go into the examination room, put these under your test papers.

Give up your test paper but keep the copy in a safe place'

When the results published in the government gazette, my name was not on the list.

My chief sent me home to fetch the carbon copy of the test for him to look at.

He got on the telegraph machine. He was agitated. He stayed on it for a long time. His fingers pounding the Morse code, he got back more codes. He banged again and again, looking at my test copy. He wrote again and again the codes coming from the other end.

My chief looked at me, he was as red as a cherry, he said "There must come a time when a man must search himself, find the truth and act according, regardless of how it used to be. I am glad that I follow my instinct and have you copy your test.

You will be my successor" he shook my hand and called out to everyone in the office, he said. "Congregation goes to your new Mr. Postmaster" I was the first Colored Postmaster in Colonial British Guiana

Before I let you go and I go for my nap, I must tell you about conscience.

There was a captain of a slave ship, who transported the demanded commodity,

Slaves, from Africa. After many trips and thousands of slaves later, the captain could not stand the terrene of his job. He quit and became a Minister in a church.

He said his conscience spoke to him. He wrote a hymn called Amazing Grace.

Believe me when I tell you that Amazing Grace has become Black people's favorite Hymn. It's the last hymn sing before committing a dead to the grave.

They sing it with such contentment, as if saying, "Thank you, we forgive you".

Datson and David questioned my absence, the days when I ran away from home? I did not want any of them leaving Mommy to follow me, so I told them that I had to go far away to get the wound on my knee taken care of.

Vincent was happy when I didn't disappear anymore. He felt safer in our yard with me present. He was sure that my three brothers still had it in for him.

"Your brother Dhia hates me. He looks at me with such anger, he told me not to go up the steps with the firewood when he is not home. He should buss he own fire wood"

"My brothers are right to be mad with you. Look what you did to their sister?"

"How come your mother don't treat me like Dhia do?"

"My mother don't have a dhulaheen-bride to protect from a bad boy like you"

I looked at Vincent, 'this is the same boy who cause me so much pain?

What am I doing, sitting on the bench, laughing and playing with him?'

I knew that I was like my mother. We are forgiving humankind with conscience.

One evening, my two brothers and I sat on the back steps while my mother cooked dinner. Buddy came home from work and went up the front steps to his wife.

I saw his wife came down the front steps with a towel over her shoulder.

She went to the bathroom, which was at the other side at the back of the house.

We watched her go back up the steps without saying a word to me. The boys don't care if she didn't speak to them. Sometimes, I think, not hearing was an advantage.

Shortly after she went back upstairs, Buddy came rushing down the steps.

He went to the ginip tree and broke a heavy branch. He pulled my brothers off the steps and started to beat them with the branch.

He hit them all over their heads and bodies. My mother ran out after hearing our screams. She tried to take the wood away from Buddy, but he was too strong.

My brothers ran in different directions in the dark, but he caught up with them and beat them. All the leaves and twigs were beaten off, leaving a strait, strong piece of wood in my brother's strong hand. He used it with all his strength on my two helpless, screaming brothers. Their screams are not like ordinary people screams, it's haunting.

Buddy was out of breath when he came from the back with the stick, half its size.

He sat on the front steps panting for breath.

My mother and I took the lantern to search for my brothers. We found my brothers huddled together in the backyard pond. They were shielding their heads and faces.

I lay on my belly, touched them gently so that they would know that it was I.

My brothers were trembling and bleeding from their heads and faces.

My mother got on her belly and reached in to them, trying to comfort them.

We held their hands and gently pulled them out of the pond.

I fetched a bucket of water and we washed my brother's mud and blood off them.

Blood was running down their faces, their arms were bloody and swollen from the blows of the wood when they tried to shield their faces.

They were shaking uncontrollably. I will never ever forget nor forgive, that night.

With all the running and trying to protect my brothers, I forget that I had an injured knee. By the time we got the boys inside and wrapped them with sheets, my mother noticed that my knee was bleeding. The stitches were busted wide open.

Buddy was still sitting on the steps, exhausted and holding on to his head.

"Buddy, what did my brothers do to you to make you so angry that you had to beat them like a pack of stray dogs?

"Your bhojie-sister-in-law said she saw them watching at her while she bathe"

"That is not true, Buddy. You passed the three of us sitting on the steps.

We never moved from there til you came and pulled them off the steps.

They never left this step. How could anyone see her in the bathroom, which is at the back of the house, if they did not move from here? Buddy my brothers never moved from the steps" I was my brothers mouth and ears all my life.

Just hearing why he nearly kill my two brothers, made me sick, so sick, I began to vomit the juices from my empty guts.

"Win, you sure dem boys na move from de step the whole time since I pass ayou sitting there?" His voice was trembling.

"Buddy, my two brothers never moved, they never moved from where we were sitting and waiting for Mommy to finish cooking our dinner".

Do you know what is the saddest part of this madness? My two dummy brothers have no idea why you, their hero, whom they and me latched ourselves to, for safety and protection, just brutalized them so badly? Worst than you would a wild animal?"

I couldn't tell you what time he went up to his wife. I left him holding his head, crying. I left him and join my mother, to attend to my brothers.

That night, my mother's food was left on the fireside untouched

We fell asleep sitting. The four of us hugged each other tighter than ever before.

I wondered what kind of curse was placed on the four of us?

The next day, a Darkie neighbor came over to inquire what all the screaming was all about? He looked at Datson's split-opened forehead and said "You have to take this boy to the hospital to get his forehead stitched. That cut is too big and deep to be left without stitching. I can see his white skull bone"

With the help of that neighbor, my mother took Datson and I to the hospital.

It was mid-morning. The hospital waiting room was full of other patients.

I remembered my brother Dhia brought me here. He fainted here.

I remember the Chinese doctor. He seems to know everyone personally.

When our name was called, my mother led us into the dressing room.

I looked around at all the stainless steel bowls, buckets and trays with huge needles.

"OK lady, tell me wha happen to these children?" he untie the cloth from around

Datson's head and asked "How did dis happen?"

"He fall on the bed iron, Doc." My mother lied. My mother who taught me never to lie, was lying to the doctor to protect her son' I thought in confusion.

I thought of what Mr. Reed told me, "One half of you do not tell, the other half of you was indoctrinated to tell".

All my life I knew only one half of me. I will do what that half taught me to do.

When the doctor looked at me for the truth, I said, "Me Buddy beat dem wid one ginip stick las night" I did what my mother taught me. She told me, 'God or me can come in the form of a fly or worm. So always tell the truth, all the time'

"Dem? What you mean dem? Asked Dr Koo

"Me Buddy Dhia, bruck one ginip tree branch and beat me two brothers til the branch tun to one lil stick" I did not know who else to explain the truth to authority.

Datson's forehead had stitched in a sign of a cross. My knee had to be re-stitched. This time he numbed my open wound before stitching it.

The Alexander family was informed. They came once again to take us away.

My exodus to Port Mourant was further delayed. I went deeper and deeper into my dunce world.

Vincent and all the other children went to school. I stayed at home to nurse my two brothers and myself.

Vincent did not mind his extended parole. He wanted so much to say "You see, I told you that your brother is a bad man, now you believe me?"

Buddy's friends from Lancaster and Liverpool heard the news that

'Dhia beat dem two gunga-mute boys so bad that one had to go to the hospital to get he head stitch'.

They came to see the boys for themselves.

"Man, we have been friends before these boys was born. What could they have done for you to brutalize them so bad? If you could do this to your own, what would you do to me or mine? These are your own flesh and blood. They are two dummy boys who cannot explain or defend themselves. You are the one to protect them. Instead you gave them lifelong marks"

The following Sunday my Buddy and his wife moved out of our new house.

Vincent and I were sitting at the back step when he and his wife came down the front steps. He was carrying a large box and she a large bundle on her head.

He stopped and looked at me. Our eyes locked on to each other.

I wanted to run to him. Hug him and beg him not to leave us. Remembering how much I love him and how much he loved us. I remembered how he cried and fainted at the hospital, for me.

In a blink, the cross on my brother Datson's forehead took my thoughts away. I turned away.

Vincent and I waited for a while, we ran upstairs. Everything was gone.

We quickly gather broom and bucket and went to work.

I brought up my mother's wedding dress and shoe, all her sari and hernee and placed them back into the bottom draw where they belonged.

I brought up our white slap can, place under the bed. The glass with clean water for her dentures and all of our stuff that belonged upstairs.

I opened the back and front doors to allow fresh air in the house.

I waited for my mother and brothers to come home. For us to sleep on a bed again.

My mother was not as excited as I; she went to look for her son and begged him to come back home. He had moved to a little grass/mud house in the other end of Liverpool. He told his mother that his wife is pregnant and that her family wants her to move away from the cursed gunga-dummy boys, for fear of the baby being like them.

"Just like how me first wife family de feel and did when she get pregnant"

All my mother had left in her life were her three mutts.

Our changing lives took yet another dive.

My mother, forty-five years old, looked doubled her age. She appeared as if the whole heavy world was sitting on her back. The dark circle around her sunken eyes looked sad and pale. Without her dentures, the double age was again doubled.

My mother suddenly became an old, old granny.

My two brothers and I never went to look for Buddy. I think from fear of rejection. My mother however, would sit on the parapet by his hut and wait to see him. Just to see him even if he did not speak to her. She just wanted to see her son.

Datson became quieter. He did not play with David and I anymore. Every time we tried to play with him, he would get vex and violent. He would chase us away.

He went to work at the rice mill, came home, go to the trench and wash, ate his dinner and go to bed without ever looking at anyone of us.

No matter how gentle I tried to reach out to him, he would growl and chase me away. The beating my brother got that night changed him for the rest of his life.

David continued to work with my mother in the fields. We played together.

I kept house and learn to cook. My first cooking was a disaster. I tried to cook fried okra with shrimp, dhal and rice. I did not know that I should not add water to fried okra.

I was so proud of myself when I served my family slimy okra, watery dhal and hard rice. All over salted.

The boys threw the food at me. Every time after that disastrous meal, if I hand them a plate of food, they looked at me until I convince them that it's Mommy's cooking.

My mother was proud of me. "In due time you will learn to cook the right way.

Today everyone loves my dhal and rice with fried okra and shrimp.

Years later, when Datson had to get a National I D card, it read on the line for any identification mark? 'Chris-cross scar on forehead'.

One morning, I saw a man standing at the gate. I thought it was a beggar, so I took a cup of rice to him-like I did for every beggar who came to our gate.

"Me come to see you mama. Me ah she brother Lungbehary" said the man who was an older David. He looked just like my brother.

"Mommy, Mommy, there is a man at the gate. He said he is your brother but he looks just like my brother David, only older"

My mother ran to the gate, opened it, and grab the stranger around his neck, he doing the same. They both began to cry and kissing each other tears.

From as far as I could remember, I heard my mother saying that her Davo was the image of her baby brother.

I watched at the excitement of my mother as she fed her brother. She kept touching him, ruffling his hair and playing with his beard. I realized that it was the first time since she was cast aside, that she was able to be so close to one of her family. She was glowing with happiness.

At least one, even if he was cast aside because of his drinking habit, came to find her.

Kasy Marage must be turning in his ashes, knowing that his two outcaste children are sitting by a holy alter, speaking in 'his language' Sanskrit-Hindi.

That day I saw some light in my mother's eyes. I saw the gold cap from her smile.

When I told Mr. Reed that my mother had lied to the doctor, he said

"Let me tell you something very important, child, telling a lie is wrong.

Sometimes you have to do something that may not be expected or accepted by others. You have to do it for you.

Your mother is a good mother. What she said to the doctor was not to protect Dhia or against Datson. It was neither for nor against her sons. She did it for she.

She was tired of having to explain to everyone all the bad things happening to her.

She did not want to hear the doctor say, "Again? What kind of mother are you?"

She did it for her, just like you did it for you when you hid in Netty's shop.

You didn't do it against your mother? You didn't do it for your friends?. You wanted something for you. You were tired of loosing everything because you don't fit in.

You did it for you. She did for she"

My mother washed my few pieces of clothes and put them into a canvas bag.

We boarded Zorena, a green and white bus with wooden seats.

It was my first bus ride. I think my mom's too, in a long time

All the way to Port Mourant, my mother warned me of what I should do and what I should not do. One of her main 'don't' was "Do not eat beef and pork, if you do, all your teeth will fall out" I thought about what she just said, I asked

"Is that why all you teeth fall out" I saw the hurt in her face from my ignorant question. She turned her face away. Still holding on to me.

My clothes in the canvas bag were placed under my grandmother's bed.

She took one look at the contents and knew that I would be the laughingstock if I were to wear them there. Aunt Eloise made dresses with matching panties for me.

My grandmother took me to Rose Hall. A town buzzing with people, cars, buses, carts of all kinds and stores of all kinds. Apollo Movie Theater and Harris ice-cream parlor were of great interest for this 'never see, come to see' child.

I never knew or imagine that there was a place with so many large, high buildings lining both sides of the road.

We passed a two-story house with a long veranda. There were several young girls, sparingly clad, laughing and dancing without music. My grandmother grabbed my hand and pulled me across the road. She said "Don't look up there, those girls are 'bad girls' that house is called 'bad house or brothel'"

We walked into Bata shoe store. I got my first shoe when I was over ten years old.

It was a black Chinese ballerina with a strap over the instep, buttoned on the side.

I was told that it was a sight to watch me walked to school in my first shoe.

I was enrolled in Rose Hall Scotch School. I was the biggest child in First Standard.

I loved being among all my family, but look forward to going home to my mother and brothers at weekends.

Every day I met new members of the Alexander family. They were so many.

At that time Uncle Bertram and Aunt Elo had five children, I became their sixth child until Bernadette came later.

No distention was made. When food or snacks were shared, anyone of us could take any plate. The house chores were shared equally too.

I felt accepted. I felt equal. I finally felt belonged.

I watched the matriarch Janie at work. To this day, I practice the values I learned from her, especially holding her family close together just like my Mommy.

One of my chore after school in the afternoon, was to go to the neighbors home to collect rice mar-Indian people cooked their rice differently, they strain the excess 'mar' that thick, white residue which the ancient Chinese invented ice cream with-

For my father's brown Holstein cow. She was different from the local cows. She was bought primarily for producing milk. Her diet was different. Her name was Janie.

While the other animals lived in the open yard or pasture, Janie had a pen fit for any human dwelling. She kept Archie from straying far from Port Mourant.

Barbara and I delivered milk. One customer on my route was the Reasat family.

One day after school, after collecting buckets upon buckets of rice mar, then having to deliver Mrs. Reasat's milk, became too much for this hungry child.

I sat under the tamarind tree, placed the brown enamel teapot spout onto my dried lips.

I just wanted to wet my throat with the warm milk that just came off of Janie's breast.

It was not my intention to drain the last drop of milk down to my large intestine.

I just could not stop. My suction organ refused to stop.

Every afternoon I sat under the tamarind tree and drank the two pints of milk intended for the Reasat's family. It's hard to stop something so good.

Janie's milk was the best cow's milk I ever had.

I had to make one more delivery of milk, but it was not for a customer, it was for little Ivan Archibald Alexander. He was about five years old. His mother was Indian of course. He was the image of us. He was another one of my father's 'half breed' flock.

I began to feel safe among my family and the diverse people at Port Morant and Rose Hall. I did not play games for fear that someone would pelt a ball at my head.

Weekends I went home to Mommy and my two brothers. David would give me the details of whatever happened for the week and I would tell him about school.

I tried not to make it look as if I was having a good time, for fear that he too may want to leave and follow me.

The first question my mother ask is "did dem people feed you pork and beef"

Datson was still grumpy. He did not pay much attention to my presence or absents. But whenever I gave him some of the goodies I brought. He stepped out of his cocoon long enough to clasp his hands, bring them up to his forehead and bow his head.

One thing I can tell you about my two dummy brothers. They know how to say thank. The way my mother taught them to say thanks.

One Sunday afternoon when David walked me to the bus, he asked me to direct him to where I am staying. He said that he missed me so much that he wants to come and see me sometimes. My fear was that once he had something like that in his head, he would do just that.

I clung to my grandmother and Aunt Elo. My many cousins were good to me.

They gave me things that I never had nor seen before, things like toothbrush, toilet paper rather than a bucket of water in the latrine, they drank coffee rather than tea, they drank porridge, cowheel soup, they bath with red, sweet smelling Lifebuoy soap. Just like Sister Mari. Yes, I loved them. I had the best of both worlds when it came to food.

I hardly saw my father. Whenever we bumped into each, there would be that strain reaction. I would give him that frightened look and he would give me that serious look.

I remember one night into my third week away from my Mommy, I began to cry hysterically, "I want to go home to my Mommy and brothers, I miss them. I want to go home now" I cried nonstop, even Uncle Bertram couldn't stop me.

The next morning, my father met me in the yard and said "I heard that you put on a performance last night? No one forced you to stay here. You are the one who kept coming here. If you want to be ungrateful to the people who care for you, take your belongings and leave. You know the way" his tone softened slightly, he said

"Or, tell your mother to come live here. I sent many people to ask her to come here so we can live together as a family. Maybe you could change her stubborn mind"

'Maybe you should go to her and change her stubborn mind?' I thought rudely.

At the end of the month, I was supposed to collect milk-money from the customers whom I delivered milk to. Every time my grandmother reminded me to ask Mrs. Reasat for the money. I never answered her. I would be lying if I did.

One day my father was in the estate yard, he saw Mr. Reasat walking towards him. Before he could ask him anything, Mr. Reasat said "Man Archie, why you no send no milk for the family for the whole month. Wa happen man?"

I got my first wiping with the infamous cow rope from the man who they said was my father. I peeped on myself. My mother never whipped me. He couldn't be my father.

My mother saw the evidence of the wiping and threatened never to send me back. "Me never beat none of me children. Me know what it feels to be beaten. Now you see why me no want you to go near dat man?" her treats frightened me. The thought of me not going back to those nice people at Port Mourant, gave me the chills. I had to find a way to soften her at this moment. I remembered what he said about being a family.

"Mommy, the man said that you and the boys should go and live with him"

"Why should he say that?"

"Because you is his wife" I lied, I knew he had other female visitors.

"Me go never do dat, me get me own new house right here" she was serious.

"Mommy, please do not stop me from going back to all the nice people who care for me. I am going to school. I am trying to learn my school lesson. One day I might be able to read and write if I stay in the school where other children don't beat me"

I had many more such beatings from my father. Some were so travels, like forgetting to put a bucket of water in the sun to get warm for him to bath.

I never let my mother know or see the marks.

Every time I saw him coming my way, I darted the other way. He still looked at me with disgust and I looked at him with fear.

Esther spent more time at Aunt Inez because she-Inez was sick and getting worst.

Children were not allowed to ask questions but Barbara would tell me whatever is being told about Aunt Inez. "They say that a baby died in her belly and they can't take it out"

"Oh my God, poor Aunt Inez. She really needs a living baby, not a dead one"

It was around this time when my grandmother took me to the Bundury Trench to collect supplies from the various houseboat people who came from the creek.

An old lady from one of the boat, wearing a straw hat and an apron with oversized pockets, took one look at my leopard spots and said

"Lad, Gad, Janie wa appen to dis choil? She fall I dutty wata or what? Wa she get all dem mark all over her like dat?"

"Ants bit her" answered my perfect speaking, almost embarrassed grandmother.

"No lie to me Janie, ants na do notin like dat to dis picknee" she went into her thatch roof boat house and brought out some raw coco butter in a small sardine can.

"Rub dis on dem marks. If dis don't clear dem out, she will have to live wid dem"

The coco butter worked like miracle. She was right, some marks stayed on me til now.

I went to visit Uncle James's home in Free Yard. I met Phyllis, their eldest daughter who was the youngest to have a scholarship to go the Georgetown – the biggest city in Guiana – to be trained as schoolteacher.

She took me into her bedroom, sat me on a stool in front of her dresser mirror.

She began to comb my hair. She did one style, then undo it, did another like a child playing with a dolly hair. I looked at her through the mirror. She was beautiful. She had a flare about her. My young mind catachreses her as young, beautiful, kind and independent. She had to be independent, or felt so, for her to do what she was doing with me, without asking permission. Yes she was an independent beauty.

When she finished her hair styling practice, she told me to take off my dress.

It was a strange request, since my mother warned me not to ever do that for anyone.

She went into her wardrobe and took out a hunter green dress. She said, "Put this on, if you do not like it, you can pick any other one. I picked this because our great-grandmother Clarabell did the embroidery on the collar and sleeves. You do not know her but I did. She was a beautiful woman" as if she was speaking to herself.

"This dress was given to me by our Gramother – so easily she made me a part of her- now I want to give it to you. I picked this because green signifies life and growth" Phyllis looked at me standing like a statue, robed in her historical dress. Her eyes were full of love and Tenderness when she said, "You will live and grow to be a big girl" she hugged me strong and close to her. She knew of my struggles to stay alive.

That hunter-green crêpe dress with bage embroided collar and sleeves became my 'good dress'. I wore it only on special occasion. There weren't many such occasions, so I kept my 'good dress' in a pillowcase under my grandmother's bed.

I mended and mended my dress so many times. Whenever I could not find the right color thread to mend the tares, I used whatever color I could get.

That hunter green dress that my cousin Phyllis gave to me in 1953, accompanied me for more than fifteen years. That is as far as I could remember.

I do not recall when or how we parted company but it will stay in my heart forever.

Rose Hall Scotch School was good to me. I was learning my Royal Reader.

I did not dear speak the 'proper English' when I went home to my mother.

She felt that every thing new I learned from those people, was taking me further away from her. She would say "Them want to make you like dem, but you will always be my Babzy and you will always be a Hindu, because your mother is a Hindu. A choil is wha ee mother is. Me ah one Brahmin, you ah one Brahmin too"

'Ya right, tell that to your fellow Brahmin' I thought but dear not say.

I knew that the deal was that I go home every weekend, but when I heard what fun my cousins have when I am away. I tried to reason with my mother to change the deal.

"Please Mommy, let me stay two weekends with them and two with you.

I am beginning to learn my bookwork. The less I move around, the more I will learn. Soon I can come home and read something to you" my mother only wanted what's best for me. When she heard that I might be able to read, she willingly agreed.

The first Sunday I spent at Port Mourant, Gramother sent me to Sunday school.

She dressed me in a nice flowered dress that Aunt Inez made for me. Not my hunter green dress that was neatly wrapped into a pillowcase under the bed.

She gave me a gill-penny-which was a larger copper coin equal to two cents.

"Put this gill in the offering plate when the catechist pass it around"

'Another Sunday school? I was not allowed in the one at Whim'.

The Sunday school at Port Mourant was different; it was nothing like the one at Whim. It had all race of children and Catechist Changa was kind to everyone.

I went through the front door and sat on any bench I choose. Not the back step.

Every Sunday I placed my penny into the offering plate.

I noticed that every Sunday on our way, my cousin would go to Balchan's cake shop, and then join me so we could walk on to Sunday school. I also noticed that she had something big in the corner of her mouth.

During prayers, she would be sucking on this big thing in her mouth.

I discovered that the penny that Gramother gave to us every Sunday, she went to the store and buy one Bullseye-a large, hard candy, which we called 'neverdone'-

for one cent and put the other cent into the offering plate.

Ok, if she could do it, I could do it too. I did just that.

The candy was so big and hard, I found myself unable to sing.

If you want to share it, you will have to use a hammer to break it apart. Even then, you will be taking a chance with your eyes and face. The candies could rictasha and smash your face or could pitch so far you would never find it.

By the time my grandmother called me up to her room, my bullseye was about half its size, after hours of sucking the pure hard sugar ball.

"How much money did I gave to you to put into God's collection plate?"

I pushed the ball to the side of my pouch like a squirrel. I answered

"A pe.. Gramother" by this time I think she saw the dark sugar coming out my mouth. She opened her eyes and looked into mine and said

"How much money did you put into the collection plate?"

I opened my mouth, not knowing what I was going to say. Suddenly the ball of rock sugar, slid down my throat. I began to see colors that no living human could ever see. The same colors I saw at the back of the school latrine and in the dept of the muddy waters. They were colors that only me was familiar with. Only a dying person sees them. The room began to get dark and spinning around me.

The hard ball of sugar imbedded itself into my throat. It was not coming out, it was not going down. Everything was dark when I felt a hard blow on the upper part of my back.

The blow sent me flying to one corner of the room and my bullseye somewhere else.

My air canal was open and I heard my lungs squeak for air. My eyes were almost out of their sockets and I was soaking wet without a drop of water thrown on me.

The red, sugary drool was all over my Sunday school dress.

"You see what happens to children when they steal from God?" asked Gramother. She sat on the edge of the bed. She too was shaken or should I say frightened by the choking episode. Or, what could've happened if she was unsuccessful?

"You opened your mouth to answer my question, only God knew if you were going to tell me the truth. He taught you a lesson before you answered.

Never do what others do, when it is a wrong do. You aught to know that if your grandmother give you a penny to put in the offering plate and you did otherwise.

When you opened your mouth, weather you were going to tell me the truth or lie, you already done a wrong thing. I hope you learn a valuable lesson" I surely did.

My mother was not keen on the idea of me going to a Christian Sunday school.

I had to live a double life from such a young age. When I was with my mother, I had to eat and speak like a Hindu. When I was with my father's, I had to eat and speak English. I was like a camellia. Change on my way to and from my two worlds.

Rose Hall Scotch School was having a concert for the coronation of Queen Elizabeth in 1953. Since I was the biggest child in 1st standard, I was picked to sing the first verse of a song.

Gramother once again took me to Bata shoe store. This time she bought me a 'good' brown leather shoe with a strap across the instep.

Aunt Elo made me a new dress with a broad sash for a bow at the back.

With my hair nicely combed back, colorful ribbons. My nice flounce dress and new leather shoes and white socks, I looked around for the photo-take outers. There were none. No one had ever taken a picture of me up to this stage of my life.

My grandmother and Aunt Elo attended the grand occasion.

I remembered standing on the stage, looking at the audience and began to tremble.

When it became my turn to sing my part, I froze.

My grandmother stood up, gave me that look, I remembered my part that says

"Twenty baby teeth they grow, ten above and ten below"

I did not hear the rest of the song. I didn't care to. My part was over. That was it.

Remember my new brown leather shoe? I packed it back into its box and kept it under the bed next to my hunter green dress. Every night, I smell the newness of leather. I waited for the right occasion to wear it again. When an occasion arose, I took it out to wear, it was unfit for my grown foot. I still smell my new brown leather shoe.

Around October of 1953, I saw the adults family members gathering in groups, whispering quietly and the women folks going back and forth to Aunt Inez home..

One such day, Barbara and I asked Aunt Mary if we could go in to see Aunt Inez? She said, "OK, just for one short minute. If she is sleeping, do not wake her"

We tiptoed into my auntie's bedroom and saw her lying on a beautiful embroider bedspread. She looked lighter than she was, almost yellow. The room had an unpleasant smell. I looked around for a used slap can or soil bedding, but everything was clean and tidy. I wondered 'what is that smell?" Not even the jay's fluid could cover the smell.

My aunt opened her eyes and looked at us. She said to me "I made some more dresses for you. They are in the shop. They need hemming. You should learn to hem" I just wanted to say something to her. I say "Aunt Inez, me know how fee hem" she smiled.

That weekend when I went home, I told my mother about Aunt Inez being so sick.

My mother went to Port Mourant to see her sister Inez. She came back home, went to her alter and pray. She cried, calling out, "Sister Inez, Bhagwan will take care of you"

Inez Viola Katick died from cancer November 9th 1953. She was 44 years old.

Uncle George, her husband, ordered the largest tomb at Aklyne Scotch Church yard.

He was certain that his turn was going to be shortly after her.

He loved his wife so very much, on his desk in the gallery, he had a large picture of her and a rolling calendar that shows the month, day and year of her passing.

Uncle George left that calendar on November 9th 1953 for the rest of his life.

I visited Uncle George in 1983. He told me most of the things that I already told you.

He allowed me to walk around the house. He seldom allowed

anyone into my Aunt Inez bedroom that was left almost untouched since her death. I was given that privilege.

I heard from others about the portrait and calendar on his desk. I saw them myself in 1983. I wondered with admiration and pity, "What are his days like? What's his night like? Could someone really love another person that much?"

He brought out a little grip from his bedroom, took out a bunch of keys from his pocket with shaking hands, found a small key and opened the grip. He took out a pair of pajamas that were so faded and fragile from so many years in the grip, a pair of black socks, and a bottle, half evaporated perfume. He said to us, my cousin Monyx who accompanied me to Free Yard that day.

"These are what I am going to her in. She made these pajamas for me. This is her favorite perfume. She bought this for me" with shaking hands, he tilted the bottle, making sure that there is some still in it. – We always powder and perfume our dead –

Uncle George, who showed me that true love, can make people do strange things, died November 14th 1986. He waited 33 years to join his beloveth Inez, in one of, and still is, the largest tombs at Aklyne Church Yard.

David decided that he was going to follow me to wherever I was going. He climbed on the ladder of the bus, the one that the conductor use to take loads to the roof, and wrapped his two arms around the metal frame as the bus moved on.

Through the glass, I kept making signs to him, telling to go back.

David followed me to Port Mourant and the Alexander's welcome him too.

He stayed with my father for a short while. He got a job as a houseboy for an overseer named Rob Christini and his wife. He was also a famous cricketer.

The Christinis loved David. They had him moved in with them.

My mother blamed me for David's leaving, but she had such a forgiving heart that soon everything became normal again. Especially when we go home on weekends.

Later she told me that she knew I had nothing to do with him going away.

Kinda like an apology in disguise?

Dhia had his first son. He asked my mother to open book and get his name.

The next year another son arrived.

Three of his children, he sleeked his mother's help in naming them according the holy book in the Hindu religion. He never took his children to his mother.

She never saw them or held them. She just opened her book to the day and time of their birth and picked their names accordingly.

Her son had six more children but she was not asked for help for their names.

The Village Office, informing her that her application for land in Black Bush has been approved. She was happy to give it to Dhia. All twenty acres

Black Bush was in the jungle that was now being cleared for human habitation.

It was infested with deadly snakes and lots of people were loosing their lives. Others were braving the reptiles and moving to fertile land. It is today's breadbasket.

He was a carpenter at the Manchester School as a. He had to pass our home on his bicycle every day. He rang his bell as he passé his mother sitting on the steps.

On payday he drop two dollars in the grass for Mommy or me to pick up.

My mother would sit on the steps morning and afternoon just to have a glimpse of her son. It was not for the money. David and Datson were bringing home money and she was still getting maintenance from my father through the Post Office.

I think she just wanted to look at him, to see her son, as he passed.

He could not stop for fear that his wife would find out that he went to visit his mother and he might have to change his route or worst, move away from Liverpool.

I think it was a relief when her son moved away to Black Bush.

She did not sit on her steps to have a glance of him or search the bushes for his pitons.

I think she was even happier for him. Now he can live with his wife and family without others knowing that he has a mother and three half-breed cursed siblings.

I think it was because of her love for her son, she made things easier, or so it seemed, for her to keep away from him for the rest of her life.

I was learning in school. The cosmopolitan environment was good for me.

I was sponging up every thing I could about my family. Every time I found someone who would take the time to talk about 'old times' with me. I soaked it in.

I loved my Aunt Elo cooking and baking. She made a better dhal, curry and roti than any Indian woman. Not forgetting her skill in making nice dresses for me.

She was my second mother. I loved her dearly.

I absorb my grandmother's behavior towards her family, and all the people around her. Her values are still in my soul. Especially sayings like - Willful waste, brings woeful want – Please and thank-you can take you through the world – Hag ask his mother 'why you mouth so long?' Mother replied, 'wait my child, your time is coming' – Don't piss too high, it would come back on your face – Don't shit of high grass, you could find yourself in deep mess - Donkey ant get no right in horse race – Don't take what's not yours, it could be a jumbee in disguise. I remember so many more parables.

I love my family. I loved the Darkies from Port Mourtant. They did the same things like my mother. My mother always told me "Always cook a little extra. Leave food in the pots, incase someone drop by. You never know, God could drop in one night after working so hard. He too can get hungry. If there is no food, He might go to the next-door neighbor. If your food wasn't eaten, it would not go to waste, you could feed the dogs, ducks and chickens with it in the morning"

By the time I got to know the Alexander, Dada had already passed on.

He died in 1944. There was a large portrait of him in the drawing room. He was a Lodge elder. Some of his sons and grandsons were and are still in the Lodge.

I went to see Mr. Reed. - Even though all the doors in the villages were never locked, it was bad manners to open ones closed door – "Who is there?"

"Is me Wynette, Mr. Reed". I waited for a long time before the door was slowly opened. My friend was slowing down.

"Me come to tell you that I can read ah lil bit, but I can count better than any one else in me class. Me always get a star for sums – mats"

"In time, you will be able to read and write. Practice writing on a piece of paper, whatever you want to tell me. The next time you come to see me, bring it for me to see" I saw that he was tired. He was dozing off ever so often. "I am going now. I will come back to see you and bring a letter for you"

"No, don't go yet, I want to tell you something.

When I say 'in life' I mean in the future. In the future you will meet all kinds of people. I mean all color, size and looks.

Treat everyone with respect. Never judge anyone by he/she looks.

You and your brothers were not given such of what I am asking you to give to others.

I am asking you to standup for what you feel is right and standup against what you think is wrong, no matter which side of you is right or wrong. Don't stifle your conscience. Remember we talked about conscience before?"

"Look across the road, you see that young man lying in the hammock? His name is Busyboy. He spends all day and a big part of the night in that hammock.

His wife's belly is big every year. She comes over for food to feed her and children, him too. Mrs. Reed and children goes hand in hand. She can't see them hungry.

Many times I ask him to do some work around the yard, mend the fence or deliver papers, where he can get some money to take care of his home and family.

He said he couldn't be in the sun, because if he sweats in the sun, his skin peels off.

"Now let me tell you about another family. Every night about 11pm,

Sugrim will pass on this road, going to the back dam – fields with his quake and castnet.

He would fish all night while Busyboy sleeps. In the morning Sugrim pass here with a quake full of fish. One hour later his wife Patti pass here carrying a basket of fresh fish to the market. She will pass back going home with a pocket full of money.

Busyboy is still living in his mother's little shack, sleeping in that hammock.

Sugrim, I am told is building a large two story house at Liverpool and is planning to send his eldest son Dewadat to England to study to become a barrister.

That is what I mean when I say 'be fair in your judgment, regardless of who it is.

I made this example, not by race, but by man's behavior. There are people like Busyboy and Sugrim in all races. It was lazy people who brought men and women from Africa and India to do their work for them free of charge; it was called 'Slavery', Indentured.

Remember I told you that during the war some of your uncles and other men went to England to fight alongside the Whites? Well, lots of Indian men went along too.

In England, both the Blacks and Indians were called 'Darkies'. They are the same in the eyes of the White man. Their strait hair makes no difference. They were all darkies"

I thought it was time for me to go, letting Mr. Reed go back to bed.

"Let me tell you one more thing. Give freely. You don't want more than you need.

Forgive quickly. The faster you forgive a wrongdoer, the faster you can move on.

Don't listen to that 'forgive and forget' saying. Forgive, yes. Forget, never.

Respect everyone's religion. I believe that at one time there was only one religion. That is why, in every religion, the women cover their heads the same way. Some change it to hats and wigs but they still cover their heads in church. That is why most of the big religious events fall around the same time of the year, for almost all religion.

When you get older, check it out, Easter/Christmas time, you will see that Christian, Muslim, Hindu, Jews and all other religion observe their own special religious holiday".

"You know something Mr. Reed? My mother and grandmother told me something just like that. My mother said that God is the Father. One day He was taking all his children to see the world that He has created. He placed them in a large tray and began to fly around. Suddenly a strong wind hit the tray with all of God's children. They were scattered all over the world that is why we have so many different religions, in so many languages. But she said, we all pray to a Father, whom we call Lord/God.

My Mommy said that the same sun dry everyone clothes without prejudice"

Mr. Reed passed away while I was still at Rose Hall Scots School.

1954 Daddy build a house at Lancaster on his birth land.

It was a three-bedroom house on 9ft stilts, the kitchen, dinning room was downstairs. The yard was fenced, it had a latrine and bathroom outside and a shower upstairs.

Archie now had his own "big house' at the back of the family's.

"I am giving your mother one more chance to come to her senses.

You tell her that I am asking her to come here to her home and be my wife and mother to her children. We have lived apart forever. Now is the time for us to be together.

This is the first and last time that I am asking her to be my wife"

He walked me through the new house. "Make sure to tell her everything that you see here. This is your bedroom. You do not have to share it with anyone. You have your own bedroom. This is for a woman and me. Preferable, your mother, and this is for the boys. You should bring her to see her new home. This is my ancestors land. Most of the Alexander children's navel cord was buried on this land. Your two brothers cord are buried on this land. Show me any fruit tree, and I can tell you whose navel cord was put into the ground before that tree was planted over it" my daddy said as he walked me through the yard as if I was his secretary taking notes.

I wondered 'Where was mine buried?'

'Now that I am going to have my own room in a big house, am I supposed to forget the way he is looking at me right now? Even the most ignorant and innocent can feel hate when it is being transmitted'. My feelings.

Why is he so hateful to me?

When I told my mother what my father said, she looked at me angrily.

"You want me to go live with dat man? After everything dat me gone through because of dat man? How could you bring such a message to me?" she waited for an answer. I had none. I was just a child-messenger.

I knew how she felt about 'dat man'. She never knew how I felt about him. I never

told her of my feelings, for the same fear that I told you before. I thought that 'Maybe if she moved in with him? I might be allowed to stay at Port Mourant with my family'.

I was willing to ignore my mother's bitterness for some sweetness in my life.

"Tell your Daddy dat since he can send message to me by you, dat me send one for him. Tell him dat his words was worst than the beatings I get from Ram"

We moved to Lancaster.

David stayed on with the Christinis. Datson was not moving away from his mother.

My mother was not moving either. That left him alone. He fought with his mother, Uncle Bertram, and Aunt Elo. He won and I had to move away from Port Mourant and Rose Hall Scotch School and the world of beautiful people from the sugar plantation.

I was reenrolled at Manchester Government School. I was in third standard.

Shortly after moving to Lancaster, my father brought one of his many visiting companion to live with us. She was Indian, of course. I had to call her auntie.

In the initial stage of her arrival, everything was nice. She was kind to me.

Later I became Cinderella without the glass slippers, nor the Prince.

The weekend deal at my mother's was bullied out of existence. His explanation was that "Your step-mother needs you here to take care of the livestock's and to learn housework and cooking. Your mother never teach you to cook or do housework"

I became the pawn between my mother and father. She, being stubborn and unforgiving. He, being a bully and unforgiving, belted out their anger on me.

The price was too high for my young life.

I soon made friends in Lancaster and neighboring villages. Children do that faster.

Most of my friends were related to me through the Alexander clan.

Remember I told you that all village people were related one way or another?

Remember Janie? The brown Holstein princess whose milk was the best?

A house was built for her too, at the back yard.

Villagers soon lined up for her milk. I kept the book of names and amount.

Two people were allowed to get free milk delivered to them, my mother and Nana Sweetie. Datson collected my mother's and I delivered Nana Sweetie's every morning on my way to school, hang the saucepan on her gate, get the empty on my way home.

Let me tell you about Nana Sweetie.

I never saw her. I did not take the time to see her. I always hurried away because I had heard from other children that she was an obeah woman who caught children, ate their flesh, drank their blood and spit the black blood in the sand. They said that they saw her dogs running around in the yard with children's bones in their mouths.

You may say I was brave, but my friends say I was crazy when I bet them one day that I would wait to see Nana Sweetie. The old witch whom many knew to be so bad, yet, many of them and me have never seen her.

I needed to know for myself if she was as bad as the children said she was?

I wanted to look inside the ugly book for myself. I have already met so many bad people in my short life, how worst could she be? Mr. Reed said, 'Judge for yourself'

On August 23rd 1954 – I remembered that date very well because it was my Daddy's 48th birthday. He started the celebration from the Sunday 22nd.

That Sunday morning as I was about to leave with Nana Sweetie's milk, my daddy gave me some meat wrapped in young banana leaf. "Give this to Nana Sweetie. Tell her it's my birthday tomorrow" He had no idea that I had never laid eyes on the 'jumbee'.

My friends watched from afar as I hung the saucepan of milk and placed the meat in the basked that hung on the inside of the gate.

I sat on the wet, soft ground and waited.

Looking through the coconut branch fence, I saw her coming towards the gate.

I saw her bare, flat foot dragging on the red, dusty sand.

She came towards me and my heart began to beat, bum, bum, and bam.

This child, soon to be twelve years old, was now face to face with Nana Sweetie.

Her two dogs began to howl in a wolf-like manner.

Stuck in cement, I could not move. I wanted to scream, but even my voice deserted me.

I made the wet ground wetter. My weak bladder exploded. I peed myself.

"Wha you ah wait fa?" asked Nana Sweetie. Her voice was old and trembly.

She was a short woman with red marbled eyes. Her wrinkled face and arms with hanging skin indicated that she had once been plump.

Her head was tied with a greasy piece of cloth. Her frock, almost down to her ankle, was from a former size; it was tied with a piece of string around her slender, bent waist.

Her fingers reminded me of the large crab legs in Gramother's okra soup.

I smell the tobacco she chewed with her toothless gums and I saw her spit the black blood in the sand. It rolled onto the dry sand like a small marble.

"I just want to say hello to you, Nana Sweetie" I said, trembling like a fevered child.

Sweat ran down my body. I was determined to prove to my friends that I was brave, or that I will die today because of my stupidity. Whichever way, I was really scared.

"Ah hear all de bad thngs people in de village ah say 'bout me. You children have no right to say tings you know nuttin 'bout" her voice was still painful to hear.

"Not me. Me never say bad tings 'bout you. Me only bring you milk and go to school. Me no say nuttin bad 'bout you, Nana Sweetie" I was pleading for my life.

My grandmother proper English went down the drain as I tried to dialogue with her.

She collected the milk, took the meat from the basked and looked at me with those beady eyes. This time she quenched them even smaller than they were. A question.

"Tomorrow is me daddy birthday. He kill ah cow" I can now speak with the shakes.

"Wait fe one lil bit, meh soon come back."

'Oh my God, she goin take me in she lil shack, drink all meh blood, spit black, obeah me, den let de dogs eat me bones. I goin never see me Mammy again" I could not move. Here was my chance to runaway, but I could not move.

I looked up and saw Nana Sweetie standing over me. With gentleness in her eyes and trembling hands, she gave me a basket full of red-breasted mangoes, plump and delicious looking with the smell of pineapple, passion fruit and guava, all mixed in one.

I looked into her eyes and saw both sadness and joy. I was too young to understand what I had missed for so long. 'If only I had done this since I came here I would not have had space to absorb all the bad and ugly things said about her' My thoughts as I took the basket of mangoes from her hands. I felt guilty and ashamed of myself for being afraid of her. I listened to others and treated her the same way people treaded my two brothers and I. With scorn and indignity.

"Tek dem mango home, make sure to show you mama befo you eat dem – from all the bad being said about her, she became overly careful. – Mek sure you bring back meh basked a manin" as I moved away from her gate, she said "Nah believe one word ah what dem a say 'bout me, it nah true. Me ah somebody, not a bad thing"

When I get back to my worried friends who were waiting at the middle dam, they were shock to see that I was still alive. They began to back away from me. They became afraid of me. They said "You spend so long wid her, she put her jumbee on you. Don't come near to us, tell us what you and she been doing all dis time?"

I sat on one side of the trench and they on the other. I explained the whole frightening encounter. I even show them the evidence of my peed dress with the mud stuck to it.

I offered them some of the mangoes, thinking that my explanation had changed their minds about Nana Sweetie.

"Stealing her mangoes, guava, cherries and other fruits from outside her yard is ok, but eating a mango that she hold wid her jumbee hands? That's a no-no"

I was afraid that I was going to be abandoned by my friends, once again having no friends to play with me because I said that Nana Sweetie was not evil.

"Did you see fire come out from she mouth when she talk to you?"

"Did she spit black blood in de sand and mek it curl up like a ball?"

"Did she smell stink from eating all those little children?"

I felt sorry for those who asked me those questions. It was as if I was on a higher Plato.

"NO, no, no. Nothing of the kind. She is just a normal old lady like any of our grandmothers. I think she likes me" upon hearing my last sentence, my friends ran away from me. I lost my young friends for a while. But I gained an inspiration for the rest of my life. I became free of fear of the old, scary woman the village name Nana Sweetie.

We met every day, she on the inside, and me on the outside of her gate.

One Saturday she said, "You want fe come in to meh house?"

"What about dem dags, dem go bite me?"

"No, dem see dat you ah me friend. Come on in"

Nana Sweetie led me into her secluded world. There were more fruit trees than I saw from the outside. She had a kitchen garden flourishing with vegetable and ground provision. On the path to her hut, lined with flowers such as Marigold, Daisy of all colors, Jump-n-kiss and Sunflowers. It was breathtaking.

At the side of the house, was a stave vat that collected rainwater for her use.

She was self-sufficient in many ways, in her little, lonely world.

I followed her, keeping closer to her than the dogs. We entered through the lone door of her one-room hut with two small wooden windows.

The kitchen was at one end; the bed-sitting room was at the other end.

In the kitchen area, on a coal pot in a cast-iron frying pan, was a fish being fried to a crisp, golden brown. In enamel bowl, on a small, wooden table, were some boiled ripe plantain, sweet potatoes, cassava and corn on the cob.

The aroma for the fish and corn made me hungry. I wondered 'Is she expecting company? She did not cook all this food for she alone?'

On the other part of her home was her double bed, neatly made with a flowered spread.

On her only two cane-seat chairs, were cushions made from colorful scraps of crêpe cotton and satin cloth, the same colors as the mats on the floor. 'Was she a seamstress?' I wondered, Aunt Inez had friends who collected scraps to make things like these.

Her few clothes were hung on the wire line that tied in a corner of the room.

Under the clothesline was a large, old, brown grip. The kind travelers carried in old movies. I wondered 'What treasure she must have in it? When did she last open it?'

On the wall was a beautiful family portrait. The woman resembled a young Mahalla Jackson. She was sitting with a distinguished-looking gentleman and two young boys standing at their sides. They were four well-dressed people with wide, happy smiles.

She had on a flowing white dress, black high heel shoes, gloves and a large brim hat.

The man had on a dark suit and socks and shoes, a large scarf tied around his neck and made into a bow – the bow was as wide as the opening of his jacket – hat on his lap, his hair neatly parted on his right side.

The two boys, one taller than the other, were dressed like the man, with hats on.

It was a beautiful family portrait. I wondered 'Who are they?'

Children are not supposed to ask question, I did not ask, but I felt Nana Sweetie's eyes on me, as I was transfixed on the photo. She gave me time to look at it and use my imagination. I could not imagine. 'Maybe it's a picture from a book of a far off family'

My young eyes were beholding all of Nana Sweetie's life possessions. There was no chest-of-draws, closet or storerooms where she could have had other possessions.

What I was looking at, were all she had.

Nana Sweetie's lack of abundance did not surprise me. I grew up in a house like this and had just about the same except we had a larger table and she had a vat and dogs.

The room with the smell of fried fish, tobacco and rose water was neat and clean.

Nana Sweetie fed me fish, provision, corn, ripe banana, washes them down with mauby.

Our friendship grew as we grew, with time.

I became her one and only visitor. "When you come tomarra, bring one comb fe me to comb you hair, dis house no 'av one for plenty years now. No need fe one" She took off her head tie to expose her baldhead. We held on to each other and dance in circle as we laughed to tears. She placed her arms around my shoulders and rests her head on mine.

She was gentler than everyone else, even my mother, when she combed my long, tangled mane. Every braid had a different color scrap-cloth ribbon, as if I was representing the United Nations, which we knew nothing about back then. Maybe someone saw my head and decided that the UN would look nice with those colors.

The softness of her touch always put me to sleep on her lap. She sat still while I slept. At times, she too slept sitting up on the chair, her hands on my head.

Whenever I went skinny dipping with my friends and had my school uniform thrown into the water by wicked children, she would iron my clothes with her flat iron, comb my hair and put salt water into my eyes to remove the redness – proof that I went swimming – She also fed me porridge every afternoon when I go to collect the empty saucepan. She said, "Never go to sleep wid a full belly ah food. The devil goin' sit pon you belly and eat the food he no work fa. You goin' be lazy ah manin and you goin' feel like somebody beat you all night" A valuable lesson, I still live by till today.

I never told Nana Sweetie anything about my troubled life. She had no way of knowing about me outside her fence and I was not going to have her worry about me.

Her home was my refuge and I was the daughter or granddaughter she wished for.

I took dried flower seeds and planted them into my yard, now I too have her flowers.

My mother and father knew of our friendship. They did not seem to mind.

When she asked about the marks and cuts on my body. I made excuses. Why should she know what the outside world has become?

"When you come on Sunday, me go show you sometin, me go gee you sometin"

Then one afternoon I found the milk still in the saucepan.

We had shared so much love and tenderness through this gate. Suddenly here I stood, shaking with fear. A fear no child soon to be fourteen years old should feel.

I looked into the yard and saw the two dogs lying by the door. They did not come to greet me like they did every day with Nana Sweetie.

Nana Sweetie met me at her gate every morning and afternoon for two years.

Today she is absent. Today I am afraid.

I ran home to fetch my father. "Daddy, I think something is wrong with Nana Sweetie. She did not take up her milk dis maning"

My father rushed out through the back gate, he said to me "You stay home. It is an order, do you hear me?" I heard him all right, but I followed him, making sure that I was at a distant where he could not connect if he pitches something at me. I disobeyed my father and did not even care of the consequence. I just wanted to know that my Nana meaning Grandmother was all right? 'Maybe she fell asleep and forget the milk?'

My daddy went into Nana Sweetie's hut. I watched and waited at the gate. The gate that still cries when opened because of lack of use. The gate where I first touch her hand and felt just skin and bones.

I watch my father come out of the house. His face was stiff and solemn. His hat was in his hand. He walked slowly to the gate. I stood there; he said, "Go home now. I have to go talk to some people in the village" Those were the gentlest words spoken to me by my father since I met him four years ago.

I was the only child among the adults who walked behind the donkey-drawn cart that carried my Nana Sweetie in a white pine box to her final resting place at Aklyne.

I cried all the way to the burial ground, carrying a bouquet of her flowers from my yard. I cried all the way home. My lost was too great. I found her all by myself. She was mine

With his arms around my shoulder, his second time holding me, my father said, "Her two sons were our friends. We grow up in this village, played ball and chase cows around here. She became strange after her husband and sons vanished in a fishing boat accident. That was many, many years ago, but she still refused to leave her home, fearing that they may come back and not find her waiting for them.

Once there was a big flood, Mother sent us with a boat to go bring her to our home.

When we went into her home, we found her standing on the small kitchen table.

We did our best to persuade her to come with us to dry land. She refused, saying that she would not want her husband to think that she has abundant him.

People in the village, especially people my age took care of her needs. I gave her rice throughout the years. Others give her fish, meat and other things that she needed outside her yard. She had a give-and-take custom. She put supplies from her yard into the basket hanging on the outside and people put whatever she needed, such as matches, soap, salt and sugar into the inside basket" My father came in front of me so that he could look into my swollen eyes. He continued, "I was told that you are the first and only person she opened her gate to since the disappearance of her family.

I am glad that she was able to cure her madness all by herself. There were times when no one could have passed anywhere near her yard. She would scream and shout from the top of her lungs. That is why till this day children are afraid of her.

I am glad you became her friend. I think the two of you were good for each other"

Some weeks later, I went to see if the flower seeds that I had sprinkled on Nana Sweetie's grave had grown? It was as if I was looking at one of her scrap work mats, spread over the mound of dirt. Every color of Daisy was swaying with the gentle breeze, just like she would have wanted it.

There was a whitewashed cross with black writing, stuck on the head of the mound.

Here Layeth the late
MATHELDA STEWART
Born October 10th. , 1853
Died August 21st. 1956
RIP

I cried after reading the words, I said out loud through my uncontrollable sobbing,

"Your name was Mathelda Stewart, but to me, you will always be my Nana Sweetie"

Nana Sweetie changed my life. I was fortunate to have laid my head on the lap of a 103 years old child of slaves who sang so sweetly in church, they named Sweetie.

She could not read nor write, had never gone to a doctor or dentist, yet she taught me so much about life, love, tenderness and when to be humble and when to trust.

From her also, I learned never to judge anyone by looks or what other may say.

From her I learned that if you eat off the earth, you could live to be 103 years old.

I could've missed the best few years of my life, the kindness, the gentleness, the honesty, the toothless laughter and stories of way back when, had I not braved the storm and taken the time to use my own eyes to look into her sad, lonely eyes.

I can only hope that in her last days, I was able to give her some of what she gave to me in what seems like a long time. I shall tell her story to my grandchildren, if I get.

I wish I had in my possession the portrait that hung on her wall, to show you my Nana Sweetie

I made one last visit to Nana Sweetie's gate. I felt an emptiness that I cannot describe. I opened the gate and let her two dogs follow me home.

I fed them and gave them lots of water. When they were finished gobbling and lapping, they ran to the back gate and waited. I opened the gate and they ran back to their home.

The next morning, when I opened the back gate, on my way to school, I saw Nana Sweetie's two dogs waddling their tails. They lived with me for the rest of their lives.

From as far as I could remember, I always had pets.

My first pet was a little kitten I found in the bushes. I named her – or was it him? –

Kafi Kandi. I do not know how I came by that name, but this 5-6 years old called her little fluffy kitten Kafi Kandi.

I remembered wrapping her in cloth and pretending that she was my baby.

She followed me everywhere. When I go to the main road to fetch water, she would be at my side. When I ate, she ate off my plate. Mommy and Buddy could not stand it.

On Sunday I was going with my mother to collect money. She began to follow me.

My mother said "Take her back to the house and close the door" I did not want her to be locked in, so I took a piece of rope, tied it around her neck and put her on the table and open the window. "Stay here, you can see me when I go and when I come back. Don't cry, Mommy would be right back"

You do not want to hear what happened. Till this day I remember the way my mother demanded that I sit on the bridge while she hurried to my hanging 'baby'.

"Oh Mommy, please, please do something. Dunk her in the trench. Remember they dat that to me? Now I am alive. Put a calabash over her and beat it like a drum – we did that whenever a chicken or duckling was sick and they would come out running – Please Mommy?

I was always allowed to have pets. Maybe they saw my need for something to talk to. At Port Mourtant, all the family had pets. Uncle Bertram's dog name was Teddy. Uncle James's was Jack. Aunt Mary-Jane had two cats name Fire and Brimstone.

At the end of 1956, my dearest, kindest, smartest, and most beautiful Phyllis died.

She contracted Rheumatic Fever. She was 20 years old.

Everyone wore black and white at her funeral at Aklyne burial ground, where she is buried next to Aunt Inez; I wore my hunter green crêpe dress with beige, embroidery.

You are becoming a big girl. At your age, I was already married".

She would pass her hand on my flat chest and say, "If you see anything strange happening to you, or, if you feel anything different happening to you, come to me right away" – that was the extent of the 'bird and the bees –

I never told my mother how hard I worked in my father's home.

If she saw that I was happy there, she too would be happy.

On Sundays she was happiest because all three of her children are enjoying her good cooking. In the largest enamel bowl, she put rice, dhal; curry vegetable, some lime achar and hot pepper. We sit in a circle. She mixed all the foods together with her fingers. One after the other, she fed us and herself, pushing the food into our mouths, using her thumb like a spoon. She says, "Good food should have some sweet, sour, bitter and hot. I mean very hot pepper, it clear your nostril and keep you regular".

She never mentioned her son, Dhia. It was as if he never existed. Externally.

"If dat man and woman work you too hard, come back home. Me na mek you for dem slave" If she only knew that from the time I wake up early in the morning, my day of chores starts. I had to take down the pozy-poty-bedpan, empty it in the latrine, wash and turn it down to dry. Open the fowl and duck pens, sweep the down and put it in a barrel for compose. Let the sheep and goats out of pens and out of the back gate to graze. Make sure that there is lots of water around the yard for the livestock. Clean and refill the lantern. Sweep the upstairs, downstairs and yard. Measure milk that Collins drew out of Janie, to customers and write in the book. Then I can have something to eat and get ready for school. Sometimes I have no time for tea. For breakfast, I would be going to my mother's for her good food.

In the afternoon after school, everything was in reverse gear. I went to my Mommy for dinner. Oh how I miss Nana Sweetie's portage - then go to my Cinderella's castle.

I had to take the posy back up. Put a bucket full of water in the sun to get warm for my father to bath. Collect the eggs, wash dishes, pen all the livestock. Sweep the yard again – She was obsess with cleanliness, only when I had to do it – Fetch water in a bucket on my head, from the pipe on the main road. Wet the plants and light the lamp.

Saturdays, was all mentioned, plus washing all the beddings and clothes on a plank of board, beating with a phitna – paddle. Polish the floor until I can see my tears. Go to the market and clean the fish. Pile firewood under the fireside for the week.

Collect milk-money and balance the book.

Like I told you, I did not care for her food, my stomach was full from my mother's.

I was practicing what Nana Sweetie told me. "It is better to go to sleep on an empty stomach" I drank a cup of warm milk sweetened with Janie's molasses every night.

"What about homework?" You might ask. I never had time at home for that.

After school, when all the children left, I stayed back in my class and do my homework. I leave it at my teacher's desk before going home.

There was an unwritten rule that when you submit your homework on your teacher's desk in the morning, you should always place yours under the ones that are already there. Mine was always on top – it was an exercise of honesty that I still see being practiced in government offices and doctors waiting rooms till today.

I still did my best to keep away from my father. I am asleep when he leaves in the morning. I pretend to be sleeping when he comes home in the evening.

The only time we made contact was when something was told to him and I had to get a whipping. Many times I never knew why? When I asked my stepmother "What do you tell my father to make him beat me last night?"

"Well, he ask me if you did all you work. Me have to tell him the truth"

"And what's your truth?"

"You ah come home late from school everyday. You ah go to you mother everyday.

On Sunday you go away all day and me have to do all you work around here. You na eat wha me cook and you hardly ah say ah word to me"

"Because me na speak to you, you mek my father beat me? Because me na eat you food, you mek me father beat me? Because me go to me mother house, you mek he beat me? Did you tell him that from the time I wake up in the morning until I go to bed at night, except going to school, I work like a slave, or is it 'like a stepchild'?

He is right here on Sundays. It is always after me finish all me work, then I go to my mother's to enjoy her good food and be with my brothers. What's wrong with that?"

I try to soften my remarks; "I go away to leave you and you husband alone"

I told you I had a whipping coming. More so for Just for talking back to her.

My father never saw all the chores I had every day. He left the home at 5am, rides his bicycle to Port Mourant sugar plantation, where he was the chief of the 'cane hoist',

After his bath and dinner the lantern blows out into darkness.

With my ear against the wall, I listen to the whispers. I wait. If I hear snoring I know that it is safe for me to go to sleep. If I hear his bedroom door open, I prepare myself.

You may be wondering 'why didn't you go back to your mother's'

Well, my father promised that when I finish primary school, he would pay for me to go to high school. My mother could not afford it, but she wants me to be 'some body'.

Here again, I sacrifice the present for 'hope' in the future.

I was working hard at school. Never late, never absent. I might be hungry from not having the time to have tea. You may see the black suet from the lampshade that I was called back to clean as I hurried off to school. Yet, I was never late nor absent.

Yes, I remembered one morning when I was called back to clean the lampshade, I was already out of the back gate, hurrying to get to school before the bell rang.

I weighed the consequences, 'be late or take a wiping? I was not late for school.

My yearly school report read, ***"Needs to work harder. Never late, never absent"***

My teachers at Manchester School were strict, with children's education in mind.

Children did not like detention because they had to explain why they came home late. You may end up with another wiping at home, for getting detention at school.

Like I said before, teachers and ministers were the most believable and respected.

Teachers were encouraged to whip and discipline children.

In those days we had dictation. Teacher would give us homework to read and study about five pages from our reading book. The next day, teacher would pick a passage from the five pages for dictation.

We were given many chances to get it right. We had it as homework. It was read out to us before writing. It was read to us to write and it was read once more for us to correct any mistake. For dictation, if you made mistakes, you get a wiping, and had to write the words spelt wrong so many times, that as long as you live, you would never spell that word wrong again. Only that didn't work for me.

Miss Erma Curlett and Mrs. George, her sister Mrs. Bowery were born and raised in Lancaster Village. There are many who made great contribution of different kinds to their county, society and individuals. I know many such people.

What I am trying to do right now – write – is to pay tribute to Miss Erma Curlett.

She taught me that a good listener is a good writer, or, is it a good writer has to be a good listener? Whichever way, she meant 'listen then write'.

Miss. Curlett was my English teacher. By the time I entered her class, she was already teaching for many years. She was unique in her method of teaching – in those days teachers were allowed to make their own curricula in the interest of good education – she made her own subjects, programs and activities.

One of her's was called 'Mental Comprehension'. She gave her class this assignment at 230pm, half an hour before the school bell rang. It went like this –

"OK class, books close, pencil down, sit up strait with your hands on the desk. Listen.

I left home this morning at 7am. About 715 I met Mama Tama at the Middle Walk Road. She was wearing a blue skirt, six inches below her knee, and a white blouse with gold buttons. She had no shoes on. She said that they hurt her bunion.

Five minutes later, on the Main Road, I saw about ten children walking on the wrong side of the road. I think they were avoiding me but I know who they are.

They were the two Cummings boys, the Henry boys, Fred, Sinclair, Urla, Olive, James and the Waldron twins, what are their names? - She was asking herself that question because we were not allowed to speak

— I also saw Hector and one of you sitting in this class today. I went to Ali's store, bought a lemonade for 5cents and a bun for a penny"

Miss Curlette continued her story. Playing with our minds, disturbing us at times.

While listening carefully, we had to make mental notes of her body language.

A pause was a coma, a short stop was a full stop, raising her eyebrows was a question mark. When she took a deep breath, it was a new paragraph.

When she felt that her story would be about a page long, like clockwork, the bell rang.

Linda, you should try it. Have someone read or tell you a long story, then go out to the field and work, make dinner, take care of your chores and then write the story told.

Imagine a young child listening to a long story like that, played with friends after school, do house chores and then try to remember what Miss Curlett said?

She is an unforgettable teacher. Devoted to her craft. Respected by all.

She produced some of the smartest and famous Guyanese, at home and abroad.

There are many writers, teachers and simple people like me who will never forget

Miss Erma Curlett and all the good teachers who are responsible for who they are.

With Mental Arithmetic, Dictation and Mental Comprehension, I was learning at Manchester School. Still the oldest in the classes, I was determined to be 'somebody' for my Mommy. I wanted to find 'hope' for me.

Miss Curlett was from my village; she knew that I was the 'reject' the 'ugly duckling' the 'raggedy ann.' of the village. She said to me one day as we walked home.

"Beauty alone passes through as people pass, but, good manners and character breeds beauty that stays in people's heart forever"

Early 1957, my stepmother's youngest daughter Mine, came to live with us.

She was my age. I gladly shared my room with her. She was beautiful, kind and detested the way I was being treated. She offered to help with some of the housework.

The outdoor dirty jobs were still mine to do everyday.

I joined the 4H club, a requirement from school, which was headed by Ms. Vesta Lowe. That privilege was given after Mine offered to some of my chores that one afternoon when I attend the class.

She questioned things like why was I wearing cheap cotton dresses while she wore better quality? Her mother told her "Her mother is poor, she can't afford better"

"But she don't live with her mother, she lives here with you and her father.

The same good quality you buy for me, you could buy for her? What you think the people around here are saying? That you are using her father money on your children while his child has to go walking and working around in cheap rags. Why the double standard? Why I have to be treated different from her while I am sharing her room and living in her father's house?"

Mine realized that it was always after her mother report 'whatever' to my father, that I get 'licks'. She asked her mother "If you know that he will beat her for every little thing you report to him, why do you tell him every little thing? Then the next morning you are rubbing her back with alcohol? Do you have to tell him everything?"

"If I don't tell him everything, he will think that I am not doing what he brought me here to do" answered her mother.

"He brought you here to report on his daughter?" she asked in disgust.

"No, he brought me here to take care of everything. He is the one who ask me every night 'wha she do today?' I have to tell him the truth" I felt sorry for her.

One of my projects at the 4H club was to learn to make slippers with Raffia-straw.

Mine gave me the money to buy supplies. – I got a wiping for asking her for money – When the slippers was finish, I brought it home and my stepmother ordered me to give it to Mine to wear in the house, because it was her money used to buy the straw.

Mine refused, she said, "It belongs to Wynette, she made it. Why should I wear it?"

"She is outside all the time, walking in all kind ah shit. She can't wear that"

My golden straw slippers, which Ms. Vesta Lowe complimented me for doing a wonderful job, remained on the window cell until it dry rotted.

David came to live with us around this time. I still feel that my father had something to do with his moving away from Port Mourant and insisted that he stayed at his house even though David wanted to go to my mother's.

I later found out that the Christinis' were transferred to another plantation and that there were other Overseers who wanted my brother to work for them but my father discouraged that notion. You see, his livestock's were growing bigger. He had lots of young calves that needed personal attention at the back dam. A job cut out for David.

My father brought his son David to the house, my stepmother brought her three years old grandson Chan to the house. The more the merrier. If he could have two of his own in the house, she too could have two.

My duties were all that I had to do plus take care of little Chan's every need.

One afternoon as I gather the flocks in the yard, I saw a little lamb in the trench. He was clinging to the parapet, water up to its neck. I took the sash from my waist, tied a muse around his neck and lying flat on my stomach, I pulled him out of the water.

I looked around for his mother. I listened for her cry for her baby. I saw or heard nothing, so, I took him home. My father ordered me to go around the villages, with the baby lamb in my arm, to find his mother or owner. I found none.

I think he was meant to be mine. He became my pet lamb 'Lammy'.

Lammy became my baby. My father did not object to me having a little sheep up in my room. Neither did Mine. He slept on the floor in his makeshift bed.

He listened to the radio. He loved music.

Every afternoon, he followed me to and from the main road, as I fetch water from the well. I think Lammy knew that he was different from the other sheep in the yard.

He refused to graze with them in the pasture. He ate rice and curry, roti and bread.

At first I thought Nana Sweetie's two dogs, I named Blackie and Brownie according to their color, would hurt the little baby lamb, but they just sniff him all over and ignored him. Lammy followed me everywhere. When I leave for school, he would bellow until I am out of his sight. When I return, you should see him dancing on his hind legs. Going up and down the wooden stairs like someone in high heels.

August 23rd 1957 my father had his 51st birthday party started. It was a Friday and it would be going on until Monday morning, when he leaves for work.

Everyone was there, I mean everyone who knew him, from the bus driver to the rice farmer. Everyone in the village was there. His special pals, Uncles Joe, Bang, Seecharan and Tigar were there from the day before.

We do not count family as guest. Family is family. Automatically they will be there.

Every kind of meat that my father reared was being cooked in large pots on makeshift fireside in the backyard. Uncle Bertram and Uncle Bhalo were in charge of the cooking – funny, women do all the cooking for their family. Men never cook at home, but when there is something big, like wedding or birthday, it's the same men who do not even go into their kitchen, cook all the food and make them taste so good –

It was at that grand occasion that I met one of the most handsome young man ever.

His name was Cecil Saul. He was a young schoolteacher who was visiting friends.

He was from the big City of Georgetown. He was surprised to know that one can go to a birthday party without being invited. "This will never happen in Georgetown" he said.

All the young girls had their eyes on him because he was so handsome. I did too.

He danced with all the girls while I watch and wondered 'would he ask me to dance?

He did, I told him that I do not know how to dance. He said, "Let me teach you. Just try to step on my foot as I move around"

"Where do you live?" he asked, trying to calm my nerves.

"I live here. Its my father's birthday"

"How come you don't know how to dance?"

"Because no one taught me how"

When the party was over in the wee hours of Saturday morning. I walked him across the slender bridge. On the road, he kissed my hand; he said, "Goodnight, could I come to see you tomorrow evening?" I could not answer. I just stood there nodding and feeling his saliva on my right hand dehydrating with the breeze. 'I need to kiss his saliva off my hand'.

The party started all over the next day. I told my step-mother that "The nice young man who is visiting from Town, would like to come to see me this evening'.

"What you mean 'come to visit you? To see what?"

She informed my father what I said. When the young man did not show up, my father say "You see what happens to girls who think that those strangers who come from the big city is 'Godsend'? Well, they just fishing in the ocean. You fall for a fisherman"

Early Monday morning, on my way to Sunday school, I stopped at Cousin Betsyann to see if the stranger, who was visiting with her son, was still there? I just wanted to see him again. I wanted to see if it was all a dream, or did he really dance with me and kiss my right hand? She said, "They left early dis morning to catch the first boat. Cecil went to your home last night. It was too dark and he fell into the water. He came back drenched in mud. I told him that he should have gone to see you, mud and all. Especially for your father to see that there are good young men all over.

These village people think that if someone comes from Town, he has to be a skimps"

My heart was broken. A prince came to my castle. He danced with me and kissed my hand. He looked at me as if I was somebody. He spoke to me as if I was smart.

He gave me a strange feeling that I never felt before. In a flash, he was gone.

Remember I told you that I was good with figures? Every week when I collect the 'milk money' I paid myself what I did not write in the book.

Every weekend I took that money to mother's teapot.

I was saving for when I finish high school, I will go to England to become a nurse.

'Hope' was all I had to live for.

My stepmother had another daughter, whenever she and her husband had problem, she would come to Lancaster with all six of her children, age ranging from ten years to six months old.

Many days there was no food left for David when he comes from the fields.

I began to bring food from my mother, hide it in his room and let him eat it in secrecy.

Otherwise you know I would get a beating and a lecture.

I tried several times to tell my father it is too much for me caring of so many children, chores, school and wondering what to feed my brother when he comes home?.

My father said that it was my mother who was making me lazy and trying to make problem in his home. He said "if she continue to tell you things to disrupt this house, I will stop you from going to her and you can kiss high school plans goodbye"

'Why is he so resentful towards my mother? She doesn't even mention him or his home on our visits' I wondered as I listened to his treats.

Oh, I forget to tell you this. Remember Charley Alexander? Clarabell and Malcome Alexander son? Mary-Jane and Sudith's baby brother? Well he got married to

Jule Gonzals. They had eight children. Wickliffe, Bibi, Sidney, Iris, Doris, Henry, Maude, and Desmond.

Uncle Charley was tall, yellow skin and very handsome. I was told that he was like a 'honey stick' that could not keep women away from him.

He also had seven other children with six different women. They were Isaac, Walter, Samuel, Elaine, James, Francis and Harold.

Did I tell you that he was one of the most handsome, charismatic men my young eyes ever saw? His charming smile stayed with me.

I remember seeing him and my grandmother sitting in her living room, holding hands and looking into each other's eyes with so much love.

I think seeing how Gramother and Uncle Charley express their love for each other, reinforced my love for my brothers.

He died February 14th. 1957. He was 62 years old.

1957 December, word got around that Gramother was sick.

Just like they did when Aunt Inez was sick, they ordered all the children to keep out of her room, only her children kept vigil over her as she lay in bed suffering from the same breathing problem as her father Archibald Hunter.

My father did not come home for days – by the way, even though he moved to Lancaster, he still kept his room at the logy – My stepmother sent me to Port Mourant on Friday afternoon. She said "Take the bus and go to Bound Yard and ask your father if he forget that he has a home here and that he has me here?"

I did as I was told. When I got to my grandmother's yard, it was beginning to get dark. – I liked that, because I was going to spend the night with my Aunt Elo, Uncle Bertram, my cousins, especially Barbara whom I missed terrible. –

I saw my father sitting under the Sankoka tree in the yard. His clothes were dirty. He needed a haircut and a shave. He looked strange. Even though I rarely had face-to-face contact with him, I knew that he looked strange.

"What are you doing here?" he asked, I looked into his swollen eyes and his sad face, this massager could not deliver. I said, "I come to see you and Gramother. You no come home for over a week, I miss you" – I lied but hope that what I said might soften him towards me - "I hear that Gramother is sick, can I go in to see her?" he looked at me again and suddenly I felt sorry for him. He was crying for his mother. He is so big and bad and mighty, yet here he is, like a little child, crying for his mother.

I realized that when it comes to a mother and a child, age does not count.

"Your gramother can't speak" were the kindest words I got from my father.

"Please Daddy, I just want to see her"

The room was full with Aunties and Uncles. The smell of disinfectant overpowers her Yardley's powder.

When my father walked me into the room, everyone looked at him with knitted brows, as if to say 'why are you bringing a child in here? They cleared the path as he pushed me through.

My grandmother was lying in a semi-sitting position. She was panting for breath. Her eyes were closed and her mouth was wide open.

"Mother, look who come to see you? Open your eyes Mother" My father's voice was trembling as he spoke to his mother.

My grandmother opened her eyes. Through the cloud of death, I saw those

Blue-green eyes looking at me.

"Take a spoonful of water from the glass and put it into her mouth" whispered my father, with his hands still on my shoulders.

'Why is he so gentle with me? Is it because he realize that he is about to loose the only woman he ever loved? Or is it the other way? He is loosing the only woman who ever truly loved him?' my thoughts as I leave the room.

Mary-Jane Hunter Alexander-Janie-Mother-Gramother died Saturday 19th December 1957. Ten months after her baby-brother Charlie. She was 81 years old.

The lady, from whom I learn how to hold a family close together. The little girl from Monstraat who waited for years, for her Daddy to come to her. The lady who married Egbert Alexander and had ten children. Her blue eyes made me think she sees everything blue. The lady, who will stay in my heart for as long as I live, was no more.

The house and yard in Bound Yard, the church and yard at Aklyne were overflowing with people of all walks of life and races.

It was her wish to be buried as soon as she passed, also 'not a piece of concrete over my grave to keep me down – no bomb'.

I remember standing in the burial-ground watching people crying and singing hymns, many of whom I never met nor knew.

My father sat on the ground next to the hole. Unshaven with clean clothes on.

I saw my mother pushed her way through the crowd and placed her hand on my father's head. He looked up and saw her. He wrapped his two arms around her legs and buried his head on them. My mother kept her hand on her husband's head.

The curious crowd, for a while, forgot that they were there for a funeral.

As soon as my father let go of my mother's legs, she disappeared.

My father went back to Port Mourant after his mother's funeral.

He stayed there for forty days before he returned to Lancaster.

That Christmas, while my father mourned his mother's death, I received my first mail, ever, from a postman.

Yes the Postman came to the gate and said, "Mail for Wynette Alexander"

I ran to collect a large white envelope. I looked at the stamp; I looked at my name and address written in longhand. I have never seen my name and address written like this on an envelope before.

I had no idea whom it was from, but I knew that someone out there think I am special to send me something and to spell my name correctly – I was the only person known to have my name 'Wynette'.- For many years I checked even the phone book for another Wynette. Only my family pronounced my name properly 'Wyn-ette'

Others called me, Lynette, Gynette, Yanette, Winnie, Whynet and anything close to, but not Wynette.-

The sender of this mail had it right to the 'e'. It read, with the nicest handwriting.

Wynette Alexander
    Lancaster Village
      Corentyne
        Berbice.

I do not think we used senders name and addresses in those days. Even if they did, I would not know to look for that. Remember, this is my first mail ever.

"Bring it here, let Mine read it" said my stepmother.

"No, why should she give me her letter? Her name is on it, she should open it"

My sweaty hands were wetting the envelope. I went up to my room and open my mail.

I found two cards, one wishing me 'Merry Christmas' and the other wishing me

'Happy Birthday' and, a photo of the boy from Town who danced with me and kissed my right hand. The boy who fell off the slender bridge, into the muddy water, trying to keep his promise to me, he even remembers that my birthday was in December.

The writing at the back of the photo read: - 'To Wynette from your friend Cecil'

I kept that picture so close to my heart. I slept with it on my chest. I kept it in my schoolbook at school. I showed it to everyone who would spare the time to look at it.

"Dat handsome boy is your boyfriend?"

"Go-dha-side, you cutout a picture from a magazine and get someone to write"

"Wha you could meet such a nice boy? Not at the market or the well?"

I kept that picture for as long as I could remember. It had dog-ears all around.

It faded and lost its feature from my wet lips and sleeping hands.

My father kept his promise. I was enrolled at Hose Hall High School 1959.

My mother was so proud, I remember her showing me off to all the neighbors at Liverpool, saying "Look at my Babzie, she go be a nurse when she go to England"

Mine offered to help with the cooking. They bought two-burner kerosene stove for her to cook on. I was not allowed to use it. I didn't even know how to light it.

Whenever I had to cook, I had to light up the fireside.

That same year my father bought a tractor and expanded his rice production and livestock. Uncle Bertram, Collins, and my father operated the tractor.

Remember the long, slender bridge that led from the road to the 'big house' and my 'Cinderella's' house? Well, Uncle Bertram and some hired hands and the tractor and trailer, fill that whole big body of water with red sand from several sand-hills in the area. The bridge was no more. Now there was lots of land for others to build homes.

My mother took me to Port Mourant Hospital to see Dr Sharples. I asked her

"Mommy why are we going to the doctor? Are you sick?"

"No, I am not sick, but I think you are. Look at you, you are a big girl and your chest is as flat as the floor. Every time I ask if anything strange is happening to you, which should be happening, you say no. I want the doctor to check to see if something is shamefully wrong with you. A tree can't fruit without blossom"

I remember the tall; Englishman dressed in white and was gentle with me.

He asked me to sit on the dressing table. He sat on a chair with wheels. He said,

"Do you eat well?"

"Yes Doctor, my mother is the best cook"

"Is there anything bothering you or hurting you?"

"No Doctor" I lied because I knew he could not cure what was hurting me.

He asked me to lie on the bed. He passed his hands on the two hard little lumps on my chest and asked, "Does it hurt? Sure, I know that they hurt. It is normal.

He pressed on my stomach, sounded my chest and back and said, "You are fine, I do not know what your mother is worried about. Some flowers bloom early, others later"

I got my second mail from the postman after looking for him all year and asking him everyday if he has anything for me and he would answer,

"When I get something for you, you would be the first to know"

Uncle Bertram built a house on the front lot of the land at Lancaster.

They moved there in 1959.

I now had my Uncle and Auntie to look over me, and Barbara to join the bus and go to the same school with me.

My Aunt Elo. Made uniforms for us. She made sure that I was properly dressed and that I have all my school supplies. She prepared meals for Barbara and I to take to school.

Before she moved to Lancaster, my mother wrapped roti and boil egg or vegetable in plantain leaf then brown paper and send it with Datson to meet me before the bus comes. Many days my friend Watty from Bloomfield Village, who always had money to spend because they had a shop, they were rich, would take me to Harris ice cream

Parlor and treat me to goodies that I could not afford to buy.

In school one day, I asked to be excused during class because I was not feeling well. As I got up and walked out of the classroom, I heard laughter from the students.

My female teacher caught up with me on my way to the toilet and said,

"Big girl like you don't know that you have to protect yourself properly?"

"I do not understand what you mean, Miss"

"Didn't you know that your period came down?"

When I saw the blood, I was afraid. I screamed so loud and began to cry. I told the teacher that I have cancer in my belly just like my Aunt Inez.

Sitting in the back of the bus, all wet and bloody, I became so angry that no one told me anything about this. Is this why my mother keep asking me if anything is happening to me? Passing her hand all over my body? That I should go to her as soon as something strange happens to me. She never said what or where.

I went to my mother. While I was crying with shame and fear, she was ecstatic,

"Ohm Bhwan, thank You for giving me my daughter" this confused child was then told the 'facts of life' by my mother, based on her knowledge.

She taught me how to tie a string around my waist, just like her mother did to her.

"People must not see anything bulky. It must always be neat and flat. It is not something to showoff, it is unclean and you have to treat yourself as such.

Wash your napkin clean and dry them at the back, away from anyone seeing them"

My mother put her arms around me and said, "Babzy, listen to me carefully. You have now become a 'young lady'. That means that if you allow a boy to come close to you or touch you down there, you will get a baby. Don't make dat happen. Wait till you meet you match and get married. I must warn you, never, never marry an Indian boy.

No matter how much he wants to marry you. Never agree to marry him.

I am an Indian, and I am telling my only daughter to never get close to an Indian boy.

I am saving you from a sure death. He might love you but his family will kill you.

An Indian woman can stray and marry out of her caste. The family will outcaste and disown her, and that would be that. But, when an Indian man marries out of his caste, or even worst, a Black woman. They never disown that man; instead they get rid of the woman and her children. An Indian man is much more important to his family.

My father and one his best friend made a match for his son and Mine.

They got engaged and as the wedding was being planned, I was told that I have to move in with David because Mine needed to have a room of her own.

Despite Mine's protest, saying, "Why should she move out of her room? I am only engaged. I have no intention of taking her room for myself, or to be here alone.

You people may not care for other people's feelings, or what other people say, but I do"

I remember making my bed on the floor of David's room. Sometime in the night I felt my brother trying to lift me off the floor and took me to his bed.

As I snuggled next to him on his single bed, I felt my brother's stomach contract and expand as he held me tighter and tighter and cried in silence.

Mine did her best to make me feel better. What she did not know, was that it did not bother me. As a matter of fact, it was better for me. I did not hear the whispers next-door and I was not taken out of David's room to be beaten.

"Wynette, I want you to be my bride's maid. I will make your dress and buy your shoes. You are my sister, you should be by my side when I get married"

She made my dress all right, a beautiful cream lace dress with satin petticoat.

In her room, we would get dress and practice our walk and smiles. We even practiced how we would cry for the crowd when we throw the rice on her and her husband.

We would lie on her bed and talked for as long as my father was absent.

She told me that she is my sister – we remained sisters until today – and that "one day that boy from Town who sends you cards every Christmas? Would come and take you away from here – She too gave me 'hope'

The week of Mine's wedding was no different from the usual wedding that goes for a week or more. It was the elaborate preparation for the grand occasion that stunned both Mine and I.

My father and her mother were beside themselves. The cooking, dancing, singing and drinking went on every night.

The day of the wedding, as Mine got dressed, so did I. Her sister helped her while I dress myself. She looked at me and said, "You look beautiful. I will comb your hair up and put the rose on top" I looked at her and said, "You are the beautifulest bride me ever see" We hugged each other and cried. I knew that I love her and she is leaving me.

My stepmother entered the room and saw me all dressed up. She did not even look at her daughter who was the bride. She said, "What are you doing in here? Where do you think you are going all dressed up like this?"

"She is going with me. She is my bride's maid. You know that all along?" said Mine, whipping her tears.

"No, no, no, no, we decided that Joy would be your bride's maid. She is better suitable for such an important occasion. She would be here soon"

Mine held on to my ridged shoulder and cried, putting snots on my lace dress.

I took off my lace dress and satin petticoat and placed them next to the brown paper bag with the rice that I was going to throw on the bride and groom after the wedding.

I pushed my way through the crowd, down the stairs, out the back yard and sat under a tree in the pasture. I did not cry. I suppose I expected that to happen. With all of Mine's genuine intention, I knew it would not happen. I did not see Mine and her maid left.

'Oh how I wish if Nana Sweetie was here'.

I went to my mother's for the rest of the celebration. The household said that I was jealous; that I could not stand the fact that Mine got married and I never would.

To this day, after 50 years of marriage and 8 children, many grands and greatgrands Mine and I still share the same love. We get on the phone and talk for hours. She is the only person I can speak to about my days in the 'castle'. She is the best 'Step-sister' one could ever have.

I still took my share of the milk money to my mother's teapot. She knew it was my England passage. "I will become a nurse. I will make you, Betose and Davo proud"

After Mine left, my room was given to her sister and six children.

David did not mind sharing his bed with me, and his space with Lammy, my pet lamb.

Janie was producing less and less milk. She was old and my father decided to retire her. He ordered that she not be milked anymore.

We got milk from his other cows. I missed Janie's milk, I would go into her pen, wash her nipples, lie on my back and suck in her rich milk. Remembering my Mommy's.

Many butchers offered to buy her but my father refused to sell his Janie.

My father and I kept Janie comfortable until her last day. We buried her in the backyard.

One evening as I fetch water from the well, a young man walked up to me, greeted me and asked about Lammy who was always by my side, every trip I made.

"What is big girl like you doing with a pet sheep? You need a boyfriend" I ignored him and went on fetching the bucket of water on my head.

I remember hearing talks that the Postman who live across the road, had a young, handsome visitor from Town, who was 'hustling' all the young girls in the village.

The next evening, he approached me again. He said, "Hello again, my dear. I asked my cousin about you because I am interested in you" with his perfect city English.

"He told me that you do not have a boyfriend but you are walking around with a picture from a magazine, telling people that he is your boyfriend. I think you need a real man.

I am available right now" He was in his mid-twenty, muscular and good-looking.

He continues to come to the well to talk to me. I kept walking away without being rude. He said, "I have been watching you ever since I arrived here. What you people do for fun around here? There are no nightclubs, no bars, nothing. How do I get some fun?

Would you like to take a walk with me tonight? Without your sheep?"

"No thank you, I do not go for walks at night"

Two days later, the gossip started. It turned my innocent world into one of the most shameful and helpless period that I will never forget, as long as I live.

The Casanova, the creep, the devil, the stranger from town, the scum of the earth, the scamp told his cousin, the postman, that he met me at the well the night before and took me into the bushes and did to me what I needed.

The postman mentioned what his cousin told him to one person as he delivered mail. The whole village was informed before his delivery was finished.

No bell or conch shell was needed to spread the news. Everyone in my little village, except me, knew that I was not as innocent as I pretended to be. That I preferred the lewd behavior of a 'town man' rather than keep myself for the right time, my wedding night for my chosen village groom.

I told you my whole world turned up side down. I kept asking myself "Why"

My father looked at me with scorn. He said I have disgraced him and his family.

He said he could not stand being in the same room with me.

My stepmother said, "tell me if your period don't come at the end of the month. I will have to take you to Mama Corte for some of her brew. This house is full as it is, I do not want another baby around here"

My friends at school, in church, on the street, all refused to speak to me.

I tried to find one person, just one besides my mother, to believe me. To see that man was lying. They believed a stranger rather than me. That hurt.

My mother went to him to ask him to stop spreading such lies about me.

He laughed at her and asked her "What are you going to do about it?"

I went to my Aunt Elo, I begged her to take me to the doctor, just to prove that I am telling the truth. She said, "Wynette, I believe you my child, but I cannot stop the people from talking. You know how it is in the village.

"Aunt Elo, I wish my Uncle Bertram was here – he was a sugar boiler who went to other countries to work for six months of the year – he would have believed me and he would have gone over to that lyre and choke the truth out of him"

I was astroziied. I was hurting so bad. I was screaming in a dream.

"Aunt Elo, you said that you believe me. Could you stand by the door and watch me walk across the road and try to bring that man to tell you that he is lying?"

"OK, go on"

I entered the postman's yard. The 'thing' was doing press-up on the landing.

He had a wide, wicked smirk on his face as he stood up to face me. He said

"I was wondering how long it would take before you come for some of this"

Holding his crouch.

"Why are you doing this to me? Why are you spreading such lies about me?

Do you know how much your lies are hurting me? Would you please go to my aunt and tell her that what you said is not true? Please, my whole world is turning up side down"

"I would like to turn you upside-down and give you some good loving. Show you what good loving is all about, but you are just one dumb country broad who is waiting for some weak-back village boy to marry you" he continued his press-ups.

I was shaking with anger. How could someone be so mean and bold?

'Why Dear God? Why?'

I began to think of a way to eliminate this creature from my not so perfect world.

'Maybe my brothers would put him in a bag and throw him into the deep canal'

He broke my thought by saying, "You are one saucy little thing. A fascinating mammal with those two little hard titties pushing out. Oh, how I want to suck on them" he was licking his lips and pulling in his drool, making a sucking sound. "Why don't you come to the dance with me on Saturday night? Give me a chance to show you passion. Stimulate you with some slow grooving, then take you to a green grass bed, jack you up and show you what this sweet city stud can do? I promise you that the next time you come into this yard, you would be begging me for more"

I was looking at a creature. For the first time in my youthful life, I was looking into the eyes of the devil. I saw fire in his eyes, a horn on the center of his forehead. He had long, sharp teeth, long nails, long stringy hair and green slime oozing from his mouth.

I was hallucinating. 'Please, someone give me a rag doll looking like this 'thigh' and the longest hat pin you can find'.

I felt my Aunt's arms wrapped tightly around me, she said, looking at him with disgust "You should thank God that my husband, her uncle is not here"

As she pushed me across the road I said, "Dear God, please forgive me, I did not know You made that kind too"

Nana Sweetie once told me "If anyone hut you so bad that you want to die?

Don't die, get a piece of brown paper, write the person name with your tears, or, let your tears drop on it while you think of the person who hurt you. Do .... with it"

It was a terrible period of my life. Not only in my home circle but everywhere I turned, people looked at me as if I was 'damaged goods'. They used shameful words and even spit on me. Just like the Indians did to my mother.

The boys at Sunday school, who used to walk me home, stayed clear of me.

Even David asked if what he was told is true?

I walked with my head down and prayed that my 'boy friend' never hear of this.

With so many people living in our house, money got missing regularly.

As always, David and I would be blamed and punished for it.

I remember one time my father received his estate bonus. He gave it to my stepmother to put away. I was told that she had visitors while I was at school and David was in the fields with the cows.

By the time my father came home that evening, his bonus was gone and David and I were accused of taking it.

I got a wiping and was told that if I do not go and bring his money back, it would be the end of high school for me.

My father sat on the steps and waited for David to come home. As soon as my brother got close to the step, my father stood up and slapped him so hard, he shattered my brother's specktickles on his face.

To this day, my dumb, deft and blind brother David ask 'what happened that day?'

Just like he and Datson always asking me what happened that night when Dhia beat them to a pulp?

David went away to my mother. I wish I could too, but I had to go to school and my father paid the school fees and bus fear.

I miss my brother so much. I miss sitting in the dark on his bed, talking with our hands and laughing in silence.

When my father asked me in the nicest way ever, to go bring David back, with the promise that he would never hit him again. I went and bring my brother, my only family in the home, my bed companion, back, against my mother wishes. I promised her that I would make sure that my father kept his promise.

'I could not protect myself, how could I protect my brother' my thoughts

Whenever Uncle Bertram was at home, life was good to me. I had him too along with his wife to look over David and me.

Whenever there was a dance, bazaar sports or any kind of activities where young people gathered, he saw to it that I went along with his children.

Uncle Isaac, one of Uncle Charlie's son, who lived at Manchester and had two daughters Elane and Lorna, would come with them to pick up all the young ladies from our yard and escort us to a dance or party.

When going to the dance, he would walk infront of us. At the dance, we were not allowed to dance with one boy too frequently. If the boys offered to buy us anything, including beers at intermission, we must not refuse, we had to take them all to him.

He drank the beers and we drank the 'sweetdrink'.

He kept a watchful eye on all of us. When the boys think that they were far away from him and would try to hold one of us closer. Uncle Isaac would tap him on the shoulder and shake his hear from side to side. The boy would have to release his grip or that would be the last time he danced with any of the Alexander girls.

We danced to songs from the Drifters, Platters, Let it be me, 16 candles, Duke of Earl, In the still of the night, For your love, Care sa ra sa ra, Don't be cool and oldies.

When going home, which was always before 'God save our gracious Queen' the closing tune, Uncle Isaac would walk behind us, holding his walking stick and flashlight, just incase some boys wanted to walk with us, they stayed at arms length.

He had a love-hate relationship with some of the young men of the village.

They love him when he brings all the girls to the dance. They hate him when he takes us away too soon, and for being so strict.

Remember I told you about Black Bush Polder? The forest that was being cleared for people to inhabit? Well Datson took a job with a gang of men, clearing bushes.

One day, a member of the gang killed a very venomous snake. They sound the alarm to be on the look out because such snake moved in pairs and if one is killed, the other will come after you. Everyone was on the lookout as they worked, but my brother did not hear the warning. He just continued working. The snake bit him.

The men heard him screamed out and went to his aid. They saw him cut his hand with his cutlass and were sucking out the venom. They helped to tie his upper arm and send a message to the Overseer to come with a speedboat to take my brother out of the forest and to the hospital.

When word got around fast. My father was the first to reach the hospital.

The doctor said, had my brother not done what he did, cut his arm and suck out the poison, he would have been dead within minutes of the bite. He asked my father,

"Where did he learn to save himself like that? He cannot hear nor talk?"

"I do not know Doc., maybe God gave him something, afterall"

Datson survived the snakebite but was never the same again. He became even quieter, but when angry, he became very violent.

In the 1960s, two good friends, brilliant scholars, who attended the same schools at home and abroad, became brilliant doctor and lawyer, they decided to fight the Colonial for independence. Which later turned Guyana into a race divided country till today.

It was the struggle for power that caused these two friends, who were Godparents for each other's children, to suddenly realized that they were different. One was Black and the other was Indian.

While Chaddi Jagan, an Indian, and Forbs Burnham, an African, were struggling for freedom from England, they were Guyanese chained together for the same cause.

But only one can be Prime Minister. Which one? That question caused a race riot that took many lives. Cities destroyed by fire, looting, strikes, bombs everywhere.

Blacks and Indians were killing each other. One could not enter the other village and come out alive, and, since Guyana's population was mostly Indian and Blacks of almost same proportion, everyone was affected.

It did not matter what one's political belief was or whom you were going to vote for. If you are an Indian, you are a Jagannite. If you are Black, you are a Burnhamite.

If you are mixed like me, you were neither nite nor mite. You would be in more danger because you will get it from both sides. You had no place to hide.

Blacks and Indians who lived in union for their whole life, were now killing each other.

The Alexanders from Port Mourant, who was few, but lived for years among Indian people, had to run to Lancaster Village, leaving their homes and everything behind.

Uncles James and Percy, Aunt Mary and their family, were lucky to escape alive and later sold their homes to Indian neighbors for little or nothing.

Aunt Lizy and her family were not that lucky. While they were sleeping in their bed at Tain Settlement, their home went up in flames. It was their Indian neighbors who came to their rescue and shelter them into their home, risking their own safety as sympathizers, until the next morning when police escorted them to a safer village.

Uncle Bertram's home, the 'big house' and my daddy's became the refuge camp for all the fleeing family. They made large tents and cook in bulk for all the family.

Both races did lots horrific things against each other. The Blacks and Indians were stopping cars and buses that had to drive through their villages. If there were Blacks at an Indian checkpoint, they would be punished. Likewise, if there were Indians at the Black checkpoint, they would be punished.

It was a terrible time for British Guiana. The bombing, looting, fires and killings.

Both leaders used the radio to plea with their supporters to stop the violence.

They made references that "We meet and greet each other at meetings and gatherings, but we don't kill each other. We are two friends fighting for the good of our country" That did not stop the hate and divide. Or should I say 'divide to conquer – to win?'

My father had to send my stepmother and her family to Tain to their Indian family because the Blacks in the village said, "If they don't want Blacks in their settlement, we don't want Indians in our village. Archie, get rid of them or you will get what Lizy got"

It was a terrible time. It was tit for tat and everyone was afraid to trust anyone.

We learned that the Indian leader, upon hearing of the burning of an Alexander's home, sent strict warning to his organizers at Port Mourant. He told them that he was born and raised at Port Mourant. He played and swam with those Black people. They are his friends and he is their friend. Do not harm any of them. Leave them alone.

It came too late for Mr. Ross, and for Aunt Lizy's home, but not one more Alexander was harassed or hurt for years of hell between Indians and Blacks.

My father and his brother James rode their bicycles through Tain, now all Indians settlement, with no problem. No one ever said or did anything to them.

Britain sent in its troops and war equipments to stop the violence and to protect its subjects and interests. They put a curfew from sundown to sunup. Anyone seen out of the house during curfew time risked being shot, unless you are a doctor, nurse or police, in which case, you would be wearing a bright yellow badge back and front.

My stepmother, her grandson, her daughter, and her six children returned.

Uncles James and Percy built their homes at Lancaster, thus making the 'Alexander's Compound', with many large houses built on their land.

There were more girls for Uncle Isaac to escort to the dance.

Early 1962, my mother asked me to accompany her to New Amsterdam. She said,

"Babzy, me hear dat me buddy son Pday come back from England. Me help to mine him when he was small. Me hear he ah doctor at the New Amsterdam hospital.

I asked my father's permission. This is my year for graduating from high school. I was not going to allow anything to give him a reason to take my 'hope' away.

I think since David walked away from him, and he had to ask me to go bring him back. Datson bitten by snake and the racial riots, he became mellower.

I did all my chores, ofcourse, before joining my mother for the bus.

On my first trip and I think her's too, to the big city. She told me stories of her life. She asked me to forgive her for not being strong enough to talk me about coming of age.

My mother gave me a lesson on forgiveness. She said,

"Babzy, I know how much it hurt you when that man from town told those lies about you. I know what people are saying about you. It is hurting me too.

I go to my alter every day and pray for him. Not in a bad way, I cannot go to God with bad things in my prayer. I ask God to give you strength to forgive him and everyone who hurt you. You have a lot of forgiving to do. If you forgive each one as it happens, you free yourself from the burden of hate. Hate is a heavy weight. It follows you everywhere. It pulls you down and sinks you in despair. It appears on your face like a mask. Hate is God's enemy.

When you forgive someone, you are not doing it for that person, who hurt you,

You are doing it for you. You are freeing yourself. You are lightening yourself.

You are the victor when you forgive" Mr. Reed told me the same thing.

We got to the hospital and my mother told the gateman that she came to see her son Dr. Pday. The man came out of his watch-house and walked us to the doctor's office.

I watched as my mother and her nephew held on to each other, hugging, kissing and speaking in Hindi. She was laughing from ear to ear. He put her to sit in his chair and stood close to her. He was the second member of her family I ever met. The first was her baby brother Lunjbeharry.

My mother was so happy; she did not let go of her nephew's hand and he did not take his other hand from her shoulder. I think she forget that I was in the room.

"Phoha – Auntie – father sister – I am so happy to see you, and who is this young lady?" he turned to me and said, "Please forgive me, I am so happy to see my aunt, I forget my manners"

"Dis a me daughter Babzy. She ah go ah high school. She go come ah nurse soon"

My mother was experiencing shortness of breath from the excitement. Especially the honor bestowed upon her by her 'doctor' nephew. Knowing how the others spit on her. Knowing how her brother forbids the other family members not to walk on the same side of the street as she.

He removed his stetscope from around his neck and began to sound her chest and back. He looked worried but did not let her see it. He said, "Phoah, I am going to arrange for you and Babzy to spend the night here. I need to give you a thorough checkup. Remember I am the doctor and you are my auntie" he smiled and left the office.

My mother and I stayed in a private room at the hospital. Nurses and Dr. Pday came in frequently to check on her.

"What is the matter with this boy? I just come to see him, not to spend the night with him. I am not sick. Why am I staying in a hospital?" she asked. I had no answer.

I was enjoying the good food, the large building, and all the modern hospital equipments. The smell of jays' fluid that clean the floors and bathroom and the neatness of the hospital staff was a learning experience for me.

I especially enjoy watching the nurses who were dressed in all white with caps. I wanted to say to them, "I am going to England soon to become a nurse like you"

My mother and I talked about when I become a nurse in England; I must come back home to take care of the people here and especially she and my two brothers.

The next day, Dr. Pday gave my mother some pills and some money, he said

"Take one of these pill everyday. Come back and see me anytime, very soon"

"Nothing na wrang wid me. I am as strong as a mule. Wha the pills fa?"

"Even mules have to be given pills sometimes Puhwa"

Datson and my mother worked in the garden, being proud of all their produce.

There was an agricultural fair where people took their animals and produce to be judged. My mother and brother got first place for producing the largest pumpkin.

Their picture was in the newspaper. It's the only picture I have of Mommy and Datson.

At that same fair, I had to bake English scones. Miss Vesta Loe, the 4H leader, gave the receipt to us. I tried to follow all the direction, but with lack of ingredients and proper baking equipment, my scones came out like 'doe boy'

I went over to meet my friend Noreen for us to take the bus together to the fair at Port Mourant estate. Her mother, Cousin Stela, took one look at my exhibit and said,

"Come here choil, let me see your scones" She looked at the six things I had.

Cousin Stella wrapped the other six scones from her from daughter's batch and gave it to me to take to the exhibition. She was one of my surrogate mothers.

Both Noreen and I received green ribbons for our scones.

Saturday May 19th I was fetching water to wash everyone's dirty clothes.

Auntie Finny, my mother's neighbor, came in a rush. She told me that her husband and son had just taken my mother to the hospital that she was on her way there.

I dropped the bucket, water and all, asked Aunt Elo for a shilling. I chase Lammy home, hopped into a bus and went to the Port Mourant hospital.

Mommy saw I was crying when I got there. She said, "Babzy, why are you crying?

Nothing wrong with me. I didn't feel well this morning, Auntie Finny think I should come to the hospital. But I am OK. Look at me; do I look like a sick person?

After examining my mother, the doctor informed us that he has admitted her for an overnight observation. 'Just like her nephew did' I thought.

I walked with her to the female ward. I helped her dress into the hospital gown.

Get a glass of water for her dentures; encouraging her to lie down, she kept protesting, she did not want to stay there. She wanted to go home, she said, "Who will take care of Betose, the garden and everything that has to be taken care of?"

"I will, Mommy. I will take care of my brother and everything else. Just do as the doctor say, so you could get better to come home"

"Better? Better from what? I am fine, nothing is wrong with me"

I sat at my mother's bedside, holding her hands, playing with her fingers. Looking at the wedding ring on her finger. The ring that never left her finger. Her joint has become so big, she was never afraid of it slipping off her finger.

I played with her long, black hair. She did not have one single gray hair on her head.

We talked and laughed for hours, until it was time for visitors to leave the hospital.

You know when the nurse began to ring the large brass bell, its time to leave.

"Mommy, I am going to send a message to Buddy that you are in the hospital"

My mother become so agitated that the nurse had to come to quiet her down. She said,

"Do not send any message to my son. I have not seen him in years. I will not remember what he looks like. He does not know what me look like. I do not want him to come here and look at me and wonder if it is me, or somebody else? No Babzy, do not bother my son" she grabbed my hand, opened her eyes wide, and breathlessly said,

"Do you hear me? Do not bother my son" I promised and tried to clam her down.

Before I left, my mother said, "You know I would not eat anything from here. Tomorrow, bring me some dhal and rice with fried sijan bagie. Cook them in my pot. Make enough for Betose, Davo and you too" she held my hand. Her hands were cold. She said, "Babzy, one last thing, take the bus and go, she gave me the direction to her sister's home – tell her who you are, tell her I am in the hospital, I like to see her"

I did as my mother asked. The lady chased me off her bridge, saying "Go away from here before my husband and neighbors see you here"

I got home as my father got home. I told him that my mother was in the hospital.

My father dropped his bag and carrier-dish on the bench, took his bicycle and rode out.

My stepmother did not like the idea that my father was going to the hospital to see my mother. I reminded her that my mother was my father's wife. She did not like that.

Very Early next morning, my father woke me, saying "Come, we have to go to Liverpool. I have to cook some food for my wife" Was I hearing right?

I show my father my mother's pots and spools. I picked the syjan bagie and my father, who I never saw go anywhere near a fireside to heat some water, was cooking a three-course meal for his wife.

Datson, David and I took the bus to Port Mourant hospital to see our mother.

My mother's enamel bowl with the hot food was in a basket on my lap.

Sundays were all day visiting at the hospital. We got there early and had all day to visit.

My mother was sitting up on the bed with her two feet dangling on the side.

She gave us her charming smile, showing her gold cap and long black hair to her knees.

I allowed her sons to greet her first. They were warning her not to work so hard, that when she goes home, she will not do anything but stay in bed. Datson said he would cook and take care of everything. My mother's laughter brought water to her eyes.

When they left to go explore the large building, I sat next to my mother and handed her the basket with the food in it.

"Daddy cooked it himself" she began to laugh again, this time with disbelief.

"No, why are you lying to me?"

"No, Mommy I am not lying to you. Daddy woke me this morning, we went to your house, I showed him your pots and spoons. He cooked this food for you"

"You mean Miky cook food for me? When he came here last night, he asked me what I wanted? I told him that I want food from my home cooked in my pots.

I never expect him to go there and cook food for me" she looked at me and asked

"Was everything neat and clean when he went there?"

We talked and laughed. She put her left hand on my lap and asked me to take the ring from her finger, she said, "I want you to put this ring on your finger, never, never take it off until I come home. No matter who ask you for it, do not give this ring to anyone. Do you hear me?"

"Yes Mommy, I hear you, but if Daddy wants it, I will have to give it to him"

"No, he will not ask you for my ring. You are my only daughter. You keep it.

When you go back to the house, look under the table, I have all my gold and silver jewelry tied in a sack and nailed to the table. Take them from there and keep them in a safe place. They are for you and your two brothers" my mother was speaking strange.

I asked her "Mommy why are you talking like that? You know that when you come home you will take care of everything"

"I know that, but we are just talking. I want you to promise me that if anything happen to me, you will take good care of your two brothers. The three of you are all I have. The two of them are all you have. Be their ears and mouth just like you have been to them all your life. God never put more weight on our shoulder than we can carry"

She looked at me with tenderness in her eyes, hand on my shoulder, she said.

"You will be blessed with children, never choose for them, especially your sons

Let them choose for themselves. You will die everyday regretting your mistake".

After some quiet moments consumed our thoughts, my mother asked,

"Did you go to my sister's and told her that I want to see her?"

"Yes, Mommy I went to your sister's but no one was at home"

My mother looked at the basket. Took her enamel bowl of food. I saw the love in her eyes as she looked at the food. She said, "let me put my legs up, I want to sit up in the bed and enjoy my husband cooking" I helped her lift her legs up, straightened her gown and put the bowl on her lap. She looked at me and said, "look in the draw for a spoon, go to the kitchen and wash it for me to eat" she threw her head back.

I did what my mother asked. While at the sink washing the spoon, it hit me, 'my mother eating with a spoon? My mother never used anything but her fingers to eat'. Even at the New Amsterdam hospital, she ate with her fingers. We never had spoons.

I hurried back to her bedside and found her still sitting but her head fell forward and her long, black hair covered her face and the food still on her lap.

"Mommy, Mommy here is the spoon. Come on, lift your head up and eat your food"

She did not move. I tried to lift her head but it fell forward again.

I screamed for the nurse. The same time my two brothers returned. The nurse felt my mother's pulse, laid her flat and pulled the red blanket over her, including her head.

"What are you doing? How would she breath if you cover her face? I asked

"Your mother is dead"

"No, no, no, my Mommy is not dead. She just spoke to me. She just sent me to wash the spoon. How can she be dead?" I was screaming, stamping and grabbing my mother. Grabbing the nurse, grabbing my brothers, grabbing the air, grabbing for God.

My two brothers pushed the nurse aside, grab the red blanket off my mother and took my mother off the bed. Trying to stand her up. They grab under her arms and lifting her to stand. Her head was turning in different directions and her hair was all over their faces.

I got on my knees, trying to hold her foot flat on the floor while they held her up.

There was a crowd of doctors, nurses and orderlies around us, and a ward full of sick women in their beds. Everyone in shock of what they were seeing.

They were crying for my two brothers.

Some orderlies grabbed my mother's body, pushed Datson and David aside, and laid her on the bed. The nurse draped my mother from head to toes with the red blanket.

On Sunday, May 20th, 1962, our mother, Tatrani Kasy-Jane Alexander-Dhero-Babe-Mommy was dead. She was 55years old.

Even if I tried my hardest to describe the scene of what happened that Sunday afternoon at the Port Mourant hospital, I will never be able to put it in words or pen.

My brothers and I held on to our mother's warm body and cried like we never did.

It was the sound of my brothers crying that caused people to cry as loud as we were.

News reached Lancaster and my father came for us. He took us to our mother's home. The four of us sat on the steps in silence. I was numb with shock

The world became dim. It never brightened again for me.

News reached Black Bush. Dhia came; ready to beat me for not letting him know that his mother was sick. My mother was right; she would not have recognized him, I didn't.

My father stood up and said, "Calm down man. Your mother went to the hospital yesterday. She forbids Wynette to send a message to you. Don't come here blaming her for not telling you. When is the last time your mother saw you? Or you see her?

She was your mother. I remember how glued she was to you as if you was her God.

I had a mother too. I have done lots of questionable things in my lifetime, but never did I allow myself or anyone to make me forget my mother. If I did one good thing in my life, it would be that I love and respected my mother. It is sinful what you did to her.

Tomorrow if any one give you sympathy, which I doubt any would, ask 'for what'"

My Buddy ran out of the yard, threw himself on the parapet and began to roll on the bush. The same bush, some years ago, his mother had to search for the allowance he dropped as he rode his bicycle passes her home.

My father said to me, "I have to go and put a death announcement over the radio.

Then I will go to Whim and inform the Burial Society office of my wife 's death"

That was when I learnt that my father bought burial insurance for himself and his wife many years ago. He paid more for her's because her final ceremony would cost much more. She was a Hindu, she will be cremated, which would cost much more for the special wood and oils required for her cremation.

Remember I told you that news got around faster than the wind.

My mother's home and yard began to crowd up with the Alexander family and villagers of both races. They brought food and drinks, cards and dominoes, hymnbooks and bhagan books. In no time a large tent was erected, and canvas spread on the grass for people to sit on. Table and benches came on donkey carts from the Manchester school.

The people gave my mother a Sunday night wake that I will never forget.

The next morning, Uncle James went to retrieve my mother's body.

They brought her up in the house where Aunties Katy, Chunu, Finie and I bath her and dressed her in a yellow sari and red hurnee. She looked as if she was sleeping beauty.

Her body was placed on a ratt – a shed built of bamboo and coconut branches on a donkey cart – there were lots of fresh colorful flowers placed all over her.

As people sang and cried for my mother, I saw a large black car drove up. A man in a black suite carrying one of the largest wreaths of bright flowers I have ever seen.

My brother Dhia went to him, the man said, "I am here to see Wynette"

"I am Wynette" I said to the stranger

"Your cousin Dr. Pday is in Canada at a conference. He sent his sympathy for the loss of your mother" he handed the wreath to me.

My mother's youngest sister Satranie, nephew John and his sister Mybee heard the radio announcement. They were her only blood family who attended her funeral.

John played an important role in making sure that his aunt had a religious sendoff.

In those days, only men attended the funeral or final place of a Hindu cremation.

The women mourners remain at the house, singing bhajans-hymns, and prepare food for the men when they returned.

My brother and his wife asked me for my mother's jewelry? I went upstairs to retrieve them from under the table. My brother grabbed it from my hand. I told him, "There is a chain and sovereign that Mommy wants me to give to Auntie Finny" my brother spread out the contents of my mother's treasure on the table. I never knew she had that many fine pieces of gold and silver- most from my father- who was she saving them for? Why didn't she wear them? She gave me some to wear. I kept them hidden.

"Take out what she said to give away" I did and my brother took the rest and handed them to his wife. – Almost forty-five years later, my cousin Mybee visited me in Florida from England, where she has been living for many years, she told me that her heart broke for me that day of my mother's funeral when she saw my brother and his wife demanding my mother's jewelry. – He then looked at my finger and said,

"Is that Ma's ring?"

"Yes, it is"

"Give it to me"

"No. Not this ring, not you or anyone else will ever take this ring from me"

It was a turning point in my life. It was the greatest lost for my brothers and me.

I no longer had a Mommy to snuggle up to. To smell the coconut oil in her hair.

To knot her long black hair around my waist, pretending that we are tied together.

To listen to her reasoning of how there are no bad people in the world, 'Just give them a listen'. 'Look them strait in their eyes'. 'Never hate'. 'Ask for forgiveness and forgive'. .

The bright light in my life dimmed the day my mother died. It is still dim today.

Everyone was gone. Everything was gone. My two brothers and I sat on the steps for hours, not knowing where to start. I knew that we have to start something, somewhere. But what? Where?

I knew I had to go back to school. David had to go back to the savanna with the cows.

What about Datson? – Who was sitting in a fetal position all the time? Refusing to eat? – What will become of him? He never left her side. What will become of her Betose?

"What will become of the three of us, Mommy?" I asked aloud.

My brothers could not hear my questions but they felt my tremble and saw my tears.

Every night, for thirteen nights, I sat in a circle with my two brothers at the alter, singing some baghan I learned from her. I had my brothers head shaved.

Just the three of us were having a 'Schraad' for our Hindu mother. For her soul to have a safe journey home.

"No one can spit on you anymore Mommy, have a safe trip and look over us. I will always need you to guide and protect us. Always I will care for your sons. My brothers.

'I have to go to school tomorrow. It is what Mommy would want'
I remember my savings in the teapot. It was not the time for that and it was the time for that now. I went upstairs and looked at the spot where my mother and I kept it.

It was not there. It was on the table. It was empty.

I gave Aunties Katy and Chunu all my mother's pots and utensils. To Auntie Finie, who was a Hindu, I gave my mother's saris and hernees, her alter items and one of her large masala brick and roller. I kept a lota, thari, brick and the empty teapot for myself.

I realized that something was missing from my mother's chest-of-draws. Her wedding outfit, it was gone. – Many years later, I met a lady from Liverpool. She told me that my mother was a good and kind person. She said, "When I got pregnant and my father insisted that I get married. They had no money to buy me a wedding dress. Your mother heard of our plight. The next day she brought a whole wedding outfit for me"

Daddy tried to force Datson to move to Lancaster, he refused, and he spent his days at Auntie Chunu and his nights in his mother's home. Passing Lancaster twice a day.

My father thought I could use my communicational skill with my brothers, to sign Datson to his house, but my brother chased me with a stick.

Before the last day of the month, students who traveled in Mr. Hing bus
Zorena, had to give him the bus fare for the next month in advance.

Back at Lancaster, I had to make up for my absence. Lammy was tied to a tree at the backyard, a large pile of dirty clothes for me to wash. They really missed me.

I had a feeling that my father was deliberately avoiding me. Every time I try to speak to him, he would walk away as if he was Datson or David.

"Daddy, I have to give Mr. Hing the bus money. Its pass due time but he has to be paid, I waited up several nights just to remind you to give me the bus fare".

The first week of June 1962, three weeks after my mother died. One months before I graduate from high school. My father said,

"You will not be going to high school anymore. Your stepmother needs you home"

If he is my father why does he hate me so much?

My mother gone. My savings gone. My 'hope' gone.

Someone please tell me the month of May 1962 never happened in my life.

Sometime in June, I do not remember when, my father instructed me to go to Portuguese Quarter, to the home of one of his friends. He said,

"My friend daughter is getting married and they asked for you to be a bride's maid.

You should go there and get measured for a dress"

My hair tied high and tight with flowers arranged around the bun.

I suppose Mine had the same idea for me, when she wanted me to be her bride's maid.

The stockings, mesh cancan, satin petticoat and three tier of green chiffon with white high heel shoes – one inch high – and white gloves, was for someone like me, who never wore that much, a culture shock.

The groom and groom's men came from Georgetown. The local girls were excited.

My escort was the brother of the groom. He was very nice to me. He put a corsage on my left hand and gave me a bottle of perfume.- the practice in those days.

He realized that I had never walked in a high heel shoe before. He supported me with his strong arm from the house to the main road, then on to the Roman Church.

The distance was too short for cars, but too long for me.

People lined the route to and from the church, Oh, how glad I was that none of them knew me. I was a stranger just like the groom and his party. Their laughter was just laugh. I did not know them so it did not bother me.

'Thank God the bride got married'. The joyous occasion began, music and dancing on the street, all the way to the house. In the house, there was a long table set for an aristocrat's dinner. There were so many items for each person seated at the table. I wondered what to do with all the different sizes of stem glasses, plates, folks, spoons, knives and napkin?.

Everyone around the table was quite comfortable, laughing and talking as if they were accustomed to everything on the table. I was staring at everything.

Some women came with large trays of food. We were supposed to take what we want from the tray as they offered. – Just like we see in the movies – My hands were shaking as I tried to do what my escort did.

I took a small piece of something in my plate. He looked at me and said, "Is that all you are going to eat?" Another server came around; he piled a heap of food in my plate.

After a prayer by the priest, it was time to eat.

I looked at everyone using knife and folk in comfort. I looked at the man next to me to see which folk and which hand he was holding it. He noticed that I was not eating. He nagged me encouragingly to eat. I couldn't, I did not know how.

I was willing to learn. I bend as if I was scratching my foot, while I look at others as they ate. It did not work. I excused myself from the table. I doubt if anyone noticed.

I went downstairs to the bathroom where I showered when I came. Changed back into my Cinderella's clothes, leaving everything in the bathroom and walked to the road.

The Lady Lindy, a bus driven by Isaac stopped for me. Everyone in the district knew the driver Isaac. He was a kind and caring man, especially to children. If you did not have money, he would give you a ride without a fuss.

I asked Mr. Isaac to drop me off at the Whim Middle Walk dam. I was born in this village. I walked this dam many times with my mother. I rescued my two brothers from drunken men who used them like freaks. I know this dam and everyone who live here.

Today I was not thinking of any of those things. I was going to talk to my Mommy.

I reached the cremation site and saw a man cleaning the area, I asked,

"Me ah Dhero daughter, where they burn her?" the man looked at me strangely. He said, "What are you doing here? Go home, this is not a place for you"

Please, just show me the spot where my mother was cremated"

He pointed to a clearing on the ground surrounded by coconut trees and lots of periwinkles of different colors. He said, "After each cremation, we clean out the area for the other Hindu's cremation. Only Hindu people are burned here, other Indians are buried over yonder" he pointed to the burial ground that I knew well.

Whenever my mother took us to the Kali Mia Temple, we and other children played 'catch ah coo'- hide and seek – hopping from one tomb to the other.

I sat under a coconut tree, braced on its trunk and closed my eyes.

I saw my mother did the same whenever she was in sorrow. I think she got answers.

I was looking for answers. My first question was for my mother.

"Matar, why did you leave me? What would become of me without you?"

I felt a gush of wind. Ashes flew all over my body. I had to shield my face to protect it from the dust. I began to cry. I cried so loud, I saw the man rushed towards me, then backed away, leaving me to empty my soul at my mother's cremation site.

I told my mother how much I miss her. How much the boys miss her. I never told her that I was taken out of school, that all her jewelry were taken from me and that the teapot was empty. Those were not things for me to tell her at this time.

I remembered many stories she told me. This one was appropriate for this time.

'Once upon a time there was a very rich and powerful king. He had many wives in many mansions. His wealth was enormous but he had no sons, only daughters.

He was a religious king, so he went to his God and begged Him for a son. He said,

"Dear God, I am the King, I can have anything I want. Everyone bow down to me. I bow down to you. I have many wives; they all have children, but not one boy.

As the king of the land, I must have a son to take my place when I die.

God, I beg of you, please give me a son"

God said to his to the humble king, "I know you are a good king. You are blessed with many daughters; can't you see any of them as your successor?

You are a blind man if you can't see the good use of your daughters.

Well, I will give you a son, not to replace you when you die, but for you to enjoy him until he becomes ten years old. On his tenth birthday, I will take him back"

The king was so happy when his son was born; he gave everyone one-week holiday.

The whole country rejoiced for their king and the young prince.

As the young prince got closer to his tenth birthday, the king ordered the largest ship build. It must be fully childproof. Nothing that would hurt a child was allowed in the boat. No rails, roof, steps, knives, not even fire to cook. All the food supplies were dried, parched and ground to powder – satwha. Water supply had to be in large drums, tightly covered and tied on the sides of the boat.

Everything was checked and double-checked before the king, the young prince and many servants set sail for the open sea, seven days before his tenth birthday.

The king told his wives, "God gave me this son but He is not going to take him from me. I will be back with my son the day after his tenth birthday"

The king and his many servants kept a watchful eye on the young boy.

There were no walls or closet for him to hide so he was always in their sight. They ate in a circle. No one was allowed to turn his back on the prince.

The night before his tenth birthday, everyone sat in a circle around the young prince bed. The king sat next to his son, held on to him and waited for the night to pass.

Suddenly a dark cloud passed over the roofless boat. By the time the lighted cloud reappeared, the young prince was gone.

I thought of a passage from the Bhagavad-Gita
"For certain is death for the born and certain is birth for the dead. Therefore over the inevitable you should not grieve"

I accepted my mother's death. She was with God. She was loyal to her religion and culture. She was the most forgiving and caring person in my life.

I was nineteen years old when I accepted my greatest lost.

After forty days of my mother's passing, my father allowed two elderly people to move into my mother's home.

He brought some of her personal belongings to Lancaster. All I wanted was the teapot.

Once again I had to be the one to coaxes Datson into moving in with us.

My stepsister and her six children moved to the small room under the 'big house'.

I had my room once again and my father promised to get another bed for Datson.

I remember the Sunday I went to coax my brother into coming with David and I.

I told him that Mommy wants me to take care of him. He said he didn't know that man.

He told me that he could take care of himself; he chased us out of the yard. I cried and told him that I need him to take care of me. My brother came with me to Lancaster.

He still spent his days at the Naga's but slept in the room with David.

My father did not ask him to do any chores. I do not think he would've done any either.

Datson allowed me to cut his thick, black, curly hair. He would take a shower when I tell him to do so. Every time I offered him something to eat, he refused, but he would bring fried fish and sometimes candies for David and me when he comes home.

Around Christmas of 1962, I came from the market and did not see Lammy.

He did not come to greet me at the gate. He wasn't bellowing for me.

I began to call for him all around the neighborhood. I did not find my pet sheep.

I asked my stepmother, stepsister and all the children if they saw my Lammy?

After two days and night looking and crying for my pet, I was told that Lammy was sold to a butcher while I was at the market. They needed money for Christmas.

My father was furious, he asked my stepmother who was the butcher they sold the sheep to? She told him. He went to Lettlekenny for my Lammy, but it was too late. The butcher said, "Archie, da lil sheep turn into curry mutton for many of my customers"

My brothers were so angry, especially David, who had become accustomed to him.

Datson was more angry with my father for allowing 'those people' to do that to me.

I used to have terrible sore throat from being in the rain and wet ground, cleaning. There were days I could not swallow even my own slaver. The pain was so bad, I could not get out of bed to do my chores.

I was accused of being lazy and faking it. Many times I didn't tell anyone of my pain.

One time it got so bad, Aunt Elo felt my head and realized that I was burning up with fever. She took me to Port Mourant hospital. The doctor sent me right away to Skeldon hospital, to have immediate operation to take my tonsils out.

Aunt Elo told me that when my father heard that I had to emergency surgery, he broke down and cried, saying, "All along, we were saying that she was faking her pain"

One day my father came home and was told something, I don't know what, I never knew 'what' Many times David and I never knew why we were beaten.

Datson was sitting on a bench under the house. He knew what was going to happen when I come from wherever I went. He was dumb, deft and quiet, but he was no fool.

As soon as my father lunged at me, my brother grabbed him around his waist. Held on to him for some minutes. My stepmother took a stick and started to hit my brother in his head. Datson dropped my father on the ground and went after her, but she managed to run inside the kitchen and closed the door before he could get her.

My father curled in pain. He could not move.

I ran for Uncle Bertram. He took my father to the hospital. First time to a hospital since he was a child. My father had three broken ribs. He had to stay home for two week.

My father never punishes Datson. He had a soft spot in his heart for his first-born son.

What was most surprising to me, was when Uncle Bertram brought my father back from the hospital, all bandaged and can hardly walk. My father went to Datson, clasped his hands and bowed to his son. A humble moment I have never seen from my father.

After my father got better, he returned to work. He had to go into the creek to dig trenches with the dragline. He and Uncle Tigar camped in there for a week or two before coming home for a weekend and taking back supplies.

During the time of my father's absence, my stepmother and her daughter called the police, complaining that they were afraid of Datson. They said that he was just sitting and searing at them and whenever they passed close to him, he moved as if he wants to attack them. They said they think he has a knife or cutlass with him. They told the police that Datson had broken his father's ribs.

The police tied my brother like a wild animal, and took him to the mental asylum.

People were questioning me all the time. My aunts, uncles, neighbors and friends were saying, "Did you send a message to your father? Why you allow them to do that to him? If his mother was here that would never had happened"

'If my Uncle Bertram and Aunt Elo were here, that would not have happened.

I think those people knew that, when they send for the police to take that poor dumb boy away. Shame on all of them"

David too was furious with me. He said that I am the one with the ears and mouth to listen and speak for them. Where was I when they took his brother away?

I told him I went to the market. That they always do such things when I am away, because I will see, hear and talk out loud for them.

My father came home two weeks later. His boy was taken to the 'madhouse'.

My father was the one who needed to be tied and taken away. He was the madman.

He chased everyone, mother, daughter, and grandchildren out of Alexander compound.

My father was going mad. I did my best to keep out of his way. I knew for sure that I would get the worst of what was happening in his head.

I miss my brother. I promised my mother that I will take care of him and I failed.

I wondered what was he doing among those sick people? Was he now going to be like them? Are they going to give him medicine for a mad person, when my brother is not mad? Are they going to make my mother's Betose into a madman?

My father gave me money the next day. He aged twice his year's overnight. He said,

"Go and bring my son back home"

I told the gatekeeper of the New Amsterdam Mental Asylum that I was here to see my brother, Mr. Datson Alexander. He looked into a large hard cover ledger, looked at me and asked, "Who are you/"

"I am Wynette Alexander. I am Datson's sister" he looked again in the book.

"OK, you are the person the doctor wants to see" he directed me to an office.

I entered and saw Dr. Pday looking up at me. He was now the head of this hospital.

I held on to him and we both cried for the pain both of us were feeling at the moment.

He said when he saw the name and realized that he was mute, he knew that Datson was his cousin, his Puhwa's son. He said that no medication was given to him because there was no need for it. He said, "We don't diagnose a grieving man as a mental case. Your brother is grieving for his mother and cannot understand what is happening around him. That is why he sits quietly in a corner. He is depressed not mad"

I went with the doctor to see my brother. I passed cages and cubicles with screaming men, some stretching their hands through the bars to hold me. Others were dancing and saying things I didn't understand.

The doctor took me to a recreational hall. There I saw my brother, dressed in a gray outfit, sitting at a table waiting to be served his breakfast.

I walked up to him; he stood up and embraced me. I cried. He did not. He consoled me.

Dr. Pday asked "Who put your brother in here? What took you so long to come for him?" He gave me some money and said, "Take Datson home. Give him lots of love".

My stepmother and her family returned. It seems my father couldn't live without them.

I resigned myself to be my brothers' keeper. I did everything right, giving my father no reason to beat on me. Give my stepmother no reason to snitch on me.

I was twenty years old and no one has asked for my hand in marriage. I was a damaged goods and no one wanted to associate himself with me.

I bid many of my cousins' farewells as they left for England to become nurses.

Hope was gone for me. I am now a barefooted, older looking village girl whose future is in this house, in this village as a spinster. No husband, no children, no nurse.

My father informed me that my mother had a life insurance and that I should go to the insurance office to collect the money for my brothers and I.

I went to Rose Hall to collect. The insurance company gave me a check for three times forty dollars. I asked the officer if he could please give me cash for two and a check for one. The man did. I went home and gave my two brothers $40 dollars each.

They wondered if I robbed the post office. I told them that it was from our mother.

I did my best to explain to them that she was hiding money away for us.

I gave my brothers so much money they never held before. I did not care what they did with it. It was theirs from their mother. They can spend it whichever way they want.

I looked at the surprise and joy in their faces and knew my mother was seeing it too.

I folded the check with my name written on it. I put it into my little teapot.

My father never asked how much we got? Or what we did with it?

I got my usual Christmas and birthday card from Cecil. In it there was a note saying that he was going to come with some youths for a church convention in

New Amsterdam. He wrote the date and time when they were going to cross the ferry.

I asked David for some money. Dressed in my 'very best' and went to see the man whom I have been loving, without seeing for six years.

I watched as the large ferryboat name Tarini docked at the stilling.

My heart was beating so hard as I watched through the crowd for him.

I saw him. I heard his laughter – he has a laughter that comes from deep within – and my hands began to sweat.

I looked at the group of young people that he was walking with.

Suddenly I wanted to hide. I did not want them to see me. I couldn't measure up to any of them.

But he was looking for me. He spotted and came towards me. He was holding the hand of one of the most beautiful girl I ever saw. She was tall, dark and had the most beautiful smile. Her smile, teeth, hair and everything about her were beautiful.

"Hi Dear, I am glad you came to see me. I was hoping you would come. I told Gloria that you would come to see me. Bytheway, this is my girlfriend Gloria"

My smile was stuck with glue. I could not move my lips or close my mouth.

Gloria saw how uncomfortable I was, she said, "I will go and catch-up with the others. See you later" she looked at me and said, "Nice meeting you" she walked away with such grace and confidence, it made me feel like a flea.

He was so kind and sweet to me. He told me how sorry he was about my mother's passing. He told me that they were planning to move to England and later get married.

I do not remember everything he was saying. I was just watching his mouth moving.

He walked me to the bus and said goodbye. I wish he had kissed my hand again.

Give me another five years of 'hope'.

Friday 27th of December 1963, my twenty-first birthday, I woke up with the world.

I was so happy, I informed everyone, even my father before he left for work.

You see there was a tradition that when a person becomes twenty-one years old, the parents give him/her the key to the door. Meaning that you are now old enough to go and come as you wish.

Cousin Claudine, Uncle Isaac's wife, who had a cake shop, promised to bake a cake and make some ice-cream for me. She told me to collect them in the afternoon.

I did my entire choirs, and then informed my stepmother that I will run as fast as I can to Manchester for the goodies my auntie made for my birthday.

It was beginning to get dark. I was not allowed to be out when it gets dark.

I collected my cake and ice cream – Cousin Claudline had a kerosene refrigerator. There was no electricity in those days – and ran back as fast as I could.

When I got home, I saw my father bicycle leaned against the post. 'Oh God, he is home' but I was not afraid, because its my big number. He knew where I went.

Our neighbor and family member, Auntie Venus, knew what was going to happen as soon as she saw my father came home and asked me? She had been watching for years, the way I was being treated. They did not call it 'abuse' in those days.

She sent her son Herman to "run and get Uncle Bertram. Something bad is going to happen to Wynette this afternoon. I can tell from the way Uncle Archie is acting"

The first blow sent cake, the ice cream, and me in different directions.

By the time my father came after me again, my two brothers were standing over me like dogs protecting their bone.

Uncle Bertram came running and screaming,

"No more Mike. Mike no more. This is the last time you will ever hit her"

My father stood up and looked at the three men surrounding me. My uncle demanded,

"Wynette, get up. Go upstairs and collect everything you have and come back to me.

I did what my uncle ordered. I quickly collected my green flounce dress, shoes and all. My little teapot with the check in it, my gold jewels from under the mattress.

I stuffed everything into a pillowcase. The cancan being the largest and bulkiest.

I Held the teapot close to my racing heart and walked down the steps of my castle.

My two brothers came to me while my uncle shield me from my father.

They put their arms around me and escort me to the gate. I got their permission to leave.

I heard Uncle Bertram saying,

"Enough is enough, Mike I brought her to you ten years ago. I know the hell she has been going through, it makes me regret my action. I am taking her away from you now"

Aunt Elo took care of my burses, and said, "You can't stay here anymore. Every time we bring you to our home, as soon as your uncle leaves, your father take you back.

I know you are thinking about your brothers. Think about you for ah change. Your brothers would be all right. Your uncle will make the decision as to where you go"

My aunt gathered some clothes from her daughters, including panties and bras – no more flour bag bras for me – and put them, including my green dress, cancan and shoes, in a large canvas bag with two strong straps.

Uncle Bertram had brought that bag for her from St Kitts. She wrapped the teapot in lots of old newspaper, put it in the pillowcase and placed it on top of my canvas bag.

I felt a gentle hand on me, shaking me to wake up. I opened my eyes and saw my uncle. He said almost in a whisper, "Getup, come on, get ready and come downstairs"

I did and found my uncle and aunt sitting at the table. My aunt gave me a cup of tea and a piece of bread. – She made the most delicious 'homemade bread – My uncle was quiet. I ate in silence, not knowing what these two kind people have in mind for me.

"OK, lets go, grab the bag and kiss your auntie goodbye. Your aunt put some stuff for you to eat. You have a long way to go. You are going to be very hungry.

Lets go the bus will be here soon" My Aunt Elo was crying as she handed me the brown paper bag. I hugged and kissed her. I thanked her for her love caring for me. I said, "Please Aunt Elo, please lookout for Datson and David" She pushed me through the door saying, "Go, go my child, your brothers are going the be alright. Just go before your father come out here to get you. Take this chance and go away. Whatever you do from this day, do it for you. For a change, go and do something for you"

Uncle Bertram was standing by the roadside, looking east for any sign of light through the dark horizon.

While I stood in the dark with my uncle, I was tempted to look back towards my home. The home where I had so many bad years. Where I stayed with the promise that I would one day live my 'hope'. I gave up living with my mother for promises made to me in that house. The house that I am leaving, where my two brothers lay asleep.

I was experiencing a strange feeling. A part of me was tearing away from me. I could not look back. I was afraid to look back; yet, I was expecting my father grab.

"Go to Georgetown. Your sister Esther lives in Evans Street. Don't forget the name of the street, Evans, or ask anyone for the 'soap factory', then ask for your sister"

We saw the light, it brighten the dark night on the east. My uncle put his hand into his pocked and put a paper money into my hand. He folded my fingers around it.

"This is an elephant. You can kill and eat it all in one day, or you can let it feed you for the rest of your life. Whatever you do from this moment on will be up to you"

We hugged each other until the bus stopped.

Uncle Bertram stepped into the bus and handed Mr. Kite. some money, he said,

"Take her to the stelling for the first boat, she is crossing over"

Egbert-Dada-Alexander, my grandfather.

My mother and Datson at an agriculture fair 1961

Michael Archibald Hunter Alexander.

Young David with his sight in 1960.

Auntie Chunu, our other mother.

My Uncle Bertram Alexander who
set me free on an elephant.

My Auntie Elouise who saw no
difference in sharing love.

A happy day when promises were made.

My Sister Esther and daughter Sharon.

Vera Alexander, we were cousins and best friends.

Cecil Saul, one of my best
friends who believed in me.

I was going to Hollywood but
got lost in Charlotte Street.

When we were three and a bump.

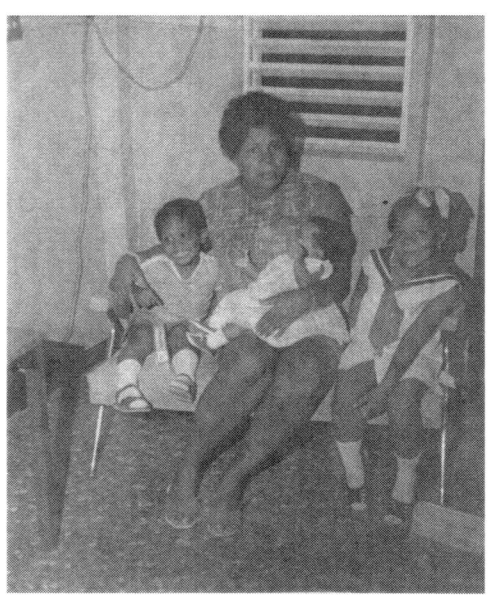

And then we were four.

We are growing- only pot doesn't grow.

Kim's first Communion. My children and I.

Daphne and I sharing a coconut.
She knows how to share.

Ada, my friend who allow me
to sleep under her table.

Bradley, the little boy who kept me sane at a maddening time.

David and I, our very first photo ever taken in 1960 at Motoo Studio.

David and I 50 years later, 2010 at Motoo Studio.

Aklyne School with my Sweetie tree still standing strong.

The path to Cinderella's Castle.

Daddy and David in 1983, my last visit with him.

Kim, Rocky and Melanie ready for America and Epiphany.

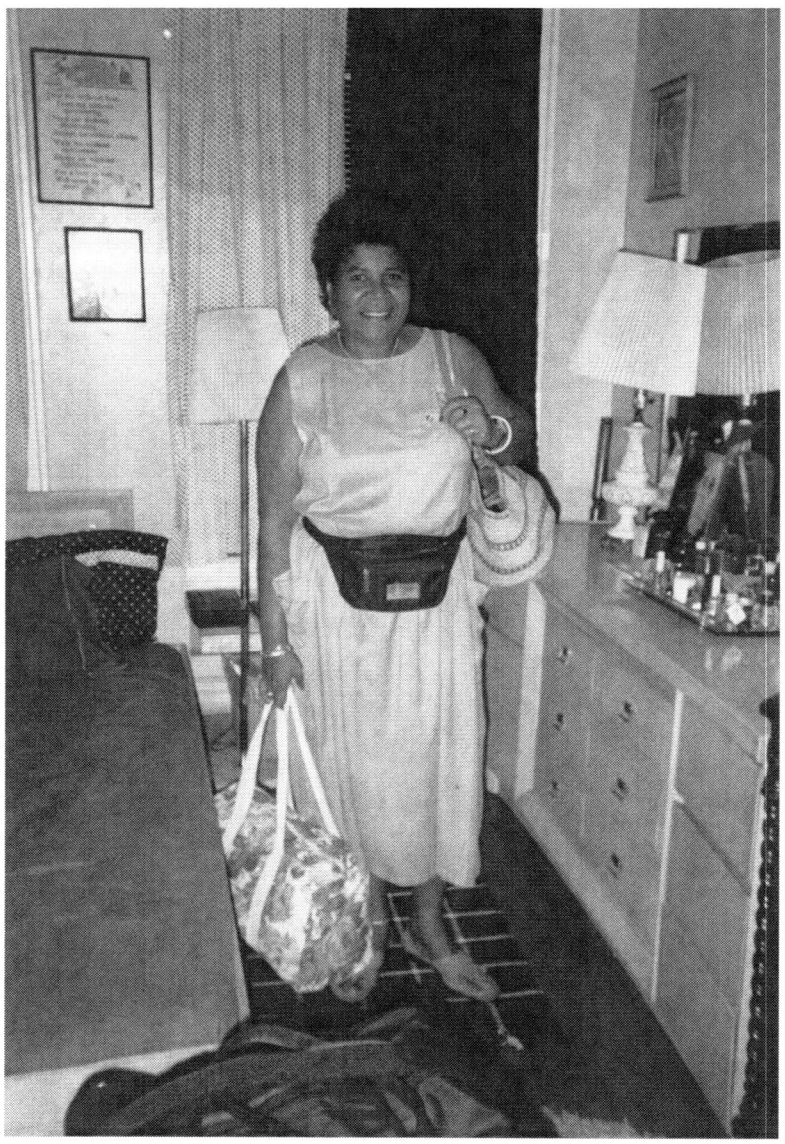

This gipsy is on the move.

Onyx, Asti, Prince, Hidi, Sabrina and Smoky. They love a camera.

Linda and the family in the beginning of my storytelling in 1996.

Linda and I having a good time in St Maarten in 2010.

We grew into our own height.

I get to hold mine, my mother didn't.

David, completely blind in 2003.

Vincent and I on a red brick road. Forgiveness is healing.

My mother's wedding gift-bank, my treasure.

Grandma the mechanic.

My constant companions.

THE EXIT

It was Saturday 28 of December 1963. I sat by the window in Mr. Kite's bus.

I kept looking back from where I came, and then I look forward to nowhere?

It was a bright day. I saw children fetching water, women beating clothes by the wells and trenches, men on their bicycles and donkey-carts going somewhere.

'They are out just like me, but they all have a home to go back to. I have none'

I dive my head into the whole of my arms and wash the window cell with my tears.

The eighteen miles from Lancaster to New Amsterdam seemed endless.

"Come-on sweetie, this is your stop. Here, take dis money to buy a ferry ticket.

You ever cross the river before?

"No Sir"

"Allright, dis is what you gon doo. You see dat cage there? Go and buy a ticket for the boat. Bytheway, where are you going? Your uncle said you are crossing over"

"I am going to Georgetown" I was shaking, holding on to my canvas bag and my hand still tightly closed with the 'elephant' that Uncle Bertram placed in it.

"Do you have money for the train?" he asked kindly.

It was at that moment I opened my hand and saw the almost soaked five-dollar note.

"Yes Sir, I have money" I held up my 'elephant' and show him.

"That's good enough. The train fare is $2.65ct." Mr. Kitt looked at me once more and said, "Good luck my choil"

I watch the sailors in stiff blue and white uniform, wishing one would take me home.

I watched as the sailors, upon hearing a loud whistle, untied a large rope securing the giant boat to the walf, it was much larger than the one my father used. It was a rope.

I boarded the train and resumed my position the window cell. The train whistle blew three times and a gentleman, dressed like a policeman shouted "All aboard, last chance"

The train began to move away slowly. I was moving away. I was moving away from

David and Datson. I was breaking my promise to my mother.

"Oh God, what a sad life I have? What awaits me yonder? Dear God?"

I had to gather strength quickly. The strength I got from my Mommy, Mr. Reed, Gramother and Nana Sweetie, my Uncle Bertram and Aunt Elo. I needed all of them to join forces to hold me from behaving like a deranged person.

I dived my head in my donut hole and sob quietly.

How strong, brave or confident can one be when all one has is a canvas bag, large enough to make a pillow, $2.35cs and don't know where this train will take you?

I have some money in my hand, I will be alright, must be alright, I have to be alright.

The train stopped at many stations in the sixty-five miles journey. I was in the abyss.

After what seemed like another life, I heard the train conductor saying,

"Georgetown, last stop"

I was the last to exit the train. My mind was mixed-up, 'should I stay on this train and go back to Lancaster? Beg my father pardon. And honor my mother's last wish?

'But how can I go back? I have only $2.35cs. The fare is $2.65cs.

I didn't have enough money to return to my brothers.

I thought New Amsterdam was the largest city in the world, with large buildings.

Georgetown spin my head 360 degree, I was still standing at the train station.

Everywhere I turned, I saw streets, allies, pavements and buildings much higher than New Amsterdam.

"Sir, I am going to Evans Street soap factory, could you please show me which direction to take?' I asked the train conductor who was impatiently waiting for me.

"Where did you say?" asked the conductor who looked at me strangely.

"I said Evans Street, Sir. By the soap factory"

"Young lady, you are standing at one end of town. Evans Street is in the other end All the way in Charlestown" He looked as me as if I just escape from a cage.

"Sir, could you please point out which one of the four directions I should take to go to Evans Street in Charlestown?" I did not want him to see how my knees were shaking. How I was squeezing them together to keep my bladder from exploding.

"It's a long, long way, you can't walk that far"

"I can walk a long way, just show where to go, please point the direction out to me"

"OK, if you say so. Atleast you don't have any heavy baggage" he looked at my St Kitts canvas bag, my right hand tightly clinched, my jewels and my frightened face.

"Take dis same street, its call Carmichael St. go strait, you will come face to face with St Georges Cathedral, this country's pride for architecture. It is the largest wooden building in the world" he looked up the street with such pride in his face.

"There are some slight turns, keep your head strait south, and ask along the way, you will reach Evans St. You will have to walk fast to reach there before nightfall"

"Thank you Sir" I said nervously, yet gratefully.

"I see so many of your kind everyday at this very train station. I know when you are running away from the country to the big city. Be careful; don't let the bright light blind you. This is not the innocent world that you are running away from. This city would devour you and spit you into the gutters, if you get mixed-up with the wrong crowd"

"Thanks again, Sir"

I followed his direction. As for walking fast and far, I knew how to do that well.

I had lots of practice. Five days per week, hopping from Liverpool to Bound Yard.

My bladder was warning me that it couldn't hold on anymore. I crawled under

St Georges Cathedral's step and relieved my bladder.

I arrived in Evans St. It was a short street with only four cross streets.

I found the soap factory, everyone knew my sister. "Wow, you are Esther's sister?

You look so much alike" said the lady who walked me to where my sister lived.

Those were good words to my ears. I was thirsty and needed to sit so badly, but that can wait now that I am on the street where my sister lives.

She lived in a one-room tenement. Her room was #3 on the right-hand side as I entered the yard.

I saw her three children sitting on the steps – remember I told you that steps took the place of chairs, which most of us didn't have. The outdoor was better to beat the heat – They were Sharon 7, Sherlock 4 and Mark 1 years old.

Sharon remembered me because they came to visit us in Lancaster that August.

I babysat them and enjoyed every moment with them.

"Mommy, Mommy, look who is here? It's Aunt Wynette from the country"

My sister appeared at the door, looked at me and asked, "What are you doing here?

She came down to where I stood and said "You getaway, right? I warn you not to leave. Now you gonna get your father coming after me"

I squeezed myself next to one of the children on the steps. I needed to take this wary body off these blistered feet. What I would give for a splash of water on my lips.

"Where are you going to stay? I have no space here for anyone else. This is a room that can hardly hold my three children and me. Why did you come here?"

"Because Uncle Bertram sent me to you" She was silent for a while, then said

"Uncle Bertram sent you to me? You didn't getaway? Did your father allowed you to leave?" 'Why is she saying 'your father' and not 'our father or 'my father'?

"No Sister Esther, I did not getaway. Uncle Bertram sent me to you"

My sister truly did not have any space for anyone else. She, Sharon and Sherlock slept on a double bed and Mark slept in a crib.

I made a bed with some bedding on the floor after everyone climbed in bed.

It was very inconvenient for them if they needed to go to the potty during the night.

It was a shelter for me, for which I was grateful.

It was my first time seeing a toilet with a tank high above and a chain to pull to flush.

"There are eleven other families living in this yard. I say hello, howdidoo. That's all. They know nothing about me and I don't want to know anything about them"

"Yes Sister Esther"

Early next day I went to the soap factory for a job. I had no 'experience' so I did not get a job packing soap, however I got a small bag with pieces of soap from the gateman.

I knew that my friend Cecil was a teacher at Grove Government School.

I rented a bicycle. I had to leave a deposit for renting it for an hour.

I had no idea how far Grove was. I knew that I was going to Grove to see my love.

I learned to ride on my father's cycle when he went away to the creek.

I asked the shop owner "Which direction to Grove?" the shopkeeper looked at me as if to say 'Who let her out of the nuthouse?' Then he pointed south.

I began to ride from around nine am. I rode and rode and rode.

I stopped several times to ask 'how far more I have to go to reach Grove?'

I arrived at Grove Village at 3pm, after six hours of riding in the hot sun.

I saw Cecil and other teachers on the public road, waiting for the bus to go home.

"Hello there, what are you doing here? Do you have relatives here in Grove?"

"No, I came to see you" I said breathlessly

"From where did you come to see me?" he asked almost angrily.

"From Georgetown"

"Oh my God, do you know how many miles you've ridden from Georgetown to here?" he looked at me with wide opened eyes. He asked, "Where are you staying in Town?" Looking around nervously for some way to help me before his bus arrived.

His bus arrived. He was the last to enter. He asked again, "Where are you staying?"

I shouted "Evans St, my sister name is Esther"

"I will come on Saturday to take you to the cinema" he sat by the back window with half of his body outside, waved to me until we could see each other no more.

The cycle shop owner took my remaining dollar and thirty-five cents. I had to promise him that as soon as I get some money, I would bring the balance to him.

He gave me the same look as before and said, "Where the hell did you go all day?"

I walked the streets, making landmarks to find my way back.

I stopped in every store, bakery, factory and anywhere that looked like people are working or cleaning, for a job. A baker-shop owner said to me,

"Why you old gals come in here and claim to be younger than you are? I bet you have a bunch of children in a room somewhere. I don't have a job for you, if you were younger, maybe, but here, take some bread to feed your children"

I heard that the Roman Catholic Church needed people to clean the benches.

I went but was told that they were looking for volunteers. I volunteer that day.

Cecil kept his promise. He came for me on Saturday. I was nervous all day.

When I got dress in my green tree tear chiffon dress with my can-can. My sister said

"You are going to a picture show not a wedding" her little children laughed when they saw me all dressed up and can hardly walk in the white high heel shoes.

I saw the surprise look in Cecil face when he saw me. He said in a kind manner,

"You are a little overdressed but you look beautiful. Lets go"

It was a long walk from Evans St to the Plaza cinema at Camp and Middle St.

The stares and laughter from people as I stumbled along did not bother me because, I was accustomed to that, remember I was a freak? It did not seem to bother him either.

I don't remember what I saw. I was in a daze, pinching myself. I didn't want to wakeup. I looked at him laughing at the movie; he is so handsome, I wondered

'Is this really happening? Am I really out with this good-looking man? Am I really free to go out and do whatever I want? Is my father going to grab me any moment now?'

After the show, Cecil bought me a large slab of Cadbury chocolate with hazel nuts.

He took another route going back to Evans St., one that did not have streetlights.

I guess he wanted to spare me being a laughingstock again, or, he being embarrassed.

My feet were on fire. The blisters were everywhere, but I was prepared to walk on fire as long as I was walking with him.

As we crossed Durban St. I saw one of the most beautiful churches on my right.

My thoughts began to race. I learned over the years that if you are in pain, you shift your thoughts from it and think of something else; soon you will forget your pain, especially if you are thinking of something pleasant, peaceful and beautiful.

'If I play my cards right, maybe he would marry me in this same church. But how?'

"This is St Stevens Anglican Church. It's famous for its record keeping of thousands upon thousands of slaves who were converted into Christianity and christened here"

With pride in his voice, he asked, "Would you like to walk through the Church yard?

Its dark but you can have an idea of how large the institution really is"

"Yes thank you," I said, holding the chocolate so close to my body. I planned to share it with my sister and her children.

We sat on the steps to the large wooden door. – In the daylight, one would see that it is painted white with red trimmings and roof. - I think both of us felt uncomfortable, for different reasons, of course. Me wanting him for myself. He is trying to be kind.

"What are your plans? Are you going to stay here? Or are you going back to Lancaster? What of your plans to go to England to become a nurse?"

I told him that I had no plans at the moment. But I did, I was planning to seduce him. I had to do something. If I will have any reason to live, it has to be with him.

As it got darker, I saw couples walking through the various paths in the garden around the tombs. Some disappeared in the dark, some sat or lie on the tombs and some came and sat on the steps where we were. 'This must be the place for lovers?' I wondered

I suppose one does not have to be experience. My youthful hormone is taking over?

I got off the steps and walked to a nearby tomb and sat on the edge. He followed and sat next to me. 'This is working, Wynette' I felt good.

I lie flat on my back on the cold concrete. Waiting for him to do the same.

'This is my chance to get him for myself'.

Cecil pulled me up to my feet. He said, "Wynette, you are a nice and innocent young girl. Don't try this with anyone else; he will surely take advantage of you.

I am not here to do that to you. I like you from the moment I saw you standing like a lost child at your father's birthday party. I asked lots of questions about you. I heard

of all your miseries, how you were stained and taunted because of what someone said.

My intention from that moment was to be your friend. If I led you to feel otherwise, I am sorry" he held my cold shaking hands into his, looking for my eyes, he continued,

"You met my girlfriend Gloria? We are leaving for England shortly to study and get married" his words were like sledge hammer hitting my head. He said, "I would like to continue being your friend. Keep your honor for the right person at the right time"

He pulled me away from cold tomb. My chocolate was left for the residents.

He held my shaking hand all the way to my sister's door. When my sister opened the door he said "Thanks for allowing your sister to go out with me. She is a good girl, protect her from the vouchers in this city." He kissed my hand and said "Goodnight"

I sat on the step, took off the shoes that has caused blisters all over my feet.

My mind was blank. I couldn't remember how many years it was since Cecil danced with me, asked my name and kissed my hand. How many years I waited for his once per year mail, I was in a daze. No more daydreaming of my prince taking me away.

"Where did you go all this time? Cinema over since eight o'clock, look at the time you come knocking at my door? Is this the kind of behavior you expect to have here?

Where have you been all this time?" my sister stood infront of me waiting.

"At the church yard, lying on a tomb" I said without thinking or caring.

In fury she threw a towel, soap and one of her old dress at me and said,

"Go take a shower, wash yourself properly before coming in here with my young children" she gave me one of those scornful looks that I have grown accustomed to.

Taking a shower in the bright daylight could be hazardous if you are not careful.

Now it is pitch-dark, I can't see what I am stepping on. Anything could be coiled up.

I had no fear; I needed that cold shower; much more than my sister think I needed it.

I threw the green chiffon dress, cancan and white high heel shoe, into the garbage heap.

I pawned some of my jewelry and bought some pieces of cloth to have my sister take me to her seamstress to make some 'town' clothes for me. – You see in those days,

We didn't have 'ready-made' clothes. Everyone took cloth to his or her tailor of dressmaker – I knew that it was because of the way I dressed and talked, I was not able to get a job. Many places I went to ask for a job, the people looked at me, and when they heard me speak, they would say "no you wouldn't do here. You're too country".

'Learning to speak like dem will take some time, but dressing like dem starts now'

My determination to make it here or anywhere else, I was making roots.

I went into a shoe store; the cheapest shoe was the imphamus 'Ballerina. The store had three colors, black, white and red. I bought the red.

I gave my sister some money after pawning my jewelry. She was so angry, she said, "Why did you do that? Do you think I will take money from you when I know that you are not working anywhere? You are my sister for Christ sake. I can give you a shelter and some food until you get a job"

One evening when I came home from job hunting, my sister told me that she got a job for me at a bar in Russell St. She said that she spoke to the owner and she wanted me to start the next day at noon. "The shift would be from four to twelve, six days per week. She wants you there at noon to show you around and explain your duties"

The first day-night, from noon to two a m, when I got home I told my sister,

"I will not be going back to that job. It started well earlier, but as the men began to get drunk, they started to pull at me. One of them threw me on the table and forced the rum to my mouth. When I screamed, the owner said 'its all in the job' I don't want that kind of job Sister Esther" She hugged me as I cried.

I heard there was a Portuguese family in First St Queenstown who needed a live-in servant. I got the job for twenty dollars per month.

I felt sad when I left my sister and her children. They stood in the yard and waved.

"Don't pawn anymore of your jewelry, you hear me? Come on your dayoff to see us. The children will miss you, and so will I"

It was a sunup to sundown job — that's what it was for live-in servants.

It was a family of six, four grown children, three boys and one girl.

They were nice to me. When the boys threw out their used clothes, I thought of ways to send them to my brothers.

My Uncle Bertram's 'elephant' was paving my path.

I gave my sister five dollars and put fifteen into my teapot alongside my cheque.

I prayed every spare moment for forgiveness from God, my Mommy, Datson and David. Every time I ate I ask God to give them something to eat, too.

When I came to Georgetown, my companion on my head followed me.

It was not acceptable to have a 'louse head' in the city.

My mistress told me to go to the drugstore and buy some sulfur cream to rub on my head to get rid of 'those things'.

I went to Twins Drugstore on Middle and Cummings St, three blocks away.

I stood in line waiting for my turn to speak quietly to the lady behind the counter.

Before I got up to her, she shouted, "What do you want?" pointing to me.

I could not answer, if I shouted back 'sulfur cream' everyone in the store would've known that I am a 'louse head'. That would've been embarrassing.

She insisted that I say what I am in the store for? I became my brothers, dumb.

A tall, well dressed in black suit, handsome gentleman walked from behind me, he walked up to the counter. He said to the lady,

"Can't you see that the young lady don't want everyone in the store to hear whatever she needs? Do you know that there is something call privacy?"

He walked back and took his place behind me.

I got what I needed, thanked the gentleman and walked out of the store.

"Miss, Miss, just a minute" it was the well-dressed Indian man.

"Where do you live?"

"I work and live in First St." I said politely.

"You are a live-in domestic servant from the country? Am I right?"

"Yes Sir" 'who is this man? Is he my Night? Or, did he too had a dream?'.

"How would you like to work at a biscuit factory? Its better pay, you will get vacation and health benefit. You are too young to spend the rest of your life being a domestic servant" His pleasant manners and smile put me at ease.

"Go to the Labor Department on Monday morning. Do you know where it is?"

"No Sir" he directed me to Camp and Murray St. and said,

"Take this card and give it to the secretary. Good luck"

I didn't know how to tell Mrs. Pereira what happened. I said nothing.

Monday morning I went to the Ministry of Labor and gave the card to the secretary.

She asked, "Do you know the Commissioner?"

"Who is the Commissioner?" I asked

"The man who signed this card. He is Mr. Fred Taharally, the commissioner of labor" she said as if I should've known him.

"No, I do not know him. I just met him on Friday afternoon at the drugstore.

He gave me this card and told me to come here for a job" I sat nervously, hoping that the secretary would hurry so that I could go back to my duties.

She turned to her typewriter and started to type. She handed me a white envelope with what she typed. She said, "Take this to the Continental Biscuit Factory, up the East Bank. Give it to the Secretary; she will know that the Labor Dept sends you."

She began to read from a paper on her desk, "Your hours will be from seven-thirty am to four pm. With one hour breakfast break, Monday to Friday. Saturday from seven-thirty am to twelve noon. You can work overtime at time and half. Saturday, Sunday and holiday, you will be paid double. Your wage will be $15.60cts per week" she looked up at me and asked, "Any Question"

"Yes Mamm. If I get the job, I will need a place to live. Right now I am living where I work as a domestic servant"

She sent me to Mrs. Rogers who rented rooms to single women. I got a room by the window for $5 per week.

I expected my mistress to be angry with me for being away from my duties so long.

When I told her the whole story, she was kind and understanding. She wished me well and game me some sheets, towels, a cup, plate and a spoon. A starter kit.

My elephant was working for me. People like my Sister Esther, Mrs. Pereira and

Mr. Taharally was clearing the path that I must walk on.

I began working at the Continental Biscuit Factory on April 1964.

My teapot was getting richer. Remember my cheque? Well I used it to buy a

Raleigh bicycle, another pair of shoes and needed supplies for my monthly use, no more clothe napkins, there was Modes, and all from the money my beloved mother left me.

Mrs. Rogers gave me a stern speech the day I moved into her house.

"This is my home, my children are grown and gone. This house is too large for a lonely old lady like me, which is why I rent out rooms.

The lady who sent you to me, knows me well, she knows that I don't take any and every kind of young women in my home.

The door lock and the light turn off when I am ready to turn in to bed.

You may use the iron once per week. You take turns with the other ladies, sweeping the house and cleaning the bathroom and toilet.

You bring no male visitor into this house. Do you understand my rules?"

"Yes Mamm"

"OK, I gave you the front room. It is smaller but you have a street view" she looked at my life possession and a tenderness crossed her face. She said

"You can give me three dollars per week this month, since you are now starting to work. Next month you pay me five dollars per week"

"Thank you very much Mamm" I remember Gramother's "Please and Thankyou will take you through the world"

Mrs. Rogers was a kind and caring 'grandmother' to me. I was the youngest in the house. I spent many nights in her room, which was the largest, listening to her stories of long ago and how things were then.

Every afternoon I had a large enamel cup of sago portage. A small Pyrex dish with rice-n-peas and fish/chicken stew, keeping warm by the wood stove for my lunch next day.

One afternoon I came home to find Mrs. Rogers laughing and chatting with a young man. She introduced him as Clive, she said that his grandmother and her are best friends and he is here in town on holiday from the mining town..

Clive came every afternoon, we sat on the steps for hours, until it begins to get dark or when Mrs. Rogers puts her head through the window and clear her throat.

He worked at McKenzie, the bauxite-mining town almost sixty-five miles away.

Many afternoons he brought popcorn, ice cream or chicken-n-de-ruff for a picnic on the steps. Everything was seen and approved by the watcher through the window.

The night before Clive left, we were both sad. I had grown accustom to him. Seeing his handsome smile, sitting on the steps when I ride into the yard, tugged at my heart.

I must've done something to him, too, because he was there everyday to see me.

We sat on the steps, holding hands in the quiet for a long time. He broke it,

"I have grown attached to you. Could I see you whenever I come to Town? Would you like to be my girlfriend?" still holding my hand, with a smile on his lips, he asked

"Yes" I said bashfully. I had no room for more words.

"To prove to you that I am serious about you, I will leave my constant companion, my radio, with you" he handed me his transistor radio in a brown leather case.

The next morning, Clive boarded the boat that would take him up the Demerara River to McKenzie.

It was on his radio, that racially hateful day; I heard that a bomb was placed in the boat. It blew up midstream. No one survived; the piranhas speared no one's body.

I held Clive's radio close to my heart. I bawl as loud as my lungs will allow me.

"Everyone good is taken away from me. I must be cursed" I cried on Mrs. Rogers' shoulder. She allowed me to lay my head on her lap while she smooth my hair.

"You are too young and innocent to be cursed" How would she know?

I mourned my loss. The first man who asked me to be his girlfriend was gone.

His radio was my comfort. It sat next to my teapot on the small table by the bed.

I listen to love songs and imagine that he was singing them to me. Songs like 'Wait for me', 'Under the board walk', 'Put your head on my shoulder' and 'I'll be there'

I spent my days off visiting my sister and the children, going to the Botanic garden and taking long rides to the seawalls.

Sometimes I get carried away, sitting by the sea and listening to my radio. I imagine that one day I would see Clive walking out of the water with a wide smile and say

"I wanted to see if you really love me" and we would live happily ever after. Just like I saw in the Indian movies when I was a child.

I was sitting on the Seawall one Sunday afternoon when I heard a strong voice.

"Be careful not to fall into the sea, or drop your radio into it. You are too disconnected from this world" He was leaning on the wall still sitting on his cycle.

His name is Stan. I told him that I was morning for my boyfriend who was killed in the boat bombing. He was compassionate. He invited me to church next Sunday.

After church we rode to the gardens to listen to the Police Band concert.

The next Sunday after church, he took me to meet his mother and two younger brothers.

Every afternoon Stan came to meet me at the factory. We rode holding hands everywhere. He helped to ease my pain, or should I say forget my pain.

His mother loved me. She also loved my long, curly hair, which was reaching my lower back at this time. She said to Stan and I "You two young people don't rush into anything and get into trouble. Wait and do the right thing when the time is right"

Stan was a decent, well brought-up, educated young man. He was a good-looking all rounder. His strong voice betrayed his age.

I don't remember if I told you this, but during this time, one day my supervisor said,

"Charlie, the gate keeper said that there is someone out there wanting to see you"

I went out and found an Indian man standing on the bridge. I don't remember seeing him before. I began to wonder if something was wrong with my Buddy?

The man, without saying a word, embraced me and began to cry. I was confused. "You don't know me. I am your cousin John. Your mother is my Mosee. She helps to raise my sister Mybee and I when our mother died. We were at her funeral. You may not remember us, but I am here to find you and let you know that we are family" He went on to tell me about the time my mother gave him a shilling to pay for writing his Common Entrance Exam. When he told his father whom he got the shilling from; they ordered him to walk five miles to give back that shilling to his Mosee-aunt.

John became the only family from my mother side, who accepted me and my family into his. His loving wife and seven children opened their hearts to us to this day.

Many others from Kasy's bloodline join John to seek and accept me and mine.

My Sister Esther found a larger room in a house over Mr. Pershaud's shop in Charlotte and Cummings St. I offered to give her ten dollars per month to help pay the rent. I was happy when she moved, especially for the children who had a house to play in. It was safer and cleaner. The bathroom, toilet, kitchen and wash sink were in doors.

I took Stan to meet my only family in Town. My sister connected with him immediately and the children loved him too too.

I introduced him to Mrs. Rogers. She liked him but it did not change her house rules.

One day at Bourda Market, I met one of the Cambell brothers. I asked him if he sees my brothers? And how are they doing? He told me that he sees them everyday. That Datson still sits at the Naga's everyday and sees David with the cows at the backdam.

I gave him two five-dollars and ask him to please give one each to my two brothers.

"Please tell them it's from me, their sister" I made the sign for him to relay to them.

I hope I get married, have a home of my own and bring them to live with me.

At dinner one Sunday at Stan's home, his mother asked me, "Why are you wearing that ring on your left hand? You are not married, are you?"

"No Mom, I am not married, it's my Mommy's ring. She gave it to me the day she died. She told me never to take it off or give it to anyone"

"I ask the question because I know that girls from the country get married very young. You should wear your mother's ring on another finger, not your 'ring finger'.

You should leave it vacant for your future husband's ring" she said smiling at Stan.

I remember the country was still divided racially. There were violence all over, between Blacks and Indians. Even with British troops and curfew, bad things were still happening around the country.

One day my sister asked me to accompany her to Alboystown, the southern end of town. She said that she did some work for a family and needed to collect her money.

"But Sister Esther, it is too dangerous to go to Alboystown. Those young Black boys are beating Indian people if they enter there. What if we don't get back before curfew? Then the soldiers may shoot us" I was afraid to go with her.

"Come on, I need my money"

"OK, put all your hair into a beret. If those people smell that you have Indian, we would be in big trouble. They may find us floating in the trench"

"What about you? You have Indian too"

"Yes, but mine is not as strait as yours. Look, I just have to use my Afro pick and I have a head full of Afro curls"

On the bridge to Alboystown, I saw three Black men sitting on the rail. I told my sister to walk on my other side, away from them. But one of them walked over to her and took the beret off her head; all her strait long hair fell down.

The other two jumped off the rail and the three men began to slap my sister around.

I screamed and begged them to leave her alone. I told them that her father is Black.

They turned on me "You got Cullie in you too? You is a Dugla like she? We gon beat out the Cullie from you too"

They slapped us around, left us on the ground and went back and sat on the rails.

I disliked all the bad people of both races who are doing such bad things in my country. I disliked the two party leaders who were splitting the population racially.

One side of me bombed the boat that carried my Clive; the other side of me beat and kicked my sister and I to the ground like some stray dogs.

By election time, I was eligible to vote. Everyone was telling me who to vote for.

"Remember who you are, you are Black"

"You are your mother's child, your mother is Indian, and that makes you an Indian"

405

"Can you see any Indian looking at you as one of dem?"

"Didn't you say that some Black boys beat you and your sister in Alboystown?"

Those stanch supporters of both party, would do or say anything to put your name on their list as a supporter of their party.

The more they pushed me to support them, the more I pulled away.

There was a third party, led by a Portuguese businessman name Peter D'Agular.

Mostly none Indian/Black supported the United Force. Such as Chinese, Whites and ofcourse, Portuguese and others who were fed up with violence and racism that the other two parties were injecting into the election. It was a small party but I did not hear that division by race thing at his rallies.

I went several times to listen to all three party leaders while they campaigned

Come Election Day, I made my choice. I voted for Peter D'Agular's United Force.

If one was to ask the Blacks forty years ago, 'How are things in the country?'

The answer would be, 'Everything is great. We have a great leader'. A Black man.

If the same question was asked to the Indians, the answer would be, 'Everything is hell in this country. I am leaving, I am going to England/America/Canada"

While the Indians exited the country, Blacks who were living and studying abroad,

Answered the call by their leader and returned home to build the country. Many did.

Now, forty years later, if you are to ask the Indians, 'How are things in the county?'

They would say, 'Everything is great. We have a great leader'. An Indian man

The Indians are returning from abroad while the Blacks are leaving again.

Peter Simms, a world traveler and foreign affairs reporter, called Guyana

'The land of six people'. Today it is primarily three people, Indians, Blacks and Amerindians. The White, Portuguese and Chinese are gone, leaving a scattered few.

African and Indians came by boats to every Colonial countries and islands.

Today, none is more racially divided than Guyana. My opinion, sad to say.

At the factory, I was doing well. I was elected chop steward for the union. I represented the workers and interpret the agreement to management when necessary.

I was selected to attend Chrichlow Labor College to do a course in Trade Unionism.

I attended many courses on Labor laws and Agreements.

Even though I couldn't read, write or spell to be qualified for these honor placed on me. None knew the truth. I hid the fact that it took me all night with two dictionaries, using a flashlight, to be able to write a short report.

I still could not read. I was able to dodge such request by blaming the insufficient light or that I forget my glasses – which I never had –

My sister decided to send her only daughter, Sharon to her father in England.

Weeks before her departure, Stan and I comforted my sister. Telling her that Sharon will one day be able to make a way for her and the boys to go to England.

The day my niece left, Stan and I accompanied my sister and the boys to say goodbye to Sharon at the Atkinson Field Airport. Stan gave her a pair of gold earrings and I gave her a gold ring. My sister cried for weeks for sending her daughter away.

Around the end of the year, coming close to my birthday, after knowing and loving Stan almost a year, he said, "If you take that ring off your 'ring finger', I would feel free to put my ring on that finger to show you how much I love you. I want others to know that you are taken, because you are mine" I was honored, excited and speechless.

I was at my sister's washing dishes when a cup full of water slipped out of my hands.

Few minutes later we heard heavy banging at the door.

I opened the door to find a tall, handsome, light skinned with red hair man standing at the door, drenched with water. His white shirt stuck to his muscular chest.

I saw the curves of his body and saw two nipples sticking out through the wet shirt.

He had those light brown, sleepy eyes that registered 'sexy'. I was freckled.

I became exited and began to laugh at the way he stood at the doorway.

"Someone from up here threw water on me" he said, with his proper English.

My sister came out of her room to see what the laughter is all about? She saw the young-man standing at the doorway, she asked, "Hi Richard, what's the matter"?

"Someone from up here threw water on me as I rode into my yard from church" he did not take his eyes from me as he answered my sister.

She looked at me crossly and asked, "Did you do that?"

"The cup of water slipped out of my hand and fell down. How am I to know it fell on you? I am so sorry for wetting your church clothes" I was laughing, he was serious.

A flash of the past struck me like a hammer. I remembered my brothers threw water on a police one Sunday as he came from church. They paid a terrible price for it.

I became serious, I said to the stranger, "I am truly sorry, it was not intentional.

It was clean water that I was going to drink. Give me your clothes, I will wash and iron them and give them back to you by nightfall" how quickly the bad past brought me to my senses. I felt bad for my laughter.

"That will not be necessary" he looked at me with those sleepy, sexy eyes.

"Do you know who is he? Do you know what you've done? Throwing water on him and then laughing about it? Don't be surprise if there is another knock on the door, this time it would be his mother" my sister said, she was furious with me.

"Who is he, Sister Esther?"

"He is Richard Greene. He lives in the next yard with his parents and three brothers.

They are big shot people. They are five boys; the eldest lives in England, there are no girls. They all have good education and good jobs. They own all three houses in the yard. The father is a foreman at Sprostons Wharf and the mother is a seamstress".

"How come you know all ah diss about the people? You just move here"

"I ask questions. I like to know who I am living amongst" If only you knew my sister. Everyone who knows her will tell you that she is one of the friendliest people.

I went downstairs, my laundry in my canvas bag, only to find my two wheels flat.

"Who would do such ah thing?" asked my sister

"I don't know, but I have to go home. I will borrow a pump from one of the ladies"

As I turned the corner, who I saw holding my pump in one hand, slapping it into the other hand like a teacher with his wild cane or ruler? Yes it was the wet cat.

I kept on walking, pushing my flat tires cycle. He caught up with me and got on his knees and pumped my wheels. I was not laughing neither was he.

He got on his bicycle and caughtup with me again by the Bourda market.

"Do you like fruits? Lets stop at the fruit-stall and get some fruits.

Pick as much as you want" my sister said they were rich, so he is showing off.

I picked some of every kind of fruit the lady had on her stand. She had to put them in two large brown paper bags. I didn't care if I was setting a bad 'first impression', there weren't going to be a second. Afterall, I have a boyfriend.

We sat on a bench in the park at Merman's Mall until 2am, some of the fruits were consumed but I still had enough to last for the week.

Mrs. Rogers gave me a long blistering speech.

"I do not get out of my bed at this ungodly hour to open door for anyone.

"Where have you been until this ungodly hour, child?" like a concern parent.

"In the Park, Maam" The last person I wanted to think badly of me was Mrs. Rogers.

I remembered how I suffered in Lancaster, trying so hard to convince so many that I was a 'good girl'. I stop trying. I do not want to see the disbelief in their faces when I tell them the truth. I just let people think whatever they may.

I came out of the factory gate to find two men waiting for me.

"Who is that handsome dude waiting for?" asked Tessa.

I looked at Stan and Richard leaning on their bicycles, looking at me. I said,

"Tes. I think I am going to ride along with you on the back streets"

When I got to my sister's, Stan was waiting for me. Breathlessly he asked

"What happened? Why did you ride the other way, leaving me standing there?"

"I don't know" I answered, looking on the ground.

"What's wrong Wynette? Did I do something wrong?"

"No, you did nothing wrong. I did something wrong" still looking down.

"There is nothing you could do to make me feel that you did something wrong"

"But I did"

"What did you do?"

"You see the guy who was standing next to you? Well, I spent most of last night with him on a bench in the Merman Mall"

I lifted my head after his long silence, I looked into his eyes, I felt so ashamed.

He placed his hand on my shoulder and said.

"That's OK. Some men are more aggressive than others. But, you are still my girl? Right?" He peeped into my face and continued "Right? You are still my girl? Right?"

Mrs. Rogers's curfew was too strict for two people who could not keep their hands off each other. Two people in love, so much in love that every spared moment were spent together. We went everywhere on our cycles. Matinee, parties, seawall rides, the Gardens and everywhere there was music playing.

He taught me to dance; we became so good that whenever there was dance or party, we would find ourselves in the middle of a circle. People just make way for us to move.

But, I had to be home by eight. Most time, was when the party or dance just started.

Mrs. Rogers, my sister and friends cautioned that I take it easy. They said I was freckled. Be careful not to end up like the 'dog and the bone', dropping the real one.

"The world is not going anywhere. It will be here when all of us are gone. Take it easy. The two of you are behaving as if you are the only people in love"

We rode the four corners of Georgetown. He took me to meet all his relatives scattered all over town. We rode with his arm around my shoulder, laughing and kissing. We were behaving as if the world belongs to the two of us.

Richard was getting tired of hearing me saying, "I have to go, it's late, Mrs. Rogers will be mad. She promised to lock me out one of these night when I am late"

"Then I will take you to my home"

The Sunday, he took me to meet his family. He said that he wanted me to go on a Sunday for his father to meet me, because that's the only day he is home.

His family was receptive and kind. His mother offered me a bowl of split peas soup, as if she had it prepared just for me. His brothers looked at me from toes to head, then hugged me and said, "We need a girl around here"

His father invited me to a game of cards, "I don't know how to play cards, Sir"

He gave me his inviting smile and said, "That's OK, sit here, I will teach you. By the way, call me Sonny or Dad, not Sir. OK"

- Over the years that followed, I could've beaten most who challenged, never him. -

His mother was a seamstress. She never measured me, if she did, I would've been a size 2, weighing 108 pounds. Whenever I visit, she present me with a piece of garment, mostly skirt and blouse to wear to work. – I never wore trousers up to this stage –

Every time I was out with Richard, I prayed not to run into Stan. I would be too ashamed to look at him. I often wondered what he thought of me when I told him that I spent the night in the park with Richard. Somehow, I cared what he thought.

If to everyone else, I was a 'bad girl' I wanted Stan to know that I was still a 'good girl'

The cloud was our carpet. We were flying high. Some women looked at me with envy, others asked, "Where did you find such a good-looking dude?" "In the Park"

I was sensitive to our color difference. I was dark and he was light with red hair.

I grew up knowing that one's skin shade makes a difference of whom you are.

He told me over and over that our color difference is in the eyes of bigots. He said that he is from a family who do not see shades of people, but people for who they are.

"You are beautiful. Your skin color represents everything that is delicious, such as Sapodilla – one of the sweetest brown fruit in Guyana – coco, coffee and cream, chocolate, honey, cinnamon and brown sugar. Everything about your color is sweet".

Our youthful hormones were doing havoc on our promise to be

patient and respectful. Many times we reached to the point of no return, then quickly, Mrs. Rogers curfew would bring us back to earth.

"I don't know how much longer I can do this" Richard said breathlessly

. "My birthday is coming up soon – April – I want a special gift from you" he held me so close, even breeze couldn't find its way between us." You know what I mean?"

My womanly feelings were at work too. I felt the same way as my aggressor.

Unknown to me, Richard rented a first floor apartment at 25th Evans St, Charlestown.

He fully furnished it with furniture from Skipper's Furniture Store.

I remember that Sunday 10th of April, 4 days before his birthday, he said,

"I have somewhere to take you" I loved him so much; I went wherever he took me.

When he took the keys out of his pocket and opened the door, stepped aside and ushered me into a stranger's home, I knew I was in a dream. I was excited. I wondered

'Which one of his friends lent him the use of his apt for the day?' I was in agreement with what was going to happen. I wanted it too.

He placed the keys in my hand and said, "This is your home now, no more

Mrs. Rogers speeches" he placed his arm around me and walked me through the one bedroom, sitting room, kitchen and bathroom apartment. It had three lights, where you had to pull a chain from the ceiling to turn on and off. It had a back door that opened to the yard and a cloth line.

Astonished, I wondered 'When and how did he do all of this? From the curtains, to the mats on the floor, to the shining pots and pans in the kitchen, when he is so busy at his job preparing for independence?' – later I learned that he seeked his mother's help while he and I worked. Despite her disapproval of me moving away from the strict surrounding of Mrs. Rogers to be on my own, she did what he asked but reminded him.

"Until you are married, you have a curfew to keep in my house" –

When I told Mrs. Rogers that I am moving out, she said, "I am not surprised. Not the way I saw him pursuing you. He is like a wild boar. I watch when he walks you to the door, just to make sure that he didn't vent his feelings on my landing"

Once again, I was on the move. My clothes in two pillowcase and my two pieces of treasures, the teapot and the radio, were safely packed into my St Kitts canvas bag.

I had my very own key to my very own home, where I can turn on/off my lights as I wish. I chanted the Indian words 'Kuch Kuch Hota Hai' 'I feel something in my heart' as I danced all over my 'own' kasha.

Richard and I became one. Our oyster was my apartment.

Saturday nights, we danced until dawn to music from Otis, Tom, Johnny, The Platters, The Drifters and Mighty Sparrow. We were so good on the dance floor.

Sundays he brought split peas soup from his mother for us to eat on my dinning table.

We went to the market regularly because I didn't have a fridge. Fridge and phone were luxury for the rich, not beginner like me. He brought ice from his home for me.

Making love, cooking and eating took up most of our spare time. He was a good lover and a good cook. Everyday he brought me something, be it from the market, the store, the jeweler or from his parents home. What else can this girl in love want?

The first few months, we had no time for anyone else. We were locked in paradise.

On workdays, we raced to see who would reach Evans St first. I did not want to wakeup from this sanctuary of love. I was assuring myself that nothing is wrong with me, that I was a woman with feelings for a man. If only my mother was still alive, I would've told her "You see Mommy, you did not have four boys as you feared. I am a woman and I am in love with a wonderful man".

After two months of pure excitement and love, I became afraid. My period did not flow. My fear was short lived. It soon turned into triumph for me. I had a big secret to keep from everyone as long as I wish. I have something no one can take away from me.

On the third month, after successfully hiding my morning sickness from all the watchful eyes, I went to the doctor. He conformed that I was pregnant. He said

"If you don't want it, this is your last chance to get rid of it. After three months, you would have to keep it" I looked at him with surprise and shock. I asked him

"What made you think that I wouldn't want my baby?"

"It's a question I ask young girls, because it is better to have it done the safe way than going to the back ally and die from septic. I feel guilty for not making this question part of my practice years ago. Before so many young girls were brought to me when it was too late" He became my doctor, friend and my confidant for the rest of his life.

On my way from the doctor, I went into Kerpalani store. I bought a pair of baby shoes and two baby books. 'This child is going to have shoes and education' I promise.

My sister was the first to confront me after she saw that my skirts were not fitting.

"You get 'catch' right? You are pregnant, right?"

When even my largest blouse couldn't hide my bump anymore, I told Richard,

"I am pregnant" I did not know what to expect. I Heard so many horrible stories of when men were told that the girl is pregnant, that he ran as fast as he could to the opposite direction, leaving her to take care of her baby. I braced myself for whatever.

Richard jumped with joy. He lifted me high in the air, spinning around, laughing and crying. When he put me down, I was giddy and he was breathless. He said,

"We are pregnant. We are going to have a baby. We are going to get married right now" I still remember seeing the joy in his eyes and me wiping his tears that ran down to his red beard. He was like a little boy who finally rode his tricycle without falling.

I was at ease from his reaction. We are still one. He is still in love with me. I said,

"Yes, we are pregnant, we are going to have a baby, but no we are not going to get married right now I have seen many wedding where people form their own opinion.

They line the churchyard just to see the bride's belly and looking for the 'shotgun'.

If you still feel as you do now, after I get this baby, I will marry you"

My sister was fit to be tied. "What you mean? You refused to get married to the man who asked to marry you because you are having his baby? Are you mad?"

His mother said, "We don't have to have a large wedding. You two could go to City Hall and get married. I want my grandchild to be legal with his/her father's name"

"We don't have to be married for our baby to be have his/her father's name.

When the baby arrives, Richard has to go to the Birth Registry and register the birth, signing his name as the father of the baby. As for the 'legal' importance? It is not important to me at this time. This baby is legally Richard's and mine. Please help me enjoy this special time in my life, without wondering what others may say or think"

The folks at my job had their say, "What did you expect? Bucket going to the well every night, one night the bottom gonna fall out". Later, they got accustomed to the fact that I was pregnant. They quenched my cravings by bringing whatever I asked.

The ladies gave me valuable advice and guidance, step by step, as if they were my mothers, and had more experience than young me.

Sister Esther was the only family I had in Georgetown. She became my other mother; she supported me all the way. I was learning everything there was to know about having a baby, from my sister, Sis, his mother and the ladies around me.

When I took Mrs. Rogers' allowance biscuits and goodies from the market, she looked at my maternity outfit as if she was expecting it. She said,

"I knew it, I knew it, I knew it was going to happen sooner than later. You young people do not have patience. I suppose I have to start knitting booties and bonnets?"

As I got bigger, she allowed me to lie on her bed, placed my foot on her lap where she massaged them. She gave me advise of her time in my condition.

Sis was making maternity clothes for me that was much bigger than my bump.

Oh, how I wished my mother were here. I would've never question her knowledge.

I know she would've been here with me. Cooking all my craving foods and massaging my swollen foot, and to see that gold cap when she laughs with happiness.

The first time I left my baby moved in my belly, I jumped off the bed to see if there was something crawling in it. When I realized that the crawling was my baby, I had a feeling of connection, a joy that I cannot explain.

It was the first time that I realized that it's a living, moving baby in my belly.

I took the baby book that I bought from Kerpalani and began to read to my baby.

I made friends with my neighbors around. All the ladies offering advice and help.

Some wanted to be Godmother, others wanted to baby-sit when I have to go back to work. I was, once again, living in a village.

I was happy throughout my pregnancy. Richard was with me all the time.

When I became too large to ride my bicycle, he towed me to and from everyday.

We did not go dancing, but we went to the movies, restaurants and market.

He bought me lots of fruits, vegetable and doctor recommended calcium and iron pill.

Mr. and Mrs. Corlett, who lived on the top floor told me "In your condition, if you are alone when the time comes, use your broom stick to bum up if you need help"

How could I be unhappy? With so much love and affection pouring all over me?"

The country was preparing for its independence. British soldiers were still here from the days of the riots. More came because of Queen Elizabeth visit for the celebration.

Richard was very busy too. He worked at the Ministry of Home Affairs. He had such a good handwriting, that he was given the task to handwrite all the invitation to dignitaries around the world. He was left-handed

That Christmas, most of my gifts were for the baby.

Richard's father, Sonny ordered a crib for the baby. He told the joiner not to paint it yet.

Early February 1966, I woke up to feel my belly as stiff and hard as an oversize basket ball. I felt heavy and uncomfortable.

I kept my clinic appointment. The midwife informed me that should not go back home. She asked for a phone number to inform my 'husband', - seeing the ring -

Richard was not allowed to stay with me in the pre-delivery ward full of women.

His mother and my sister took turns sitting by my side, sapping my head with lime rum.

It was a long labor. I was dilating slowly. Two days and two nights of pain.

In those days, women had to bear their pain until they were ready to deliver. There were only three nurses to take care of a large ward of screaming women. If there was, however, any sigh of danger in a delivery, a doctor would be summoned.

The nurses wheeled me into the labor room.

In my delirious state, I heard one nurse say, "this baby better come before seven o'clock, I have to go listen to Dr. Paul" – radio soap opera –

My bouncing baby girl arrived into this world at 6.45pm.

I heard one nurse saying, "Oh Lord, this is another White soldier baby"

Remember I told you that there was lots of British army officials in the country?

Well their presence, Mulattos, was showing up in labor rooms all over the country.

I was wheeled into a large, open ward with about twenty beds for new mothers.

My bed was between an Indian and Black women. When the nurse placed my little baby girl into my awkward arms, I saw the two women, crane their necks to look at each other, having the same thoughts as the nurse "Another soldier baby"

Richard, his mother and my sister, granted me the special moment that I needed to introduce myself to my own flesh and blood.

They allow me to cry as I held her against my cheek, placed her little body in the valley of my chest and let her heart beat against mine. Just like my Mommy did with me.

She is a Lightie and I am a Darkie, and she is all mine.

I am feeling her warmth from my womb. She just came out of me. She is mine.

Holding my baby in my arms was the most emotional experience of my life.

My visitors too were crying and laughing with joy. Sis said,

"This little princess is the first girl in our family. I had to deal with a houseful of boys, now I have a girl to sew pretty little dresses for" I felt a touch of jealousy.

Richard gave me jewel box full of gold jewelry. He whispered,

"Thanks for my gift. We are getting married as soon as you leave this hospital.

Tomorrow I will go and register my daughter. Do you have a name yet?" I looked at my baby and said, "Her name is Kim". He kissed me, took the baby into his awkward arms and said, "Hello Miss Kim Greene, I am your Daddy Richard, you are my Missy"

The next day, nurses, patients and visitors lined the windows of the ward to catch a glimpse of the motorcade of Her Royal Highness, Queen Elizabeth, passing on New Market St. – most of the baby girls born during her visit were named Elizabeth –

I stayed in my bed, cuddling my own little princess, getting to know her and working on getting her to latch on to my breast.

We went home five days later to a home fit for a princess. Everything was pink.

A pink crib with pink lace canapé. Pink shimmies, booties and bonnets.

When Kim was nine days old, I asked a friend to take a picture of her.

I vowed that my baby was going to see what she looked like as she grows.

She was not going to be like me, whose first picture was taken at eighteen years old.

Sister Esther was working for the Archbishop of the West Indies, Dr Alan John Knight. She asked him to christen her niece. You see in those days and up to now, you could not take a newborn baby out to visit unless he/she was christened.

Kim was six-weeks old when she was christened into the Anglican Church.

The christening party was too grand. Richard, brothers and friends built tents and benches in the yard. The large crowd celebrating her coming into this world.

"My mother wants us to set a date for the wedding. She needs to start making preparation. Remember I have a large family and my parents have lots of friends"

"Yes, me too have a large family. I want to take my baby and you to Lancaster to meet my family. I cannot make any plans for a wedding before you meeting them"

Why was it so important that I go back to Lancaster before I take such an important step? I already have a child, which was more important than getting married.

I wanted to go back to Lancaster to see my two brothers, most of all. I want them to see my baby. I wanted Richard to see that I too have a large family. Until now, my sister and my two nephews were the only family I have while it seems as if half the population of Georgetown was his family and friends.

"When are we going to meet them?" he asked agreeably.

"When my baby is six months old. Around August Monday weekend, I may get a few days from the job, then, we could go for a week"

"Job? What Job? You are not going back to work at that biscuit factory.

I am capable enough to take care of you and my daughter. No more work for you"

"I am going back to work when my baby is two months old"

"Why do you want to wait so long from now to go to the country?"

"Because that is how long I want to wait" he didn't know that I wanted to go to Lancaster when my Uncle Bertram was home. You see, I never told Richard much about me, except that I have two brothers, Datson and David and that they are mute.

Going back to work was hard. Leaving my baby was even harder.

Since she arrived we have never been separated. Now I have to leave her for hours.

Sis offered to take care of her during the week and I could have her at weekends.

That didn't sit well with me. Eight hours away from her would be bad enough, five and a half days away from her? That will never happen.

I asked Ada, a middle-aged hairdresser and her elderly mother, Mama to care for Kim. Ada had no children; she was a devoted daughter to her mother.

"They live across the street, while your mother lives across town. I need to be close to my baby every spare moment I have" I told Richard.

I cried so hard when I took my baby over to Ada's. Mama had to take Kim inside while Ada pushed me through the door to go to my job.

Mrs. Joseph, my supervisor on the job, saw that my blowes was soaked with milk. She sent me home to nurse my baby and returned. – That was not in the union agreement – I took my lunch break everyday and went home, ten minutes away on my cycle, to nurse and play with my baby, giving myself ten minutes to return to work.

Many days, Richard joined me to be a part of the joy of being with our daughter.

After three years of leaving Lancaster, I was in the train going back home.

It was a much better ride than the one I took so long ago.

Richard and his mother had never gone to Berbice. This was their first trip.

Kim was the center of attention in the carriage. Everyone was smiling and waving to her. She was a pretty baby with a head full of curls. I did to her what my Mommy did to me; I divide her hair in four and twist twenty-five curls on each quarter.

If I were thinking that we would surprise the family at Lancaster with our unannounced visit. It did not happen. Someone in the ferry took the news faster than the wind can blow. "Me see Wynette in the boat. She been wid a man holding a baby"

My family, Uncle Bertram, Aunt Elo and their family, Uncle Jamesy, Aunt Georgie and their family, Uncle Percy, Sister Bea and their family, my stepmother, her daughter and seven children on the bottom floor of the 'big house' and Mr. and Mrs. Chance and family on the top floor, Uncle Patrick and Aunt Venus and family, then, my Cinderella castle, with my father, Datson and David. That's how many people now lived in the Alexander's' compound. They all greeted us with open arms.

Uncle Bertram and Aunt Elo said that we would stay at their house.

Datson with his hair longer than mine, and a face full of hair, did not frighten little Kimmie. She grabbed his beard, wanting to kiss her uncle.

My brother's eyes glowed with happiness, through all the hair around his face.

I placed the baby into his arms. He looked at her, then at me and signed

"Why is she so white?" I showed him Richard. He shook his head, understanding why.

The smile from Uncle Bertram put me even more at ease. His eyes told me that I came back home at the right time.

Richard and Sis were truly surprised to see where I came from.

Looking at all the large houses, the families who came out to greet us, left them trying to behave like country folks too. They were seeing what 'village' living is all about?

When the news spread around the village that the 'Prodigal Daughter' has returned.

They came to greet me and to see what they can do for me. That's village living.

I looked at the two 'city folks' and wondered what were they thinking?

I hope that no one tells Richard about my past. I would do that when the time is right. Not because we are madly in love and have a baby, that I have to spill my past.

Uncle Bertram knew that my father got the news that I had arrived, but he was in no hurry to take us to him at the 'back house'.

I told myself that I am not afraid. I was a big girl now. I am trying to forget that path. I have Richard's strong arms to comfort me if need be. But I was afraid. My heart was pounding, my hands were sweating and I was shivering, walking the worst path of my past that is leading me back to my father and that house of horror.

Uncle Bertram saw my condition, put his arm around my shoulder, gave me a quick squeeze and said, "Its OK, you don't have to be afraid of him anymore"

"Mike, where are you? Openup, you have visitors". shouted my uncle.

My father aged more than I could ever imagined. He sat proud and upright as a king in his old Berbice chair. He was sixty years old and had just retired from the estate.

He assumed my tasks of doing things around the house and caring for his companion who is now bedridden with Parkinson Disease.

I placed my little girl into my father's arms and took a seat next to Richard.

The silence was too long for others not to suspect that something is wrong.

I looked around the living room where I once kept so neat and tidy with the floor shining that I could've seen my sad face on it.

The same living room where I peed myself so many times when the rope hit my back.

"Archie, who come da?" my stepmother broke the silence from the 'big room'.

"Dem an't come to you, go back to sleep" my father spoke. Even his voice changed.

Richard and Sis introduce themselves to my father. He was receptive with a smile.

"I cleaned your room as best as I could, for you and the baby. Your companion can stay where they are, but you stay here. Whatever you do in Georgetown is up to you, but here, you don't disrespect me by staying anywhere but here" he was not looking at me, but I knew he was speaking to me.

"You and no man are sleeping in any house in this family compound, unless you are married. Even if you have a child," said my father. 'Look who is talking' I thought.

I was not afraid of him anymore. If I do stay in this house, it would be because I will be sleeping in the same house with my two brothers.

"I wanted them to get married from the very start, but Wynette was not ready"

"Was your son ready?" my father asked Sis.

"Yes, he and his whole family were ready for a wedding. We are ready right now"

'Do not force anyone to get married' Archie said sternly.

David sat on the edge of the bed; he had brought in some mosquito coil to protect his niece from mosquitoes. He watched me coaxes little Kimmie to sleep. He was happy to have her; he kept kissing and squeezing her. He told me that he was proud of me.

We tiptoe to the steps, our onceuponatime meeting place for comforting each other.

He brought me up-to-date with everything that had happened since I left.

He told me that Daddy went loco after I left. – He used his index finger, pressed against his temple and twist in circle, meaning crazy

— He told me that he and Daddy did all the chores around here. He said Datson does nothing but sleep here, that whenever Daddy offered him some food, or try to communicate, he would grunt angrily and walk away.

David told me that Datson is so angry with my father for selling our mother's home,

Even though Daddy gave them some of the money and ordered new clothes for them, Datson is still angry with him.

My brothers still walked barefooted like my father, if I was still here, me too.

I asked David if anyone comes to help with my stepmother? He said her daughter-in-law Raj and daughter Mine comes once per month to give her a bath.

What about her daughter and seven children who live a few yards from her?

He told me that one of her granddaughter comes once in a while to see her.

He said that my father takes care of all her needs, did all the cooking and he David did the cleaning, washing and taking care of the livestock.

I was trying hard to block out all the misery I went through in this house, but they kept bumping into me. In the kitchen, I saw the kerosene stove that I was not allowed to use. Now, brown with rust and cobweb adorn it. On the landing I saw the plant pots with dried, cracked dirt that once had my beautiful houseplants that decorated the living room. The dried, cracked dirt transcribed, "Wynette don't live here anymore"

The next morning, my father brought up a bowl of rice porridge; boil eggs and a large enamel cup of boiled cow's milk. He said, "There is plenty of fresh, warm milk on the fireside. Give the baby as much as she can drink. Forget that powdered thing from the can. I put a bucket of water and soap on the landing for you to bathe her".

I was looking at a completely different person from three years ago.

My father has become humble and quiet to me. He was always

humble and quiet to others, not me. He would be having a good time but as soon as I appeared, his whole demeanor changed with disgust in his eyes. Oh, how much he has changed?

As if we have no past. We still manage to avoid each other eyes.

All the aunties in the yard invited us for meals at their homes. I took my brothers along. They did not leave my side and certainly I was not going leave their sides.

My father and uncles took Richard for drinks. Richard drove the tractor to the fields. He came back with bags of coconut and ground provisions. He and my father were having a good time. I liked that. Now you see why I did not tell him my about past?

I tried to block out the haunting sound that was coming out of the 'big room' as long as I could, just like I was doing with all the bad things that happened in this house.

Richard and his mother were experiencing country life. People from the country are giving people. One only has to ask for something; a villager would get it for you if he could. They always want to give visitors something to take back to remember them by.

Sister Bea told me that she sends a pot of split peas soup every Sunday for daddy and the boys. Homemade bread every Friday, and that her daughter Elane helps David with the washing. She assured me that I don't have to worry about my brothers, because they have a yard full of family who would not let them go hungry. She said, "Your father is too proud to ask for help. He should demand that your stepmother daughter do more to care for her mother, after all her mother did for her? But he does it all himself"

"That's life Sister Bea, that's life. Its his choice" I didn't want to say anything else.

She said that she sees Datson in the morning when he goes out of the compound, and in the evening when he comes home. He spends his days at Auntie Chunu's and at Tara Stand, where he sits and waits for Auntie Chunu who sells fish at the market.

I coaxed Datson one morning into cutting his long lucks and beards.

You see, Linda, we Dugla-mixbreed-multyracial people, if we let our hair grow long, it stays straighter. If we cut it short, we get a curly Afro.

My brother sat as quiet as my Lammy and allowed me to cut off all his long, strait hair and bushy beard. A good long shower and a change of clean clothes did it.

No one recognized him when he walked through the yard with my baby in his arms.

"How did you get him to agree for you to do that?"

"I did not ask him, I just told him that Kim is afraid of his looks"

My brothers brought all kinds of goodies for Kim. Some she couldn't eat because she was too small. Datson asked to take her out every morning, I gladly obliged.

Despite everyone's objection, I knew that my brother would protect her with his life.

Our week vacation was winding down. I spent a long time with Uncle Bertram.

I thanked him for setting me free. I told him that I didn't want to get married until I came home. I wanted Richard to see that I too have a large family, and that I didn't drop off a coconut tree. That mine too has large houses and spoke proper English.

My uncle gave me that smile that would calm a volcano. He said, "I am proud of you. You did not let me down, like some said you would. They did not know you like me and your Aunt Elo did. You made us proud of you"

One day when I was alone in the house, I stood outside the door of the 'big room' for a long while, listening to the sound from within. Wondering, should I go in? Or should I just go back home to Georgetown? Carrying the same tonnage on my shoulder?

I opened the door and went in. I stood strait with my arms folded.

When I saw what my stepmother had become, I heard my mother's voice.

"Only when you forgive, can you truly be free"

I took up the cup of ground barley and fish soup, made by my father. I had to hold her head steady with one hand, to get the cup to her lips without spilling from her shaking.

I said, "We were someone's children. Even if you were doing what you were asked to do, like reporting my every move in this house, for which you became a victim yourself, you could've seen that we were our mother's children, not three dogs.

I have to forgive you for all you did to us. I am speaking for my brothers too"

I knew that I would not allow anything that happened in this house to provoke me anymore. I have my baby to live for and I am saving 'hope' and time for her.

My father was sitting in his Berbice chair when I came out of his room. He handed me an envelope and said, "I had to sell your mother's house. People were vandalizing it.

I gave your brothers equal parts and kept this for you, if you should ever come back.

I didn't take a cent from it for myself. It belonged to the three of you. I only wish that Datson could understand that I could not let him live there alone"

The silence was painful. I did not know what to say. I did not know what to do. I stood still, holding an envelope that has my share of my mother's labor.

The day before we left, I knew I had to make one visit outside the compound.

I got Datson and David to accompany Kimmie and me to Whim to see Auntie Chunu, Uncle Naga and their family. Auntie Katy had already passed away,

I gave Auntie Chunu one hundred of the five hundred dollars that was in the envelope. We hugged each other, laugh and cried. She was still my loving Auntie.

I stopped at Sahardat store and bought three pairs of leather sanders for the three men in the 'back house'. They had the same height, six foot + and the same size foot.

Remember I told you of one summer when I went to play with friends? Well we had to pass their house to go back home. The girls said, "Wynette, come with your baby"

I crossed the bridge and entered that yard after so many years. They were still my friends and I was happy to see them.

I saw their father sitting in a hammock. I didn't say anything to him. I greeted his wife.

We were laughing and talking when I saw the man got out of the hammock and went over to where Datson was holding my daughter. I rushed over, grabbed my baby from my brother's arm and stood face to face with the man in the dark window. I said,

"Don't you dear touch my daughter. Don't you dear touch my baby".

My friends looked at each other and their mother bow her head down.

I gave one hundred dollars to Sister Bea. She said, "Wynette, you do not have to pay me for what we do for them" I said, "No Sister Bea, I can't afford to pay you for what you and Elane are doing for my brothers. I am just thanking you"

Uncle Bertram and Aunt Elo refused to take anything from me..

I asked my father, "If I decide to get married to Richard, would you come to the wedding?" I had to get this question out. It is one of the reasons I could not make a decision before. Every girl needs a father to walk her up the isle and give her away.

"Where are you going to get married?" my father asked

"In Georgetown, that's where all of his family and friends are"

"What about your family? A girl is supposed to get married from her own village to wherever her husband comes from. Most times it used to be from one village to the next. Nowadays people stray so far from their family, they make the other side think they don't have family of their own"

"Would you come to my wedding in Georgetown, Daddy?" I wasn't looking up. I wasn't looking down anymore. I was looking strait into my father's face.

"No, I have never been to Georgetown and I am not going to Georgetown"

As I turned to walk away from the man who would not be at my wedding, my father threw a cold spear through my heart. He said,

"You are following in your mother's footsteps. She too had no one on her side"

On the train ride back to Georgetown, Richard and Sis spent most of the time talking about the wonderful time they had and how large and kind my family is.

They can hardly believe the amount of bags and boxes of country goodies, such as rice, coconut and eggs from my father's. Other family cooked and baked. There was plenty to eat, such as fried fish and chicken with that rich 'home-made' bread.

We were so loaded with country kindness; we had to rent a 'special hire' car.

Kim too, had her share of gifts. My father got her a pair of gold bangles.

Others gave gold rings and earrings. I pierced her ears, when she was nine days old.

The Greenes were busy planning a wedding.

The wedding invitations were printed and ready for delivery. – In those days, most wedding invitations were hand delivered. Only the ones for out of town were posted.

Country people never post an invitation. They send verbal message of the occasion.

I went up to Lancaster one weekend to tell my family that I am getting married on November 19th, Then I gave them the printed invitation for keepsake.

It's an insult to post an invitation to a family, because an invitation is an option.

My father still refused to attend my wedding in Georgetown.

Uncle Bertram was going to be away at that time, so I asked Uncle George Alexander,

Commissioner of Police in Georgetown. He is my father's cousin and grandson of Malcolm Alexander. He told me that he was honored to oblige.

I took an invitation to Stan's home. Even though I have not seen him in more than a year, he and his family are still my friends. His mother visited me regularly.

He brought a wedding gift to my apartment. We sat at my dinning table, wordless for a while. He just stared and me through his specktickles, as if he was saying,

'Are you sure you are happy?' Then he said, "I would've accompanied my mother to your wedding, yes, she will be there. You know she still loves you like a daughter?

But I will be leaving for Canada that same morning"

I felt sad and ashamed. I wondered, 'Am I doing the right thing?'

Sister Esther, once again asked the Archbishop to conduct the ceremony in his chapel at Austin House.

People asked," What is your connection with the Archbishop? Local people don't even enter his home, more so to get married and christen your baby in his chapel"

"I have a blood connection to the Archbishop"

I used the remainder of the money from the sale of my mother's home, to buy eight yards of Brocade and satin at Bettincourt Store, for my wedding dress. I even got my shoes, stockings and gifts for my bridesmaids from the money in the envelope. As if my mother stretched those few dollars to cover everything for her Babzy's wedding.

"Richard, what's going on? It seems as though you are the only one getting married. Every time I go to Charlotte St. I feel as if I am in the way of all the busy folks getting ready for your wedding. You and your family have decided on everything so far. The wedding date, who will be in the wedding party? I have two friends on the job whom I would like to be my bridesmaids but is seems that everyone has already been chosen.

Things that I think I should decide on, has already been decided.

My sister tried to get involve; your mother told her that she has everything arranged.

Richard, what's going on?" I had rehearsed my question over and over for days.

"Wynette, what do you mean? Everything is going well. We are getting married in two months. I am busy on the job. You are busy on yours. My mother and our family are busy doing for us what we cannot do for ourselves"

"What about my family?"

"How many of your family are here?"

"My sister Esther is a shout away from your home. She offered her service. What's the matter? She is not good enough to be involved in her sister's wedding plans?"

Richard and I had our first quarrel. Am I ready to go through with the wedding? I was very happy the way things were. What difference a wedding would make?

Richard sensed my unhappiness. The next day, he and his mother met me in Evans St.

Sis said, "I know you don't have any relatives here in Georgetown, that's why I get my sisters and family involved in the preparation"

"I have my sister here, she offered to help. I have friends on the job that would be willing to help. I have neighbors around me who would help. I am not alone"

"Tell your two friends to come to Charlotte St. to be measured for their dresses.

I will go talk to your sister. Anyone else who are willing to assist, please send them.

Aunt Harriett came to town to help with my wedding preparation. She stayed with my sister. Boy, could my Auntie cook, bake and decorate?

The night before my wedding, my little apartment was bubbling over with my sister, auntie, friends and neighbors. They came to do 'qua qua', a traditional African ceremony where the people sing folks songs and dance around the bride-to-be.

The day of the wedding, I was nervous, very nervous. There were many women around me, trying to do things for me that I normally did for myself. I should enjoy the pampering? But I was too nervous to understand that today is the most important day in my life and that I should allow myself to be pampered.

My first bridesmaid Elane came to dress at my home so she would be there to assist me.

Ada did my hair. She said, "Richard, warned me not to use any makeup or lipstick on you" she softened it by adding, "but you don't need any of them, you are a beautiful bride without them"

Uncle George was early. He was so handsome, and so handsomely dressed, he left the women speechless.

He let me take his arm as he led me to his car. His chauffeur opened the back door and Elane helped with my long train. I looked around before entering the car. I saw a large crowd standing around just to have a glimpse of the bride.

The driver took the longer way to the chapel, giving others enough time to arrive before we get there. "A bride should be the last to make an entrance," said my uncle.

When we arrived at Austin House, in Kingston, I couldn't believe my eyes.

Where did all these people come form? There were so many cars and bicycles along the street, as far as I can see.

The crowd cleared a path for us to walk. The wedding party was waiting by the door to follow me up into the chapel.

Ada carrying baby Kim, my little flower girl who threw rose petals on my path.

I was queen for the day. All eyes were on me. The music played 'Here comes the bride' as my uncle walked me into the chapel and stood next to Richard and his father.

The chapel was packed with no more standing room left. The men stood along the walls, allowing the females to sit.

The Archbishop asked, "Who giveth this woman to be married to this man?"

Uncle George answered, "I do"

We said the marriage vows and promised to 'Forsake all others, love and obey each other in sickness and in health, as long as you shall live?'

433

During the ceremony, I tried to focus on some of the faces in the crowd.

I saw my sister Esther, Sherlock and Mark, Aunt Harriett, Aunt Nora, Ronnie, uncle Rick's son from Suriname, Ulrick, Uncle Bertram's son, James, Uncle Jamesie's son. Brooksy, Uncle Percy's son, and Alvin, Aunt Wini's son.

My mouth was stiff from smiling all the time. I continued to survey the chapel when I saw him. Tall and upright, dressed in black pants and white long sleeves shirt and a dark tie. He was looking at me and I was looking at him. My smile turned into laughter.

"I have family on my side, Daddy, and I have my very own Davendra-David too"

As we signed the register, Richard whispered in my ears, "Sign your name for the last time. From this moment on you are mine, with my name, Mrs. Wynette Greene as long as you live. No one else can love you or dance with but me as long as you live"

After speeches and cake cutting, I danced with my husband to the tune 'Tonight you're mine' which he selected. Then I danced with my Uncle George – he was such a distinguish man, all my bridesmaids asked about him. "Is he your father?" "Who is he?" "He is so handsome" all the women had their eyes on my uncle. I told them,

"He is my uncle and he is married with children but there are lots of single men in this hall. I have six of my own who are just as handsome but not married"

I walked over to the table where David was sitting with my side of the family.

I motioned him to dance with me. He told me that I couldn't dance. I challenged him, because he was a good dancer. He learned the steps from watching movies at Chundon theater and by feeling the vibration at dance halls. I stamped on the floor to get my brothers' attention if they were in another room. They felt the vibration.

My brother and I took to the dance floor. I threw my long train over his shoulder, we held each other close, and others cleared the way so that David can show off his moves.

While we were on out honeymoon at the Belair Hotel, family members from both sides, moved my stuff from my little apt. Into a larger two bedroom bottom flat right behind where I lived. Richard had arranged with the owner to rent the flat since the two-story house began construction. My husband carried me over the threshold.

Kim's first birthday was another grand affair. Her grandmother made the cake and dress fit for a princess, with smocks and embroidery. The entire neighborhood and my friends from the job's children attended the birthday bash.

Richard and I were inseperatable. The only time we were not together was when we were at work. Love was plentiful. Friends and family called us a 'perfect couple'.

Getting married didn't change our nights out of dancing and movies. Ada was always willing to keep Kim. As a matter of fact, Kim wanted to be with her all the time.

We went back to Lancaster several times after the wedding.

Richard and my father were getting along like buddies. I remember Richard saying on our first visit after our wedding, "Now I get to sleep with you in your room"

Uncle Rick had retired in Suriname, decided to return to his homeland and his family in Lancaster, especially his 'partner in crime' Archie-Mike.

They lived together in the 'back house'. My father was once again like a little kid.

Aunt Wini too moved to Lancaster in the 'big house' with her family. She did the cooking for the 'back house'.

Once again the Alexander compound was buzzing with happiness. Now Rick, Archie, James, Winifred and Bertram were all living with other families, on the land on which they were born. Where their umbilical cord were buried under the fruit trees.

The smile on Uncle Bertram's face tells me how happy he was to be with the added siblings. I can only try to imagine what it was like when there were ten of them growing up in this yard with Gramother and Dada?

435

A crowd would gather under Uncle Bertram's house where there were benches and tables to eat, drink and play cards, dominos and talk old time stories.

Except Uncle Brother and Uncle Percy, everyone else drank rum and water in moderation. You don't dear call them 'alcoholics' "Alcoholics misbehave, they beat their wives, they stay in bed all day and drink all night. We don't do any of those. .

"Mike, you remember the day when we went to fetch water at the big well at Whim? You knew that I had problem with Bowel boys, but because you were in love with their sister, you disregard my feelings and stop to talk with them?" asked Rick

"How could I forget that day? You slapped me so hard that the lard bucket full fell off my head and flatten on the ground" answered Archie.

"Yes, and Mother took us to the Police Station for the corporal to give us five lashes each with the catalane tail on our bare backside. I remember what she said to us on our way home, still rubbing our asses. "Do you know why I took you to the police?

Not because one hit the other that I could've settled at home with Dada's belt. I took you to get a lashing because you smashed my lard bucket. Now I have to go put my name on a list in Manoo's store and wait my turn for another empty lard bucket"

"Jamesie, you remember when we came from school at breakfast time, if Mike don't see smoke coming out of Mother kitchen from a mile away, he would throw himself on the ground and role like a wet bore, kicking and screaming "Mother na cook, oh God, Mother na cook. Me na see no smoke coming out of her kitchen. She na cook"?

He who have the smallest gut, had the biggest mouth" The laughter was healthy.

"Ayou remember when Mother and Dada give Bertram to Auntie Sudith? Oh yes, everyone crying, watching our little Bert following Auntie across the narrow bridge"

"It was a sad day for me. He and I were babies at home". said Aunt Wini.

"Bert, wa happen with you and Auntie Sudith that day?"

"I don't remember. I was too small. Mother said that I refused to go into Auntie house, that I sat on her step and collected everything that she used to coxes me into the house, put them into my pillowcase and said, "People picknee want to go to him home".

I heard that she get someone with a donkey cart to bring me back here at midnight"

He gave everyone that victory smile. Oh God, I loved him so very much.

"Alyou remember the time when Mother give us rice pop-portage for tea, breakfast and dinner because things were bad and money was scarce?"

"Oh yes, Mike boasted that if Mother give him any more rice-pop, he will not eat it.

Well, Mother put that bowl in front of him every meal, even after things got better and we get real food, he had to eat that portage before he got food"

"It was hunger after two days that made me eat Mother's warm and warm back rice pop. It was the best rice pop I ever had and the best lesson I ever learnt as a child"

The roar of laughter would draw others to join in the 'longtime stories' telling.

I was happy that Richard was there to see what a loving, respectful family I have.

Our habits, food, culture and tradition and kindness are unique of village people.

Linda I must tell you of this tradition that both sides of me carry on till now.

Whenever there is a special occasion such as the birth of a child, bonus from the estate, harvest of rice or anything that brings joy and money, we would put aside a certain amount of money to "Feed Beggars' like thanking God for His abundance.

People would go with their donkey cart to Rose Hall to pickup beggars who would be under Swamber's drugstore shed. They would take them home, wash their hands and feet. Put them to sit on new white sheets on the floor, feed them with a healthy vegetarian meal and lots of fresh fruits and homemade drinks.

Each one is given a dutchna-gift of new clothing and taken back to their hangout.

These days the new beggars don't go in buses and don't eat vegetarian food. They want meat, rum, cigarettes and music to dance. Some get drunk and misbehave.

We still keep that tradition of sharing to all the little children instead.

We do the same to them and give them new clothes and school supplies.

Our first and second wedding anniversy were spent at the Belair Hotel.

I remember the owner saying to us, "If you continue to come here for the next five years, I will give you a whole week, meals and all, for the other three years, with a party on your tenth annivercy. You seems so much in love, don't allow anything to change"

That December, my brother-in-law was having a fashion show in McKenzie.

Richard and I went up the Demerara River to the bauxite town, sixty-five miles in a small speedboat. I was scared to take such a trip, remembering what happened to Clive.

Richard assured me that I have nothing to worry about; I had him to protect me. He held me into his arms all the way to McKenzie, soaking wet with the river water.

Anywhere there was a close door or privacy we would make love. On the floor, in a chair, on the table, in the shower even in the yard to feel the damp grass on our bodies.

We were like two wild animals in heat all the time. Our hands were on each other all the time. We squeezed each other butts as we walk on the streets. We kiss as if it was the first time. The world was evolving around the two of us. I loved him more than me.

Halfway into the show, Richard whispered, "Are you as board as I am, watching what we know anything about? Lets go back to the hotel and make a baby boy"

We did.

Remember I told you that had Uncle Rick stayed in Guyana he would've been a famous cricketer? He was so good at the game. Every time there were big matches playing in Guyana of the West Indies, he would come form Suriname to attend.

Now that he is retired and live in Guyana, he did not miss any game.

Early 1968 there were a big Test Cricket match in Georgetown. He had prepared to travel in a few days when he complained of not feeling well.

My father and Uncle Bertram had to almost tie and drag him to the hospital.

The doctor admitted Uncle Rick and told him that if he rested for two days and bring his blood pressure down, he would discharge him in time to go to the game.

Uncle Bertram took tea for Uncle Rick, he found him already up and waiting to take a shower. "Two days are up, I feel wonderful, get me out of here"

"Did the doctor discharge you? I can't unless he did" asked Uncle Bertram.

"No, he was here. He said I have to stay afew more days and that I should not shower without an orderly. But I am going to take a shower and get out of here now.

I feel wonderful. I have never been in a hospital before. I am getting out of here.

The youngest brother followed the older brother to the shower after trying to talk him out of his stubbornness.

As soon as Uncle Rick threw a basin of cold water on his body, he fell into the arms of Uncle Bertram and died.

It was a big shock for the family, especially my father. Uncle Rick was his best friend, then his brother. All his children, family and some friends came from Suriname.

Richard and I went up to be with the family. I was three months pregnant with my son.

Uncle Rick was buried at Aklyne Church yard among his ancestors. The words on his tomb are written in both English and Dutch.

By the time I was six months pregnant, people thought I was ready to give birth.

439

Even the nurses at the clinic could not tell if I was having one, two, or three babies.

My last trimester was difficult. Richard was with me all the time. He did everything possible to make me comfortable. I told him that the baby seems to sitting on my lower organs, that I have to keep pulling it up to get some relief from the pain. His mothers made a contraption that I strapped under my belly tie it over my shoulder like a sling.

The doctor put me on bedrest, earlier than the two months that I was entitled to.

No one knew the sex of the baby before birth, in those days.

The pain and stiffness started, but I was in no hurry to go to the hospital.

I remember how long I was there before Kim was born.

Richard was at my side throughout the labor. My pain was less with my darling, my love, and my husband at my side. I loved him so much, I would wash his foot and drink.

When we did go to the hospital, they kept me into the holding pen again until the next day when the head nurse brought the visiting doctor to see me. They took me right away to the theater and did an emergency suzerain to take my bouncing baby boy.

He had the navel cord wrapped around his neck. He weighted ten pounds and had to be placed into an incubator for days because he was blue from lack of oxygen.

When my baby boy was placed into my arms, I was looking at my brother Datson.

My baby was brown with strait black hair and a small, strait nose. I looked at him and said, "Master Rocky, you are from my side of the family"

When we got home, the pink crib became blue with no canapé.

Richard was beside himself. He was celebrating every night with his friends.

My father-in-law presented his grandson with a silver five-shilling coin, the same as the one he gave to Kim when we brought her home. He thanked me for his grandson.

Rocky too was christened at the Archbishop's Chapel and had a grander party.

When we took him to Lancaster, my father called him Rick. He said that his brother came back as his grandson.

I called my son Rocky from the time the nurse handed him to me.

I was in a solid place in my life. I had a wonderful husband, a beautiful daughter, a prince and a home full of love. Everything was rock solid for me. No one could wish for anything more in a home or in life.

Everyone agreed that Rocky resembled Datson so much. When I told my brother that the baby looked liked him, he showed no surprise, he just shuck his head as to say

'What do you expect? He is mine'

I listened to everyone's advise as how to raise my babies.

"Make sure that you squeeze all the milk from the baby breast"

"Why do I have to do that?"

"Because if you don't, that dried milk can cause big problem when she/he is older"

"Do I have to do that with the baby boy too?"

"Ofcourse, men too have problem with that dried milk left in them as babies"

"Just squeeze the milk out of every baby's breast as soon as he/she is born. Every

Newborn baby has milk in their breast. Gentle squeeze it all out"

"Use fresh coconut oil on dem hair and to massage dem body"

"No, not coconut oil. Use olive oil from Swamba Drug Store for dat"

"No, use crab oil from the Bush people, that is better for the tender skin"

"Remember, you have to protect your boy baby so much more than girls"

"How so?"

"You have to make sure that you don't make one drop of breast milk fall on his?"

"Why"

"Choil, because if breast milk fall on his 'wily', he can never function as a man.

Always use nuf bedding to cover that part of him, whenever you are feeding him.

If some women only know how much more care a mother take to prepare her son

for a wife, they would wait until they get their own son to know a mother's love"

"Tie asifeter – dried dark garlic – on the baby at all times to keep away dem bad

Eye- evil eye and oldhigg-vimpia from dem.

"Whenever you are out with your baby, when you return home, always go in with

Your back and call the baby's name and say "you are home', then close the door,

Leaving out the jumbee-spirit that may following you and the baby home"

"Always keep your bible open to the 23rd Psalm, under your baby's head"

"As soon as your baby start eating food, feed dem everything that you eat.

Hot, bitter, sour and everything else, they would not develop kinna-alagies"

"You baby get 'good hair', no put no grease on dem head. Grease blocks the growth No wonder people who use grease and block their pores have picky-picky hair. Only Black people put grease pan den hair. Indian put oil on dem hair everyday".

"Just give the picknee nuff fresh fish and greens to eat, and wash dem hair regularly with okra leaf or bitteraloes and some fresh coconut oil"

Never open umbrella in the house, don't put hat on the bed, never sweep after dark.

. Never sleep with your foot to the east. Only dead people foot should point to the east.

I wish my Mommy were here, she would've been doing all the above and more.

Our neighbors, Hector and Doreen Edwards, became Rocky's Godparents. And Doreen took care of him when I went to work. No one was paid to care for children, you just have to take the baby's supplies, and if you didn't, they will use their own.

Ada and Mother did it for Kim. Doreen, Hector and their four children, Averill, Fenton, Hector jr. and Annie did it for Rocky. One could never put a price on a good neighbor; you can only try to makeup at Christmas or birthdays with nice gifts.

Richard and I resumed our nightlife. Dancing and movies on Saturday nights, Sundays we took the children to visit their grandparents, my sister and Mrs. Rogers.

What a perfect family we make. I am still asking myself if this is real?

Uncle Phillip, my father's cousin, and his wife, Aunt Nora, lived with their two children, Mack and Patsy in a little cottage in Hadfield St. Lodge.

We heard that they were moving to a new settlement with larger houses in South.

We asked if we could get the cottage to rent, now that our family has grown to four?

We got the cottage and moved in time for Rocky's first birthday.

It seemed as though every new home I move into, I get pregnant.

Yes, I was once again pregnant and still the happiest wife and mother.

I remember right about this time, I noticed that my husband was not meeting me on the job. He was not waiting for me at home. He was not calling to ask if I was feeling like he was feeling, so I would race home and make passionate love.

I remember one evening after I prayed with my children, put them to bed; I got dressed in something nice, shoes and all, and went downstairs. There was an old, rusty car that Uncle Phillip had left. There were lots or rubbish in it.

I crawled into the car and waited. My plans were that when my husband comes home and don't see me, he would get into a jealous rage, rush out to look for me.

Mosquitoes were having a good night. I felt something long with many legs crawled on my foot; I sat still until it crawled away. I don't remember how long I sat in that rusty car, I fell asleep in it until Richard's bicycle leaned against it and woke me up.

I watched him go up the stairs and I waited to see him run back down, grab his cycle and go looking for me. He never did. He did not even know that I was not in the house. He crashed in the couch and went to sleep.

My father came to Georgetown for the first time; he stayed at Aunt Wini, whom he said he missed very much after she moved away from Lancaster to Queenstown,

I went to see him. He saw me from the window and said to his sister,

"Oh Laad, she is in the 'family way' again. Look, three and a half of them on one bicycle" 'How did he know that I was pregnant? I had no bump yet?'

At this period, I think my father was doing everything he could to makeup for the years of physical and mental abuse I went through with his doing.

He supplied us with meat, rice, coconut, eggs and whatever where in season.

Once per month he sent my supplies with a 'hire car' that made trips to Georgetown.

I, in turn share them with my sister Esther, Sis and friends. I never ate my bread alone.

My father bought a car when Uncle Rick came. Uncles Jamesie and Bertram drove it because my father could not drive a car. He drove a tractor because he passes the test. But failed the driving test for a car. He said that the examiner wanted a bribe, which he refused. – My father always hated bribery and what it can do. He said 'bribery corrupts'

After Uncle Rick passed, no one wanted to go out driving anymore.

My father gave the car to Richard. At first I objected, I told my father that we are happy the way we are. He said, "How could you be so ungrateful and selfish? You prefer to ride a bicycle with soon to be three children rather than have your husband drive his family? A car that I am giving him free of charge, for you and your children?"

We went up one weekend to get the car. Richard was like a little boy with his first toy. He spent hours cleaning, polishing and wiping off fingerprints from the car.

We drove back to Georgetown in our shiny green Ford, #PL96. The children and I were so proud of Richard, watching him drive, he looked so handsome and professional as if he had been driving all his life.

The man was so adoptive, skilled, and smart; he always surprise the pants off me.

In a matter of a few months after Richard got his car, things began to change more.

I still ride my bicycle to work and carrying my children around.

My husband said he is busy with the job and driving around looking for parts to improve the looks of his car. Fancy rims, mirrors and so on.

Mrs. Joseph, the supervisor on my job would come into the lunchroom and ask if anyone wants to work overtime? I would be first to put my hand up.

You see, every penny I made, every penny given to the children on any occasion, was given to my husband to 'put up' for when we are ready to buy our own home.

He gave me market money. I had to ask him for money if I needed. It was our decision since we got married. It was all right with me, even though my sister thinks I shouldn't trust any man that much. Even his mother didn't agree with my 'stupidity'.

But I trusted my husband with my life. What is money in comparison to my life?

Every time he went to the bank to deposit our savings, he showed me the book.

What else could a wife want?

But now when I put my hand up to work, I hear remarks among the women.

"Lord, some of us never learn. How dumb can she be?"

"Yes, the more she give him, the more he has to take the women to the seawall"

"All good things come to an end with these no good men. She's too good for him"

"Don't you know the wife is the last to know what's going on in her marriage?"

I asked my good friend Olga, "Who are they talking about?" She snugs her shoulder.

Things were happening that never happened before.

I was still riding my bicycle while my husband drove a car. He comes home in the afternoons with bags of new clothes and cologne. Get dressed and says he has to go to a meeting or something to do with his job.

For his birthday that April, I planned a surprise party for him. I invited our family and friends including his pals at the Fire Station. Our little cottage was full of exciting people waiting for the 'Birthday Boy' to come so we could all turn on the light and scream "Happy Birthday"

Well we waited, and waited. My brother-in-law stood by the roadside, every time he saw a car turn the corner he would signal us to turn off the light.

I was melting with embarrassment. I did not know what to do or say. People were looking at me with sympathy. I could not look at anyone. I was ashamed of myself.

The next day, my husband told me that he was celebrating his birthday with his friends at the Fire Station. He said he got so drunk; he fell asleep on the billiard table.

I never told him that those friends were here with me, waiting for him to come home.

I found myself being alone with the children and a belly growing bigger. Still it was for the good of our future that my husband had to be away from us.

It was an abrupt change, but what can I expect? With my big belly and all?

Denial taken hold of me, I was not going to admit anything. Its better that what I had.

His parents and brothers warned him, "Don't be surprise if she drop you as soon as she drop her load. We would encourage her to do just that. You are shameless man"

Every time I go to Charlotte St my in-laws would ask, "Where is Richard? You still riding bicycle with children, when your father give him a car to alleviate this problem?"

My father-in-law said, "Child, the apartment in the front house will be empty.

Tell Richard that you want to move here. You and the children need to be close to us. When you are so far away from watchful eyes, people tends to stray"

I began to wonder, is my darling husband, the man whom I know is mine and mine alone, doing something wrong? No it can't be. We promised God and the Archbishop that we would only love each other until we die. I am not dead yet. My husband did not break his promise. Some of them are jealous because we are so much in love.

I was six months pregnant when we moved to Charlotte St.

The children were happy to be with their grandparents and other relatives.

By this time, Ada had gone to America and every time Kim saw a plane in the air, she would cry, saying Ada is in it leaving without her. It was a sad time for her and me.

Before, when I was pregnant, Richard and I went to the movies, stop to get ice cream and walk around town window-shopping, especially on Sundays.

This time I go alone to the movies, and then take my two little children for ice cream

Something was happening around me, but I don't know what? I don't know how to behave. What I should say to my husband without hurting his feelings?

I never wanted to upset or hurt my husband feelings. So, I will stay humble to remain his wife. I will keep my side of the promise and I am sure that people are wrong about my husband. We love each other too much for anything to go wrong between us.

About a months before I go out on maternity leave, I became too large to ride to work. My friend Alga and I took the bus on the back street.

One afternoon while we waited for the bus, I saw a large, fancy car slow down, and then reversed to where we stood. I saw him exit his car and walked up to me.

"Hi Wynette, how are you?" It was Cecil. He was one of the many who studied abroad and answered the Government call to come back and develop the country.

He was a General Manager and was living with his wife and children in South.

"Hello Cecil, how are you?" he saw that I was lost for words. I wanted to put my arms around him and let some of this fluid that was flooding my brains flow. He said,

"Come, let me take you and your friend home. I know where you're living.

You see, even though you may not have heard from me, I kept abreast of all that was going on with you. My brother and your brother-in-laws are good friends from church,

Through him I hear all about you. I see you are populating the country".

One Sunday afternoon, I came home with Kim and Rocky and whoever was about to exit my belly, a lady came up to me, she said, "Are you Mrs. Greene?"

"Yes, is something wrong?" I wondered if something was wrong with Richard?

I sent the children in to their grandparents and stood on the bridge to listen to her.

"I am so sorry for you, with your condition and such small children and all. But I have to tell you what I came here to tell you. Your husband is going with a policeman wife right across the canal from here; she is an older woman with quiet a reputation.

That woman is bad. She broke up my home by doing the same that she is doing with your husband. I hear that your husband used his position on his job, to transfer the lady's husband to the interior so that he can be with her all the time"

The lady was talking, I was watching her lips moving, but I couldn't hear anymore.

Things were tingling all over my body. Insects were biting me. My sight was clouded.

I couldn't move, even after the woman left, I still stood on the bridge. Can't move.

Like a zombie, I walked over to the address where the lady told me that I would find my husband. I saw my father's green car parked in front of the house.

I walked up the steps and knocked on the door. A woman opened the door partially.

She opened her mouth in shock when she saw me. She whispered, "What are you doing here? Look at your condition, you should not be here" 'How did she know who I was?'

I walked back home like a zombie. I went into labor but felt no pain.

I was twenty-seven years old; I was dying from inside out. All my shakers crashed.

I died that Sunday.

Sis brought the children and found me in bed, my belly hard and stiff, she said,

"Its that time again. Where is that boy with the car?" she called out to my sister and Doreen, my neighbor from Evans St who now lives upstairs in Charlotte St.

The three women fuss over me. "Her bag is packed, lets take her to the hospital"

All signs said I was ready to have the baby, but I was not dilating. One nurse said,

"She is not showing any sign of feeling pain, which she should at this stage"

"It seems as though she just shut down"

That late September morning, the doctor who made the early rounds, said,

"Listen to me, and listen good. You have to snap out of whatever you are in, if just until you push this baby out, then you can sort out your problems.

I am taking you to the labor room now. If I don't do this now, that cut on your belly could rupture. I do not recommend operating on you again. You see when they did that to you with your pregnancy; they cut you the old fashion way, up to down, thus cutting your abdominal muscles. Since its been over two years, and you seemed to heal well, I am hesitant open it again" he smooth the wet hair off my face, looked into it and said

"Come on, let's do this together, think about your baby"

At 8.15am my beautiful baby girl, eight and a half pounds, entered this world.

Melanie is the stamp of Richard, red hair and dimples and all.

Richard was around, but I didn't see him. I was more ashamed to look at him.

My sister and mother-in-law made barley in soup and porridge for me to drink to produce milk for the baby, but none came. I tried to force my nipples into my baby's mouth. She struggled to clamp and suck, but nothing came out. My sister took a comb and began to comb my breast, an old fashion way for releasing milk. That didn't work. She placed hot compress that did not do it.

We had to give my days old baby a bottle; I couldn't breast-feed like I did the others.

The Archbishop, in his chapel, once again christened Melanie.

Everything went on as usual, the big party with lots of food and drinks. I was playing the part as best as I could. I kept that artificial smile when others were around. I even allow my husband to put his hand on me in the presence of others.

I was not fooling everyone, especially my father-in-law. He felt the lukewarm vibes.

I kept two of monitory gifts from the christening, gave Richard the rest to bank.

I boarded a bus with my three children, for Lancaster.

Everyone was happy to see us. They asked, "Where is your husband?" "He's busy"

I stayed longer than before. People were beginning to wonder what was going on?

I was tempted to ask my father if I could stay here with my children?

Then the baby got sick, vomiting and derriere. It was getting worst even though everyone tried their old fashion remedy like boiling pomegranate skin, guava skin, clove, and whatever he or she could think of.

My father got the 'hire car' to make a special trip to Georgetown to my family doctor.

I knocked on Dr. Saywar's door after twelve midnight. He came down in his robe, angry but concerned. He looked into my baby's eyes then the diaper, he said,

"There is not much I could do at this stage. You waited too long its 'gastro enteritis'.

Dr. Saywar walked around his office, holding his chin and thinking, while I am praying. He told me, "I am going to give this baby an injection, she is too young for such, but I have no alternative. I will advise you, however, to stop at the public hospital.

Just so that if and when it happens, they don't have to do an atopicy on this little thing"

I asked the driver to take us home

The small bottle of Lucazade doctor gave; I put two drops into my baby's mouth.

She was so weak; her eyes didn't close as she slept. No sound came out when she cried.

Every time I put the liquid into her mouth, I look for vomit or stool.

I sat up with my baby in my arms for the rest of the night and the day. I would not allow anyone to take her from my arms. If she is going to die, let it be in my arms.

I consider myself religious. I pray every morning and every night. I pray whenever someone is kind to me. I thank God everyday for all the good things that has happened to me, and, as I held little Melanie in my arms, I did what I never did before.

I made a promise to God that if He allows me to keep her, "I would never forget your kindness. I would always be reminded of this promise that I am making to You"

"Please, Dear God, Ohm Bhagawan, You are One. I beg of You, save my baby"

My baby drank the whole bottle of Lucazade and still had a dry diaper.

"Thank You, Dear God. I will always take good care of her"

I returned to work after two months. Doreen took care of Rocky and Melanie.

Sis took Kim everywhere she went. Especially at the church where she taught sewing to young girls. She loved it when people asked her if Kim was her daughter? Because, even a blind person would feel the resemblance with Kim and Sis.

A friend at the factory's welding shop made a bicycle carrier to hang over the handle, for me to carry Melanie in. Now I can carry all three of my children on my cycle.

Around this period there was buzz in the country. Everyone were talking about the picture show name 'To Sir with Love".

Schools were taking children by the busloads to see a Black Guyanese teacher in England whose name was Mr. E.R. Braithwaite teaching almost all White children.

Just the fact that he was from Guyana made everyone proud and wanted to see him.

The cinema was sold out all three shows everyday for months.

People were claiming Mr. Braithwaite – which is pronounced three different ways –

To be their family. They were going over and over to see him in the movie.

Even after Sidney Poitier came in another movie where he said, "They call me Mr. Tibbs" people were still call him Mr. Braithwaite from Guyana playing another role.

Today some people still Sidney Poitier is a Guyanese who played another Guyanese.

My father-in-law said, "I look at Kim and see what my wife looked like"

To everyone else, everything was hunky-dory. We appeared like a normal married couple. Only in the confine of my bedroom, things were not the same.

I wore pajamas at night; I never let my husband touch me ever again.

We never discuss what happened. We lived in a freezer.

I warmed up in the presence of my children and others. Richard used those moments to his advantage. He would hold on to me longer. He would try to kiss me, but that meckanizism inside of me has frozen and died. I didn't feel anything anymore.

We went to the wedding of Bridgett, Richard's cousin. I sat with Sis and the children and watch my husband flirt and danced with the women at the reception. I said,

"Sis, hold the baby and watch the children, I am going into the food area to help serve and do whatever I could to help. I want to leave this hall".

When I returned, I sat next to Sis and took my baby in my arms. A nice looking man came to me and asked if I would like to dance? I said no, I showed him the baby in my arms. Sis took the baby form me and said, "Getup and go dance with the young man"

As soon as I stood up and about to go into the outstretched arms of the man, my husband pushed himself between us and said, "Hi buddy, there are plenty of women in this hall. Why would you pick my wife? My wife don't dance with anyone but me"

Sis caught the man as he walked away, she said, "Sir, come back" in the presence of Richard she said, "Please dance with my daughter, as many times as you wish"

One day I was over at my in-laws when the phone rang. My father-in-law answered.

Suddenly he was angry, he was agitated with the person on the other side. He said

"Let me tell you something, woman. Do not call on this phone for my son anymore.

Do not call for my son anywhere, anymore. My son has a wife and children. Leave him alone" he slammed the phone down.

Richard was his only son who was married with children.

After Richard realized that there was nothing he could do to 'turn me around',

He began to be arrogant. He would insult me and threaten me. He said

"You want to be a stubborn fool. Go right ahead. But remember, those three children are mine. Don't ever think of taking them away from me. Remember where I work"

How could I forget where he works? He works in the Ministry of Home Affairs,

the ministry in charge of all Law Enforcements among other portfolios.

"Don't try anything on me. Don't tell anyone our business. I will play along with you if you play along with me. When you are ready for me, I'll be right here with you.

You don't want to be childless on the street, do you?"

I was looking at a stranger. Someone I never knew before. I wondered what went wrong in such a short time? Because I refused to accept changes? I'm too old fashion?

Every time I saw a woman looking at me, I wondered if that was she?

Richard would invite friends to the house. I would cook and serve them.

If any of the men try to speak to me, he would quickly interrupt by saying things like,

"What are you standing around here for? Here is out of your league, go back to the kitchen". Some of his friends did not like what he has become. One in particular, used to always come to the house when he knew that Richard was not home.

He would tell me how sorry he was about what was happening. He would ask if there was anything he could do for me? He told me that he always had a soft spot in his heart for me. Then one day he placed his hand on my shoulder and tried to kiss me.

I pulled away from him and said, "I promise you that I will not tell Richard about this, only if you promise me that you will never come back into my home?"

Kim was always having terrible coughing. Many nights I had to sit, holding her in my arms, rubbing her chest and back with camphor and coconut oil.

I took her to Dr. Saywar who informed me that my baby has 'asthma'.

Even though I was fearful of that news from watching my brother-in-law, Richard's older brother suffers from asthma. I was not going accept it. Not my baby.

I told the family what the doctor said; they said she inherited it from her uncle.

I said 'Hell no, my daughter do not have asthma"

I went upstairs to Doreen and Hector, crying and telling them what I heard.

They informed me that their eldest son was diagnose with asthma some years ago, they said they bought a bottle of cough medicine – in those days all our drugs came from England.- "It worked but that was a long time ago"

"Do you still have the empty bottle or remember the name?" ask this hopeful mother.

They told me the name, then Hector said, "let me look in the old barrel to see if the bottle is still there" I held my breath until my friend came back with the little brown bottle. It was empty and even the paper label was faded.

I held on to the empty bottle as if I have found the cure for my child's asthma.

I poured one tablespoonful of water into the empty bottle; waited awhile, then shuck it vigorously. I knew that I was taking a big risk not knowing what the outcome can be.

I put the bottle to Kim's mouth and poured every drop of whatever was in the bottle.

She was fine for a while, then, suddenly she began to cough and cough none stop.

I became so afraid; I was hanging on a balance. My friends were afraid too.

Suddenly Kim vomited all over the kitchen floor. On the floor, with horror, we were looking at a large piece of something that looked like liver or octopus, or sea sponge.

I told you, my child was not going to suffer like her uncle. I was lucky.

I go to the Bourda market with the children every Sunday mornings to give them an outing and to buy fresh fruits and vegetable.

Mr. Burnham, the Prime Minister can always be found at Bourda market on Sunday morning selling his party newspaper, The New Nation. Remember I told you that we were friends through the union, not through politic. He said to me,

"So I hear that you are not a party member, that you didn't vote for me?"

"But you are the Prime Minister, my vote would not have made a difference"

"But why you are not active in the party?"

"I am not active in any party. Look at me. I am a Dugla. I love both sides of me.

But I don't like the racial divide caused by both parties. Its hurting both my people"

"OK, lets put politic aside, what's going on with married life. I see you are populating the country" he looked at my children. I did not answer. I wanted to cry.

He saw my reaction and insisted, "Is that man misbehaving? Is he still working for Desmond?" "Yes" "OK, leave it to me, I will find out what's happening"

One month later, Richard told me that we are going to Africa.

I pleaded with my husband to go alone, I said, "Leave us here, your family are right here, they will look out for us. I will continue to work and live right here with the children. You never know, maybe when you return, we could be like it was before"

"You don't understand, our government is opening a embassy in Zambia. I am going as a diplomat for my country. I have a wife and three children. They know that before they appointed me. They would not let me go alone and leave my family behind"

"So, what do I do now?" I asked, not expecting this.

"First, we have to go and get pictures and birth certificates for the Ministry to get passports for us. Then we go to the Ministry of Health and get some vaccinations"

It was after getting my birth certificate; I discovered that I was not born on 27th of December. I was christened on the 27th of December.

All my life, I knew my name to be Wynette. On my birth certificate there was no Wynette. My father registered my birth with a name of his choice.

My mother gave my godparents the English name Wynette because my Hindu name is Basmati and the church will not accept it.

"What a confused life? I told you I have a story to tell? Linda"

My cousin Eddy, Uncle Rick's son from Suriname was celebrating his fortieth birthday. My father sent the invitation to us to attend.

We used our passport for the first time to go to Suriname.

The evening of the party, Richard and I were getting dress in the bedroom next to my cousin's master bedroom. Richard said, "Remember, when we go downstairs, you only dance with me. In other words, you do not dance with anyone else. Your cousins, maybe, but no stranger. Do you understand?" As if he was scolding his little child.

"But Richard, my cousin and his wife are both important people in this country.

You see from all the preparation and gifts and so on that is going on here, tells us that important people will be attending. Are you saying that if someone asks me to dance, that I should refuse and insult my family in his house?"

"You hear me. I said no dancing with strangers"

"But what do I say if someone asks me to dance?"

"Tell him that you have a bad toe"

"But I don't have a bad toe"

My husband, who was already dressed in his shining black hard shoe, stepped over to where I stood barefooted, he placed his shoe heel on the big toe of my right food and with all his weight, he smashed it like a grape. Blood spilled in every direction as I screamed and fell back on the bed. He said, "Now you have a bad toe"

Eddy rushed into the room, his face covered in shaving cream, and asked,

"What happened?" he looked at all the blood on the floor and shouted, "What the hell happened in here?" I couldn't answer; I was trying to catch my breath.

Richard said, "She is so clumsy, she dropped the iron on her foot"

My husband told the children and everyone who asked why my toe was bandaged?

The same story and I never made them any wiser. For the balance of my life, I never had a toenail on my big toe of my right foot.

I am trying my hardest not to be my mother's daughter

"Wynette, I was informed that I have to be ready to leave here before Christmas.

You and the children will join me as soon as we get settled. In the mean time you will move in with my parents and my brother Rick and family will move in here"

"What about all our stuff in here? My sister and some friends want to buy some of them. If we sell them, we can get some money to put in the bank for the children"

No, we are not selling anything. I give everything to my brother.

Saturday, December 23rd, 1972, Richard was getting ready to leave. His flight was in the afternoon, he said, "Wynette, don't try anything foolish while I am gone. I leave the passports with my mother. She will give it to you on the day you and the children are coming to join me. I did that because I don't want you to take my children away"

"Where would I go, Richard? With what can I go somewhere? You have all the money in the bank. You give all my stuff to your brother, free of charge. With what I can take your children and go somewhere?" I felt helpless and victimized. I was empty.

"My parents will assist and you are still working. You will get my salary while you are here. You will be all right.

I am going to get a haircut and shave. I left everything on the bed, pack my suitcase"

I packed his suitcases and among his stuff, I found the bankbook that we opened jointly in 1965. Before Kim was born. Before we got married.

I sat on the bed, holding the little black book in my hand, thinking, 'this is the only thing that join Richard and I at this moment. Our children's savings and my hope for a home of my own' I opened the book and began to look through the pages.

Richard made deposits almost every month with no withdrawal.

I kept turning the pages until I reached the pages that showed from 1970 'withdraw' 'withdraw' 'withdraw'. Until the end that said 'Balance $35.

Government vehicles lined Charlotte St to take Richard and who ever were going to the airport to see him off. "Aren't you coming to the airport to see me off? What you think people would say if you don't come?" I handed him his packed suitcase, knowing that the first thing he will see when he opens it would be the bankbook.

I stood in the flat, looked around at all the pieces of furniture that I bought by paying 'susu', something like the pyramid. 'Compulsory saving'.

My mother did it with Aunties Katy, Chunu, Dull, and all her other friends.

I always like the last and first collection, because I had enough money to buy something piece of furniture or something from the large department store, for my home.

I gathered myself and the children's belongings, my radio, teapot, the large hatbox that Mrs. Rogers had given me; I now keep our jewelry, and walked over to my in-laws home. The spare room was cleared for us.

My father-in-law Sonny did not go to the airport. He said to me, "Child, you know that we love you like our own daughter? You give us so much joy with those three children. I can't help but watch you weathering away in front of my very eyes.

What can I do to make things a little better while you are here?"

"Daddy, I do not want to sound ungrateful, but I want to go to Lancaster with the children, stay there until its time to go to Richard" Maybe if I cry, I could ease some of this pressure that is bearing down on me, but I could not cry. I never cried since that Sunday night, two years ago. Something inside of me died. I don't have a cure.

"There is nothing ungrateful about you wanting to go to your family. I want you to know that if you ever want to talk to me, I am here to listen" "Thanks Daddy"

Mr. Scott saw me on the street, he looked at me sadly, I wondered if it was because Richard was gone and he wanted to know who was going to pay for the educational insurance that we bought for the children? I said, "Don't worry about the payments being made. I will pay it every quarter as usual" he shook his head and said.

"Mrs. Greene, didn't your husband tell you? There is no more insurance. You see your husband did not pay the premiums in over two years, despite my going to his office to collect them. There is no insurance for your children, its forfeited" I had no room for shock anymore. I asked, "Mr. Scott, what if I come into the office and see you? Could you accept the payment and restart my children's insurance?"

"I wish I could, but, it's out of my hand and out of the records. I am so sorry"

I resigned from the Continental Biscuit Factory. Parked my bicycle under my in-laws house and took the bus to Lancaster.

The 'Big house' was empty since Aunt Wini moved to Georgetown.

My father and brothers cleaned it and made it comfortable for the children and I.

My stepmother had deteriorated to the state where the 'back house' had an unpleasant smell. My father was doing his best, but the odor was overpowering.

I enrolled Kim in Aklyne School, the same school that I attended twenty some years ago. Oh how things have changed? There were so many Blacks and Duglas among the Indian children. 'Who would believe that at one time, I was the only mixed child among only Indian children in this school?'

Rocky went to a little kindergarten at Liverpool. Melanie and I walked around the villages and did things with the family.

One can live in the village with little money. My father supplied me with most of what we needed. The money I got from the job and Richard's salary I got from the Ministry was more than enough for us to live comfortable.

It was on this occasion, I was more open to talk with my father. He came every evening, the children and I would sit on the steps and talk for hours - the same steps that my mother and Auntie Katy sat and talked for hours – David would be right by my side, asking me 'what are you two talking about'. Datson was an early beder, but during the day he would walk Kim to school and bring her back home.

I was getting a few drops of honey in my bitter tea.

When Melanie and I came back from taking Rocky to school, my father was waiting for me in the yard, he said, "She is gone, I am going to make arrangement to burry her"

My brothers and some cousins came over to help my father clean, throw out and burn most of the things from the 'big room'.

I used some of the money to buy my father a new mattress and beddings.

I asked Sister Bea if she would cook for my father and the boys? I said,

"Daddy would supply you with rice and meat and whatever he brings from the farm.

He would give you some money from his pension and I would give most of what I have with me"

Most of what I told you of the past about my grandparents, uncles, aunts and old times, I got from my father around this period. We talked about the way things were when he was a little boy growing up right here in Lancaster. He showed me the fruit trees in the yard where all his siblings 'navel cord' was buried. His was buried under a lime three that never stop bearing large, yellow, juicy limes.

We never spoke of my mother. I wasn't ready to hear anything from him about her.

We never spoke of what happened to me in his house. I wasn't ready for that either.

"Daddy, is it true that there are good and bad spirits roaming the place?"

"Yes, there are. I would not tell you a lie. I experienced them several times.

One such time, I heard that some of my calves are being stolen and branded as soon as they are born. I went to the savanna to spend some nights with my cows and try to catch the thieves. As I slept in my banabe -hut, I heard the cows mooing and moving around.

I saw a very bright light in the distant. I knew the thieves were there to steal my claves. I began to shout and curse and threatening the thieves. I picked my cutlass and went towards the pen. The light was gone, the cows and their babies were all there.

I went back to my hut and fell asleep.

I swear to you my child, something big and heavy sat on my stomach. I tried to breath but could not. I tried to fight it off this thing, yes it was a thing. I realize that I was dealing with a 'suckanani' an 'olhigg' a 'bloodsucker'.

I remember that Mother had put some limes in my bag for me to make swank-limeade. I reached for the lime and squeeze it with all of whatever strength I had left.

They don't like lime and garlic. Yes, they do exist. They live among us in the day, and become what they become, in the night"

"Daddy, do you mean that the suckanani-vampire is human?"

"Yes, it could be a neighbor. That is why most people keep limes, garlic and manicole broom over their doors and windows to keep them out. If you have a lime tree in your yard, they will never enter"

"You mean they are like a vampire? They fly like a bat?"

"Yes, something like that. I don't want to frighten you, but lots of babies put to bed good and healthy, and found died in the morning, from having all their blood sucked out of them. The marks are there for everyone to see.

"Should I be afraid to stay here with the children?"

"You don't have to be afraid around here, we have too many lime trees around. There are manicole brooms over every door in this compound. As for garlic, you can find that in every home. You see, suckanani only attack people who challenge them, like I did, or people who do not protect their babies with asifetter-dried garlic pinned to the baby all the time. They love people who don't have lime and garlic in their blood"

Another night, I told my father a story my mother told me.

"Mommy said that she was coming home one night when she saw a man dressed in all over white bracing on a telegram post. She thought it was one of young men who lived down the dam who may have had too much to drink after the cricket game.

She said to him, "Jacob come on, lets go home, I will watch when you cross the bridge"

Mommy said the man in white didn't move, so she went on her way. She looked back and saw him following her. He didn't cross his bridge but continue to follow her.

She was at her door and the man in white was on her bridge. She said a strong wind with sweet smelling perfume hit her. She realized that it was not Jacob. She calmly said,

"I am sorry I disturbed you. Please go back where you come from"

She said the thing in white turned around and walked back towards the main road.

"Yes, there are spirits or ghosts around. Especially if they died untimely"

"Do they hurt people?"

"No, people get excited and make a big deal of it but they don't harm anyone"

Remember I told you that I would tell you more about Mrs. Jordan? Well I visited her some years ago. She was in her late ninety; she had a strong voice, good memory.

We talked about my grandmother's young days and about Clarabell and Sudit, whom I never met, but was always ready to hear about my ancestors.

"Your grandmother Mary Jane had the bluest eyes I have ever seen"

Mrs. Jordan had three generation from one family as her servant over the years.

First the mother, who worked until she died, then the daughter, worked for the Jordan's until she died; now, the granddaughter is working for Mrs. Jordan. She was young and beautiful. Elaine was a second cousin of mine. Mrs. Jordan's nephew Bert, whom she adopted - she had no children - fell in love with maid, and married her under the nose of Mrs. Jordan, despite her objection Elaine gave birth to twelve children.

She was David and me best friend.

Mrs. Jordan spent her last days watching twelve little half-breed children running around in her house. She said, "Without these children, I would've gone along time ago.

They keep me alive. I love them dearly. I wish I had some years to enjoy them"

Those children inherited all of Mrs. Jordan's, the wealthiest, land and wealth.

Future has a way of making us submit to our weakness and make us stronger.

Someone from the Ministry of Foreign Affairs came up to see me. He brought Richard's salary and some letter from him. The officer said to me,

"I see you are quiet comfortable here, but I am here to inform you that you should come back to town to be close by when we get the order to send you and the children to your husband"

"I am not going to Africa. I will wait right here until my husband comes back"

"I don't think that is an acceptable decision. The 'Old Man' would not like that"

"OK, I'll take my licking, but I am not going to Africa"

I was proud of myself for not letting anyone see the smoke from my volcano.

I kept a calm demeanor. I never told anyone of my unbelievable experience.

I think I was ashamed of myself for being such a looser, after being the envy of many.

It was most important for the children not to even sense that there was a problem.

I read their father's letters to them. If they asked question about him, I will be as normal as any mother who misses her husband would be.

I thought of taking my children across the border to Suriname where I have family.

But we had no passports; my mother-in-law would never give them to me.

I took the children to meet all my remaining aunties in Whim. I told them about my childhood days in Whim. I tried had not to tell them any of the bad things that happened to my brothers and me. I will tell them later, when they are older to understand.

I showed them the empty lot where I was born; I took them to the Kali Church.

Datson and David walked with us throughout the villages, showing off to villagers my children and me. They were happy to have me back. My father too.

The children, now almost two, four and six years old, were enjoying country living.

The next month and a half, more letters and money came for me. This time the officer was more serious. He said, "You have to come down to Georgetown by the end of the month. Arrangements are being made for you and the children to travel to Zambia by mid April. If you chose not to go like you said, then the government will send Mr. Greene's children on that flight" he walked away from me angrily, then stop and said, "Remember, get the children to Georgetown by the end of this month"

We went back to Georgetown two days after the end of the month. I went to the Barclays bank in Water St and opened an account and arranged with the Ministry of Finance to deposit my husband's salary into my account.

I remembered Richard telling me that when we go to Africa, we will live well with the living allowance provided by the government to people they send abroad, that ones monthly salary remains at home. His goes into my bank account now.

I placed the bankbook into my teapot and packed them into my large hatbox that had pictures and jewelries, along with my radio and gave them to Doreen to keep.

My father-in-law took me to the Royal Bank of Canada and withdrew seven hundred dollars for us on our trip. It was a lot of money then. I deposited it into my account. I didn't need any money where I was going. I would need it right here when I returned.

We left Guyana twelve days after, on 14th of April, Richard's birthdate.

We intransit in London for almost twelve hours. My brother-in-law Cedric met us at the airport and took us to his home. Boy, was I glad to have him at that time. All three of the children had vomited and I was a mess trying to cope with three crying children.

After cleaning up and ate 'fish n chips' Cedric took us to shop in London.

We experience our first bout with the cold weather. We were shivering in April.

To this day, forty years later, I still have beddings and other things from Marks and Spenser. They just don't fade tear.

We arrived in Lusaka after a long flight. The children were excited to see their father. I too, played my part for all in the welcome party to see.

I couldn't believe that I was in Africa. I thought Africa had only Black people wearing grass skirts and running around with painted faces and shields and spares.

I saw more Whites than Blacks at the airport. The building was well furniture with leather chairs in many lounges where mostly Whites were sitting.

We went out to a parking lot packed with Mercedes and other expensive foreign cars.

My husband even had a showfare in uniform waiting for us.

Our flat was not ready. Richard said, "I asked my friends, Ossie and Chris for the children to stay with them and their children. You will come to the hotel with me while we wait for the house promised to us. It should be within a week of two"

"That's OK I will stay where my children stay. You stay at the hotel"

We moved into a three-bedroom apartment in Makashi Rd. it was nicely furniture with all the modern facilities. The children loved the TV most of all. It was our first time seeing one. I couldn't get them away from it.

At this juncture, I could've changed things between Richard and I. I could've licked my wound, bury my pride and start a new life with my husband and children.

But, I couldn't. The 'trust' was gone, I was dead inside. I was stubborn.

The first night into our own home, Richard attempted to make love to me. I said,

"I am here because of my children. I have been living in pretence for more than two years. I can continue to live like that. Whenever you touch me, you burn my skin.

We have been doing well so far. For the sake of my three children, please let us continue to pretend. I never thought that your betrayal could make me into what I've become, but it has, you will have to take me as I am. Lifeless and feelingless"

It was the first time I said so many words to my husband in a long time.

"You must be crazy if you think that I am going to pretend to be your husband while you lock your legs, refusing to perform your wifely duties in my bed. You got to be out of your --- mind"

"If you ever force yourself on me, don't ever fall asleep.

"What are you going to do?"

"Try it and see if you would see or feel what I did"

"You are crazy"

"You made me crazy"

After my husband attempted some more advances on me in bed. He became so angry, he ordered me out of the master bedroom, saying, "This is the master's room, I am the master. You choose not to be my mistress, get your ass out of here"

I moved into the small back room. When the children asked why I moved? I told them, "Since Daddy came to Africa, it seems as if he adopted some of the animals sounds. He snores like a hippo. I can't sleep in the same room with him" that worked.

I tried to do everything right and do my best to keep out of Richard's way, just so that he did not snap at me or insult me in the presence of my children or anyone else.

Chris, Ossie and their three children were our only visitors. I asked them about school for Kim? She went to school in Guyana and I did not want her to fall back from what she already learned. They told me that she should have no problem if the embassy requested it. They said other people have problem getting young girls into school.

I spoke to Richard about Kim going to school; he said that he is working on it.

Few days later, he told me to get Rocky ready for school the coming Monday.

"But Richard, you got it mixed up, its Kim who needs to go to school, not Rocky"

"You're not listening to me. I am telling you to get Rocky ready for school not Kim"

"But why? Kim is six years old and already attended school. Rocky is four years?"

"Yes, but the law here is that boys gets first preference to attend school.

I watch Rocky go off the school, while Kim stay at home. I was desperate to keep my daughter from being a dunce like me. I began to teach her as best as I could at home. We sat together at the breakfast table, away from the telly.

One day I gave Kim some words to spell. When I asked her to spell them back to me She spelt most of them wrong. I lost it. I began to scream at her. I picked up the rolled paper that I used to threaten or demand calmness when my children misbehaved.

I began to chase her around the table, screaming and crying at the same time.

She ran from room to crying, I was right behind her crying and begging her not to be like me, "Spell the words Kimmie. Spell the words, don't be like me, I cannot spell"

She ran into the bathroom, I followed and found her fainted on the toilet seat.

I grab some water from the sink and threw it in her face. I sat on the floor of the bathroom, cradling my first born in my arms; I cried my heart out for the first time.

I couldn't stop. Everything that was bottled up in me was flowing through my eyes, nose and mouth. I did not know how to tell Kim, as she threw water on my face, that she had nothing to do with the pain and anger that I was feeling.

Let me say this right now, I never beat my children. Never. I screamed at them, I punish them by sending them to stand in the corner, or send them away from the TV.

Beat my children? Never. I had enough from my father. I did not want my children to feel about me, the way I felt about my father.

If I tell you that I never spank them on the hand or the bottom to keep them from getting burn by playing with matches or hurting themselves or each other, I would be deceiving you. I might be saving the world from another arsonist or bully.

Now, when I hear people say that if you were beaten as a child, you would do the same to your own children, that you are not expected to be a good parent?

To those experts I say, "You are so wrong"

Three months passed before the children and I went out of our home. Rocky went to school and back, but we never went anywhere.

Depression and anxiety was working on my very being. I began to feel sick.

I thought it was the change of whether it would pass.

I asked my friend Chris for something for fever. I told her that I was burning up and had no energy. Nothing helped. My temperature was not coming down. Richard would come into the room, look at me and the children sitting around me, keeping my head cool, and he would walk out of the room.

I was getting weaker and couldn't cook and attend to the children. Richard took over and did the cooking and taking Rocky to school.

"Richard, I think I need to go to a hospital. I am feeling terrible"

"The only hospital you need is in my bed. You need to be my wife again, or else?"

One evening, the deputy ambassador Pat, stopped in to see how we were adjusting.

The children brought him into my room. He physically lifted my light body and took me to his doctor. The doctor said that I had malaria and I had to be hospitalized.

Chris took care of my children until I was discharged from the hospital.

One day, Richard's friend Gabby, a Colored Zambian, came with his girlfriend Daphne. She was from Trinidad. You see in those days, lots of single females were imported from England and the Caribbean to work as secretaries for the government.

Daphne entered the house and the first words that came out of her mouth, I expected to be "hello, I'm Daphne" or something like that when we meet someone for the first time. Instead, she said to my daughters, "Go get the comb and brush for me to comb your hair. It looks as if your hair never comb since you left Guyana"

I stood with my mouth open. By this time the two men had gone away, leaving this rude stranger to order my children around. Then she looked at me and said, with a smile, "Hi, I am Daphne, my boyfriend and your husband are friends. I decided to come and see you and the children, hang out with you, since they are going gallivanting"

You see, Zambia had four races of people, Blacks, Whites and Coloreds and Indians. Coloreds, is what we called Mulatto. Colored were considered a stage up from Blacks. In Guyana it was not as blatant as it was here. Richard was considered Colored in Zambia, because of his light complexion. He attached himself to them more than the Guyanese and Caribbean people.

Richard said to me, "We would be moving from here to a new house in Olympia Park. The children will have a large fenced yard to play in, and you can plant a garden. We will have a houseboy and a gardener. Maybe there you can stop being so stubborn. You know every time we move into a new home, we increase our flock?" his arrogance shoved me farther away from him. We still never mentioned what cause the problem.

I knew that he was the cause of the cause; he lost moral and inner debt.

It was a beautiful house on a hill, far away from the city, with no neighbors close by and no telephone. What else could be more appropriate for a loveless marriage?

Kim was finally accepted into Northmead School where she and Rocky were in the same class. Rocky being the youngest in the class, had become the assistant to

Mrs. Bajad, the teacher. She told me that he needed to be in the kindergarten, or beginner's class, but they put him to her class. He plays at her desk and hand out papers to the students. She said that he was too short to clean the blackboard.

It was so lonely and desolate, that every time I saw someone on the road, Melanie and I would go out, try to have a conversation even though most didn't speak English.

Richard bought two dogs name Nixon and Zee, from an American.

Nixon was a Rhodesian ridgeback and Zee, a German Shepard. We had to build a concrete cage for Nixon. He was not friendly to anyone. I had to push his food through the metal gate of his cage, with a long stick. He was good for security but not anyone else. Only Richard could've approached him. Let him in and out of his cage.

Zee on the other hand, was a friendly, loving family dog. She became our companion in the house.

We were safe when Richard went out in the night. With Nixon

roaming the yard, we could not go out the door. With Zee in the house, I cuddled with my three children and prayed for daylight.

We never had visitors in the night, so whenever we saw a light coming up the hill, the children would get excited because their daddy is coming home.

Daphne, Ossie, Chris and their children visit us. Their children were the same age as my children and they bonded quickly.

The lot next to our house was cleared to build a house for the Canadian embassy.

An old man who was the 'watch man' at the building site, befriended my children and I.

Even though he did not understand a word we said, and vice versa, we became friends.

At nights before Richard comes home and loose Nixon, we would sit on our side of the fence and eat roasted corn from Amdala-Grandfather.

Even though the three men were from different tribes, Barnaubas and David our houseboy and gardener, gave Amdala the utmost respect. Barnaubas, who spoke a little English, explained that Amdala a high priest. He said he was a medicine man, a counselor, and chief in his village and a messenger-peacemaker. He said that Amdala was a highly respected and trusted by every tribe, and that every tribe has one like him. "He is a very honorable man. He has eight wives and fifty-three children and hundreds of grandchildren"

When the house was completed, he asked if we would give him and his wife Mama, the vacant room. We did and he and Mama moved into our yard.

Melanie, being the only child at home, became very attached to him. She followed him wherever he went. She ate whatever he ate, refusing to eat my food.

Amdala broke his tradition that a man never sit and eat with a female of any age.

He ordered Mama to "stop telling her that she cannot sit and eat with me" she was confused. In her old age she was seeing tradition and customs broken by her husband.

Melanie ate caterpillar, rain flies, kapenta-small dried fish and whatever strange and different looking food. The basic was enshema-white maze-corn meal and relish-vegetable, most of which they got from my garden.

In the day, there were people moving around in the yard, but at night no one dear venture out because of Nixon. They peek through the windows in the morning to make sure that he was locked in before they would come out to start their fire to cook.

We had other pets, a cage full of guinea pigs, multiplying every other day. Turtles that we found on the road lying on their backs. A little goat kid we named Willy that Amdala brought for Melanie, and numerous birds that we put out food and water for.

Zee and Willy sat in the couch with the children, watch television and eat snacks.

Daphne saw that I was bored with nothing to do and nowhere to go, she said,

"Your birthday is coming up, ask your husband for a typewriter"

"What am I going to do with a typewriter? I can hardly write, more so to type"

"Just ask him for a typewriter" she demanded.

I did and I got a typewriter. Daphne brought typing, shorthand and office books.

Every afternoon after work, she came in her red two-seated 'spitfire'.

She began teaching me to type and write shorthand. She gave me homework from the Office Skills book. "You will not be bored, you have learning to do"

One day Daphne handed me a receipt with my name from the Lusaka Secretarial School. She said, "You are ready to go kick some butts. Trust me, I know you are"

"Where and how do I get there?"

"Your husband will take you. He has a car"

When I asked Richard, he said, "Hell no, you don't want to be my wife in here but you want me to play the part of your husband and take you to and from school so you can get an education that your father denied you. Hell no. Get your friend who is sending you to school, to take you. Unlike you who is dead, I have a life" he was mad.

Many days I got a lift from Ed, the Canadian neighbor. Other days I walked to the main road and thump a lift. Daphne brought me home in the afternoon.

Since I had servants to do everything, I took the opportunity to do something for me. I studied hard and long. I did the first elementary Pitman exams in typing, shorthand and office skills, all paid for by Daphne.

When the results came back from England, I got First Class in all three examinations.

Daphne was a smart, classy young woman. She loved to dress in African outfit. Always had her makeup on. She was really beautiful, kind and compassionate.

She studied nursing in England, then change to secretarial and came here on a contract to work for one of the top Minister.

She had her own flat but she said that life can be lonely here if you are not a 'player'

She loved my children and pitied me. Even though I never told her or anyone else about my problems, I think that I was only fooling myself. Everyone knew, they see my husband with women all over town. There were many young girls who had a flat but no man. Men were in demand and my man was able and available.

Daphne invited us to a Christmas party at her flat. Ossie, Chris, Richard and me went to the party. I was so nervous; I didn't know what to wear? How to comb my hair? I know one thing; I didn't dear put on anything on my face, like makeup or lipstick.

I didn't have any, anyway. I kept asking Chris, "How do I look? This is my first time going out, do you think I look OK?"

We got to the party; Richard dropped us off and drove away. I followed my friends into a packed apartment with mostly young, beautiful, nicely dressed women, few men.

The women were dressed in sexy, skimpy clothes, lots of halter-tops, showing lots of skin, and thigh pants. Lots of makeup and shinny faces and eyelids.

I was over dressed with my long skirt and turtleneck long sleeves top, with no makeup.

I felt like an old Chaperone to a room full of young models.

There was a Zambian man who was a TV announcer, he knew Chris because he an Ossie worked at the same TV station. He greeted her and me. I was stuck to her like a fly under a leaf.

After he danced with Chris, he asked if I would like to dance? I hesitated but my friend hunched me to go on and dance.

As soon as we walked to the center of the dance area, and began to dance, Richard appeared from nowhere and grabs my arm roughly from the man and told him,

"This is my wife, she don't dance with strangers" The man walked away in shock. and Richard walked away, leaving me standing in the middle of Daphne's living room.

All eyes were on me. I prayed for a whole to open so I can drop into it. I was numb.

I walked slowly to the bathroom and lock the door. I had nowhere to go but within.

I had been saving some money since I came to Africa. Every time Richard dropped his pants, I went into his pockets. Every time he emptied his pocket on the dresser, I picked out the largest notes. Every time I needed stuff for the children or did the food shopping, I quadruple the amount I needed and save three quarter of it for me.

I kept myself and the children's passport in a square wooden box. I think Richard didn't care that I had them or that he forget that I had them.

In the same box I stocked my US dollars and pounds. I did not save Quasha, the local currency. I could only use it here.

Daphne tried to probe into what's happening with Richard and I? Even to my best friend, who's doing so much for me, I could not open up. I said, "Nothing is wrong.

He just gets angry and loud at times, but nothing is wrong"

"Do you have any idea what people are saying about your husband indiscretions?

They are saying things like",

"Who is that 'plain Jane'?

"We never sees him with a wife nor children. I thought he was single"

"Look at the way he humiliated her at your party?"

"But she is so plain. Someone should've dressed and put some makeup on"

"Wynette, what's going on?" My friend began to cry. I put my arms around her and whispered, "I just want to go back home"

Am I my mother's daughter?

I had befriended the driver of our embassy. I asked him if he would put a letter for my father, in the mailbag and send it to Guyana for me, without letting Richard know?

He said he would, I gave him a letter with three hundred pounds addressed to my father.

In it I asked Daddy to go to the BOAC airline office and buy one adult and three children one-way tickets form Zambia to Guyana. I wrote, "Please don't tell anyone about this. I miss home and wants to come back"

With my freedom on the works, I concentrated on my studies and Daphne began to teach me to drive in her stick-shift two-seated car.

When she thought that I was ready, she took me to the police station to get my driver's license. I passed the rigorous written and driving test – if you are a woman in Africa, its harder – I passed the test and Daphne paid for everything.

Even she did not know about my wooden box and savings.

When Richard saw that I now have a driver's license. He lost it, and for the first time others saw how angry and insulting he is. Daphne was shocked that a man would want to keep his wife from getting an education and becoming independent.

I took the intermediate Pitman tests at school and passed with flying colors.

Daphne said, "You see? You can do anything that you makeup your mind to do. Now do one more thing for me. Bake two dozens of muffins every Monday to Friday, I will take to work every morning" I did not ask any question. How could I? With all she had been doing for me? Making some muffins, that's costing me nothing? Is the least I could do for this caring woman? Richard pays for all the food that we bought in bulk.

My cousin Noreen, a nurse in England came to Lusaka to work and lived with us.

Now, Daphne and Noreen shared a room in our house. I had more company; I hoped that my husband would be less insulting to me in their presence.

One day Noreen walked into the kitchen and heard Richard saying to me,

"You should've had the same curse placed on your brothers, then your behavior can be accepted" Richard was twisting the knife every moment we were alone. I was taking it with a grain of salt, because I know that my children and I would be leaving soon.

"What did you just say to her?" asked Noreen in shock. He told her he was sorry.

Noreen bought a car, on her day off; she would let me drive to school.

One such day, the traffic was heavy and I got caught on the train line. I panic after seeing bystanders pointing to the speeding train coming my way. I moved my foot from the clutch and the engine cut off. I knew there was nothing I could do; the train was already on me. I heard the whistle. The last thought at that moment was my three children. I covered my face and waited, ready to go. To this day, I don't know how the car moved off the track seconds before the train passed.

People gathered around me, some angry, some sympatric but all wanted to know why did I move off the tracks so late? What they didn't know was that I had a flood.

I called that incident my second miracles. Remember I told you about the fishes?

Northmead School had flimshow every Thursday evening. Richard dropped the children off some evenings and picks them up after. The children said that their father come too late for them. They said that sometimes all the children are picked up, they had to wait long period, in the dark, for their father to come for them.

During the winter one Thursday, the children asked Richard to take them to the show.

It was the only outlet they had, besides going to church on Sundays with Brenda.

I pleaded with my husband, "Please Richard, if you know that you cannot pickup the children on time, leave them at home. It is too cold to leave them outside too long"

"What makes you think that I would leave my children out on the cold? Your mind is so twisted, you imagine only bad things about me"

I made sure that they were well dressed warm enough for the cold weather.

So far, I've been able to deceive everyone, especially my children. They love their father; I did nothing to discourage that, even if I had to do it with much agony.

My three children were my life. I lived for them. I submit like a beaten dog, to the worst kind of verbal abuse and torture. Yet, I am here because of my three children.

They were supposed to be home by eight-thirty, the latest. Nine-thirty, ten-thirty no children. It rained and I prayed that they were not in the rain on this cold night.

At about eleven o'clock I saw the light coming up the hill. I looked at my children.

They were drenched and shivering. Their lips were blue. Rocky seemed worst, because when the rain came down, he gave his wind blazer to Melanie and brave the elements.

You see, when the picture show is over, everyone has to leave the schoolyard for officials to lock the gate. Leaving the children to wait for their late parents outside.

I took my three children strait to the bathroom, gave them a hot shower, while Daphne made some warm soup. We got on our knees and prayed, like we did every night. I hugged and kissed them more than usual. I was telling them 'goodbye'

I went out to the sitting room to find Richard fast asleep on the couch; I could smell the whisky on his breath. I went into the kitchen and took up the longest knife, returned to the sitting room. I stood over him, looking for the right spot to plunge the long, sharp stainless steel onto this 'thing' that is causing me so much pain, driving me to madness.

I felt two strong arms grabbed me from behind, I heard, "Wynette, don't do it. Think of your children. What would become of them if you are in jail?" Asked Daphne.

Remember the muffins I was making for Daphne? Well she brought an envelope with cash every Friday. She asked me to keep it for her. I kept them with mine in my square box in the safety of Mama's room. Every time I had money I deposit it in my box. I never did withdrawal from my box until when Daphne asked me for envelopes that I was keeping for her. I gave them to her with no question asked.

I had no reason to worry about Mama being my safe keeper. She probably never saw a US dollar or a pound all her life. Put simply, she was too honest to even look into it.

The next afternoon, I saw two cars in front of the house. One was Daphne's, the other I did not recognize.

I walked out to her standing with a strange man. She said, "Open the gate for us to park your car" Daphne handed to me the keys to a two-doors Fiat with its engine at the back and the trunk at the front.

I stood next to the car, holding the key in my hand, looking at Daphne, I wondered,

'Who is this person? Why is she doing all of these things for me? What does she want from me? What is she up to? No one has done what she has done for me. What is her gain in all of this?' I kept looking at her and she kept smiling in an awarding way.

Now, it was 'catch me if you can'. My children, Zee, Willy and me in our little car name Suzy. We went everywhere. Picnics, zoo, parks, villages and any place of interest. Sometimes Chris and her children joined us, two adults and six children in little Suzy. She was oozing sweetness in my life, by just seeing how happy my children were in her. I fill her up with the same amount of gas as a motorcycle and drove all week

It was around this period when I collected lots of wooden carvings and stones such as malaki, tigers-eye, amities and ivory, most of which I bought on the street or from people who walked around selling their beautiful crafts and paintings.

I did my last Pitman advance exams. I got first class in everyone.
'How did I do this?'
"Now, you are equipped and ready to go face the world". said proud Daphne.

Let me tell you a little about Zambia while I was there.
Most of the people were honest and humble. It rained once per year. Villagers come with large pales full of water and ask if they can place them under the lights around the house to catch 'rain flies' a good source of protein.
After I saw that David and Amdela had their wives, I asked Barnabus when is he going to bring his wife? He told me that she is too far away, that it would take days to go and come back. I told him that its alright, he can go and get her.
A week later, I look down the road and saw Barnabus coming up with his tie flying and a briefcase in his hand. Several feet behind him was his wife who had a large bundle on her head, two bags in her two hands and a baby strapped to her back.
I walked to the gate and found myself looking at beauty that only God hands molded.
She was dark with the smoothest skin that I saw only when my babies were small.
She smiled, exposing the whitest teeth. She wore a chatenge-wrap around her waist, leaving her firm, pointed breasts exposed for the convenient of little James on her back.
Lena had never seen herself in a mirror, only on the reflection in the lake. She never used soap or cream, yet she moved around with the beauty and innocence of someone unreal in this city where women are using bleaching cream to get lighter.
We loaded Suzy with all the clothes and shoes that my household didn't use, along with foodstuff from my pantry and garden and take them to villages.
We never came back empty. They in turn gave us eggs, vegetable and

peanuts, but the most important and satisfying gift is their appreciation, smiles and friendliness.

Melanie continued her close relationship with Amdela. Many days he had to jump the fence to escape from her, if he could not take her where he was going.

The children had large birthday parties with lots of children from school, friends and neighbors. Plenty of food and drinks. I always invited the houseboys' children around the now developing hill.

Someone offered to take me to a witch doctor to control my husband's wild behavior. I told her, "I didn't know that he has a wild behavior. I like him the way he is. He is a good father and husband" She looked at me as if I was the one who needed it.

I heard many strange stories, this one I will share with you. It is true.

Two people working in a bank became lovers even though they were both married.

The husband of the female found out about it and confronted his wife. She denied it.

The roamers and evidence continued.

He went to her parents, the elder in his village, everyone whom he taught could help.

She continued to deny having an affair with the married man.

Her husband finally went to the witch doctor. The witch doctor told him that he has to be absolutely sure of his accusation, because what he will do, will be irreversible.

The witch doctor opened a large sisears in the center of his hut. He told the husband that if his wife was having an affair, the sisears will close, and whatever happens, he would not be able to undo the result.

The sisears closed one night and the no one could've separated his wife and her lover. They were taken to the hospital. The result was fatal.

Richard's arrogance never ceased. He was angry at all my

accomplishments and the freedom that I was enjoying. His insults fell on deft ears and that made him angrier.

One Saturday evening, the young ladies living in my house were getting dress to go to a party. – There were lots of parties, because there were lots of Guyanese and West Indians, most of whom were young and single women.- I remember my days at Lancaster, when I watched my cousin prepare for a dance. Paper curlers rolled their hotcomb hair. I was not allowed to go with them. Only when Uncle Bertram was home.

Richard came home very agitated. He called the houseboy and told him,

"Stay in the house with the children, Madam and I have to go out" 'Go out? I have not gone out with my husband since Daphne's party'

He said to me in a demanding way, "Come on, lets go" the children asked, "Daddy can we come for the drive too?"

"No, you can't come where we are going" I was not afraid of him anymore. I asked,

"Should I change my clothes? Like get dressed or something?"

"No, no one will notice you where we are going"

It was a long, silent drive at high speed. I had no idea where I was being taken to, but I was immune to fear. I made some side-glances to see his demeanor. I saw only anger. Still, I was not afraid. 'This man could never hurt me anymore'.

'My husband had become strange, mostly because of my refusal to accept his behavior, but he would not kill me. He is not that kind. I know my husband'.

He turned into a large parking lot opposite a hug building that looked like a hospital.

He took out an envelope from his glove compartment. His hands were shaking. He said,

"This letter came for you from your father. When and how did you write him?"

"I wrote it some time ago. I don't remember when"

"How did you post it?" he demanded. I did not answer.

He opened the envelope and took out four tickets and shoves them into my face.

"Take a good look at them, they are the tickets you ask your father to send for you.

You are planning to take my children away from me? You think you can getaway with it? I took your crap for more than four years, just because you are the mother of my children. Ah man stray and get a piece of pussy, and the whole world dried and died"

"No Richard, not the whole world, just me. You are still enjoying the world"

"Who are you? Look around you, you know how many women's husband are out there every night having a good time with other women, yet go home to their wives who are not dead cold like you?"

"I'm not those women, I am me. Was it the piece of pussy that made you squander all our savings and robbed my children's future by not paying their insurance?"

"No, you are not them. You are a stubborn jackass, who is as dumber than a jackass.

If you think that you could take my children away from me, think again.

I would rather see you dead than let you go away from me. Remember, "Till death do us part?" He pretended not to hear my question. I asked

"Is that why you left me to die with malaria?" He was stunned from my question. "I will do better next time. You see that building over there? Its called Chinama. You ever heard of Chinama? It's the mental home where men commit their wives when they want to get rid of them or who don't behave themselves, like you are doing.

In this country, men have the final say. I'm your husband, and a Diplomat. I have the final say. When I deposit you here; no one will ever see you again. Not unless I say so. You can kiss your daddy and those dummies goodbye. I have Diplomatic Immunity?

You will never see your children again and I will never want to see you again.

Take a good look at yourself. You're a fool to think that because you can type and drive, you are going to be somebody? Look at you. No one would hire you to be a charwoman to clean their office floor"

He threaded the four tickets and threw them into my face.

"Hate will hold you back" my mother's words.

Sunday morning I got my children ready for church. I kissed them goodbye when Brenda came to get them – Brenda was one of the single girls who came from Trinidad. She kept the children at her flat some weekends. She loved children and church. –

The rest of the residences were out. I wrote a note and placed it on Noreen's bed, asking her to please take care of my children. I went to the medicine cabinet and empty every bottle into my mouth, locked the door, ask God to forgive me, I went to sleep.

Noreen came back home because she forgot her identification badge to enter the hospital. She found the note and could not get into my bedroom.

She ran outside screaming for the men. She ran over to our Canadian friend, who came to help the other men to break out the iron bars from the windows of my room.

Ed and Noreen rushed me to the hospital. My stomach was pumped. I was in coma.

I saw my mother, Mr. Reed, Clive, Gramother, Phyllis, Lammy and other pets.

I tried to reach out to them but they turned their backs on me. I tried to call Lammy, but he too walked away in a smoky white cloud. I kept following them but found myself in a tunnel with white cloud. When I reached the end, they were gone.

I began to cry, that's when I heard her voice saying the same words for the second time, "Wynette, who will take care of your children" Daphne was holding my foot and crying. My three children were with her.

Priests and councilors came to talk to me at the hospital. They made me promise that I would never attempt such a dangerous thing again.

When I returned home, the men and women in the yard came into my bedroom and sat around the bed, for hours, dead silent. No one moved or said a word.

Barnabus told me later, that there were so much crying among the women and anxiousity among the men. They wanted to go to the hospital but didn't know where. He said they were worried that they may have to leave their beautiful home and all the help they got from me. He said Amdala counseled them that I would come back home.

I didn't know how much my children understood what happened or what was told to them. We never discussed the incident.

Richard kept away from me as much as he could. His insults ceased for a while.

I went on enjoying my children, and give thank to God for rejecting me.

One day, Ed's houseboy ran over to me and said, "Madam, come quick, Bwana no look right" I ran over and found my friend sprawled on the chair holding his chest.

I got the men around to help put Ed into Suzy. I drove as fast as I could to the hospital.

I remember going to see him, he said, "Thanks for taking care of my boys, and thanks for bringing me here. I guess our children are the only thing on our mind when something serious happens?" I said to my friend, "I guess so. The feeling is mutual"

His ambassador thanked me for doing what I did. I said "He did it for me first"

About three months later, Fred, the ambassador came to visit me. He said,

"We have to pack and move back home. It has nothing to do with you and what happened. I hope the 'Old Man' never hears anything about it, but you have nothing to do with our order to leave. The Zambian government requests the change. I guess I did not tell them what they wanted to hear. It's a high level dispute"

I was feeling lighter and brighter. I couldn't take the smile off my face.

- In life, things have to happen, before things happen -

He continued in almost an apologetic way, "I am so sorry that things got so bad for you here. I should've paid more attention to what was happening. I heard and saw things, but once Richard did his duties at the embassy, that was all that mattered.

Let me tell you, he is good at what he does. He can stay away four days, comes in on Friday, and completes the whole week's work in time for the mailbag on Saturday.

I have nothing to complain about. The man is good at what he does.

He would be quick to remind us that it doesn't matter what day he did the job, as long as by the end of the week it's done. He is right; his duties are done faster that some of us who are in daily.

I would arrange for you to stay in England for a while until things cool down, then you and Richard may return home with your children as one happy family".

Richard gave Nixon and Zee back to the American who he bought them from.

I made arrangements for the people who were replacing us to keep my three families whom I have grown so close to. I love and respected them very much.

I shared most of the foodstuff and meat among them. I gave them all the Kwachas.

Amdela kept saying that we are not taking Melanie. Many times I had to get Barnabus to explain to him that Melanie is my baby and she has to go with me.

He said no, that she is an African child and no one should take an African child away.

I knew that it was because he had grown so close to her that he is behaving this way.

I asked Barnabus and the houseboy next door, to explain to Amdela that I know how Africans feel about their children being taken away, but Melanie is not an African. She was not born here, that she was born far, far away from Africa.

The packers came and packed our things including all the crafts I collected.

Remember my wooden box that Mama kept for me? I retrieved it the day we were leaving. I wrapped all my crispy currencies in many layers of soft tissue and place it flat on a private part of my body.

I arranged for all my people in the yard to be taken to the airport to see us off.

They have never been to the airport before. I was happy to oblige. Even the neighboring houseboys and their families came along to say goodbye to us.

Melanie refused to come in the car with us. She sat between Mama and Amdela, in the bus. At the airport, she sat on Amdela's lap; Mama dressed her in ivory necklace.

When it was time to board the plane, I hug and kiss everyone who came to see us off. I tried to take Melanie from Amdela, but they wouldn't let go of each other.

Richard had to intervene and actually pull her away from Amdela's tight hug.

She kicked and screamed all the way, did not stop even when the plane lifted off.

I should be the happiest person in the plane. I wanted to leave long before I arrived.

If only I could have this screaming child to stop. Other women in our group took Melanie to quiet her. Nothing worked. Richard walked with her up and down the isle.

About one hour in the air, I felt that Melanie was warm. I asked the other mothers if they had something for fever?

She began to get worst. Fred asked the hostess if there was anything she could do.

She gave us some ice and a towel to keep her cool. It was not working.

She was behaving strange. Her eyes were turning up and getting red

The ambassador asked if the pilot to call ahead to Kenya, where we had to in transit,

And call Dr. Haynes, who was a Guyanese, living and practicing in Kenya, to meet us.

Dr. Haynes met us at the airport, prepared to see a child with high temperature.

After he examined Melanie, he told us that he was looking at a seriously ill child.

He asked why we didn't take her to the hospital in Lusaka when she got sick?

We tried to convince him that she was not sick when we left home.

He told us that he would give her something to lower the fever and that we should continue to keep her head cold and give her more of the medicine every four hours.

He said that he would call London and have Dr. Fang Afat to meet us at the airport.

"Dear God, what is happening to my baby? Does she have Malaria like I did?

Dr. Fang Afat met us at the airport and whisked Melanie and me to the hospital.

The Whips Cross Hospital doctors isolated both Melanie and I because we just landed out of Africa. They did all kinds of blood and fluid tests. Spinal tap and drew fluid from her knees. Nurses and doctors were asking me questions that may be able to help them.

The doctors and nurses were dressed in long blue overalls, with masks and gloves.

Dr Fang Afat told me that we are in good hands now, and that he would check with the embassy for news of my sick child. He left.

I didn't know where we were, how would others know where we are? But at this moment, nothing else mattered. I was watching everyone in the room. I began to talk.

"Dear God, You answered my plea four years ago. I kept my promise. Even when it seems to other that I am practicing favoritism among my children. I never broke my promise to You that I would cherish every day that You allow me to have her.

I come to you once again, my Dear Father, please take the fever away from my baby"

By nightfall, the doctors shake their heads in doubt, all the tests they did revealed nothing. Yet Melanie's temperature kept above dangerous level.

She was placed on isolation in a cubicle at the Princess Margaret Ward for children. She was naked with the window open to let the cold March wind cool her room.

She was washed every hour with ice chips in a basin of water.

I sat in the sitting room, confused, hungry, alone and afraid. All I did was pray.

The next day, my brother-in-law Cedric took me to his home to see my two children.

I learned the bus route and went everyday to spend with Melanie.

Nothing has changed. They were able to bring the temperature down, only to see it shoot right back up. Her chart looked like shark teeth, up, down, up, down.

I spoke to the doctors' everyday; I get the same answer, "Mrs. Greene, we have and are doing everything possible to make her better. If we can find the cause, then we can treat it. But all the tests show no cause for her fever. I must tell you, she is not getting any better. It's been more than two weeks and there is no sign of her improving"

"Dr. is there another place we could take her? Or another specialist could see her?"

I realized that I should not ask those questions to a doctor who has been doing everything for Melanie since she was admitted. I humbly apologized. He said he understands how I feel. I don't think anyone can understand how overwhelmed I am.

My sister-in-law was very helpful caring for Kim and Rocky.

Before I left for the hospital every morning, I help to clean the flat, bath the children and cook. I bought lots of books for them to read. I did my best assuring them that I love them very much. They always give me a note or drawings to take for Melo.

Two months has passed and Richard did not go one day to see Melanie.

He told his brother that he could not bear to see his baby in isolation.

Melanie has gotten to skin and bones. Even though she was being fed intervenes, every drop was just passing out as it enter her vein.

Melanie never spoke a word since we left Africa. Every time I try to make contact through our eyes, it seems as if she was not my baby, she was someone else.

The doctor told me one morning "Mrs. Greene, it is not easy for me to tell you this, you will have to prepare for the inevitable any day now. There is nothing more we can do for Melanie" He sat on the bench with his arm around my shoulder.

When the doctor left, I remain sitting, lost in myself.

"Hello" I looked up and saw a woman dressed in a long African outfit. She said,

"I hear about your baby in isolation. I see you every day when I come see my son"

I was in no state to form a conversation with anyone. She continued

"I hear you just come from Africa? I am an African. My son is in here because I fed him bad meat, I don't know if he is going to live" she began to cry. I realized that she was in the same sinking boat with me.

I began to talk with her. I told her of our time in Zambia and how much Amdela and Mama loved her. She held my shoulders and turned me to face her, she said,

"Madam, your baby did not come with you"

"What do you mean? My baby did not come with me?" I am willing to listen to anything. Anything, no matter how dumb it might sound. She continued

"You see, after what was done to African during slavery generations ago, people all over Africa promised never to allow anyone to take an African child out of Africa'

"But Melanie is not an African. She went there when she was two years old"

"Amdela sees her as his own African grandchild and he kept her spirit"

"But I have my child. She is very sick, but she is my child. She is lying in there"

"Yes, you have your child but Amdela has her spirit" she shook me as if to wake me.

"If what you are saying is true, what can I do to get back my baby?"

So far, this lady is the only one who seems to know something about my child.

"Go into that room. Get on your knees, hold your child hand and speak to Amdela.

Bear in mind that he is not a bad man. If, in your plea, you sound mad or angry, he will not listen. Speak to him, plea with him. I cannot tell you the words, you should know what you would say to someone who wants to take your child away form you"

I thank the African lady. She went to see her child and I went to see mine.

One could count Melanie's ribs and watch at the skeleton outline of her tiny body.

Her eyes and lips were dried and cracked. There was no movement from her.

Her eyes half open and mouth wide open. They had already taken her chart out.

I got on my knees, held my baby's cold hand and spoke directly to Amdela.

I do not remember every word I said, but I transformed my mind to see Amdala in Melanie's little body .I spoke softly. This was my only chance; I have to do this with belief. I have to believe what the lady said; I have nothing else to hold on to.

"Amdela, I am begging you, please to release Merre to me, I will take good care of her. I know you love Merre; sometimes we have to give up someone we love.

I love you like my own father. Merre, Kim and Rocky love you as if you are their grandfather. We will always love you and Mama. I am begging you on my knees, please let go of Merre; I promise you that I will take good care of her

It was hard to pick my words carefully at a time like this. I tried.

The nurse said to me that evening, as I leave. I was not allowed to stay with her. M

"You know we did everything humanly possible to save your baby? I am so sorry that we could not even reach her in anyway. I am sadden for her and you" I looked at the beautiful Irish nurse with blue eyes, I saw genuine sadness in them.

I kiss my baby goodnight and say to her what I say every night when I leave her.

"Melo, Mommy Wynette is going home to see Kimmy and Rocky. I will see you tomorrow morning, OK? Mommy love you"

I went into the chapel of the hospital to have a conversation with God.

I made the same promise that I made four years age, this time I asked God for one more favor. "Dear Father, if it is your wish to take her, please give me the strength to stick around and take care of my other two children. I know my baby will be in good hands, if that is Your wish"

I sat that night in a chair by the phone in the sitting room, all night.

I informed Richard, Cedric and Agata of what to expect. I never told my children that their baby sister might die that night.

It was still dark when I sneaked out of the home to catch the first bus to the hospital. I quickly put on isolation protections that I had to wear to enter Melanie's cubicle. I entered and found a nurse; she was collecting lining soaked in blood, from the floor. I asked what happened? She said, "Melanie had a terrible night. All this blood is from a nosebleed and bowel movement. Yes, all blood, I didn't think she had so much blood and fluid left in her little body"

I knelt at my baby's bed. For the first time in two and a half months, she spoke.

"Mommy, Amdela gone"

I tried to find the African lady, but no one seemed to know of her or any sick child who ate bad meat. "Who is she? Where did she go? Where did she come from?"

Melanie spent another three weeks recuperating in the hospital.

After she gathers some strength from drinking lots of Lucazade and other nourishing drink, she had to use a baby walker to learn to walk again.

She couldn't eat solid food because of not eating so long and the soreness of her suffices. Her voice changed. To this day, she still has her childish voice.

I thought of the African lady. I needed to thank her. I went to the admission office, no one knew of my description. Even the ladies, who clean the ward, never saw her.

Belief can cure.

All the nurses, doctors and other workers, gathered to say goodbye to Melanie the day she left. No one expected this day, after what they saw for so long.

When Cedric opened the door, Melanie stumbled her way strait into the arms of Richard. She never knew that he did not go one day to see her in the hospital.

I allow the charade to continue for the sake of my children and my pride.

My cousin Enid, Uncle Isaac's daughter, who is a nurse in England, came to take me out. She took me into a hosiery store. The gentleman behind the counter knew her well.

He greeted her, and then looked at me and asked, "Is this your mother?"

I was thirty-one years old. Enid was older than me.

As soon as Melanie became strong enough to go out, I took my children to go and look for my niece Sharon, Sister Esther daughter who came to England years ago.

We kept in touch, I had her address. We got in two buses to reach the place.

When we got there, all the buildings were boarded. No one lived there anymore.

I was frantic. Every time I think of a way of escaping, something always blocks me.

We went to the grocery store and asked if anyone knew her. Someone told me to go across the street to the movie theater that she worked at before she moved.

I did and was told that my niece had moved close to the airport, which was many miles away. I was sent to a friend of hers whom may have her new address.

I got her address. 'Now, how do I get there? I have to find her' I am desperate'.

Sharon friend Betty offered to take me there the next day. She said that her older daughter would look after the children, while we go looking for Sharon.

We changed many busses to get to the area. We asked everyone in the area to tell us where is this street call Hazlet Road? We were sent on more busses. We asked police, postman and everyone who gave us the time – let me tell you, English people are kind and helpful to strangers. One man even got on one of the busses, just to show us where to go – We did not find Hazlet Rd. Betty said it was night, that we should go back.

Heavy heartedly I agreed with her. We boarded the bus. She wanted to go to the upper level, but I was too tired to climb the stairs. We sat on the back seats.

Suddenly I heard a woman asked, "Is this seat taken?" I began to scream at the top of my lungs. My niece Sharon scream too. We began to hug and dance in the moving bus.

That was the fourth time in my life; I had no answer for what happened.

The fishes in the hole. The train line. The African woman. Finding Sharon.

We did not go back to Hackney for weeks. Sharon's two daughters, Vanessa and Marcia bonded with Kim, Rocky and Melo. At last, my children and I were having a wonderful time in London. I was winding down but still very impacted. I would scream at the children, even spank them for the slightest misbehavior.

I saw my niece daughters looking at me strangely. When my children cried, they cried.

Sharon took me into the bathroom, she said, "Aunt Wynette, you are not yourself. Please be my loving auntie again. The one I knew and loved all my life" we cried.

I almost felt my being, revamping. Like if you were constipated for a long time, then finally you get it all out. You feel the ease from your head, down. You even want to kiss the toilet bowl for accepting all that waste.

Sharon helped me to release a lot of years of pent-up emotion and pain.

I went on my knees, hugged my three children and begged them for forgiveness.

She showed the children and me almost all of London.

One day we went to one of the largest park, I don't remember the name, but it was large. One can walk all day and still haven't seen the whole park.

We went to the water fountain, everyone drank but Melanie was too short and still abit weak. I used my hand to catch the water and put to her mouth. When she drank enough, she said to me, "Mommy, you are the best water catcher" her words took me back to when I was her age. I said, "Mommy had lots of practice, baby, lots of practice"

Cedric and Agata came for us. They told me that Richard was angry that we went away without telling him where we were, and how upset he was, and how much he missed us. I kept a still tongue. I was happy and I was changing.

I think the man at the hosiery store, snapped me back to life.

The children started school at the Hackney Primary School.

Melanie celebrated her fifth birthday by having a tea party with all her classmates.

I worked with Agata at home. She was a seamstress; she worked for a large clothing factory. They cut the garment in the hundreds and bring them for her to stitch.

She paid me well, unknown to Richard. I hid that along with what I brought from Zambia in a secret place in the sewing room.

Richard informed me that we have to leave. I wished there was somewhere I could take my children and hide from him until he goes away.

In other words I wanted my children to stay in England and continue school. They were doing well and even their accent was all England.

I pleaded with Cedric and Agata to keep my children. They had no children of their own. They grew close to my children and the children in turn love them both.

I was willing to go back home with Richard if he would allow the children to stay.

Richard refused, asking them if they thing that his children are coffins"

We went back home to a different Guyana. Everything you could think of was banned. I mean everything that was once imported, was now 'contraband'

I was glad that my mother was not around. All the food she and the Indians ate, were banned. No more flour for roti, split peas for dhal, chana, garlic, onions and many others basic food and household items. Dhal was my mother's only source of protein.

The Indians were angry and hate was further festering.

Blacks were hurting too; they didn't get most of their foodstuff either. Flour was their main staple for bread and bakes, even toilet paper, soap, pigtails and salt beef.

They would say they are making a sacrifice to support their Comrade Leader.

Once again, a split between my people. The Indians complained and make do with what they could. They crossed the river over to Suriname and risked their lives, jail, just to buy some flour, split peas and garlic. Indians can't live without those three items.

It was hard to bring three children, who have grown accustomed to all the basic niceties, to where there was no soap the bath them. They would ask for some butter or cheese or peanut butter, only for me to tell them there were none. "We are in Guyana"

There was also no room in the inn for us. My brother-in-law and his family were living in what was once my home. Another one of my brother-in-law, his girlfriend and two of her children moved into the spare room at my in-laws home.

The children and I had to sleep in the smallest room in the house, where Richard's older cousin Aubrey, slept. The children slept head and tail on a small cot. I had to climb to the top of the bunk where Aubrey slept below. Richard, whenever he came home, slept on the sofa in the sitting room. Still I told myself.

"You take what you get and don't get upset. In time, 'This too shall pass"

I got the children enrolled in Dolphin Government School. My sister-in-law taught there and her husband took my children when he took her to school.

I took my savings to the bank and informed the Ministry of Finance to stop depositing Mr. Greene's salary into my account.

Richard hit the sky when he found out that his salary was paid into my account.

"It was just payback, Richard. I took what you took from my children and me"

He screamed, began to sweat and punching the walls. His mother ordered him out of the house, while I continue to play cards with Daddy Sonny.

When Richard stamped out of the house, Daddy said with a wink, "You did well, my child. I am happy to see that you came back here, changed. You are braver and stronger. Always take the right side in life. Not your friend or family side. Take the right side"

I couldn't take the living arrangement. The house was too crowded.

I asked Richard if we could get an apartment for the children to be more comfortable?

"I'm quite comfortable here. When you lived in a big house, you were lonely. You brought people to live in it. Now you are in a full house and it is too cramped? What the hell do you want?"

I didn't retrieve my treasures from Doreen; instead, I deposited all that I brought from my trip abroad, into the hatbox for her to keep.

I packed a small BOAC bag, told Sis and Daddy that I am going to my cousin Doris, Uncle Charlie's daughter, who lived in Queenstown. I promised them that I would only sleep there, that I will come every day to take care of my children and help around the house and wash their clothes. This way, Rocky sleeps on the top bunk, over Aubrey.

Neither of the two objected to my leaving. Sis said, "Do what you have to do child"

Daddy said, "Go my child, even if you don't come back. Go with my blessings"

I came every morning; sometimes the household was still asleep. I packed my children lunch kits and get them ready for school.

When they are gone, I pounded the pavements looking for a job. Any kind of job.

I had in the large brown envelope in my hand; thirteen 'first class' Pitman certificates to show that I am qualified. All I need is a chance. 'Please, someone give me a break'

I get back to Charlotte Street in time to see that the children did their homework. We spent quality time together, either by going for walks or to the market for fruits.

We sit on the steps; talk about Africa and England, and how they wish they were there.

Only after we kneel and pray, and I kiss my three children goodnight, would I leave to go sleep at my cousin's home.

Old Years Day-New Years Eve, morning, with my brown envelope, and told Doris,

"Today is the last day of this year, I am going out there to look for a job. The New Year has to be better for me. I cannot go on like this. I am loosing my mind".

My first stop was at the PNC-the ruling party office. The secretary asked for my membership card? I explained that I never had one. I showed her my papers but she was not interested in them, she said, "Comrade, are you telling me that you are not a member of this Party, but you wants to work for us?"

"I just want a job Miss. I was told to come here because you find job for people"

"Don't call me Miss. Where the hell have you been? You address everyone as Comrade; it means that we are all one. We are brothers and sisters. Colonial days are gone" OH, how much things has changed? But I still need a job. I said, nicely,

"OK, Comrade I understand all that you told me. We are sisters, could you give this sister a job? I am willing to do anything you see fit for me" She became softer,

"It's the rule, I cannot employ any nonmember in here, for security reasons"

I walked on to the Bank of Guyana where someone I knew as a child, had a high position. He told me that the ladies who worked in the typing pool have years of experience in typing and shorthand. Since I have none, he could not hire me.

Lost in my world of desperation, I remembered that my 'longtime' friend Cecil was

General Manager for the Guyana Marketing Corporation.

As I walked up Lombard St. that rainy old-years day, crowds of people were hurrying down the street. Going home to prepare for old-years night parties.

The security guard too was in a happy mood, he directed me to the GM's office.

I knocked on the door, shaking inside. Saying to myself, 'This is my only chance'

A lady opens the door and told me that the GM will not be available to anyone until the second week of the New Year.

I pleaded with her that its important that I see him today. She closed the door.

I stood outside Cecil's office door. Like a zombie, I did not move. I refuse to go

Every time the lady would look through the glass window and sees me still standing there, she shooed me away, but I was going nowhere. Once Cecil was in his office,

He has to come out sometime. This is my only chance. I am going nowhere.

'What did my father-in-law say? That I came back stronger and braver?'

Some drunken men on the street were behaving badly, making lots of noise.

Cecil came out of his office, into this secretary's office to look through the window, down to the street. He turned around to go back into his office and saw me through the glass door. He stood there with his mouth and eyes wide open. He asked the lady how long I was out there? It would've been about four hours, but it doesn't matter now.

He put his arm around my shoulder and led me into his office. He told the lady,

"I do not want to be disturbed" 'OH God, thank You, Persistent pays '

We sat on a couch and he offered me something to eat and drink. I couldn't show him how much I needed it. - Gramother said, "No matter how hungry you are, don't let anyone know that you are hungry for their food. Be a hungry pretender"-

"So, Wynette, tell what's been happening? How was your tour abroad?" I reminded my self that I did not come here to cry or beg. I came here to ask for a job.

"It's been alright. I am here to ask you if you could give me a job. I know you have to hire only party members. I am not one, never has been but I just came back from serving this government. On that ground I think you have no problem hiring me"

Cecil began to laugh, he laughed so hard with his foot in the air, I was feeling foolish. He said "Wynette, understand something, I hire people according to their qualification. For those who are not educated enough for clerical jobs, I hire them for their willingness to work, not because they are party members. I do not adhere to that order. In this Corporation, there are people of all races. I don't care of their party.

Cecil called the Personal Officer, Mr. Johnson, he introduced me to him and asked him to look at my papers and see if there is a position that the corporation has to offer?

After the interview with Mr. Johnson, he promised to get in touch with me later.

Cecil drove to Doris's home. I told him I was staying there until we can find a place.

Two weeks later I was employed as a Customer Relations Officer for the GMC.

I danced without music; I just needed some proper clothes to dress for the position.

I had two pieces of clothing suitable to go to work with. The yellow pants suit I wore Monday, Wednesday, and Fridays. The brown and white dress I wore Tuesday, Thursday and Saturdays, until I got my first paycheck and got more clothes.

My photo and announcement was in every newspaper. The Corporation assuring their customers that they now have someone to address their problems to.

A friend told Richard that he saw my picture in the newspaper. He asked

"Where, in the obituary"

I was proud of myself. I was determined to make the people who throw this lifeline to me, be just as proud of me. My children and my job were all I had to live for.

Every month I gave my boss Mr. Stewart a full detailed report of the problems.

He was a smart Marketing Manager; I began to learn about marketing from him.

Because I worked closely with the other Marketing Officers who studied abroad and had degrees in Marketing, I was sucking up their knowledge. Whenever one of them went on vacation, I did his job and mine too. My boss liked what I was doing.

I was sent all over the country to open new outlets for food distribution. I interviewed and hired applicants from the areas to work in the new outlets.

We opened one in Manchester Village. I asked my boss if I could hire my brother David? Because he was mute, I had to get permission to hire him under the code of disabled worker. David became one of the hardest working employee. Because he could not hear nor speak, he did not sit and gossip or listen to gossip. He did his job well.

When I worked at the biscuit factory, the union encouraged us to apply for low-income houses. I did but left the country before others were given their home.

I went to the Ministry of Housing and met with the Minister Singh, who knew me from my union days when he spoke at several seminars. He said,

"We sent you many notices to your address on the application. You never answered, and then I heard that you got married and went to Africa. All those houses are gone now" he looked at me sadly and continued, "However, we are building in a much nicer area up the coast call Atlantic Ville. The view of the Atlantic Ocean is to die for.

I will arrange for you to have one on a nice spot" 'Thank You Dear God, Thank You'

"Mr. Singh, you will never know how grateful I am to you" I said as I stood to leave.

"You know that you will have to bring your husband in to sign the contract. You would've still had it if you were single, but now that you are married, the law requires that both party sign jointly" said Mr. Singh.

I told Richard about the house. He said, "I don't need a house. My father has three houses in the yard. I can live in anyone of them. I don't need a house"

Early one morning I was hurrying to Charlotte St to get my children ready for school when I saw a young man jogging on the street. He began to talk with me. He was very handsome. The wet shirt stuck to his muscular body. His eyes were blue and his smile was flirty. I dismissed him as another young man hustling an older woman.

The next morning he was on the road again. I spoke to him. He told me that he is here writing his teases for a master's degree in Boston. He told me that he had been in the country for a while, and is enjoying his homeland. He said he couldn't believe how the country has changed from when he was raised here and attended one of the top schools.

He was modest; he talks about himself and how nice it was growing up in Essequabo among the six races of Guyana in peace and harmony.

He sounded intelligent. He wanted to know everything about me. I told him some, not a lot. I will always be cautious not to tell anyone everything about my life.

I was surprised when he asked me out to a club. I said to Doris, nervously,

"I have not gone out on a date since a lifetime ago. I feel stupid going out with a younger man" Doris looked at me, straiten my dress and hair, pushed me out, and said,

"Go on and have a good time. Men don't get nervous or feel stupid when they go out with younger girls. Do they?"

Every night I went out with Ron. He was pumping youth back into my old, swizzle life. He treated me like a lady, with respect and kindness. He was tender and loving.

He waited at evenings in Charlotte St. we walked hand in hand. Not giving a damn

He met me on the job at lunchtime, we went to some 'hole in the wall' to eat local food. Every night we hit different nightclub. Boy, could he dance? Dancing make me free.

I was so full of energy; I would sleep from four to six in the morning and still be ready to tackle the rest of the day full of life. I was afraid to close my eyes and miss the light.

Ron took my children out for dinner and walks in the park. He took them to shop.

Ask any woman, if any man shows love to her children, she can't help but love him.

Melanie told Richard that a blue-eyed man took them to dinner and was holding Mommy's hand when they walked in the garden. Richard looked at me scornfully, said,

"So, I hear that you are behaving like a fool all over the place, with a young man?"

"Yes, I am making up for lost time. I am taking all that I can get. I am enjoying every moment of it. He is young and full of good loving. I am hungry for what you and I had before you found 'a piece of pussy' and turned me off cold all these years.

I thought you were the best lover and dancer. I am thankful I will not die believing that.

I was longing for a good omelet. Yes, I am making a fabulous omelet by beating some fresh eggs into my life. So, while you are still looking in the shadow for your old bone, I am enjoying a real young juicy bone. You like yours older, I like mine younger"

Ron was five years my junior.

I noticed lately that everywhere Ron and I went, Richard would show up.

He did not make any disturbance but he would let us know that he was watching us.

Ron and I were having fun. I was behaving like a child who had all the candy from the store. We went for long walks on the seawall and the garden. He manicured my nails. He would tell me about England, where he studied at Oxford. He was so knowledgeable about the government here. He encourages me to read, read, read.

He bought books for me to read. He was never condescending, or showoff.

I wondered 'how come a young man like this can be so smart, yet so simple?'

When we walked on the streets, people in high position in the government would stop and talk with him. He would say after, "Oh, he is someone I knew in another time'

For the first time in six years I feel like a woman again. I was walking with my head up. Ron straitened my drooping spine and assures me that I am a beautiful woman.

We ran hand in hand to catch a bus or car; we even hopped on a moving dray-cart once.

Laughing and giggling like two school children. I remember 'Roman Holiday'

He admired me the way I am. No makeup, lipstick or nail polish, he said I had beauty.

Every good thing comes to an end. Ron had to leave. I knew that he had to leave, that was why I collected all the nectar I could get from him to sustain me when he goes.

On the way to the airport, Ron stopped at my job to say bye. He said,

"Wynette, I'm going to miss you. Let the sky be the limit. Don't settle for anything less. Your life is the only thing you own. Live as if you are proud of what you own

He took my hand and placed his collage ring on my finger.

Later, I learned that Ron was a writer. He published a famous book in Guyana.

That he was the right hand man and adviser to the leader, until he decided to go abroad to study against the wishes of the 'Old Man'.

I received a notice not long after, to go to the Finance Dept to put a down payment for our house. I did not have the amount required. I blocked out the fact that I have a bank account. I was not going to touch that.

I went up to Lancaster and asked my father to loan me the money. He did.

Richard still had to sign before the keys were handed to me.

Richard was playing 'payback'. He said lots of nasty things to me, but eventually he went and signed the contract and I got the keys to my new home.

Now, I have a home for my children. A home of my own. My very own home.

I got some carpenters to build cabinets and cupboards and paint the inside of the house.

I bought a double bunk for the four of us to sleep on until I could furnish the rest of the house. I had a one-burner hotplate to cook on.

The children were excited as much as I was. I took them up every afternoon to see how our new home was coming along. They knew which was whose room. The blue was Rock's, the pink was Kim and Melanie's and the front yellow room was mine.

I had a long talk with my children. I told them that their father might not come here to live with us because he needs to be close to his important job. That moving up here would be too far for him to get to work on time. – I was a lousy liar –

Mr. Stewart recommended that I be given a loan to buy a car. He told the board that I have been doing a lot of traveling and I needed one to do my job effectively.

I got my brand-new, yellow Toyota Corolla, PBB299. Am I moving on up or what?

I am driving while my husband is walking. Does that remind you of another time?

I was earning more money than my 'big shot' husband.

The sky opened and God was touching my head, He was answering my prayers.

On Christmas Eve of 1976, Daddy Sonny went into the hospital and died a week later. I lost a father and my children lost their grandfather. A good and kind man.

A man whom I thought would live forever. His Lodge gave him a wonderful sendoff.

That same Christmas Eve we had planned to move into our new home.

When we went to the car, Richard was sitting in the front seat. He said,

"I want to see where my children are going to wake up on Christmas morning" I couldn't let my children see what I failed to show them for so long. I couldn't let them see how angry he has made me; after all he is their father. Because of my three children, I have been, and may have to, endure Richard's mental abuse forever.

He occupied the front, largest room of my house. He never left.

Cedric came home for his father funeral. I bought a double bed for him to sleep on. I set it up in the pink room, so when he leaves, the girls would move into their room.

When Cedric left, Richard moved the bed into the front room, which he kept locked.

I could not put my purse down without him taking out my money. When I confronted him, he said, "What are you complaining about? I am just doing what you did to me. Besides, you are making much more than me. Its call 'tit fa tat' my dear wife"

I found a safer place in my desk draw at the office.

I was officially assigned Marketing Officer. I received a pay raise and allowances just like my graduated comrades. I put my paycheck into the bank and lived on my allowances and mileage payments.

When I had to go out of town and was paid to sleep in a standard hotel, I stayed with friends, family or the cheapest hotel, save, save, save. I have three children to educate.

I saw Cecil at Board meetings and if we bump into each other, he would complement me of the job I was doing. He would say, "I know you have it in you"

He and Rocky had the same birth date. I take two important men in my life to lunch at the Pegasus Hotel. Rocky is allowed to spend the rest of the day with the GM

Cecil told me that he was born on a Sunday at twelve noon. I said, "So was Rocky"

We were opening an outlet in Bartica, a large town in Essequibo. I was going to be there for about three month. The Corporation agreed to send my children by plane every Friday afternoon after school and bring them back on Monday mornings in time for school. I parked my car in the GMC yard, which left Richard to walk or catch a bus.

You see, he didn't only take the best room of my house, but every

Before I Forget

morning, he sat in the front seat of my car to be taken to work. I just had to bite my lips for my children.

It was in Bartica, that I think I saw a Nazi or soldier. I never knew about those people until years later. When I look back now, I am sure that I met a Nazi in Bartica.

There was an old White man who spoke very little English. He lived with an Amerindian woman in the woods, and sold produce in the town. He had no children and was proudly showing off what he called bullet holes on his body which he said that he got from running away in World War 11.

Not until years later when I learned about Nazi and how some of them escaped to South America and integrated with the local people, that I came to that assumption.

If you were to ask my children now, many years later, to name one of the nicest and happiest times they ever had? They would tell you, it was in Bartica.

They remember Mrs. Paris and her good cooking at the Government Rest House where we stayed. They talked about the fun they had in the river when I went to work, and Mrs. Paris watchful eyes on them. They would tell you how we sat on the sand in the afternoon and watch the sunset over the water. They would tell you how good I was in explaining an old movie to them or telling them about my childhood, removing the bad part and telling them the fun I had with my two brothers.

I taught my children the importance of praying. We didn't go to church every Sunday. But we prayed regularly. When we awake, we eat, and when we go to bed.

I mediated every spare moment I had. Mediation took me out and away from bad karma. Every time after mediation, I see things much clearer and I am calmer.

There was a period back then, I gave up on meditation. That was when I was sinking in the abyss. I couldn't see clear. Now I have magnified clearness.

My calmness angered Richard everyday. I gave him no reason to extol himself, no matter what he did. It was like throwing water on duck back.

He knew that he could not lay a hand on me, and frankly, I honestly

507

think that he didn't have it him to hit me. The only physical hurt he did to me was what he did to my big toe in Suriname. Here in Guyana, he was careful not to provoke me to go to the "Old Man'.

During this period, Richard was sent to the interior to do a course of 'Leadership core' I called it 'Brainwashing'. During his absence, we were having a good time. The children invited some friends in the neighborhood, for a little party at our house, since they were invited many times by their friends but never invited anyone in return.

With the house full of children, I could not turn on the stereo for them to dance. I asked my neighbor to see if he could fix it? He could not. I had to borrow a boom box from a friend. Come to find out Richard had taken out a fuse from the back of the stereo so that we couldn't use it in his absence.

The job sent me to Barbados to meet with some purchasers and arrange to sell produce to them. I took the opportunity to buy some banned items. Remember everything was banned in Guyana?

For dinner one evening, I cooked some potatoes, onions, garlic and a can of sardine. All the items mentioned were banned. But it beat phalli minion, which only the 'big ones' ate. It was the most delicious meal we've had in a long time.

When Richard came home that weekend he saw the empty sardine can. He became so angry. He grabbed me and all the other items, down the flight of stairs, made me dig a hole and buried the can and everything else. He said, "You are playing with my job. What do you think would happen to me if the government finds out that my wife has banned items in my home?" I was looking at a man I do not know. His hair and beard was long and knotted. His eyes were red and wide-open, staring strait ahead.

I could not take Richard's barefaced arrogance anymore. Even the children saw that what he was doing was wrong. They saw that he had occupied the room, which was to be mine. He is sleeping on the bed that was to be the girls. I was sleeping on the floor when he is on a bed. They saw that I was paying for everything, while he only ate and slept here. They saw that I wash and iron his clothes that he puts outside the door before locking it. They asked, "Why does Daddy lock us out of the front room?"

Nothing goes up in a strait line forever. Children grow up, knowing right and wrong.

My children's love was all I lived for. Just like my mother and my grandmother.

I decided that enough is enough. I was going to divorce Richard, get him out of my house and live happily every after with my children like we were in Bartica.

My lawyer discouraged me. He said, "I must warn you, it is not common for a woman to file for divorce. It's tougher because of your husband's position in the government.

I disregarded his warning and ask him if he will take my case or should I go to another.

He took on my case and told me that I will have to be present when his secretary hands the petition to my husband. I would have to point him out to her.

"That's not a problem. Tell me which morning she would go over to the Ministry of Home Affairs gate, and I will deliver my darling husband to her"

As usual, Richard sat in the front seat of my car. I dropped off the children at school then dropped off my husband. The young lady was standing at the gate. I said to her,

"Miss, this is Richard Greene. My husband" I watched as she handed him the papers.

I sped away as fast as I could, looking back on my rearview mirror. He was still standing by the gate looking at the papers. The young lady was gone.

I knew there would be fireworks in the house, I sent the children out to play.

Richard came home earlier than usual. – You see, he gets into my car in the mornings; I have no choice but to drive him to work. But in the afternoon, I pick up my children and head home. Many times I passed him walking on the streets. I blow the horn and move on laughing to myself. – 'After one time is another'

"So you have money to waste? You know that I will never give you a divorce"

"Why? Because you are enjoying the best of all the worlds? Free food, free house, free car ride to work and free money to steal from me? What would make you want to miss out on all those goodies?"

"You are my wife. That's enough. That's all I have to tell the judge"

"You are shameless. You have no conscience. You broke the trust that a man and a woman promised to keep. You've become so angry and poisonous, because I am surviving, even though you are willing to see me dead. You are a master manipulator, using my children as shield. I need to get you out of here and stop the poison of hate that you are pouring into my being, since you broke the trust that I had in you"

Richard stood with a glass of rum in his hand, shaking the ice against the glass.

"You can talk from now till neverweary morning. You still can't get rid of me"

"You are nauseoustic. I want to vomit all over you.

Imagine there was a time when I loved you so much, I breathe in all your carbon monoxide, rather than move, and let you release your grip on me while you sleep.

I stayed awake, watching you sleep and thanking God for you. I thought you were the best dancer and lover, that no one could be better than you. Oh how wrong I was.

They say, 'When you avoid the truth, you become a slave' I have been your slave because I refuse to believe the truth. I gave you everything I had. That's what slaves do.

Things had to happen for things to happen. I could've lived and died thinking you were the best dancer and lover. Today, if you just brush pass me, I feel my flesh on fire"

Our first date in court, the judge said "Lady, go home to your husband"

The second date, the same judge said, "This is a joke. You are living and cohabiting with your husband in the same house, and come here for a divorce?

Are you making a fool of this court?"

I asked my lawyer, "What was that all about?" I was angry while Richard smiled.

My lawyer said, "Your husband said that you sleep in his bed and have sex with him. No judge would grant a divorce if that is true"

"But it's not true. I sleep with my children, while he sleep in another room"

"It's your words against his. He is the man, remember what I told you?"

"What do I do now?"

"Move out"

"Move out of my home? And leave Richard in it? When he never put a sent for it?"

"Yes, if you want a divorce, you will have to move away from your husband"

I had nowhere to go. I fought the devil to keep me from sinking again.

Every holiday or long weekends, I drove up to Lancaster with the children.

In the ferry one such day, I was a woman holding a little girl. The child was the spit resemblance of Melanie. I got our of the car and walked over they stood, I asked,

"Is Richard supporting this child?" She looked at me. She knew me alright. They always know the wife. She held her head down. I asked again. "Does he support her?"

With her head still down, she said, "No" I went back to my car, get some money, gave it to her. I told her to get herself a lawyer and take him to court for support.

Richard was waiting when I got home. He was red with fury.

"So you are going around giving people money to take me to court? You did it and got nowhere, now you're looking for company?"

"Children should be taken care of financially by their father. You don't give a cent towards mine. I do that all by myself. You had been getting everything free for so long, you don't know the meaning of responsibility anymore.

You don't even know which school your, I mean my children are attending? You don't know how they are doing at school. You don't know anything about them". I said.

"You are pissing me off. I am warning you, stop before something terrible happen"

"What else could happen to me? I went up, down, east, west, north and south already. What else can you do to me?"

"Watch yourself. Be careful how you eat or drink in here. Remember you tried it before? This time you may succeed with your weakness for suicide, without doing it yourself. Watch yourself. I'm warning you. I have evidence. You shouldn't be driving heavy machinery without having it checked out every time". He was dead serious.

He took my car that night while I slept, and crashed the front of it.

It was the first time my children were angry with their father. That's how long I shield them from the monster that I lived with, and his torturous ways.

I went to visit my Aunt Wini in Laluni St. I heard that the tenant below will be leaving and that the three bedrooms apt will be available. I went on my knees and begged her to rent it to me.

I drove back home one day, just before Christmas, and collected my children, their

Clothes and books along with some of my personal belongings put them in the back of my car. Wrote a note to Richard, telling him "I could not live like this way anymore. I was going, leaving everything I own, because when the court case is settled and the judge ordered you out, we will return to my home"

That night, my children and I huddled in one room, door locked, afraid that he would come and kick down the door and demand to take my children. He did not.

I catch the Christmas sales and furnished my apartment. My children were happy, I was more at ease and I felt safe being in the yard with my family above us.

On the job, the Manager for the Ware House was being sent to England on a course.

Mr. Stewart recommended me for the position. It was an honor, because it was a demanding and responsible job, every purchase made from farmers around the country for produce and livestock, was done through the Ware House. I said, "I can do that"

One Friday afternoon I got home and found Richard in my apartment, with no shirt on. He said, "I need to spend time with my children. I see you did well for yourself here" He did that every weekend, he slept in my bedroom and I slept with my children.

We went back to court for the third time. I was confident that I had all the winning cards to make the judge grant me my freedom.

Richard's lawyer produced the note that I left in the house when I moved out.

She read the note minus the part where I wrote that I would return home after the judge grant me a divorce. Then she directed her question to me,

"Mrs. Greene, could you tell the judge where your husband had been sleeping every weekend since you moved out of his home?"

I was dumbfounded. I couldn't say a word. She continued the blows.

"Are you telling this court that my client is good enough to sleep with you on weekends, but not good enough to remain your husband and father in his own home?"

I walked out the courtroom, my knees beating each other. I held on to the rails for support. I was really weak and confused. I felt cheated I wanted to scream.

Richard caught up with me on the steps; he had that smirk of victory, he said,

"I told you not to waste your money. Now look what happened? Winner takes all"

My friend Cecil was always at the Courtyard waiting, he knew I'd need his shoulder.

Richard never came back to spend another weekend in my apartment.

Kim passed the Common Entrance, The examination that qualifies a student to high school. The scores determined which school she/he is qualified to attend.

She was within the highest marks. She was qualified for Queen's Collage.

In the colonial days, Queen's College and Bishop's High School were the cream of the cream. Only Whites and very rich attended. The two leaders attended Queen's College.

Queens College was an all-boys school, while Bishop was an all-girls school.

I couldn't contain myself when I saw my daughter dressed in her kaki uniform, yellow tie and socks and shoes. She would be identified by everyone as a student of Queen's College. Just the uniform alone says, "She is smart"

I am proud to tell you that Rocky followed Kim to Queen's College, later.

Melanie chooses Bishop's High School when she became qualified.

I lived less than a year in my new home in Atlantic Ville. It was horrible.

Now we live in Laluni St, my children and I are happy. We were just happy and free.

I hurried from work, picked them up and drive as fast as I could to catch the six o'clock movie at the Starlight Drivin Theater. We listened to music, news and soaps such as

Dr. Paul and Poacher Faces Life, on the radio. We had no television or phone, but we were contented with what we had. We were happy and the children were doing very well in school. Educating my children was the utmost in my agenda. I was obsessed.

I must tell you, no one in this world will ever love my children more than I do.

But, I never spear the rod or spoil my children. I imbedded into them the values of honesty, courtesy, good manners, respect and everything that children needs to learn.

Rocky and Melanie were partners in crime. They got into all kinds of trouble.

They would drink the condensed milk from the fridge, then full the can with water.

They climb over high fences and went into neighbors yard to pick their fruits.

I punished them by sending them to stand in the corner. Sometimes I find them enjoying it by sitting on the floor playing cards or marbles. But they are in the corner.

Kim, I must say, was the 'big sister' who did no wrong. She was Miss Goody- twoshoes. I always find her in a corner, reading Mills and Boons and Nancy Drew.

They knew if they brought home a button, they had to show me where it came from.

Remember I told you that we went to the drive-in theater? Well on days when I know that we will be going, I will ask the children to be ready, so that when I come to pick them up, we could leave rightaway. I hate to miss the trailers and cartoons.

Melanie had a habit of always being late. She can't find whatever she wants to wear. Many days we were late because of her. One day I warned her that if she were not ready when I come, I would take the other two and go, leaving her at home.

So be it. I came to get them for the movie; Kim and Rocky were ready,

"Where is Melanie?"

I drove off and left her at home. Melanie came out and stood in the middle of the street and began to scream for all the people in the neighborhood to come out to see what's happening? People were coxing her, offering to take her to their home.

I knew she was safe, my aunt Wini lived upstairs, they were watching her.

The doctor who lived across the street asked me, "What kind of mother are you? Leaving the child at home while you took the others out to the movies?"

"I am the best kind of mother for my children"

Do you know that whenever we are going out again, Melanie was the first in the car?

When it was school holidays, my children stayed home while I went to work.

Kim was in charge. Rocky and Melanie would bank on her, but she stood her grounds.

I gave them passages from their schoolbooks, to study. When I come home, I give them a dictation. I could tell who studied and who did not. They had to do it over and over until he and she, or he or she got it right. No matter how late that night.

Both my girls had long, soft hair, but I was no good at breading their hair.

Most times my neighbors or friends, wherever I lived, did their hair. Here my aunt or her daughters did their hair. I got so many complain from Aunt Wini about Melanie giving them a hard time to comb her hair. I warned her that if she continued, I would cut off all her hair. I supposed she wanted me to cut off her hair because she refused to go up to get it comb and breaded. She stuck all her hair in a hat instead.

One afternoon, I cut it all off. To my surprise, the girl loved it and she looked beautiful.

Melanie and Rocky were very close. I think it started since she was a baby.

He said she was his baby. He was two when she was born. He always wanted to hold her and feed her whatever he was eating. He said to me, "Mommy, look, baby holding she daddy hand". Every time she cried, he was the first to reach her crib.

If Rocky did something that deserved punishment, Melanie would ask to take his punishment. That's how tight those two were.

I remember, it was Christmas Eve; I was in the kitchen busy preparing all the many dishes that we prepare for Christmas, such as pepper-pot, garlic-pork, ham, bake chicken, rice-n-peas, black cake, sponge cake, ginger beer and lots of traditional dishes.

The girls inform me that I need to go out and warn Rocky not to be jumping from the top of Aunt Wini's steps, down to the ground, which was about ten feet.

He was with another boy from the neighborhood.

I went outside and warned both the boys to stop jumping. I told them that they are jumping into a rubbish dump and that there may be sharp things that can cut them.

I came out two more times to warn them, but as soon as I went inside, they continued.

Suddenly I heard Melanie screaming, "Mommy, come out here, Rocky foot cut

bad. Mommy come quickly" I went out, there was blood everywhere. I looked at his foot, decided that it was not life treating, I left him outside and went back to do what I was doing. I could not concentrate on what I was doing. I went back outside and said to him, "Rocky, I came out three times and warned you to stop the jumping. What do you think I should do to you now?" I saw that he would need stitches for the deep gash.

His Godfather Hector, took him to the hospital, he got twelve stitches.

Christmas morning, when the four of us should be sitting at the table, thanking God for His abundance, and enjoy our Christmas breakfast. I had to take his to the room, because he could not walk. He said, "Mommy, are you mad with me?" I said,

"Yes Rocky, I am very, very mad with you. I warned you three times that you are jumping into danger, but you had to showoff to your friend that you could do what he did. Now you know, those who don't listen to warnings have to feel the consequences.

I am very angry with you because I am feeling your pain. But, I still love you, Shun"

Kim and Melanie became his nursemaids while he was on bed rest.

We were happy in Laluni St. With my aunt and family upstairs, I felt safe.

My children and I went to picnics in the park, for drives in the country. I took them to the job for them to see how I am able to manage all these sometimes-rough men.

Cecil brought his children to spend weekends with mine.

My friend Cheryl, the telephone operator on the job, lived with us during the week and went home on weekends. We had several children parties and adult parties without being afraid of anyone. I went to clubs with my friends and dance till closing time.

My father came down and spends a month with us. I brought David to see the eye doctor. His sight was failing. Dr Grawall told me that there was not much he could do.

I couldn't think of anything else I needed. My children were doing well in school;

I was doing well on the joy. I was saving more money for my children's future.

I was free to dance.

There was no question that everything I did; I did for my three children.

They were my reason for living. I am so much like my mother and her three children.

When each one on them were babies, and had running mucus, I put my mouth to their noses and gentle pull the mucus out, just to make them comfortable

Kim was thirteen years old and in two more years, she would have to join the

Nation Service, a military training camp where youngsters go away from home to live and train in the jungle. I heard of so many abuses of young girls during this training.

I didn't want any of my children to become brainwashed like their father.

Things were getting worst in Guyana. Foodstuff scarcer and politic was dangerous.

There was a cane cutters strike, rather than negotiating with the laborers for a raise. The government ordered every government employee, from the top to the bottom, to go into the fields and cut the cane. If anyone didn't follow that order, he/she and the person who were to see that that order was carried out, would be fired. It was a frightening time. People were snitching on one and others, most times falsely. People were afraid to speak up for fear of being labeled as disloyal to the government. 'Unpatriotic'.

A farmer, one Saturday, brought a crate of plucked chicken to the warehouse for us to purchase. I took one sniff and rejected the purchase, because they were spoiled.

An hour later, I got a call from the 'chief whip' Margaret, from the Prime Minister's office, she said, "Comrade, we encourage farmers to farm, assuring them that we would purchase everything they bring to us. I have a comrade here; I will send him back to you. Do what the government is paying you to do. Pay the man for his product.

It was Saturday everyone was gone half day. I had to pay the farmer for his rotten chicken out of fear of loosing my job.

Cecil was so angry with me that he ordered the finance department to deduct the five hundred dollars that I paid the farmer, from my salary. He called me into his office and said, "In life, we have to stick to what is right, regardless of the consequences.

We cannot put our heads between our legs everytime someone threatens us. You are lucky that you still have a job. I hope you learn an important lesson from this"

I went up to Lancaster to see my family, and to visit the Manchester outlet.

Daddy told me that David never missed a day on the job. He said even on holidays, David went to see for himself that the outlet is closed.

Going through the books, I discovered that for three years, David never took a sick day or was given vacation. I asked the supervisor, who grew up with us in Lancaster and whom I hired for the job. "How come Mr. Alexander never had vacation in three years?" He said, "If he don't take sick leave and ask for vacation. What should I do?"

"He is mute, deft and going blind. You yourself wrote in your report that he is one of the best employees in this outlet. Yet you never saw that he is entitled for two weeks vacation every year? I remember sending replacements for you, when you went on vacation every year. Everyone here can read and hear their rights for working here, except David. All he knows is that he has to come to work every day. Sick and all"

While I was at the outlet, I asked for a meeting with the employees, Three female employees told me that when the large trucks come with heavy bags of rice, sugar and other heavy loads, David has fetch them all on his back, into the store, while the male employees played cards in the back room. They said that if the supervisor in charge didn't see that it is wrong or unfair, how could anyone else say anything?.

I asked them, "What about you? You could say something to the supervisor, or to one of the Officers who visits the outlet. You don't have to watch advantage being taken on anyone of your co-worker and not say anything, for fare of loosing your job.

Do what is right, regardless of the consequences. Let your conscience be your guide"

After my weakness for not standing up for what is right, and had to pay for it.

I learned from my best friend Cecil, that if I don't standup for what I believe, other would always see me as a weak fool. I am standing with my head high, for my brother.

I was hurting for my brother. What I heard, took me way back when we were children at Whim, when people used my two brothers to fetch their heavy loads.

I took David down to Georgetown for six weeks. I told him of all his rights on the job. I told him that he alone should not fetch all truck loads of supplies, that there are other younger and stronger men to help him. If he gets sick, he is entitled to stay home.

I had to assure him everyday that he will still have his job when he goes back.

He got his six weeks vacation pay from the office in town and the supervisor got a warning letter for taking advantage on a disabled employee.

Yes it was personal. I am my brother's mouth, ears and eyes. Its personal pain I feel.

Things were worsening. Even though I worked in the food distribution corporation.

I could not help but wonder what will happen in the country with the dwindling production of produce and the ban on all basic imported food.

Exports such as rice, sugar and bauxite, which were our only means for foreign currency, were screeching to a dangerous holt.

Foreign currency became scarce. One could not be caught with US,

UK or Canadian money. If you were going out of the country, you were allowed $15 Guyana, which was equivalent to $0US. If you are caught at the airport with more than that, yes they had their way of finding it, wherever you may hide it, and, you can kiss that trip goodbye.

You will be placed on a block list. You will never be able to leave the country again.

Some people bought lots of gold items to sell when they go wherever they were going.

When the authority discovered that, they took that away too, but allow the people to go.

During early1978 I was tempted to join the People's Temple-Jim Jones. I heard that the organization was rich and people were enjoying a good life in the interior.

They were driving large, beautiful vehicles in Georgetown, living in large houses in the upscale areas and seem to be happy and free. They purchase produce in large bulk from

us. I asked one of the members, "How do I join your Temple?" She said,

"You can't. Only American are allowed anywhere near our compound"

November 18th 1978, more than 900 Americans died in the cult let by Rev. Jim Jones.

One weekend when Cecil brought his son to play with my children, I asked him if he could sit for a moment. I told him that things are not looking good in the country. I said,

"I am seeing the Warehouse getting emptier and emptier everyday. Things are looking bleak. I want to join the massive exodus out of here, for the future of my children. What do you think?" As if he was expecting it from me, he said,

"Wynette, if that is what you want to do, go for it. Where do you want to go?"

"I am thinking of the States, that's where most of the people are going.

I don't want you to think that I am abandoning you, but when you see a hole in the boat, its time to secure a lifejacket. You throw me a lifejacket three years ago. I will forever be indebted to you for giving me that big chance when I had nowhere else to go.

You are the only person I am expressing my feelings to. What do you think?"

"I'm seeing the same hole that you are seeing. I left England with my family to come home and build. I can't build without material. It is harder for me when I have to deal with the politicians. But I am looking at the hole closely too"

I went to the US Embassy and got a multiple visa. I discuss my plans with the children then I asked Aunt Wini if she and the girls would take care of my children?

Sister Esther was willing to move in with the children so they can stay in their home. I knew that I had to discuss my leaving with Richard. He was still the father of my children, all under eighteen years old. He said,

"If you want to jump off like all those rats who are leaving because we are going through ruff times, go right ahead. But, my children stay with me, in my house.

I would not put your name on the list at the immigration. I would hope that you would come to your senses and work towards taking your whole family, which includes me.

I'm still your husband, legally. Maybe we could work things out, be family once more"

The hypocrisy of my husband made me want to throw up. He too is willing to jump ship. He is willing to use me and my children to do so, but no one should know this.

Daddy called to tell me that Datson was not feeling well and that he took him to the Port Mourant Hospital where they admitted him.

I secured the children with my aunt and drove up to Lancaster to see my brother.

I missed the last ferry and had to sleep in my car until the next morning.

I went to the hospital. It was still somewhat dark and everyone was asleep. It was quiet. I walked into the male ward and woke the nurse who was sleeping with her head on the table. I told her that I was here to see how my brother Datson Alexander was doing. She took up a flashlight and led me to my brother's bed. She shun the light on his face, he seems to be sleeping in a fetal position. I touched my brother and he was cold. He was stiff. He had to have died for hours for regamortist to step in and make him so stiff. My brother was dead for who knows how many hours, no one knew.

I balled so hard. I woke the whole hospital. "How could you people not know what time he died? He was just left in a bed to die with no one at his side. How could you not know when he died? What time of death are you going to put in your report, when all of you were asleep? My God, what is happening here?

I drove up to Lancaster. It was sad to see how my father broke down and cried for his first-born son. He aged double in front of our eyes. David and I held on to him and cried for loosing our Datson. My mother's companion, her Baldeo-Betose.

Richard brought the children for the funeral. There were a large crowd of relatives and villagers gathered in the yard, before going to the Aklyne Church Yard for burial.

I saw a group of people surrounding someone who was crying so hard. I went over to find Auntie Chunu sitting flat on the ground, holding her head and crying like a mother would for loosing her own child - I think after his mother, she was his only other love.

We put my 'quiet' brother Datson Egbert Alexander, my mother's Baldio-Betose into the ground at Aklyne on February 10th 1979. He was 40 years old.

After the funeral, my father looked as if all his blood was drained out of his body. He walked slowly from the burial ground and went into his bedroom.

David and I sat on the steps to reminist about our beloved Datson.

He told me that he was a better climber on the coconut tree, while Datson was a better swimmer in any dept or amount of water.

I reminded him of the time when we were small, living with Mommy at Liverpool.

One day, Datson was going to catch crab at the seaside. I asked him I could go with him? He said no. I followed him anyway. He kept chasing me back, I stayed a safe distant behind him, I knew that if he catches me, he would put a good licking on me.

When he reaches the canal, he crossed to the other side, leaving me standing.

He sat on the dam watching me. He used his index finger to scowl me for not obeying him. When he thought that he had punished me enough. He swam back over and put me on his back and swam over to the other side.

We went to the seaside where there were lots of crab holes. Datson pushed his hand deep into the holes and brought out large 'buck crab' and put them into the quake.

I noticed that he was testing some of the holes. He held me down and pushed my hand into one of the large holes. The crab latched on to my hand. I pulled my hand with the crab still latched on. My brother began to laugh while I screamed. He used his index finger again to warn me that I should listen to him when he tells me to stay home.

He eventually releases the crab's tentacles from my hand.

We had a quake full of large, juicy crabs. We began to walk back to the canal.

Datson got into the water with the quake, swam over and went away, leaving me alone.

'What can I do? If I scream he would not hear me. How could he leave me on this dissociate dam? I had to walk about a miles to Whim, got on my belly and crawl on the long, narrow plank across the deep canal.

When I got home, my brother was sitting on the step, sucking away on curry crab.

My mother said, "That should teach you a lesson. When you big brother tells you to stay home, you don't disobey him"

Datson knew he was the oldest, he demanded his authority be recognized.

We were four at one time, now we are two. We held on to each other tighter.

An employee from one of the outlets introduced me to her brother who lived in the US. He asked if I would pay for some of the gold jewelry he is planning to purchase for him and his family? That when I go to America, he would reimburse me in American equivalence. That was like music in my ears, because it would be the only way I would get some money to start off with in America.

Lots of people were doing the same thing, in order to get some spending money abroad.

I trusted him because his sister was my friend. I paid thousands of dollars for all the gold he ordered for himself, wife and children. Even the goldsmith was surprised of the items this stranger was ordering and he wondered if I knew what I was doing?

The man gave me his address and phone number, and promised to pay me in the US.

He even offered to let me stay with him and his family until I settled in.

I bought my airline ticket from Pan American Airline, to leave Saturday 10th March.

Daphne and Ingebridgt, her Norwegian husband came to Guyana to visit us.

I resigned from the job, deposit most of money into my bank account. Gave my father and Sister Bea some of it, and the remainder to Aunt Wini for if and when my children come for any assistant. I gave my three children an amount to keep for themselves. Remember I could not take any more than $15-0US

Kim was thirteen, Rocky eleven and Melanie, nine years old. I did my best to assure them that I am leaving them to open a better door for them. I encouraged them to study hard and remember everything that I thought them, especially good manners and the three don'ts. 'Don't lie, don't steal, and don't hate', good etiquette, honesty, respect and consideration for others, and never forget to say 'please' and 'thank you'.

Everything in my apartment were packed in a truck and sent to my house in Atlantic Ville for the convenient of my children. I arranged for Pam, Richard's cousin, to go up every weekend to wash and iron for the family. My sister promised to visit them often.

Richard asked, "Where is the car? Who has the car keys?"

"I was not leaving the car with you. I sold the car" I was enjoying his looks.

He was getting red with angry. I knew that he was demanding to keep the children because he thought I would leave my car for him.

"What the hell you're telling me? How would your children go to school?"

"The same way all other children from the Ville whose parents do not have cars, goes to school. My children are adjustable to changes. They are like me. We accept changes. It's been a big part of our lives. You should try it. Walk with your children"

Cecil took my children, Sister Esther and me to the airport. It was hard to tear myself from my children. I kept reminding them that I am doing this for them.

I left Guyana with a bag no bigger than the one I left Lancaster with. I had no money, not one cent in my position. I was playing safe at the custom and immigration.

Only when the plane lifted off the runaway, did I know that I was free to leave. – During this time, lots and lots of people, including Cecil were taken off planes by authorities –

MY AMERICAN EXPERIENCE

It was cold in March; I was not dressed for such weather. I followed the crowd to the exit. I didn't see the man who promised to pick me up, the one with the golden promise. I sat in the waiting area for hours, looking at the sliding doors, hoping it's him.

The area became empty except for one lady, sitting a few chairs from me. I wanted to ask her if when her people comes for her, if they can take me to this address?

The lady saw me walking towards her; she grabbed her handbag and said,

"Don't come any closer, I will scream" She had a foreign accent.

I kept walking to the telephones, looking at them closely. You see, it was my first time seeing 'touch tone' pay phones. It said to drop a dime into the slot then touch the numbers. I had no dime. I didn't have a penny-cent. I got on my knees and began to search the carpeted floor, just incase someone dropped a dime. 'What's a dime?'

I saw a pair of shinny black shoes standing next to me. I looked up and saw a man wanting to use the phone. I looked at him keenly as he made his call. When he was finished. He asked, "Can I help you with something?"

"I came from Guyana since early this afternoon. The man who promised to pick me up never came. I do not know what to do. I have no money"

The tall man with kind, gray eyes took out from his pocket a handful of silver and handed them to me. He showed me how to use the phone. He wished me well and left.

I dialed, he answered, I said, "This is Wynette" the phone went dead.

I was cold, shivering, lost, homeless, penniless, scared. I missed my children.

I wondered, 'What would become of me in this cold country?'

I remembered that I had Ada's phone number. I dialed it and she answered. It was two in the morning, but she sounded surprised that I was in the country without informing her so that she could come and meet me. She directed me to take a taxi to her address on New York Ave. Brooklyn, and that she would wait outside to pay the fare.

Ada dressed me in layers of sweaters and pants. She was smaller and shorter than I. Long socks and gloves covered the parts of my body that were exposed. She wrapped me with blankets and placed a knitted hat on my head. She put me to sit inches away for the radiator. A hot cup of tea began to chase the shakes from within.

I told Ada about the children and that Kim was going to Queen's College. It gave me joy to see the pride in her eyes for her Kimmy.

When I told her about the gold deal, she was ready to throw me out for my stupidity.

"Don't you know never to trust those cons? Do you know how much family robbed their own family by promising to bring and keep all their savings until they come over?. The same happened to you, you will never see nor hear from that 'gold thief'

"Ada, I have nowhere to go, can I stay here until I get on my feet?" I begged.

"You see how small my apartment is? I don't know what my husband would say. Even so, where would you sleep? I don't have the room for another person in here"

"Ada, I can sleep right here, in this dining room, under this table" I plead.

"Let me go talk to David. This is his apartment. He has to give that consent"

While Ada was gone, I got down on my knees and prayed that

David, whom I don't know, would be kind and allow me to sleep under his table.

Ada came back with additional comforters and pillow. She said, "Make yourself comfortable, the toilet is down the hall. Have a good night, I should say good morning"

It was cold for me who just came from 80-90 degree to cold March in Brooklyn. I had to pee regularly. Every time I walked to the bathroom, the floor cried. I didn't want to anger my kind hosts, so I took up my bed and settled on the floor closer to the toilet.

Some hours later, I heard a strong masculine voice asking,

"What are you doing, lying next to the bathroom?" David was a tall, light skin man.

He opened a door and ordered me to "Make yourself comfortable in here"

It was their sitting room, beautifully decorated with lots of ornaments, plants and lamps.

There were sofas and couches, all covered with clear, stiff plastic.

I made my bed on the carpet floor and went to sleep. The next day Ada said,

"Are you lucky or what? David doesn't allow anyone to come into his sitting room.

You can see, those chairs don't get anyone sitting on them. This is his private showroom. I can only come in to clean and wet the plants. Wow, he allowed you in it"

I began to pound the pavements of Nostrand Ave., asking for anything to do?

Mr. Reed told me "The only job that starts from the top is grave digging"

I look in the papers and saw an advertisement to clean an apt in Manhattan.

It was St Patrick's Day and Ada offered to take me on my first subway ride.

We got into Manhattan and I could not believe that the land could stay afloat with all these high concrete buildings?

We went up in God knows how many flights on the brass shiny

elevator to the door of the would-be employer. Ada rung the bell and a bending old man opened the door.

Ada left me in the safety of the apt. She gave me a token and said, "When you are finished, take the A train downtown to Nostrand Ave. don't be afraid to ask directions".

The apartment was a mess. There were boxed with old ratting food piled in the sink.

I began to clean the kitchen first, but the old man said, "Leave the kitchen, start in my bedroom. I followed him into his bedroom; he put $20s into my shirt pocket.

He touched my breast every time he stuck the money into my pocket. I said,

"Sir, I came here to clean. Please let me do my job and go. I don't like you touching my breast. Please allow me to do the cleaning then you pay me" He pushed more notes into my pocket and now trying to play with my legs. I ran to the door and out of there.

I didn't check the notes in my pocket until I reached Ada's home. There were five crispy twenty-dollar bills. That was my first of many job experiences. It gave me a start. I gave Ada two of the notes and I kept three.

Several other job interviews I went to. Some were unforgettable. I will tell you about one or two. I went on the Long Island train to meet a lady who was willing to sponsor me to become a legal residence. There were lots such offers in the papers. Many women were coming to America for such an opportunity.

The lady was young and beautiful. She had a husband and two children, three and one years old. She said that she had a lady who didn't speak proper English and that she wanted her children to be around people who can speak 'properly'

She told me what my duties would be. I would work from Monday to Saturday half-day. I would start working from six in the morning to prepare breakfast and get the older boy ready and take him to kindergarten. I would work for the rest of the day, and go to sleep after I cleanup the dinner dishes. She walked me around the house, pointing out all the dos and don'ts in her home, then she said, "Come and let me show you where you will sleep. She led the way down some stairs into the basement. There was a room with a single piece of furniture. A cot against the wall, nothing else. She said.

"After you are finished, you will have to do all your bathroom duties upstairs before coming down to sleep, because we lock the burglar gate that leads upstairs"

I thought, '1979 there are still cages to lock some of us in, while the master sleeps'

"So, what do you think? Will you take the job? I will sign your working papers"

"Yes, I will take the job. I have to go home and collect my things. I will come back tomorrow" if I didn't say that, she would not have given me the train fare back home.

When I told Ada about my visit, she told me that she experienced worst than that.

I went to several Domestic Agencies. Many of the prospective employers made just about the same demands as the lady in Long Island, except the cage. Some wanted to pay half the legal wage. Some said no day off, any vacation. One even offered me room and food to work for no pay, and she will sponsor me.

One day the lady at the agency, probably seen me once too many times, said,

"Sit here and wait, I have someone for you to talk to. I think she'll be good for you"

She called me into a small boot and told me to pick up the phone and speak to the lady on the other end. I spoke to Mrs. Heller. I felt as if I had known her all my life. She made me feel so comfortable. We spoke about our children. We were the same age and had three children, two girls and one boy. 'I think I like this lady; her voice is ringing in my head. She sounded compassionate and kind' I told myself. I agreed to meet with her.

Dan, the Heller's driver, met me by the clock at Grand Central Station. He was very friendly; he had praises for his employers that I would feel likewise if I work for them.

It was a long drive to Westchester. I asked Dan, "Why are all the trees so bare? They all look like so dry, like firewood. There is no water to wet them?"

"No, it's not like that. You see, it is still cold from winter. Its just weather change. It happens every year. You will see and soon get accustom to the changes"

We drove into the driveway of one of the most beautiful houses I have ever seen.

I wondered, 'how many people live in this big house? I saw this house in the movie'

Mrs. Heller met us on the driveway. As soon as I saw her, I knew I made the right decision. She had something about her that I called 'honesty and compassion'.

She was shorter than me and petite. She had red hair and eyes that looked strait at me when she spoke. She was different from the others that I met and had interviews with.

I agreed to take the job to and start right away. She took me to my living quarter above the garage. It was a large apartment, with all convenient to make me comfortable.

It had a fully equipped kitchen, living room, large bedroom and bathroom.

I sat on the large king bed with four wooden posts, and wondered if I was dreaming?

Little three years old Bradley stole my heart the moment I saw him. He had his mother's red hair. He held on to my index finger and led me into the main house.

He told me about the animals and their names, he was a chatterbox.

Still holding my hand, he led me to the dining table to sit and have dinner with the family. He introduced me to his family by saying, "This is Wynette, and she will be living with us. She will take me outside everyday to play with the butterflies"

I thank God everyday for directing me to the Hellers.

The husband, wife and five children became my family from 1979 to this day.

They began the process of sponsoring me the first week on the job. They had to publish the job in the newspaper for three weeks. If within those three weeks, an American applies for the job, they will have to let me go and hire the American.

A few people called, but none wanted to come so far to work for a family of seven.

Mrs. Heller and I had some things in common. We were the same age, we had two daughters and one son, and both our daughters were the same ages.

The obvious difference was that she was White, an American, and rich. I was Black, hoping that she would make me an American, and I came to her country penniless.

She and I became the best of friends. I never forget that she was my Mistress, and she never reminded me that I was her servant. We, the Princess and the papa per.

Both husband and wife were married previously and had two children each before.

Little Bradley became the apple of everyone's eyes. All his siblings treated him as such.

Every Saturday, Cheryl would link my children to speak to me on the phone.

One such Saturday, about five weeks into working with the Heller, Kim said,

"Mommy, please thank Mr. and Mrs. Heller for the box they sent for us"

"What box you're talking about?" I asked in surprise

"You don't know? They sent us a large box full of clothes, shoes, candies and the whole secrecies of Little House on The Prairie and letters from all their children to us"

"No Kim, I have no idea that they did that. I am so very surprised to hear this"

"Mommy, you must be working for some very nice people, if they would send so many things for your children all the way to Guyana and you don't know anything?"

Now I know why every morning when Mrs. Heller and I sit around the table in the kitchen, having our coffee for her, tea for me, she questioned me in details about my children sizes, what they like to read, what the temperature is like there and so on.

I considered myself lucky to be working for the Hellers. They paid me more than the required domestic pay. From the very first week, they paid tax and social security for me. I went to Brooklyn from Saturday afternoon and returned on Tuesday midday.

They paid my transportation to and from Brooklyn.

I met women on the train who are doing the same job, I listen to their stories, I know how lucky I am. One elderly woman worked for many years with the same family. Starting with the parents, then daughter, now granddaughter. She watched babies born, grown up, married and gone. Three generations, and she still got far less than what I was getting. The employers never paid tax, social security. 'Mrs. Jorden'

Most of them went home on Saturday afternoon and return on Sunday after church.

I was way ahead of many women who were in my position. I see most of them on Saturdays when we board the train; almost full of domestic servants, from New Cannon to Stamford. Hearing their stories, made me quiet. One should not boast at this time.

In my heart I know I was working for a good, compassionate family. Humankind

Ada found a studio for me in Macon St for $20 per month. I missed being with her and David on weekends, but I love my own space too. I can cook all my Guyana food including curry and dhal without worrying that spices can smell in a house for days.

My cousin Vera, Aunt Mary's daughter, came to America. She shared the studio with me. I took her up to Westchester and Mrs. Heller found a sponsor job in the area for her. We were close to each other, she walked over to me some nights and we slept together, talking and laughing. We went to Brooklyn on Saturdays but she had to return on Sundays, while I returned on Tuesday. One Sunday morning as she got ready to leave, she said, "I wish I could find a nice family like yours. You have the best boss"

1979 was a grieving year for the Alexander and me. First my brother Datson died in February, I left my three children to come to America, then Uncle Brother, Daddy's older brother, died in April.

One day around the end of May, I woke up feeling depressed and sad. I went out the back door, under the apple tree to sit on a bench.

I put my head into my hands and began to cry. I cried and cried but I could not tell you why I was crying. Mrs. Heller opened the door and called out for me. She said I have a phone call. It was Cheryl. My heart began to pound in my chest. She said,

"Wynette, I went to the airport last night and say your cousins there. They told me that they are waiting for the plane that is bringing the body of their father who died in St Kitts. Wynette, your Uncle Bertram is gone" she continue to talk but I didn't hear anymore. Mrs. Heller took the phone from me and finished the conversation.

I walked back to the apple tree, sat down but never cried. I had already cried just moments before, for my beloved Uncle Bertram, who gave me the elephant of freedom.

I called it a 'preminission'

I could only imagine the pain my father was feeling, first his son, then his older brother then his youngest brother? All tree gone in about forty days apart?

I could not go to my Uncle Bertram's funeral because if I leave, I would never be allowed to come back into the US. I have to wait until my papers are approved before I could leave this country, that is, if I want to reside here.

Many women in my possession could not go home to attend their parents or children sickness or funeral, for the fear that they surely would not be given another visa.

I noticed lately that whenever I spoke to my children, they sounded fearful. As if they could not speak to me as freely as they did. I asked them, "What's the matter?"

"Nothing, Mommy. Everything is alright" but I noticed that Melanie was kept away from speaking to me. There was always an excuse for her not speaking to me.

I called my friend who lived next-door to them. I told her that I could feel that something is wrong and if Melanie was OK? My friend said,

"Wynette, your children are forbidden to tell you, but your husband brought an Indian woman to live in your home. They keep Melanie from speaking to you because she threatened to tell you that her father brought a maid to take care of them but she is sleeping in his room? You see, Richard told the children the woman is their maid.

Melanie asked why the maid is sleep with him? She is banned from speaking to you"

"But Pam was going every week to clean and wash for them. My sister too, was going to do things for them. What happened?"

"Your husband told them not to come back, that he has a fulltime maid"

I didn't tell Mrs. Heller what's going on, my other life with Richard was blank. I gave her the impression that I am here to make a way for my husband and my children.

When the Labor Department approved the application for me to work here legally.

I asked the ladies in the train for a good immigration lawyer to start my papers which should take about two years, then I would be able to go back to see my children.

They told me about one in Brooklyn. I had to pay him $20 every week.

Every week I join a line of Black women going to pay this man for doing their papers.

Every week, I would ask him "How is my papers coming? Did you send it in yet?"

"Yes, yes, your papers are in. just keep making your weekly payment"

Two years passed. Mrs. Heller was just as anxious as me about when will I hear good news from my lawyer? She once asked, "Wynette, are you sure that this lawyer is any good? You should've heard something from him by now, it's been over two years"

But whenever I go to him, he told me the same thing, "Your papers are in process"

Vera moved away from Westchester and got a better job in New Jersey. Her papers started a year after mine and she already had a letter from the immigration, acknowledging receipt of her application for permanent residence. I was devastated,

'How could this be happening? I came here before her; my labor permission was granted before hers, three children waiting for me to get them. What's happening?

Aunt Eloise came to visit Vera and I. We did our best to make her happy.

I took my two weeks of vacation and took her to Washington, Atlantic City and many other trips. I know that I would never be able to repay her for all she had done for me,

But I did everything I could for her. Did my best to show my gratitude and love for her.

She too, told me many stories that I am now telling you.

One afternoon, I was in the kitchen and saw a car drove up the driveway. I saw two men dressed in black suits and dark shades. – From experience, whenever Vera and I saw men looking like them, we would run the other direction and hide in any hole we could find, because they could be Immigration Officers. That would mean the end of our stay in the country – I ran through the back door, down to the horses' stable where

Mrs. Heller was mocking the stalls. Breathlessly I said, "The Immigration Officers are here to get me. Please Mrs. Heller, don't make them take me away. Please, please"

"Wynette, calm down. No one is taking you anywhere. Not with me present"

I hid in the stable while she went to meet the men. She came back, put her arm on my shoulder and led me up to the house where the two men were sitting in the breezeway. "Wynette, these are Mr. Pick and Mr. ….'I don't remember'. They are here to talk with you. Don't be afraid, you did nothing wrong" said Mrs. Heller.

Mr. Pick said, "The lawyer you have been paying to process your papers, was disbarred some years ago. We found out that he was still cheating thousands of women like you. We raided his office and took away all the files. That's how we found your file. We are here to give you your file, Get yourself another lawyer.

As soon as your petition comes to us, we would work on it.

You are not alone, trusting crooks like that" he saw that I was still shaking with fear, he said, "Don't worry, you will be going home to see your children soon"

In the mean time, one baby was born and another came later in my house. I asked my mother-in-law, "Sis how could Richard take a woman into my home with my children living there? All my personal belongings are in there. How could any woman agree to move into another woman's home with the woman's children in it?"

"What can I tell you? I told Richard that it doesn't look good, and it's not a good example he is setting. I am praying for you to come and get your husband and children out of here as soon as possible. By-the-way don't tell anyone that he will be going too"

I continued to pay the mortgage for my house, sent hug barrels and boxes for my children. I even sent clothes and shoes for the baby girl. She was not responsible. Children are innocent victims of their parents' indiscretions. My too are.

I dreamt one night that I went back home to Atlantic Ville, I saw a lady on the steps and asked her for my children? She said that they are downstairs. I told her that I just came from downstairs but there are no children there. She said that I should go back down and lift the coconut branches and I will see my children.

I found my three children lying with their arms across their chests. They were dead.

I screamed so loud, all the lights in the Hellers' house turned on.

Mr. and Mrs. came running with their robes flying behind them.

"What's the matter Wynette? You had a bad dream? What's wrong?" she placed her hand on me and said to her husband, "She is soaking wet. She is shaking"

I told them about my dream. They dialed my home and demanded that Richard wake up all three of my children and give them the phone to speak to me.

In Brooklyn, Ada had a little birthday party. A lady who had just come over from Guyana, said to me, "Girl, I am so sorry for you, it must be very hard for you to be here while all these bad things are happening to your children back home"

"What are you talking about? What happened to my children?" I was lost.

"You don't know?" she looked at me strangely.

"Know what? Please tell me what you are talking about" I feel something cold.

"Two of your children had terrible accidents. Your son lost a finger when a crowd trampled on him in the National Park, and a motorcycle hit your baby daughter. She is badly burnt" My belly was 'running water' as the saying goes when a mother is in pain for her children. That was what my nightmare was all about.

I called Sis immediately. She conformed what the lady told me. She said,

"We agreed not to call you because we know you would leave everything and come back here. That would jeopardize Richard and the children chances of leaving"

I never called my mother-in-law again.

For the years I've been away from my children, I sent each one of them to Trinidad to spend the August holiday with their Auntie Brenda-from Zambia- and her family. Kim went first, then Rocky and finally Melanie. They never stopped talking about what a good time they had and how nice the Henry family was to them.

The next day after those two men visit, Mrs. Heller drove me to the city to meet their family lawyer. Three months later, I got my notice of approval to go home.

Between Mr. Pick and the new lawyer, they were able to do my petition in such a way where I would be able to bring my family back when I returned.

Normally the woman goes home, gets approved if she is lucky, and comes back to America work for another required, two years before she could apply for her family.

Because of the crooked lawyer who held me back two years. I was given that concession.

I couldn't tell you who was happier, Mrs. Heller or me. She wanted me to go home and bring my children as much as I did.

For the four years I worked for the Hellers, not one day did they made me feel different from them. The children were kind and respectful. If I seem down and one of them ask, "What's the matter Wynette?" little Bradley would answer, "Can't you see that she misses her children?"

Bradley and I grew very close. We were together most of the time. He loved the outdoor. We would play in the woods and pick berries and feed each other.

We would lie on the grass and look for angels in the sky.

One such day, he said, "Wynette, why are you different from us? You are Black and I we are White. Why are you different?" We were in the woods, I thought of my answer,

"Brad, look at all the butterflies that are flying around us, they are all different, right?

Some are white, some are black, some are black and white, some are brown and white, and some are brown and black. Besides their color, what else do they have in common?"

"They all can fly" His innocents captured my heart for the years I spent with him.

"Despite the difference in color, they are all butterflies. You see how they are flying around together, not seeing difference in colors? Its because they are all the same.

Well, you and I have different color, but we are all human being. We are all people" It was the best way I could answer this five-years-old, question.

One day I told him, "Brad, when you grow up, get married and have children, I will take care of your children and love them just like I take care and love you" he said,

"When I grow up, I will marry you, because I love you" out of the mouth of an innocent child who helped me to keep my sanity while I long for mine.

When his parents are away, I am to sleep in the main house with the children.

I remember the first night I had to do that, I went to read to Brad and tuck him in.

He took all his stuffed animals from his top bunk, put them neatly on the floor and said,

"You see, you can sleep in my bed and I will sleep on the top. That way, I can protect you. You don't have to sleep in the guess room all by yourself" it started when he was three years old. He had no idea how much he was protecting me from going nuts.

For the four years I worked with the Hellers, I deposited one hundred dollars every week, after taxes and social security deduction, into an account at the Chase bank.

Every year I got a raise and every week when Mrs. Heller took me to the train, she gave me an extra $20, she said "If I forget to give you this token, remind me" I never had to. You would never imagine how helpful that precious 'token' was for me?

I rented a one-bedroom apartment in Brooklyn, 96th St. next-door to Uncle Phillip and Aunt Nora, in preparation for bringing my children.

I don't think Mrs. Heller ever went to Brooklyn before, but she loaded her Suburban with furniture, took them to my apt and helped me setup for the arrival of my children.

Mr. Heller rushes for a camera whenever he sees a Cardinal on the feeder.

At Christmas, I couldn't fetch all my gifts on one trip. Every week I took home fruits and vegetable from their garden and fresh eggs.

I get gifts for the family too. I went to Delancy St. and bought sweaters for the children and Mr. Heller. For Mrs. Heller, I bought a bottle of Charlie.

I never saw the family wore what I bought for them, but Mrs. Heller wore her Charlie. Later on when I checked the label of the clothes they wore, none of them were polyester.

How should I know that there is a difference between cashmere and polyester?

I started buying pen sets for all of them and Charlie for my best friend.

They even got me my own pet kitten I named Caesar. He sits on the grape harbor and waits for me every evening. We go up to my apt, eat and then he sleeps in his bed next to mine. In the morning he goes out, roams the property, chasing squirrels and birds.

One Tuesday when Mrs. Heller picked me up at the train station, she sat on the passenger's seat and handed me the car key, as said, "Wynette, you drive" she was serious. I was even more serious, I said, "But, Mrs. Heller, how can I drive? I don't know how to drive in this country. You drive on the wrong side of the road. Your steering wheel is on the wrong side of the car. I could never drive here" she had a Rabbit.

"Did you drive in Africa and Guyana? Well, you will have to drive here.

If you are planning to live here, this is the best time to start. Lets go"

They trusted me with the lives of their children. When the children urges me to drive faster. I told them, "The police would surely spot me from a distance and stop me for driving over the speed limit" They would say, "But Wynette, you are driving 25 mph?" I would answer, "Yes, because that's what the road sign said" they would laugh among themselves and tell their parents that I drove so slowly even the turtle is faster.

One morning, I stood on the driveway, as Mrs. Heller was about to drive off, she said,

"You will have to pickup Brad from school and take the others to horsehiding lessons"

"But, Mrs. Heller, how do I do that? You are going with the car"

"The Suburban key is in the mudroom" she drove away before I could say anything.

She was so much like Daphne. She made me do things I never thought I could.

She joins with people like my mother, Gramother, Nana Sweetie, Mr. Reed, Uncle Bertram, Cecil, Daphne and others, who drop some honey into my bitter tea.

I learned from Mrs. Heller, the American way of not being afraid of anyone or anything, once I adhere to the rules and laws of the land.

I finally got a date to leave the country and an appointment at the Guyana Embassy.

The whole family took me to the airport. They all wrote letters to the Immigration Officers in Guyana, expressing their love for me. Little

Bradley even put a picture of himself into his letter. – I still have that letter and picture. –

The day before I left the US for Guyana, my mother-in-law called me, she said,

"Wynette, I know that you are coming home tomorrow. I want you to go to your home with your children. I told Richard to cleanup his mess before you get here.

Your place is in your home with your children while you are here"

My cousin Patrick brought my children to the airport to meet me. They were good for my sore eyes. They were so grown. Four years made such a difference.

Kim, soon to be seventeen, turned into a beautiful young lady. She held herself and the other two, closely with the hope for the future that I promised them,

Rocky was a typical fifteen years old. He was excited to see me and wanted me to tell him, right then, everything I went through for the past four years.

Melanie, thirteen, just wanted to know how soon she would be leaving for America? Because she already told all her friends at school that she is leaving?

After much hugging, kissing, laughing and crying, Kim, still crying, said,

"Mommy, Daddy said to tell you that, 'if you don't want to be embarrass, don't go up to Atlantic Ville'. Uncle Patrick had to promise him that he will take just us three back home, or else we would not have been allowed to come to meet you" she held on to me and sob so hard, the other two joined her and the four of us held on to each other and empty our souls. We had no time for words; we just released some of what was pent in.

"Don't worry children, I'll be alright. I will go to Aunt Wini's family in Laluni St. – Aunt Wini had passed away during the time when I could not go back to Guyana –

You can come and see me there tomorrow morning"

I knew I was back in the lion's den; I will do nothing in my being, to anger him.

Our heads are in his mouth. If I do not play it cool, he would snap our lights out.

I spent the days with my children but let them go to Atlantic Ville to sleep, otherwise Richard would stop them from coming to see me.

I kept my appointed date with the Embassy. The Officer told me to come back in a month's time, while they investigate if I really worked as a domestic in this country?

I was heartbroken and afraid, because so many women came back home, just like me, but never got their papers to return to the States. Some even committed suicide.

The only consolation I had was that I told the truth. I've been a domestic when I should've been in school. I clean, wash, cook and babysat for people, long before I was old enough to do that. My record of being a domestic in Guyana was proof able

I remember Gramother and Mommy saying, "Only the truth shall set you free"

I informed my employers of my plight. Mrs. Heller told me that the lawyer assured her that it is routine. They are going to check if I was really a domestic worker.

There were many cases where professionals such as doctors and lawyers sent their wives to work as domestic servants, just to join the exodus out of Guyana. Others who had family who were American Citizens, were luckier, their family sponsored the whole family to the US. They never have to run and hide from authorities or do domestic work.

I sat on the steps of my family's house, with my three children, just like my Mommy did with her three. I saw sad eyes on Kim. It must've been quiet a burden at such a young age to care for her brother and sister. She said to my questions, "Mommy we will talk when we leave" as though she didn't trust wind or anyone to hear what she has to say.

I look at Ricky's hand and said to myself, "I made a perfect baby boy with all ten fingers and toes. Now my son has to spend the rest of his life nine fingers. He wanted to be a pilot since he began to talk. Would he be a pilot or serve in the army?"

I look at Melanie's scars from the burns she got when the motorcycle hit her. They were marks that she would have to live with for the rest of her life. With her lighter complexion, they stand out more visible to the eyes.

My heart was pounding with pain. "What have I done to my children? Did I do the right thing leaving them and going to pave a better future for them? Would they ever get over whatever it is that Kim promised to tell me later?

They seems quiet happy and contented with me being here with them"

The first working day after my arrival, I went to Richard's place of work.

He was just another person I needed to talk to. I asked him for the children passports?

"What passport? I am not sending my children anywhere unless I am going with them. You can't run to the Old Man, you know how he is against people leaving?"

He was right. I had my head in his mouth. I had to play it cool. I said softly,

"But Richard, I did your papers too. Your mother knows that, I did for you too.

She told me not to tell anyone that you will be going to America. I have your paper, tomorrow, I will bring it here to show you" I did, he promised to get them up to date.

I went up to Lancaster with the children to see my family and spend Christmas/New Year with them. Especially being with David and having the children being with him.

I promised Mrs. Heller that I would clear up one of the most horrible period of my life. That I would confront my father as to why he treated me so bad when I was a child?

Lancaster was not the same without my beloved Uncle Bertram.

After all the excitement of seeing the family and they seeing us, I made an appointment with my father. I sent the children to Aunt Elo's and told them to stay there.

We sat face to face, he in his Berbice chair, me in the rocking chair, both by the windows. This was hard for me, but, she said, "It's the only way you can release yourself from the years of pain, wondering 'what did I do to deserve such abuse'. Ask your father"

"Daddy, I have some questions that have been following me for years.

I am forty years old, for thirty years, I've been carrying around these question,

Daddy why did you hate me the way you did? What did I do to hurt you so badly?"

My father sat erect in his chair. My question surprised him, puzzlingly he said, "What are you talking about? What kind of question it that" 'Has he lost his memory'

"Come on Daddy, this is me, Wynette, who lived in this house with you and your family. This is Wynette, who you beat with the cow rope until my back was as hard as cardboard. This is Wynette, who had to wear rags, walk barefoot and do every chore in this house and yard, take care of your livestock, and then rub bare rice in the empty karahee-stewpan, just to get a flavor of what been cooked, for my brothers and I to eat?

After Mommy and Nana Sweetie were gone, I was hungry; I took a piece of food out of the boiling pot. My mouth was so badly burnt; I couldn't close it or speak for a week.

You came down to where I was washing clothes under the tree, as loud as you could, you said, "I hope you didn't tell anyone that you are hungry in this house? Now you can open your mouth with no sound, feel how my boys feel, not being able to speak" Daddy I wondered why so loud when we were so close, then I looked upstairs and saw why.

This is Wynette, the little piggy who stayed at home. Whose dream you shuttered.

This is the same Wynette who you refused to allow finishing high school, one month after my mother died and two months before I graduate. Why Daddy? Why?"

My father remains sitting strait, giving me his undivided attention. Saying nothing.

"Daddy, you believed everything bad said about me. You never give me any credit.

I did so much to get your affection. Or even your attention. You would be laughing with my cousins and other children, but, as soon as I pass by, your whole demeanor would change, as if I was your enemy. You showed only distaste for me. I wondered why?

Whenever there was a party or banquet at the center, I would work even harder, to make sure that everything was perfect. I even catch the animal's dong with my bare hands and buried them in a hole so that you don't smell anything; I did it, just to please you, to keep your promise for me to go out. What do you do? The day of joy, I am told

"Your father said for me to tell you that you cannot go to the center today" You couldn't tell me that yourself but you always made sure you came home later those nights.

Why Daddy? Why did you hit me so hard with a piece of wood that I still, to this day see little silver sparks that no doctor can diagnose? You slapped me so hard on my ears; I lost some of my hearing. People have to repeat what they are saying to me.

Daddy you have to clear this muddy water that's drowning me, before I can drink again"

I had to speak fast. I had years of rehearsal and didn't want to miss anything.

"I don't know what to say. I thought everything was alright, that we had no problem these past years. We have been doing well. Now you come with all these longtime story. Things I tried so hard to forget. Why are you doing this to me at this time?" he asked

"They may be things that you forget, but they are things I am trying to forget.

Daddy only you could make me forget what happened to me in this house. Only you can help to wash away my pee that flooded this floor every time you beat me with the rope.

Until you help me to understand why? I will never be able to move on.

When the man across the road said such horrible things about me and tarnished my life. You did nothing to help me; instead, you condemned me as the worst thing.

You helped your brothers when their children to England to study nursing, its one of the qualities of this great family, to come together and help each You were aware that my only dream was to go join my cousins in England and become a nurse. It was my mother's desire too, that was why she agreed for me to come here and be a slave for you and your extended family, just so that you would pay for me to attend high school.

What did you do Daddy? Not a month after my mother's death, two months before I graduate from high school, you dropped the gelatin. You left me dunce.

Do you know that every night I went down on my knees and prayed for you not to come home? I wished for a jumbee to come out of the Aklyne burial ground and take you back into its tomb. Then I will end my prayer by asking God to please forgive me?

Every time I try to come up for air, something pull me back down, reminding me that I belong in the dept, because my father put me there. Be a slave in rags for his household.

Daddy, please help me, I will be going away soon, taking my children with me. I need to be able to raise my children without thinking that it is all right to brutalize them the way you did me. So far, I've never done it and I beg God, never to do it, I do not want my children to feel about me, the way I feel about you. You know that I was afraid to speak?

Do you know how much I wished that I too were dumb and deft like Datson and David? Because I realized that whenever I spoke or laugh, you would strike out at me, violently?

Every night my tears drained into my ears as I lay waiting for a beating, and after one.

Yes Daddy, my tears flooded my inner ear and brain from the years of abuse from you"

I thought of something that would move this stubborn man and bring him to a confrontation with me, but he just listened. So I continued.

"Do you know how much I wished for Uncle Bertram to be my Daddy? How jealous I was of his children and all your brothers and sisters children who were so happy with their parents? Daddy, do you know that to this day, some of my cousins remind me that I was the only one in the family who got more wiping than anyone else. They say that they get spanked with a belt or a whip but me; I get the mighty cow rope. Yet they all think that you're one of their best uncle? You are kind to them. You took the time to talk with them. They never saw the side of you that David and I knew" I got his attention.

"How did David come into this? I thought this was about you and me?"

"David suffered just as much as I did. He couldn't hear or speak, but he felt the pain.

To this day, he doesn't know the reason why you shatter his glasses on his face with a blow? For years, he been asking me that unanswered question. 'Why Daddy did that?'

I went close to the latrine the day after; to tell you who took the money that my brother was accused of taking. You know what you did, Daddy? You chased me away, saying I am a troublemaker. You refused to believe any truth about us.

Datson, David and I suffered equally. Even though they did not hear or speak, they were 'fatherless' just like me. We didn't have a father to protect us when we were used as freaks and slaves. Not because you put some money into the post office you are a father.

You were not there when I had to hold on to David for dear life when he took a knife to cut under him and Datson tongue so they too could speak.

Datson never accepted you as his father. Uncle Naga was his father and when Mommy died, he clung to Auntie Chunu as his mother. He came here because of David and me.

Do you know it is when I look into the mirror I am convinced that you are my father?

You used David and I just like those loveless people in Whim. When it was useful to you.

While you were going on with your carefree life, my mother and I were dealing with life.

Daddy, do you know how much I wanted you to put your arms around me, like Uncle Bertram did all the time? You held me three times in my short miserable life with you. I wanted to glue myself to you, but you quickly reminded me that I am rejected.

I glued myself to the first man who held me tightest. He was not much different from you. He didn't allow me to dance, and like you, he didn't want me to have an education.

There is nothing we can do to undo the past, but you could help me to understand.

Daddy. I need to move on. Help me. Please Daddy, help me" I began to cry because it seems as if I will leave just as full as I came. All these reminisce and pain for nothing.

My father got up from his chair; he began to walk around the room. I saw how much he has aged from the time when all those abuses were done to me. He said,

"You come here to clear my conscience or yours?" He went back into his chair.

"My conscience? What did I do?" The question had me puzzled.

"You were born with ears to hear and mouth to speak, my sons were denied such"

"Am I to be blamed for my brothers being the way they are?" what a shock to me.

"From the moment I heard that your mother got a girl and that she could hear and speak. I hated you. I hated you with such a passion, that now, I am glad that I didn't hold you when you was a baby, because I am certain that I would've strangled you to death.

Every time I heard of what was happening to you, when the Indian children tied you in the ants nest, when the Black children threw you in the trench, when the boy cut your foot, and all the bad things that were happening to you, when a father should be there to protect his child, I was wondering, 'Why didn't they finish her off and ease my hate?'

Whenever I head your voice, head your laughter, all my blood turned acid. I wanted to choke the very life out of you, knowing that my two boys couldn't hear to laugh.

Yes, everything you said is true. I did all those things to you because I didn't want you. But since you were forced upon me, I used you to vent my hurt. I am ashamed of it.

Over the years I tried to change. I beg God for forgiveness. When your uncle sent you away, I cried, begging God to bring you back, so I can beg you pardon. I never thought that I could love you, after all that I have done to you. How I wish for you to come back so I could tell you how sorry I am and how much I love you" My father was on his knees, repeating himself over and over, banding his head on the floor, creeping over to me.

He grabbed my leg and placed his head on my lap. I got off my rocking chair and joined him on the floor. We locked together. He kept repeating, "Please forgive. Forgive me. Forgive me my child, forgive me. We wept until the muddy water became clear.

Linda, this was the hardest chapter of my life. I never dream that it can get harder.

I was not responsible for my brothers being mute but I felt my father's pain.

There was nothing to forgive. I understood his pain.

I knew that I had to make one more visit before leaving this country. I went to Black Bush Polder to see my brother Dhia. My Buddy.

Years after our mother died, I got married, I took my husband to meet my brother and family. Richard even got one of Dhia's sons a job in the Ministry of Foreign Affairs, and he lived with us in Charlotte St. until we left for Africa, then he moved to Sis, at the back.

Richard and Dhia became good friends. They had one thing in common. Rum.

They would drink rum and coconut water until they pass out under the coconut tree.

I took my brother under one of that coconut tree, no rum or coconut water. I said,

"Buddy, we need to talk. There are so many unanswered questions I need to get answers from you. I am going and taking my children away from here, but I can't leave without making this visit and hearing what you have to say to me.

Did you know that you were the hero of our lives? My two dummy brothers and I had no other man in our lives. We worshiped you like our God. What happened? Why did you turned on us the way you did. Why did you beat my two brothers so brutally, leaving scares on them to carry to their graves?"

After the long session with my father, talking to Dhia was easier. I was not afraid to ask questions. I was not afraid of anyone anymore. I continued,

"Why did you treat Mommy so bad? Do you know she died not wanting to see you?

When I asked her if I should get you, she said that you don't know her and that she may not recognize you, after not seeing you for many years. I shouldn't bother you?

Do you know how hard it was for Mommy to say that about her son?

You and your wife got nine children; she was not allowed to hold one in her arms.

She gave you this land, but was never allowed here. Your wife sees her in the market, walks the other direction. She shows everyone that your mother is not connected to her in anyway. The same person whom your mother choose for you because she loved her.

It was my mother who chooses your wife for you, despite your rejection. Yet, that same person turned on my mother as if she had the plague? Afraid that my mother's curse would fall on her children"

Why is it so hard to get men to dialog when I need answers? My brother instead of saying something to me, called one of his son to bring some rum and coconut water.

"Buddy, why did you and your wife take all of Mommy's jewelry, without giving me or the boys a single piece? Did you know that it is the custom for the daughter or daughters of the dead woman to get her jewelry? Do you know that people thought I got all my mother's jewelry? Who took all the money out of the teapot? It was my savings.

When snake bit Datson, I swear to God that you would come to see him.

When he died, l looked around the crowd for you, because I swear again, that you would come to your brother's funeral. Many of your friends were there.

Buddy, did you ever see us as your own? As your brothers and sister?"

The rum began to work; my brother was getting flush in his face.

"Wynn, do you know how hard it was to be an Indian man living in a house with an Indian mother who was married a Black man and had three Black children? Two of them cursed by their grandfather, a Hindu priest? A father curse on his daughter came true.

Every day I walked with my head down, in shame. I suffered too, being a part of your family. You will never understand what it is like to be family with Black people?

Even now and here as we sit under this tree and your children are playing in my yard, all my Indian neighbors will be questioning, who you are and what you are doing here?

This Black government hasn't made things any easier for Indian people"

"But I am not the government. I am your sister. We come out of the same womb.

You refused to take me to the buttonwood walk for crab dogs to eat me. That was love?"

"No, I was old enough to know that if I did it I would be hanged for murder"

"Is that why you befriended and used Richard to get your son into the same bad government? You had lots of Black friends when I was growing up. Was that wrong?"

"If I move to China, what kind of friends you think I would have?"

"Do you know that David still thinks that you are his hero? On occasions like this, I am glad that my brothers could not hear the hate that comes out of the mouths of people they love. Like the name you called us when I couldn't keep them away from you at the cricket field when you won your big game" my brother was getting ready, rum working.

"How come you didn't ask me all these questions before? You came here several times before. You took my son in your car on his wedding day. Why questions now"

"Because I am going away for good. We may never see each other again.

This is the time for me to get answers to the questions that has been plaguing me for years. I need to hear from you, Buddy, why Datson had to go to his grave with a cross on his forehead? Why Mommy had to die, not wanting to see you because she had not seen you for many years. I need answers before I can forget and go away with my children"

Then my Buddy, my brother, my hero, hit me with a sledgehammer strait to the heart.

"My mother was a Brahmin, the high caste of all Indians. She should've been stronger and rather die than taking me to live in Black people's house, yet, still thinking that she was a Brahmin. When she move from so high to so low, she never accept her downfall. I was a Brahmin, but no Hindu would let his daughter marry me, because my mother is married to a Black man. I had to take her choice for me, a Madras, who became afraid for her children becoming like Datson and David. You think my life is easy?

My mother was my mother until she married and got children for a Black man"

I got up, ready to collect my children and get away as far from here as possible.

This is one load I will not be able to unload. My brother has it all figured out.

I looked down at my brother, who was almost in a lying position. He was crying.

I went down on my knees, put my arms around him, pulled him back to sit up. I said,

"Buddy, we were both entangled in a web of hate, because of ignorance and belief.

I would not leave without letting you know that I will always love you. You will always be my Buddy. You saved my life. I remember the first and only time my mother hit me on my mouth, was when I refer to you as 'Dhia' and not Buddy. She said "Don't you ever forget that he is your Buddy. I remembered how you cried and fainted when Vincent cut my foot. That was love. I knew then and I know now that you loved us.

I remember when I was little and my tooth was shaking, ready to be pulled out, I will hold on to it until you come home, because only you would put your hand into my mouth, holding me gently in your arms and take out each one of my baby teeth without any pain.

So Buddy, as I am about to take my leave, I want you to know that you answered all the questions that were eating at my being. I feel freer because I've been untangling all the bondages that have been tying me down" my brother looked at me with red eyes, said,

"Wynn, in order for me to justify all that I did to my mother and the three of you, I had to justify my actions. I lash out on my mother, even though I was with her all the way. I live every day, realizing that a lie told to me, caused me to almost kill my two brothers. Rather than facing my demons, I saw you guys as the demons. It was easier.

These days and for years, she has been paying for all that she made me do to my family.

Do you know that it was my mother who choose her for me? My mother loved her so much. Even when I did not want anything to do with her. I ask myself everyday,

"What went wrong? Where did the 'cobra' that poison us all, come from?

You see, from the day we got married, she thinks she was my mother. I could never speak about my mother and my family in her presence. Yes I wonder everyday, 'how did I allow this to happen?' but I did, I allowed her to rule me. But guess what? She made not one but four daughters who are the image of my mother, they look, walk and talk like my mother. So you see, I am seeing my mother in four of my daughters everyday and its haunting me. My mother denied me the only chance for me to beg her for forgiveness.

I know she would've forgiven me, but she didn't want to see me even from her dying bed

You think your life was hard? Try to live with my life for one day"

"Buddy, no one made you do what you did to us. You have to face your own demons. . You will always be my Buddy and I will always love you"

Is this going to be my last visit? No, I still have my David and my humble father.

The compound was still alive with Alexander family. I asked my father.

"Daddy, did you love my mother?"

"I pitied your mother. You have to understand, your mother was screaming for help.

It just so happen that every time she screamed, I was there to help her.

Your mother was too high for my reach. Being a Black man, she was like 'untouchable'. But we kept crossing path. My mother had a lot to do what happened after.

You are a big girl now, I can tell you this, do you know that I went to your mother three times because it was my duty as her husband? Do you know that all three times I got the shakes? I trembled as if I was touching someone whom I was forbidden to touch?"

"Did you know that my mother was like a doctor? Whenever we had ringworm, she would heat a penny in the fire, rub the hot copper on the spot and then rub some lime.

Whenever we had vomiting and running, she gave us charcoal or burnt roti to eat"

"Daddy why you never had a Black woman? All your women were Indians"

"I love one Black girl with all my being. I was not good enough for her.

When her husband died years later, I took my donkey cart full of meat and provision for the wake. That was the first time I ever spoke to her, but I loved her all my life.

It was during this time that my father told me most of what I told you before.

He even told me that a famous family son from Port Mourant wanted to courting Esther.

He said he forbid it because he knew that no Indian man could marry a half-Indian girl.

My father told me the same thing my mother told me. "His family will get rid of you"

"They will outcaste a daughter, but do everything to regain their son. Even murder"

"Daddy, remember you told me the story about something sitting on your chest when you went to take care of your calves at the Backdam? And I told you the story that my mother told me about the person in white that followed her home? Well I had an encounter with one such spirit.

I got a live-in domestic job with a family; I had my own quarter to stay in. The very first night, something huge sat on my chest, holding my two hands down on the bed. I screamed and fight so hard. When I woke up, all the bed linen was on the floor.

I decided that I would not keep this job. I went to tell the lady that I am leaving, the little child asked, "Why? Because you met our friendly ghost?"

"Yes, he was not friendly to me" I decided that I was not going to let a little ghost frighten me away. If I can fight off so many living 'badguys', what is a ghost?

I went to the store and bought lots of garlic, placed them all over my living quarters and open my bible to the 23rd Psalm. Mr. ghost never bother me again for four years, until the last night before I leave the job for good. I packed my bible away and said, "Well I am leaving, thanks for not bothering me anymore.

That night he came back on me with a vengeance. I was bruised from struggling. I saw the huge dark figure walked away from me into the bathroom.

I was told that many years ago, before the present owner bought the house, that the first owner had an untimely death. I was glad that I was not mean to him"

If you have not seen someone in many years, Whim market is the place to go.

I took the children to see what country market is all about?

People were calling for me, "Wynette, come and buy something from me"

"Wini, you na memba me?" I was happy to meet them, even if it was difficult to remember their names and faces.

One lady was sitting on the ground, selling shrimp. Her face I could never forget.

She played in my life. She was smiling with the children and me. She said to the children,

"Look at this, your mother did this to me" she was holding her lobeless ear.

"Mommy, you did that? I can't believe that you did such a horrible thing to this poor lady. When? Why? How did you take off her ear like that?" they were looking at me as if they were seeing me for the first time, they were waiting for an answer.

Savitri too was looking at me, laughing how she got back at me, through my children.

I never told them when, why, and how Savitri lost her earlobe.

While we were there, Manchester school had a dance. Barbara and I went.

On the dance floor, we saw my father and Cara Bowel dancing and laughing.

They finally had each other in their old age. He got his girl after waiting a lifetime.

Daddy went to the local goldsmith and bought lots of gold jewelry for the children and me. – Guyana is the land of gold and Guyanese love to wear gold, even in their mouth.

Sir Walter Raleigh lost his head for not finding El Dorado, but it's there in the interior- He gave the children money to shop in Georgetown for whatever they wanted.

David seems too skinny; I got him some tonic and ask Daddy to see to it that he eat properly. Sister Bea was doing a wonderful job, cooking good nutritious food for them.

I told my father that Richard might give me a hard time taking the children away. That he may not give me their passports, and since they are still under the age of eighteen, he must sign for their passport and give permission for me to take them out of the country.

"If he gives you trouble, call and let me know, I will take care of it. I have friends too"

We said our goodbyes, while waiting for transportation to take us to Georgetown.

"Am I ever going to see you again? Would I see you again? Asked my feeble father.

"What you mean, you not going to see me again? I will be just a plane ride away"

"Yes, but that is a far way for me who never left this country on a plane"

"You and David may come and visit us one day. Feel the cold that we have to live in.

Daddy, thanks for opening up to me. We both suffered in different ways. You help me to shed a lot of weight that I've been carrying around for years. Thanks Daddy"

He held me close to his chest, squeezed me with all he had, for the last time.

The children went back to school and I went to see Richard to collect their passports.

He had none to give. He said, "I change my mind, I am not going to let you take the children, I will bring them when I am ready to come" God, what is happening to me?

"Richard, why are you doing this to me?"

"Because I am the man, God made me first. Why you never fight for me? Why you didn't come up with the children to your home and raise hell and let people see that you are fighting for your husband and your home? I was certain that you would do that"

"Yes, He made you as the rough copy. I once fought for you. I allow centipede and tarantulas crawled all over me in an abandon car, you never noticed that.

I was not allowed to wear makeup, lipstick and nail polish, but I wash them off your clothes and handkerchiefs as quickly as possible so no one else would see them. I hid all your abuses from the children. I lied about my toe being crushed. Your touch burns me.

You were too busy to see how I was fighting for you. Now, you are nothing to fight for"

"I still have everything. You have nothing" I was looking at the hurt on his face

"No, you don't have everything. You don't have me. Remember I was your 'everything'? Until I was strong enough to fight you, I stood beside you in public.

I got my strength for things I stand for. You got your weakness when you fail to stand.

While the shit flies feed on you, I have honeybees following me. I am 'persistent'.

Everything in life is temporary. It's how you use your life will make a lasting mark.

Mahatma Gandhi said 'There is sufficient in the world for man's need but not for man's greed" Your greed for power and hostility left you with nothing. You have nothing"

I had to keep reminding myself, 'He who angers you, controls you'

I had to move as fast as I could, because the date for our appointment at the embassy was coming up. I have to present up-to-date passports for our visas before we leave.

My father called an old friend who was a Police Commissioner in Georgetown.

I had to secretly take the children to Acme Photo Studio, get their picture taken, and then take them to this person at the Brickdam Police Station.

I begged my children, especially Melanie, not to say a word to their father or anyone else about their pictures being taken. This is my battle; I am fighting like hell to win.

When I worked for GMC I befriended Mrs. Hoyte, Richard boss's wife.

I went to her house to speak with her. Most wives have the first and last words with their husbands before they go in and out of bed.

I explained my predicament to Mrs. Hoyte and for her to ask her husband help for me to take my children away, without putting me on the block list, as Richard threatened.

Two days later, Mrs. Hoyte called me at my family's phone. She said,

"Mrs. Greene, Desmond said that you should go on doing what you are doing.

He said no one would stop you from taking your children out of the country. I think he made that clear with your husband too. Good luck my friend" – Let me tell you a little bit about Desmond Hoyte. He was the Minister of Home Affairs for many years.

He became President after Burnham died few years after this period. He changed the country back into a less divided place to live in. He lifted the ban on imported foodstuff, which made the Indians, especially, very happy, because now they can have their traditional foods and not limit their invitees to weddings and other ceremonies, for lack of flour, split peas, garlic, onion, chana and Indian spices, like they had to, when everything basic, was banned. They even named him 'Desmond Pershaud' –

Now that I was free from fear, I went to pay Richard for a final visit. I didn't ask him about passport or anything to do with the children. I said,

"There are two items in Atlantic Ville which I would like to get, my mother's little teapot and her small masala brick. You can keep everything else"

"Whatever is in my house stays in my house. You can't go to anyone to make me give you what's in my home" He was pissed, and I didn't care. I asked,

"Richard, what make you turn into this monster that you've become? You are so hateful, resentful and down right scary?"

"You know the answer to that? You made me the monster I am. A man gets angry, hateful, resentful and downright scary, when he is rejected. You did that to me for years. Now you want to know why I am so resentful? You took everything from me and now you are taking my children from me?"

"Yes, you are scary. For you to say that I took everything from you, you are scary.

That house you live in with your woman and making babies, belongs to me, you took it.

Everything in that house, belongs to me, you took them all. You brought a woman to live in my house with all my clothes, pictures, jewelry and even my underwear. Do you know how invading that is? You got everything, yet you want to go to America with me.

You said I am taking your children from you? You've always used them as a pawn.

Before we ever had children, I begged you, should we have children and I should die, that you would never give my children a stepmother, because of my experience as a child with a stepmother. One should never ask a woman to love or care for another woman's children. I am still alive, but my children had four years with a stepmother

You talk about rejection? I was born in rejection but I am not hateful and resentful"

Richard sat in his chair, turning from side to side, with a smirk on his face. I said,

"As I sit here, I will tell you the truth. At the beginning, you were my life. No one else could've measured up to you. You had me so tight in your hands I didn't want to move.

I didn't move. I breathe into me what you breath out of you. You were my reason for living. Richard, you changed that. You open your fingers to pickup more than you can hold, and I slipped right through. Once you started, you couldn't stop. Like when a dog gets the taste of egg, he never stops raiding the chicken coop.

I told you already, your part in my life is over. I wouldn't leave my parashoot near you.

I worked for days to do a report for the course I was doing. The morning of my presentation, my report disappeared.

I had the company's petty cash to take to an outlet the next day. When I get to the store, there was money in my bag. I knew you took it. You were doing everything to pull me down. Everything to make me fail or loose my job. You made me stronger.

You are living and making babies with one woman and yet you are having more babies, same age, with other women. You brought yet another woman to sleep in the house, telling resident woman that the visiting woman was your Auntie Virgie.

The children knew that you were lying, but couldn't say anything. When the resident woman finally met the real Auntie Virgie. You exercise your bullish trait. You are scary.

Do you know all the years of your abuse; I never let my children know what was happening? Even when you crushed my toe, I lied to them. But, I couldn't protect them from your indiscretions over the four years they were with you. What example did you set to them? What example did you set to your son? That it's OK for him to do the same?

Richard, there are men who are in jail for stealing bread to provide for their children.

You on the other hand, stole from your children. I am looking at one right now.

Look at the watch on your hand. It's the watch I sent for Kim's sixteenth birthday.

I put it in a box of cake mix, so that no one else could find it. But, because when the boxes and barrels come for them, they never see the contents that I sent for them.

Before I left four years ago, I took my children to Maurice, the goldsmith to make jewelry for them. Today they have none. They said they got lost in the home you live in. Enjoy all that you took from my children and me. They are material things. We have me.

You need to stay in your jail of 'no conscience'. Alas, I am free, I am rich, I have everything. You dealt me the winning hand. You can't hold my children ransom anymore

You see, my dear husband, you have been enjoying quantity sex, as many as your open fingers can grab, or should I say open your crotch? Me on the other hand, enjoy a good quality loving. If I can't get it, I go into hibernation until I can get what I want.

Richard, do you know that I loved you so much that I was willing to forgive you? I told myself that it was just the experience you seek.

It was your denial, arrogance and robbing my children, turned me off" finally I said,

"You told me that when you are finished with me, 'not even a stray dog would lift its leg to piss on me'. Well I am finished with you, but I don't wish you bad because I pity you. For the sake of my children and what we had in the beginning, I wish you well.

Let me tell you what Lord Krsna asked Arjuna. 'For the uncontrolled, there is no wisdom. For the uncontrolled, there is no concentration, and for him without concentration, there is no peace. And for the unpeaceful, how can there ever be happiness?' I wish you peace"

Sunday 6th March 1983, we were ready to go to the airport for a nine o'clock flight.

My Sister Esther came to go with us. A mutual friend of Richard and I offered to take us.

Suddenly Richard arrived at Laluni St. he said that he wants to children to go with him.

That he will take them to the airport in a car that someone lent him.

I told him the time of the flight and ask him not to be late with the children.

We arrived at the airport and waited, and waited. No children.

The airline began to announce the last call. The lady at the counter told me that its time for me to board. I told her, "Please give me my bag, I would not be leaving.

My sister saw that I was going to callasp any moment. She gave me a tiny pill to place under my tongue.

An Immigration Officer approached me and said, "Mrs. Greene, where are your children? I just got a call from the Minister to escort you and your children to the plane"

"I am waiting for my husband to bring my children" I could hardly speak.

He stood by my side and waited while the plane waited for my children to arrive.

Finally Richard arrived with the children. My sister screamed at him and called him some names that could put her away. His friend looked at him and shook his head in disgust.

I reminded myself 'Wynette, don't let him anger you. Forgive him, wish him well'.

The Immigration Officer hurried the four of us to the plane.

I was too exhausted to speak. I asked the children to buckle their seatbelts and sit quietly until I catch my breath. Even freedom can be exhausting.

COMING TO AMERICA II

During our five hours flight, I dress my children with the jewelry my father gave them.

I looked at them and wondered, how was my life different from theirs? Would they be able to cope, after all the baggage they collected for the past four-year?

I prayed that my children enter America as empty from such, as we are right now, with only the clothes on our backs.

It was snowing when we arrived at Kennedy Airport. Vera, Winston and Eve met us with coats and hats. It felt good to enter my warm apartment. It was full of family and friends waiting for us. I walked around the apartment in astonishment. 'This is not how I lift it one month ago?' Vera informed me that Mrs. Heller came here while I was in Guyana, and brought all the things I was looking at. The fridge and freezer was full of goodies. Cupboards lined with foodstuff. In the bedroom, there were sheet sets and comforters and winter sleepwear for all of us. In the sitting room was the largest surprise of all. A 26-inch Magnavox TV wrapped with a red bow. I told you they were the best.

The children were excited to be in America. Seeing their relatives and looking around the apartment they asked, "Mommy, whose place is this? This is nice and warm"

"This is your home. Here is where we will have a new start together. Just the four of us"

The Hellers called and welcome us. They spoke to the children individually and welcome them to America. They said they are looking forward to seeing them soon.

After most of the welcome party left and we finished a delicious dinner, I decided its time to have a long talk with my newcomers before they get too comfortable. Vera said,

"Wynette, not now, hold your talk for later, let the children settle in for a while"

"No Vera, they had enough time to settle down. I need to talk to them before they wake up to their first day in America, how things are going to be here.

I sat my three children in one couch and I sat on a chair facing them. I started,

"Kim, Rocky, Melanie, I have to talk to you. I promise not to be long, but I ask for your ultimate attention. You three waited for four years to come to this country.

I kept my promise. You are here and you will be good, respectable, law-abiding citizens.

This country is overflowing with good opportunities for everyone who is willing to take them. Also, this country has lots of bad things. Things that can destroy your lives.

You and only you can pick which way you want to go. But, for now, while you are in my charge, I choose your path. I pray that you don't let me down. It will not be easy.

We will pray everyday, thanking God for all His blessings.

I promise you that I will do my best to feed you, house you, and give you the best education that you can take. You will have to take good care of your health. Cover your head and feet well when you go out in the cold. We don't have health insurance.

In this country, you can be anything you want to be, and, you are going to be somebody. I will see to that, not for me, but for you. Here is your chance. Take it.

You have to grow your own height, no matter how tall or short your parents are.

I will not lie to you, things will be tough, you will see lots of things that you want and can't get because we can't afford them. I am asking you to work with me and together we will make it here in America. Lets make gratitude one of our daily attitudes.

'Please' and 'Thank you' will take you through this world as a better person.

Back home we greet everyone me meet. Here, some will return the greeting; some will look at you as if you are crazy. I say to you, greet everyone, whether they answer or not.

You can speak, use it, two of your uncles couldn't speak but they greeted everyone

Take 'can't' out of your vocabulary, that is lazy people's word.

Remember every time you pass the US Embassy in Main St. there are lines all around for blocks away? Well that doesn't happen only in Guyana. It happens everywhere in the world wherever there is a US Embassy. Why? Because everyone wants to come here.

I want to stress one very important point. In Guyana, we had mostly Blacks and Indians. Here in the 'United States', we have many, many different races of people. Many come from all over the world, to make this country their home, just like us.

The important thing I need to drum into you, is, do not judge anyone by his or her looks or race. See everyone as a human being first. If their character-behavior is not what you think is right, walk the other way from them. You don't have to be friends with them.

But don't judge anyone because they look different than you. Keep your religious and political opinions to yourself. Soon you will become eligible to vote. Listen to the facts and vote with your head, not with what others say-so. Be an independent person.

If anyone of you should join bad company, accepting the temptation out there, and do anything wrong, like pinching-shoplifting, drinking alcohol, smoking or do drugs, which you could find right outside the halls of this building, to disgrace this family, disappoint the Hellers and be a bad statistic in this country, I will cut you into little pieces and flush down the toilet. You see the toilets here are so powerful, that when you flush it, within seconds, whatever you flushed, can reach miles away from here, all the way to New Jersey. Your 206 bones will be placed in a garbage bag and buried in the bushes. No one can trace your parts. And, since you just got here, no one will even miss you"

I looked at the white of six wide-open eyes staring at me, but I couldn't stop myself.

"We are now four in this family. Each one of us has the same rights and responsibility.

If there is a problem, lets discuss it together, and lets solve it together.

We're a team, we are a package I beg of you, never allow anyone to break this team.

I don't want to hear from anyone of you that your grades are bad because 'the teacher don't like me'. Then is when you will see how much I love and appreciate your teacher.

Your teacher has your future in his/her hand. I have your life in mine, don't mess with us.

Tomorrow, I will give you pen and paper for each of you to write your father.

We will walk to the post office and post them. Always remember your father will always be your father. All children come into this world by both a mother and a father.

OK Roc, do the honors, turn on the mighty TV"

My memory replayed the past. I had to face my father, brother, husband, Savitri, Mildred who pushed me into the Manchester trench, and Vincent.

I did it, not against them, but for me. I need to keep 'hope' alive and cleansing myself from the hate that followed me all my life. I slain the demons. I purged the hate.

I had to burn the field, in order to see green again. I forgive them all.

Now I pray that my imagination will preplay a better future with hopes and dreams for my children and I in this new beginning, in this blessed United States of America.

Our one bedroom was cramped. With a double bunk, a double bed, a highboy and a dresser, there was just a narrow path to enter the room and crawl on to the beds.

When we retired to bed sometime pass midnight, leave it to Rocky to discover that there was another smaller TV on the dresser. It was yet another shock to me, but joy for the children. You see, they have not seen a telly since they left England.

I don't remember if anyone slept that night. Rocky on the top bunk, Melanie on the bottom, Kim and I on the bed. By morning however, all four of us were on the double bed, holding each other close. My heart was bursting with joy and contentment.

They had their first, full course American breakfast with hot chocolate milk, pancakes, bacon, eggs and orange juice. I said, "Don't expect this every morning. This is a welcome breakfast, present of Mrs. Heller. I will not be able to give you this kind of breakfast often. I will do my best to feed you well, but you will have to understand that we are poor, but proud. I promise you that I will never go on Welfare or collect Food Stamps. Not that they are bad, they are useful for people who needs it, not for young, healthy people like us. I didn't bring you here for that, I brought you here for a better life and good education. Leave everything else to me. All I ask is your understanding.

After breakfast we went out to play in the snow and to familiarizes them with the neighborhood. Everything was strange to them, but they were not over zealous.

They took everything in stride. Sometimes I catch them showing each other how the stores are packed with stuff they have not seen since they left England..

Apples and grapes were their favorites, scarcest and most expensive fruits in Guyana.

They pasted their letters to their father. They never ever got a reply from him.

A few days later Mrs. Heller came in her Suburban to fetch us to Westchester.

We saw the biggest snowfall. All the children had lots of fun sledding down the slopes and making snowman. She told me that Caesar went away when I went away.

Mrs. Heller took us shopping for more winter clothes, lots of socks, gloves and hats.

After a week of fun in Westchester, it was time for me to take them to Brooklyn.

She and I sat at the kitchen table, just like we did every morning for four years. She said,

"Wynette, we are letting you go. I would've loved to keep you always, but your children need you more. While you was away, I searched around as far as Stamford for an apartment and school for the children. The rent is too high for you to pay here.

I would not be able to live with myself if I were to have you leave your children in Brooklyn alone, to come here to work for us. I know what the labor rules are, but I could terminate your service. You paid your dues to live in this country with your children.

I will give you letters of recommendation. You will always be a part of this family

You must go and take care of your children. Any time you need me, I will be here"

We had dinner with the Heller family in the main dining room. There were lots of hugging, kissing and crying. My children had a first hand look of what America is all about, that there is good humankind in all races.

Mrs. Heller drove us back to Brooklyn, the Suburban loaded with everything she bought and other household things she got from the basement and gave to us.

When we got there, she handed me an envelope and said, "This will help you until you get on your feet" I heard the praises of my children.

"Mommy, the Hellers are such nice people. How did you find them?"

"God found them for me. I needed some good in my life and He give them to me"

Fun time is over, time for school. My Cousin Joslyn recommended the Epiphany Lutheran School. She said her two children are going there and are doing very well.

I took the children and their school records to meet Pastor William Sherman.

He looked at Kim's report and asked, "Why do you want Kim to attend high school?

She is over qualified for high school. With eight GCEs – General Certificate of Education from England – she is ready for any college or a good job. She don't need to be here"

"Pastor, I want her to get an American High School Diploma and to know American history. This country will be her home now; she needs to know about it. My children will learn the Pledge of the Legion, the National Anthem and everything else that they need to know, to become decent, law-abiding citizens of this country"

He looked at Rocky and Melanie's reports and said, "Your children has good records. This school has lots of teachers from Guyana. I like them for their strict discipline"

"Yes Pastor, I heard that one of my teacher is teaching here. Mrs. Bowree is from my village, she taught me in school. It would be an honor if she should teach my children"

"Mrs. Greene, how do you plan to pay for three children to attend a private school?

This is not a free school. You will have to pay for each one of them.

How are you going to manage that, when you are not working anywhere at the moment?"

He was blunt, but beyond his bluntness, I saw kindness in his emerald green eyes.

"Pastor Sherman, I promise you, I will never be late on paying my three children school fees. Even if we don't eat, their school fees will be paid" I couldn't help the tears, remembering my own hunger to have an education, and my promise to my children.

"OK, this interview is over. You will hear from us" He was emotional too.

One of the good things about New York City Subway is that you can put a token, pass the turnstile, and you can now live and ride all the trains for the rest of your life.

Rather than going Downtown we went Uptown and rode all the trains, all over the city. To Manhattan to the Bronx to Queens to Far

Rockaway to Coney Island. Underground, overhead, underground and then overhead to Sutter Ave, our stop.

The phone rang, it was Pastor Sherman, he said, "I have been calling you for hours. I thought you went strait home?" 'What is this? Who does he think he is talking like this?'

"Thanks Pastor, I took the children on their first train around the city"

"I was calling to have you come back with the children. It is too late now. Come with them tomorrow morning at 9am sharp" His bark was bigger than his bite.

"Thank you Sir. We will be there tomorrow morning 9am sharp"

"Mrs. Greene, I've decided to accept your three children into Epiphany. Our rules are very strict. No nail polish, no short skirts, except for PE, no chewing gums, no lightering on the streets, no loud behavior and no lateness even if the snow is covering the school.

This is a discipline school and I expect anyone coming in here, to follow the rules.

Kim will work in the office after classes every afternoon. That should cover her fees. You will have to pay for the other two. Fees are paid in advance.

They start on Monday. Oh one more thing, we don't tolerate tardiness even on payment"

"Thank you so very much Pastor. We will not let you, this school or church down"

"Before you leave, take the children into the storeroom and see which uniform will fit them. Take as many as you wish. You see when student graduate, they denote their uniforms for children coming in to the school" He forget to say 'poor children'.

I bought one set each new uniform. I went to the goodwill and bought three blazers, change the buttons to black, sew on the school crest and have them dry-cleaned.

Monday morning, my three children dock out in their new uniform to their new school. I still have the picture to show you. My chest was bursting with pride.

We took the #2 train together, I said, "You will make friends, choose the right ones. You are old enough to know good from bad. Eat the meal serve to you in school, it is better than the fast food on the streets, besides, we don't have money for fast food".

They came off at Eastern Parkway, and I went on to start pounding the pavements.

Mrs. Heller was pounding the phone too. She called and told me to go to Fifth Ave. to meet an old lady name Mrs. Abe. I went and got a job working Monday to Friday, from 10-7, for far less than what the Hellers paid me, but it was a start.

I spoke to the supervisor at DaGastino supermarket and got two hours, Monday to Friday, from 730-930am, washing and tying vegetable in the storeroom. Every little bit helped.

We went to the North Shore Animal Shelter and adopted a puppy and a kitten.

Nixon became Rock's responsibility to walk, hoper-scoop and care for him.

Kit kit the girl's charge, to empty her litter box and keeps her from falling into the toilet.

Our weekends were happy ones. We clean, wash at the Laundromat, grocery shopping with a list combined by all four of us. Only if there was an irresistible sale, did we buy what was not on our list.

There was a fast-food restaurant on Sutter Ave. Once per month we would go there, each one using his/her own money to buy whatever we wish. – They got an allowance from Uncle Philip every week. – Rocky the miser always left his wallet at home. The first few times, we got together and paid for his choice. Let me tell you, that boy could eat.

He was the skinniest in the family, but boy, can he cleanup?

One Saturday was one too many, we girls discussed among ourselves that we will teach him a lesson. We went into the restaurant, picked up our trays and got our stuff.

Rocky was right behind doing the same. We paid for ours and went to sit. He stood by the cashier, pointing to us, but we weren't looking at him. We were eating our food.

Later we saw him outside, looking in at us. Melanie holding up french-fries to him.

We had a weekend of laughter that lasted for years. He never forgot his wallet again.

We collected extra packets of ketchup, mustard, mayo and paper napkins for home. We went into a department store. I needed to get some underwear for the girls.

There was a man in that department, as I approached the salesman, Kim ran out of the store. I went after her to find out what was her problem? She said,

"Mommy, how could you go to a man to ask about women panties? That's not manally. It's like asking a woman for shorts for Rocky"

"Kim, these are the different changes you will have to live with here in America.

What would happen later when you have to go to a gynecologist who is a man?"

Whenever I find a weekend job from a tenant at Mrs. Abe's building, I would go and work, leaving the children to do their school assignments, house chores, go to church-one of their school rule was to attend church every Sunday. Matters not which church as long as the minister signs their 'church card'- and spend time with Uncle Phillip, who teach them about baseball, and Auntie Nora, who was the best cook and baker. Kim in charge.

Remember my savings at the Chase? Well I never touched it. I pretended that I didn't have it. That was for, if God forbids, we have a medical emergency, because we had no medical coverage. They took good care of their teeth. We never went to a dentist.

My children were disciplined. They did their school assignments and had good reports. They understood I didn't have money to buy name brand things for them.

We frequent the Salvation Army Stores and wholesale meat market; their things were much cheaper. We parceled out the chicken in four pieces each and freeze them.

Stew or curry with some potatoes and vegetable made the one piece of chicken each looked plenty. We were contented with whatever we had. We didn't have choices.

One day I was in the kitchen, I heard Melanie telling the others that her friend at school told her, "If your mother ever spank you, dial 911 on the phone and the police will take her away" I waited to hear if the others had anything to say. I said,

"If any one of you do anything that deserve a spanking, I will give you one.

I have done that before and I will do it again. None of you will grow up to be arsonist or serial killer because I allowed you to play with matches or allow you to hit each other.

You can dial all the 911s. I don't care. I have papers to live here legally, you, not yet.

The police will send you on the next plane back to Guyana; I will not go back for you.

By the way, Melanie, who does your advisor lives with?"

"She lives with her family, they all go to therapy. Mommy what's therapy?"

"I don't know. I've never been to one. But let me tell you something, follow the rules in my home and we will all avoid going where your friend and her family goes"

Kim had her High School Prom. The whole family went to shop Downtown Fulton St for her outfit. Her classmate Stephen took her in a limousine to the dance.

My regret was, that I couldn't get the afternoon off to watch my daughter dress for her prom. Mrs. Abe said, "I am happy that your daughter is going to the prom. Hopefully she will graduate from high school and go on to college.

She will understand that you have a job to do. Ask a neighbor or friend to help her.

You will be home to see her when she get back from the prom"

Stephen and Rocky became friends. He recruited him into the Civil Air Patrol.

I took Rocky to the Army, Navy Supply Store on 14th St. and bought all his uniform and other camping supplies. I was so proud to see my son in his military uniform.

Steve became a regular visitor to our home. He was mostly friends with Kim, because they were in the same class and Rocky, because they were about the same age and in the

Civil Air Patrol together. Melanie was too young, at thirteen; she was not interested in being friends with him, but she thought he was quite.

Mrs. Abe got sick and was hospitalized. I went to see her one afternoon, she said,

"I know I owe you for two weeks, take this" she gave me a check for $1500.00.

"But Mrs. Abe, you made a mistake, this is too much"

"No, take it and go, I need to rest" I went to work the next day and found her son.

He told me that Mrs. Abe had passed away. I gave him the check that his mother had given me by mistake. He took the check, but never paid me what was owed to me.

Few weeks later, I met Mrs. Abe's granddaughter at the grocery store, she said,

"Hi Wynette, I hear you give my uncle the check that Gramma gave to you?

You people will never learn, would you? That check was for you from Gramma.

She discussed it with us before writing it for you. Why did you give it to him?"

"Because we people never learn"

Without a job, the children were concern. Rocky asked if he could go pack bags at Patmark Supermarket? I told him that I spoke to the delivery person at DaGastino and said that I should take him. He would deliver groceries to apartments, pushing a wooden cart. Rocky was excited, "Mommy I could do that, when do I go with you?"

The man took one look at my son and said, "Lady, take this boy home. Bring him back after you fatten him up some. He would not be able to push those carts of groceries"

My reported earnings with the IRS for 1983 was $1,111.11

On Mondays off when I worked for the Hellers, I did a Nurse's Aide course.

I took my diploma and Mrs. Heller's letter of recommendation, and went applying in Nursing Homes and hospitals. I got call from two Nursing Homes in Far Rockaway.

Both hired me to start the following week after I attended a one-day orientation.

I accepted both jobs. The Homes were minutes apart. I could work both shifts.

From what I heard from other works, it would not be difficult to work two jobs.

"You just speak to your supervisor and offer to void your fifteen-minutes break, for coming fifteen minutes late. You can work at both homes. They are one of the same, anyhow" The excited family went out to buy two sets of white uniform, sneakers and socks. This would be my first well-paid job since the Hellers. I told the children,

"I will be away longer than before. Each one of you will have to take care of each other. Kim will still be in-charge" Melanie asked, "Why she always has to be in-charge? She spends most of her time reading her book. What kind of charge is that?"

"She had been in-charge before you was born. She has done a good job so far; I want to keep it that way. If you and your pal-in-crime do what you have to do, there should be no problem for the person in-charge or me, should there?"

I couldn't stop singing praises of what good and cooperative children I have.

Every day I had to tell the children how my friends-residents were doing? It was important to me, for my children to know the value of caring for the less able.

They knew the names of all eleven of my patients. They were as sadden as I was, when one of them passed on.

I told them about Maria who shared a room with her husband Adolph. One day the ambulance took him away. He never came back, but every time she saw an ambulance drive into the yard, she ran to her room and straitens her husband bed. She said,

"Adolph is a dentist, he has all these people sitting here waiting for him" She took chairs from other rooms and lined along the wall of her room. When they put another female into her room. Maria pulled the resident into a wheelchair and took her outside.

There was Lana, short and tiny. She was proud of her homeland Budapest. She told me stories of her childhood and how she came through Ellis Island with just the clothes on her back. She said she and her husband had a store in Brooklyn, until he died. She had no other family. I had to search under her pillow every day for the bread she hid.

I told her I am her family, I will give her fresh bread everyday. I meant it.

I told the children, "I see true love in the eyes of those people. They couldn't speak or do anything for themselves, not even wipe their drools, but they give me love"

In the Nursing Homes I learned about the 'revolving door'. Once they leave for the hospital, they seldom come back. I did my best to give every resident the utmost respect. It was at that period of my life I learned and accepted the meaning of,

"When God put a period-full stop, I have no right putting a question-mark"

I stood in front the mirror looking at my all white uniform and stet cope around my neck.

"Mommy, look at me, the Nurse Aide. I take care of people just like I always wanted"

One winter Sunday, it snowed so much we could not venture out. The four of us cuddled into one bed and my children opened their floodgates. I never questioned them of what happened for the four years I was away from them. I wanted them to tell me if they so choose. Once one started, the conversation began.

"Mommy, you must've been thinking that we did not care, when we spoke on the phone. But we had to watch what we say to you, because the lady stood right over us"

"Whenever you send barrel and boxes, we never see what's in them.

"Rocky went to Aunt Wini and I went to Auntie Megan at lunchtime to get something to eat. Miss Kim here, stays in the liberty, reading through"

"I couldn't play with the boys because I had to carry a baby on my hip all the time. The boys refused me in a team because they said I will be called away to baby-sit"

"Did anyone of you told or ask your father what was happening?"

"I did, he said that our mother is telling us to say those things. He made you out to be the bad person, though we were seeing all that were done. He called us 'trouble makers'"

"Mommy, one night I was washing our school uniforms downstairs. I had to wash them at nights so we can go to school with clean uniforms the following day.

Daddy came home, went upstairs, rushed back down to me, took my head and hit it against the concrete post, and went back upstairs. To this day, I don't know what I did"

"What about when I was in the shower and he beat me with a belt? I don't know why he did that. I asked the two of you what I did? Remember?"

The one good thing came out of the 'talk'. They were at ease telling their stories.

As if it needed to come out when the time was right. No tears or bitterness, just ease.

You see why I begged Richard not to let my children walk in my footsteps?

Our apartment was getting too small for us. Our winter gears alone fill the lone hallway closet. Rocky was sixteen years old and had to move into the living room to sleep. That was only official, because he found himself every night into our room.

A co-worker gave me a phone number for low-income housing. I called and went with all the necessary papers for an interview. The line was so long, I was determined to keep faith and hope alive. I was given a number to call to check on my status.

I called that number every working day. I ask for the name of the supervisor.

I called her every day. I think she got tired of my calls, she sent an inspector to inspect our apt. "You will hear from us" he said. 'No you will hear from me' I thought.

I called everyday until one day, as soon as the phone rang, the supervisor said,

"Mrs. Greene, come in tomorrow morning 9am. Bring x# of dollars"

We began to pack that same night. We didn't know where we were going and we didn't care, once we had a little more space to live in.

"Mrs. Greene, we are going to give you a three bedroom apartment in a newly renovated building on Amsterdam Ave. and 141st St. Its Uptown Manhattan. Far away from where you live now. Your job, the children school, no pets, all may be affected.

You will not be allowed to see the apt until the day you move in. Trust me, its better than where you live right now" I was given a letter to give to the Super when we move there.

The address was on the envelope. '1640 Amsterdam Ave #4' .We took the A train to 145th St, came out and walked to the apt building on Amsterdam Ave. We liked what we saw, even though we could not go into the building. We were moving up.

It was a sad day when we had to leave Uncle Phillip and Aunt Nora who promised the children their continuous allowance and for them to visit on Fridays for baked stuff.

The most hurtful thing was, having to leave Nixon and Kit kit. They would be in a good home with my uncle and aunt, but they were our pets, it hurts to leave them behind.

We arrived in the moving truck and met Super Ray. He was a short White man with a friendly, helpful mannerism. He explained that the reason why the Housing Dept doesn't let tenant see the apt before. It's because, "people wants 'that one' 'this one' and they cause problem. This way they have to take what is given to them, and be thankful" We were so thankful when we walked into our new apt, the smell of the new carpet, everything new, spacious living room, three bedrooms, one self-contained for 'moow'.

The Super left, I needed to ask him a question. I sent Rocky to catch-up with him ask him to come back. Rocky ran out, then ran back in and asked,

"Mommy, what do I call him?" We didn't call adults 'full mouth' not even a stranger.

"Call him Mr. Super" The Super commented several times of how manally they were.

One of the changes we had to deal with was greeting everyone we met. People looked at us as if we are from another planet. We never stop saying 'Good day' even with response.

Rocky was the first to put a bold sign on his bedroom door, 'Keep Out' He kept everyone out of his room, but he never kept himself out of our rooms.

We discuss the facts of what it would cost us for 'move up?'

Kim got a weekend job at Kentucky Fried Chicken. Rocky at Lampston, and Melanie went to Queens every Saturday to help an old lady with the grocery and laundry.

Once they were working, I gave them a bill to pay; I called it 'responsibilities'.

Kim paid the electric bill. She walked around turning off all the lights and asks everyone to iron once per week, because ironing every day pulls more currants.

Rocky paid the phone bill. He wrote a sign, 'Only for 911/ incoming calls only'

Melanie provided the quarters weekly for the laundry. She too asked, "Why because I am paying, we have so much more clothes to wash and dry?"

They always keep four needles threaded with different colors for me to mend and patch whatever is torn or missing buttons. We are poor but proud people.

Every time I went into the girl's room, Kim side would be neat and well organized.

Melanie's half would be a mess. I scowled her; that I will pick up her stuff from the floor and put them in the garbage. Nothing seems to work. One Friday night I said,

"Melanie, I did everything I possible could for you to keep your room tidy.

Now, for this whole weekend, you will make a bed out in the hallway and sleep there.

Maybe that would teach you the lesson of keeping your surroundings clean and tidy"

She said nothing. She didn't protest. When night came, she made her bed in the hallway and slept. The other two knew better not to come pleading for her.

She did it Friday night, Saturday night, Sunday night, Steve and his mother visiting.

Before the company left, Melanie made her bed in the hallway, where the visitors have to pass to go through the front door. She pretended to be asleep when they were leaving.

I must tell you, she keeps a neat and well-organized home. None could do it better for her. She passes on the same warning to her children if they did not 'cleanup'.

Whenever we saw a line at the church, we join in, because we will get stuff such as four, rice, cornmeal and other foodstuff for poor people, most importantly CHEESE.

We ate cheese in every form you can think of. Every meal had some cheese in it.

One day I even tried to make pizza. I saw the children throwing a plastic plate to each other. They were ducking and laughing. They were mocking my pizza, the danger of it.

Whenever one asked, "What's for dinner?" another answer, "Something cheezee"

We bought our first car. An old, two-door Buick Skylark that I drove to work at

Far Rockaway. I thought Kim and Rocky to drive in that car, at the back of City College.

Kim writes SAT and had the highest scores. She graduated Valedictorian 1984.

She received the Borrow President Award from Mr. Golden. The Senator's Award. Presented to her by Senator Markwitz, and several other awards. She was named,

'Outstanding American Student'

Uncle Phillip told me that I should go to the Vista Hotel by the World Trade Center that they are hiring and it would be better and closer for me. I did and got a job cleaning rooms. The money and conditions were better. Especially the tips, if you catch the guests before the supervisors do. Nowadays maids have personal envelopes in guess rooms.

I still remember something from the Vista Hotel that I will never forget.

I had to take care to the 'President' suite, which was on a top floor.

There was a guess from Saudi Arabia who was going to be there for a month, he was kind, we spoke about our children. When he left, he gave me an envelope with $500.

In our apartment, they said no pets, but we sneaked three small pets in.

We had Prince, a Chiwawaa old boy, who understood only Spanish when I found him wondering on Riverside Drive. Melanie took over. He bit everyone who touches her.

She took him everywhere in a small Avon bag. He knew when to hide down in bag on the train or in a store. I had to use a broomstick to wake her, for fear of him biting me.

Jasmine was Kim's gray cat we got from the shelter. She was truly a heartstring puller. She sat on top of the TV; her arm and tail slapping on the screen, as we watched a show and not paying attention to her.

Chris was Rock's green lovebird. We bought two from the pet store, but one died.

Her cage was never closed. She walked around the house and slept in her cage.

It surprised everyone who visited us, to see a cat, dog and bird walking around in the house and drinking from the same water container. "We are a peaceful household".

Rocky and Melanie went to school in the train with a teenager from the neighborhood. The boy attended Brooklyn Tech.

They were good friends until things started to change. Their friend dropped off from school. He was always standing with a group of other, not so nice, guys.

I've been hearing frightening things that their friend was involved in.

I asked Rocky to keep away from the corners with this guy, because almost every night there was shootouts on the corners. Many nights we have to take cover in the bathroom.

There were always lit candles and flowers at the corner for falling men.

It was every mother's nightmare, raising a son and keeping him alive.

One day I came down the street and saw Rocky with his friend at the corner.

I walked up to him and slapped him on the face. At that same moment, a police car was cruising along. The police asked me, "Why did you do that. Lady?"

I grabbed my son by the collar and said to the officer, "I am doing this now, so you don't have to justify your action when you shoot him down, just for standing here".

Remember the guy that I bought all the gold for him and his family? Well I met him at a funeral. He is a preacher somewhere in the South, still dressed in all the bling-bling.

"Mrs. Greene, I am calling from Colombia University. We are reviewing Kim's application and would like to speak to you. How soon could you get here?" I had just started working at the Vista Hotel; there was no way I could ask for time off.

"I finish working at four, would that be too late?" I was sweating and shaking.

"That would be alright. I will wait for you. You know how to get here, don't you?"

"Yes, I pass your beautiful buildings every day. I prayed for this day"

I went back up to finish my fifteen rooms to clock out on the dot of four.

I think I told every maids, linen men, and even guests that "My daughter would be going to Colombia University. The famous school on 116th Street" I always jump the gun.

In the train, that day, I remember telling everyone who sat next to me, the same words.

Mrs. Connor said, "We are reviewing Kim's application. Everything seems good so far. The only thing we need, is for you to bring us a reference letter from someone who is a US Citizen, acknowledging that they know her and that they would recommend her. Reason being that Kim has been in this country just under one year".

I walked out of the office and called Mrs. Heller on the payphone in the hallway.

The next morning, Mr. Heller personally dropped off a letter to Barnard College.

I accompany her to her dorm. I met her roommate, clean and packed away her clothes and books and reminded her of our rules of being a decent and respectable person.

Some roommates came and left. Just when she thought no one would share her room, she was blessed with Lynn who remains her best friend for almost 27 years and counting.

Kim studied Environmental Science, her love for the environment, pushed her to it.

October 19th I got a call from Guyana, my father was sick. The next day I got on a plane. It broke down in Miami; I had to spend the night there. I got to Guyana on the twenty-second morning. My father, Michael Archibald Hunter Alexander died before I got Lancaster, October 1984, one and half year after we said goodbye. He was 78 years

Sister Bea said, "Your daddy waited for you. He refused to go to the hospital. He sat in his chair, looking out the window, asking "When is Wynette going to get here?'

His first and only love Clara was by his side.

He walked into his bedroom, lie down, called out your name and died peacefully"

Uncles Joe and Tiger, his two remaining friends, dressed my father for his final trip. There were all races, mostly Indians at my father's funeral. And there was Clara, his first and only love.

Uncle Joe stayed with us for nine days. He told me all about the 'team' and their love.

In his will, he left everything for me with the provision that I take care of David.

Once again I had to leave my loving brother David, in the good hands Sister Bea.

Two years after Kim graduated from high school, Rocky did, and received the highest SAT scores. He was Valedictorian in 1986. He received the same honor and awards as Kim. He got a scholarship to Valparaiso University. A Lutheran College.

I went to Indiana with him. We stayed at the Holiday Inn. It was there I saw Oprah on TV for the first time. I said, "Rock, look at this lady? She looks like our Kimmy?"

We went to the college and met his roommate. I packed away his things on his side of the room and reminded him of our rules, plus begging him to be careful. I said,

"Son, you are going to be so far away from the family. Please be careful. I don't see too many people looking like you, but that shouldn't be a problem. Remember to take

'Can't and won't' out of your vocabulary. Be respectful and attend church service.

Sort your clothes into three category, white, gray and dark, otherwise all will be gray"

"Mommy, don't worry. You didn't make a spineless son. I will make you proud.

I made a deal with all three of my children that I will assist them financially while they are in college, as long as I get a report of their progress, from the school.

I knew of a co-worker who was sending her hard earn money to a child whom she thought was attending college away from NY. After many years, and thousands of dollars, she found out he dropped out of school years ago, cashed her check every month.

There is a saying 'When your neighbor house is on fire, cover yours with water'.

We agreed that my check goes strait to the school; and that the schools will then send the report to me. It worked well. I never had to feel the hurt my friend felt.

When Rocky became a senior, I did not receive a report. I called the school. The secretary said, "Mrs. Greene, Richard requested that we do not send his grades to anyone. He is of age to make such a request. We have to honor it" "Yes Mam, I understand.

Two questions? Is my son still in school? Is his grades OK?"

"Yes, Richard is still with us. He is involved in lots activities. His grades are excellent"

Well, he broke his promise, so I broke mine too. I didn't send a check to school.

One day, while I was on the job, I got a call from my son, frantic and breathless,

"Mommy, you forget to send the check. I can't enroll for the next semester until they get a check from you. Mommy please send your check as soon as possible"

"No Rock, I didn't forget to send the check. We have a deal, your school report and my check has to exchange hands. You think that you are old enough to change our agreement, then you should be old enough to write your own check"

The next day, I received an overnight mail with my son school report.

He graduated with double major. I told you I would do anything to make it happen.

Two years later, 1988, Melanie did exactly the same as her sister and brother when they graduated from high school. She received the same awards as her sister and brother. Prince, her dog had to be present at the graduation in the church, while she gave her speech. I had him in the Avon bag try not to strangle him for fighting me to go to her.

Many parents, upon hearing about Kim and Rocky and watching Melanie receiving her awards as Valedictorian, surrounded me to ask, "Mrs. Greene, how did you do it?

Three children, all Valedictorian, and awards from the Borrow President and the Senator.

How did you do it? What did you do?" I was a puddle, my children made me so proud. They never asked for things that I could not afford.

They were contented with whatever I gave them. As teenagers, they never asked for 'name brands'. They never expected allowances from me. The only money I had to give them was a nickel each per day for them to use the bus ride from the subway at Nostrand Ave to their school at Lincoln Pl.

I said, "I never hid the rod. Even though I never had to use it, it was always in clear view.

The credit goes to my children. They are like ducks, they march one behind the other"

Melanie sent only one application to only one college, Colombia University.

When Kim graduated from Barnard College in 1988, Melanie entered Barnard College.

She told advisors at the College that she has taking her sister's recommendation.

While my daughters were in college, they received a financial assistant for books and other expenses, from the Jewish League of Women, recommended by Mrs. Heller.

Kim went on to Seattle to graduate school to do a Master's degree in Science.

At this stage of my life, I had three children in college to financially subsidize.

Kim found a small apartment; she and I went to a garage sale and furnish the whole apt with everything needed to make her comfortable. The people who had the sale were so happy, they gave us new, unwrapped bed linen and towels, they even delivered them.

She sold Time Life Books and did other jobs to support her while away from home.

The nest was empty of my children, but our three pets kept me happy.

I found add jobs anywhere and everywhere to keep afloat and my children in school.

While Kim was in Seattle, our date for citizenship at the immigration came up. I could not afford to pay $800 for the airfare for her to come to NYC to receive it. We agreed that she would get it the next time around.

Mrs. Heller just happened to call to see how we were doing. I told her we would be going to get our citizenship. She asked why Kim would not be there. I told her my plight.

She asked for Kim's address. That night, Kim called me, all excited, she said,

"Mommy, guess what? Mrs. Heller sent me a return airfare. The travel agent here pushed the ticket under my door. Mom, please call and thank Mrs. Heller for me"

Yes, the Heller's never cease to amaze us. Their kindness never stopped.

Did I tell you, from the time the children came, the Heller sent us a smoked turkey and ham from a company, every Christmas?

My Aunt Elouise passed away in England in 1991. I attended her funeral.

She gave me unconditional love at a time when I needed it most. She was my second Ma.

My supervisor from the Vista was leaving and going to work at the Mayflower Hotel on Central Park and Columbus Circle. I followed her. It was a smaller, beautiful, old fashion hotel. Three months later, I was appointed manager of the laundry.

In my heart, I still wanted to work with patients. Take care of people. Nurse people.

I applied and got a weekend job with the Florence Nightingale Nursing Home on 96th St.

I got Kim, Rocky and Vera, working there part time and summer break jobs.

I resigned from the Mayflower Hotel to work fulltime at the Florence Nightingale Nursing Home. Two years later I got a pink slip. I could've gone back to the hotel, but I didn't. I worked at many Nursing Homes in the Bronx and Riverdale.

When I told the children that the unemployment office told me that I am eligible for Food Stamps, they asked, "Who's going to the store with food stamps? Mommy, remember you told us that we didn't come to this country for welfare and food stamps?"

I left my phone # with many doormen in the rich district. Just incase someone was asking for a cleaner? I got a few cleaning jobs in Fifth Ave. area.

Every Sunday morning, I went to an apt to clean and wash for a couple. They always left the $20 on top of the fridge. – Sometimes I cleaned three apt on one Sunday. Starting from 7am-7pm – I discovered one Sunday, there was no money on top the fridge.

The next Sunday, same thing, the third Sunday, after cleaning, washing and ironing.

I was sure that there would be three $20s waiting for me-you see, I was so dumb, I didn't look for the money before I did the work, always after – There was none. I wondered,

'How could these people, who are so rich? Who drive a fancy car with a silver jaguar sticking out the front? Who opens their door for me every Sunday? Leaving me to clean and wash while they go out to brunch? How could they forget to pay me three weeks?'

I waited for them to return. I had two other jobs to go to, but I needed to see them.

The silver jaguar approached me; the lady came out while the man drove down to the garage. She said, "Wynette, what are you waiting here for?" she was surprise to see me.

"I am waiting for my money. You have not paid me for three weeks, you open the door"

By this time the husband join us, he asked the same question. He said,

"Its my wife fault. I told her weeks ago that we can't afford a maid anymore"

The couple began to walk away from me. I caught up with them as the doorman opened the large, brass and glass, spotless door. They looked at me as if I was disturbing them.

"I come to your home every Sunday morning when most people are still asleep.

I clean your whole apt. Change your bed after you left all your fresh semen that gets on my hands. I wash and iron, all for $20. You spend more than five times on your brunch. Do you have any idea what $20 means to me? Do you know how much $60 is to me?

You are just another one of those who are still fly on the wings of slavery"

I stuff my scarf in my mouth to quiet my cry, as I watch the sympatatic doorman close the door behind them.

There were also the many kind people during this period. There was a young attorney who refused to believe that his maid has three children in Ivy League college at the same time? He did everything he could to help me with kindness and free advise.

I went to a large hospital on Broadway and fill an application for Nurse's Aide.

I got the job and worked from 3-11pm. Many days I ate the discharged patient dinner.

From 7am-2pm I clean and wash for a young attorney in downtown Manhattan.

So from 7am to 11pm I worked five days per week. I got every other weekend off from the hospital. On that weekend off, I moved into an elderly lady's apartment and care for her from Friday midnight to Sunday midnight.

Yes, I was doing three jobs at one time to keep my three children in college.

I spoke to a co-worker whom I ride the bus with every night. She lived in Convent Ave. in a nicer building, and since my building was getting crowded in the hallways and stairways. I wanted to move to a somewhat safer ground.

My friend told me that it is not easy to get an apt in her building because it was a

Co-op and everyone in there owns their apt. She said that when the building became a Co-op, all the residents paid $250. for each apt. Only when someone dies or move out, an 'outsider' can rent or buy an apt for more than what they paid for it, but, she said that there is a ceiling that no one can go above because they are 'low income' apts.

"How could I own one?" If you don't ask, you wouldn't know. I am persistent.

"You have to buy it, if there is one available. It is very difficult for anyone to get into our building. Even if one is available, you have to prove that you could pay the fees"

"How could I get an application? Who should I talk with when I go to the building –

You see, once I set my mind on something, I peruse it even if I fail. At least I tried. –

"But you don't understand, with your kind of income and three children in school, you would never be able to afford to live in my building. Besides, Convent Ave. is the

Oasis of Upper Manhattan, it's a Historical District. It has some of the most beautiful 'Brownstone' buildings. Not any and every one can afford to live in Convent Ave"

"Just give me the name of the person whom I should speak to?" I am persistent.

I met the secretary for the building, Mrs. Burchett. Filled out an application and was interviewed by the Board. Everyone wanted to know how would I be able to pay?

They didn't know that I was a 'save bat'. That I have been saving from the first week I worked in this country. That there is a saving account in the Chase Bank that has not been touched since I met the Hellers.

The night after the interview, I got a phone call from an elderly lady who was on the Board. She saw that there was no way I could to get the Board to approve me for an apt.

"Mrs. Greene, my name is Lena. I was one of the people who questioned you tonight.

I feel compassion for you. You are trying to uplift yourself and children. I want to help.

I have an offer for you. I am thinking of moving back to my home now that my husband is passed. I will sell my apt to you. Come see me tomorrow. I am in #1. Lets talk about it"

"Thank you, thank you, thank you. This is music for my children and I to dance with"

"You are welcome, but don't start dancing yet, lets meet and discuss business first"

I danced with Prince, Jasmine and Chris. I called the three children and asked them to join me in praying and dancing. I told them about my interview and the upcoming meeting. Their voices told me that they too were dancing.

Nowadays, the more I am told I can't do or have something, I always prove them wrong.

We now have our own piece of the Apple. All four of our names on the Certificate.

Peter, the young attorney, did the search and closing for me, free of charge.

One evening while I was moving stuff from Amsterdam Ave. to Convent Ave. I saw

Wally the handyman, he said to me, "Mr. Greene, you have done the best thing leaving this building. It is getting worst with the drugs and the traffic in the hallways. When you come tomorrow, I have a house-warming gift for you"

The next morning, Willy was dead, shot during the night while trying to chase the drug dealers from the building. He was an army veteran and a descent humanbeing.

When Ray the super came to check the apartment before accepting the keys, he said,

"Oh my goodness, this apt looks like no one lived here. You and three children live here for four years and I don't have to do one single thing before bringing another tenant in here. The fridge and stove look as if they were hardly used. Did you ever use the oven? You really took good care of this place. You should see some of the apt after some tenants moved out. I have to throw everything out and bomb the cockroaches out"

The Hellers never gave up on us. Every time the children graduated from high school or college, marriage and arrival of grandchildren, they received generous gifts from them.

For Bradley's Bamitzsa, my whole family stayed in a fancy hotel in Connecticut. Limonene took us to and from the service and party. All paid by the Hellers.

In high school, he had an assignment to write about someone who has influenced him.

He chooses me. He came to the hospital and interviewed me.

He got an A+. His teacher told him that he would've liked to meet me. I have that paper.

He was doing his internship working at Madison Square Garden. He invited me to have lunch with him. He placed my hand on his arm as he walked me through the building. Everyone who hailed him, he introduced me as his 'Second Mother'

I danced at his wedding. He and his wife have two beautiful little daughters.

On a visit to Guyana, I stopped to see Auntie Chunu on my way to the ferry.

She held on to me and began to cry. I taught that she was happy to see me. She said,

"Wini, dem come through the window and tek all me diabetic medicine. Now me have no mo pill" I looked at my watch, if I didn't leave soon, I will miss the last boat.

I forget about the ferry. I took my loving, caring auntie to the doctor then drugstore.

We came back to her home. I went to Lancaster and get David for us to spend the night with her. She told me more stories about my mother and her three children.

"You know that this house that you and the boys grow up in, once belonged to your grandfather? Oh yes, this used to be Kasy Marage house. Here is where they had a funeral puja for your mother, put a black flag right there by the fence, while she still live.

This is the house where he put a curse on her for marrying your father, a Black man.

Wini, you remember when you were little; your mother took the three of you to the back dam to work in the rice field? When you all had to stay in the woods seven days?"

"Oh God Auntie, how could I forget that? We worked all day on the man rice field.

My brothers fetched pyra, my mother bagged and sew the paddy bags, and I sweep and pickup the remaining paddy on the ground for our ducks and chickens.

The man put his bags of paddy on his little canoe and told my mother that he would be right back for us. No one came back for us of seven days.

I think, looking back now, that my mother had a feeling that he was not coming back for us, because she asked him if he could leave his box of matches with her? She protected it with everything she had. She kept it under her breast, from getting wet when it rained.

We were on the bank of a wide, deep, alligator infested canal. My brothers and mother could swim, but it was too far and dangerous to carry me across on her back.

For one week we slept on rice straw bed in the open sky. We ate roasted and boil fish and coconut. She used a rice bag to lore the fishes to pieces of coconut in it. There were plenty of coconut trees around. My brothers used their teeth to tear the fiber off the hard coconut. Datson used his little penknife to clean the fishes.

If you were to make a picture of us, you would see a mother holding on to her children, even though she knew that we might never make it out of the wilderness.

After a few days, the boys became restless. They threatened to swim across and go get help, but my mother showed them the alligators in the water"

In Guyana there is a long ream-grass that we call 'bizy-bizy'. It grows in shallow water. If you pull it strait up, you can get about six inches of soft, white, nutty root.

My mother fed us with bizy-bizy root. She boiled weed with the canal water in her aluminum saucepan, for us to drink something hot every morning.

There was a banana farm across a small trench that was not as wide or dangerous as the canal. We saw the bananas yellow on the tree. We pointed them out to my mother.

She told me, "Babzy, those bananas belongs to the person who planted them, if we take them without permission, we will be stealing. You know, we never steal?"

At nights, she lit a large bonfire to keep the snakes and animals away while we slept. She and the boys covered with rice bags but she covered me with her flourbag skirt.

When the last match used and rain ousted the firewood, she knew we were at the end.

She prayed with us sitting in a circle. She said, "If we are to die, we will die together"

Am I my mother's daughter? Did she love her children any less than I do mine?

Uncle Naga was at the rum shop when he heard the drunken man talking that he left the Brahmin woman with her three Kaffar children for the animals or alligators to eat.

He said that he is doing the village a favor and himself too because he don't have to pay her for working in his field.

Uncle Naga and Auntie Chunu came in a boat to rescue us that same night.

"Auntie Chunu, I remember everything, but the part that I will never forget is when you and Uncle Naga came in the middle of the night, calling out our names in the dark.

I would never forget that light from your boat and the looks on my mother and brothers faces when they saw you and Uncle Naga. Do you know that people look more beautiful in the dark? Do you know that for as long as I live, I will never forget you, Uncle Naga, Brother Joe, Sister Mari, Moses, Simon and all your children? You treated us like your own"

"What you talking about? You are our very own"

I am glad that I missed the ferry that day. It was to be our last meeting.

"See yea that light yonder so shines a good deed in a naughty world," said Shakespeare.

The children and I had a code of how to keep in touch. Thanks to the telephone.

I did this every morning to all three of my children in Seattle, Indiana and New York.

It was my way of knowing that they are safe and they are where they should be, free.

I bought my very own piece of the Big Apple, at Convent Ave, across the street from Alexander Hamilton Country House. Every Sunday there are bus loads of tourist walking up and down Convent Ave., taking pictures of the beautiful three-lined avenue and all its beautifully designed brownstone buildings.

At one corner, it the landmark church, The Convent Ave. Baptist Church, on the other corner, another landmark church, The Convent Ave. Anglican Church. Less than a block away is the famous New York City College. It's a 'Historical District'

After doing some renovations, we moved into our very own 'cassia', in time for

Christmas 1988. It was one of our best and happiest Christmas and New Year.

It is a small apt. With two bedrooms and a large sitting room, it was right at a corner, on the first floor. The building is beautiful with a lobby well lighted and clean. The brass trimmings shine and the marble seats and steps made my new home look like 5th Ave's.

All the tenants welcome us. I promised them that we would not disappoint them.

Once again, my young adults share one bedroom. They were happy to keep me out.

It was at this juncher, I told my children the story that my father told me, that his mother told them about the tree and its strength or weakness based on the decisions made by its branches. I said, "I know that I have only three branch, but we have a strong beautiful tree with lots of room to grow three more branches, and many smaller ones.

Please, don't leave me lap-sided. Lets add, not subtract from this family"

If we went out to a restaurant, ate the same food and everyone got the running, they would ask, "Mommy, how come you don't get sick? You ate the same food?"

I would say, "You guys never ate the dog and hag food when you were little.

Animal poop can build your immune system. In Guyana's septic tank, we put some horse poop, it will breed some maggots to keep the septic tank clean continuously"

Here is a true story.

A young boy went to the temple to talk to the holy man. He said,

"My father keep beating my mother, there is nothing we could do to stop him"

"Your father? No son, your father can't beat anyone. He is too sick in bed to move"

You are wrong, just before I came here he was chasing all of us out of the house"

"Son, by the time you get back home, your father would be dead, he is that sick"

The young man was so happy, he hopped and jumbled all the way home, only to find his father still keeping the family out of the yard, but the man next door just died.

We went to the North shore Animal Shelter and adopted a six-weeks black Labrador We named her Onyx. She was the love of everyone's life. She was the sweetest, smartest, most loving dog we ever had. When we walked with her on the street, people asked how could they get one like her. We sent them to the shelters.

We also adopted a little gray kitten, which we named Topaz, to join Jasmine.

I made room on the hallway for each of my children to store their boxes from college during their summer break.

Kim stocked her boxes, Rocky did the same, and Melanie didn't bring anything. I asked, "Mel, when are you going to bring your school stuff home?"

"Some of my friends and I are planning to rent an apartment for the summer.

Mommy, I am a junior now and I need to 'find myself'" I remember another senior.

"You have to find yourself? What do you mean? I didn't know you were lost?"

"Mommy its a group of girls planning to live together. I am a big girl now"

"Yes Baby, you are the big one, but I still sign the checks to your school.

Now, I am not going to order you to come home and bring your boxes. You are a big girl. Come September, take your own check to your school, because you've found yourself"

The next day her reserved space in my hallway was occupied. Call me what you wish.

Later in the summer, she told me stories of how the girls were not getting along. I said,

"Maybe they needed you to keep them from loosing themselves?"

Oh yes, they called me many names such as, 'The Dragon Lady', 'The Barracuda'

'The Old Fart' 'The Iron Lady' 'The Sergeant Major', but I didn't care. I had promises to keep. I had three youngsters whom I promised God and myself to do my best for them.

I had curfew in my home. When I get home at 12 midnight, I expect everyone to be home, except if I know in advance that they were going to be out.

It was a dangerous period. Young people were being killed on the streets every day and night for their jewelry, shoes and coats. It was a difficult time for parents.

They knew that whatever they did away at school, I have no control over, but in my home, I am all the above, plus head of our household, and their mother who loves them.

Rocky knew the rules. One night he went to visit a girlfriend and forget the time.

When he got home, I was already there and the chain was on the door as usual.

His sisters stood on the hallway, looking at me as if I was the one who broke the curfew.

I heard the knock on the patricianly opened door, stopped by the chain.

I looked at the girls with that 'Hatchet Woman' looks. I went into my bedroom, leaving them standing on the hallway, close to the door.

I heard movement in their room. I knew that they wouldn't open the door for him and they knew better than to come to ask me to open the door for him.

They passed pillows and blanket through the window to him. He slept in the lobby.

I am thankful that I have a safe, clean, warm lobby. I knew he would be safe.

Rocky has never been late in my home again. I am thankful that I still have my son.

I constantly reminded my children that each time I gave birth; I tore a piece of my heart and placed into them. I told them I have only a quarter of my heart and they need to stay safe and alive to keep my heart alive.

Remember my mother's wedding ring? I wanted to share it with my three grown and responsible children, one Christmas I announced my intention to entrusting them with it.

"We will start from the eldest. I will entrust upon you, one of the most precious piece of keepsake, my mother's ring. Every Christmas when we meet. The person next in line will wear it for one year. If anyone of you does not wish to wear it, you don't have to, but, if you agree to, please do not loose it. You can't put a price on my mother's ring"

Kim graduated from Washington State University with a Master Degree in Science.

Came home to New York, and could not find a job.

She decided to study Science one Sunday when the family was watching a morning program, where the interviewer asked the guess, who was from the EPA,

"Why aren't' there more minorities in this Department?" He answered,

"Because they all want to become Computer Analysis. No one wants to study Science"

She took her resume everywhere. Everyone wants someone with experience.

Kim, who graduated from Colombia University and Washington State University, found a job in a discount store at Broadway and 145th St. for $3.35 an hour.

I coxed her depression and told her to keep hope alive. I said,

"Education is the best thing one can have. Things may not be going the way it should, but do not despair. No one can take away your education. 'This too shall pass'"

Kim is now married to Dennis, and has a son Jared Michael Alexander. She has two Masters in Science and Education and has been teaching for over fifteen years. She said,

"Mommy, now they can't say that minorities don't study Science. I am teaching them"

Kim, Melanie and I decided that us girls would go on vacation together.

We went to the beautiful island of St Maarten for the first time.

I remember a group of young men asking my daughters, "Where is your other sister?"

My daughters replied, "She is not our sister, she is our mother" I am alive again.

After all three of my children graduated with Masters, MBA and Bachelors, I went to New York University. My children were most supportive. They were as excited for me as I was of them. I was a supervisor in the Food Service Dept. at the same hospital.

Every Friday evening was family time. I cooked their favorite meal while they play games such as Scrabble and Monopoly. We eat together, laugh and discuss any problem and our plans for the future. They were so smart; they talked about opera, theater, classical music and arts, museums and computers. I was certainly not in their league.

When they watched Jeopardy and race to answer, with pride in my heart, I sit quietly. I wish I could've saved that period of our lives together, in a bottle to show you what true happiness and family togetherness was all about. Shouldn't good things last forever?

Melanie graduated 1992 and started Medical School at Colombia University.

She too worked at the same hospital in the evening.

Linda, allow me to warn you, if anyone comes into your happy home and says,

"I envy you. I wish I had a family as close and loving as yours" Don't take it as a compliment. Show that person the door. Nothing or no one could put your close, happy family together again. You would be asking yourself, "Why didn't someone warn me about this?" I forgot.

I AM MY MOTHER'S DAUGHTER

I graduated from college, my two daughters were there cheering for me, giving me flowers and gifts with tears of joy. It felt like I made it, finally, after my three children.

In the midst of my celebration, my supervisor called me that Saturday, my weekend off, asking to come to work two days because two supervisors called in sick.

I protest, saying that I was planning to celebrate my graduation with my family. That it's my weekend off. She said. "This is not a request, it's an order. I have no one else to call"

I had to run the whole hospital, from the second to ninth floor, with limited staff.

That Sunday afternoon, as I went from floor to floor to make sure that all the patients had their right dinner, I stepped out of the elevator on the 7th floor, not knowing that someone had spilled some alcohol on the waxed floor. I went sprawling to the ground. My left arm came out of its socket from grabbing the rail. I was flat on my back and could not move.

An elderly man, a housekeeper, was the first to come to my aid. He saw that my arm was out of its socket. He actually sat on me, tore my sleeves off and screws my dangling arm back into my shoulder. He later said, "In Jamaica, dat is wat we do all de time when ah man throw out him arm playing cricket. The faster you put it back, the better fe when de bleeding and swelling start" The doctors agreed with his quick actions.

A group of doctors were making rounds at the same time. They came and took care of me. On the stretcher to the emergency, I asked the chief, "Dr., would I be able to walk again? Please say that I am not paralyzed. Oh God, please don't make me paralyze"

I was fifty years old and could not work anymore? I was 'disabled'?

Me, Wynette, who loved coming to work everyday? Who have never been late or absent? Who received letters from Management warning that if I didn't take vacation and time earned, I would loose them? This Wynette is now 'disabled'. I cannot work anymore? Is this my 'life sentence'?

I had to use a wheelchair, a walker, then and a cane. The MRI showed my damaged lower spine. I did all kinds of therapy for a long time. I had Epidural. They tied sandbags to my arms and feet, to try to pull my spine back into place. Hang me upside down.

I still cannot put my arm to the back of my head. I live everyday with back pain. I drank so many pain medication that I began to bleed in the stomach. My world has turned upside down and I was frightened.

I had planned to work until I get my turn for a rousing retirement party at 65.

What is going to happen to me now? I have no job, no medical insurance.

I could not keep my appointment with my Primary Care Dr. Lucak.

She called me at home to ask why I did not show up? I told her that I no longer have the health insurance to cover my visit. She said, "Wynette, please come in to see me. It would not hurt me to see someone who cannot pay me. I am your doctor, you are my patient. We have a relationship of trust. If I cannot assist you at a time like this, what am I doing to the trust that you have in me? Come to me every time you have an appointment.

Don't worry about paying me. Things will get better for you. Until then, come to me"

What a lady? What a doctor? What a friend? She treated me for my back pain until I get Medicare, then she recommended a good doctor who accept Medicare.

Some doctors recommended surgery, others said no.

It was recommended that I sit in a tub with water as hot as I could take.

One cold morning, the pain was more than I could bear. I decided that maybe a hot soak would ease my pain. I got into the tub around 8am. When I was ready to get out, I could not move. My legs were stiff, every attempt I made to move, caused ribbiting pain.

I sat in that tub for hours, afraid that I may fall asleep and drown in a tub full of water.

The water had gotten cold and getting colder. I did not know what to do. I just prayed.

My life companion, Onyx stood with her head resting on my hand to keep them warm. She ran to the door, barking, then returns to me, licked my face then ran back to the door.

It was Onyx furious barking and running through the house that woke me up.

Kim came home and Onyx bit her coat and pulled her into the bathroom.

She couldn't get me out of the tub. She had to call 911 for paramedics to take me out of my frozen tomb.

Rocky got married and moved far away from us. Someone heard the part of the wedding vow when the preacher said, "Forsake all others" and took it literally.

Melanie got married to Stephen in November – Yes the same Steve who was our friend from the time they came into this country when she was just thirteen years old. –

She involved her entire family and me in every step of arranging her wedding.

Kim was her Maid of Honor, Rocky was a Best man and I had the privilege and honor to walk and give my daughter away to Steve.

Steve became my other son. A new branch was added my tree. .

They had a large and beautiful wedding. Family and friends came from all over.

The Hellers attended the wedding, which was held in Brooklyn.

After the reception, I walked them to their car that was parked on the street.

We found that the windows were shuttered and their phone was stolen.

Those thieves have no idea how much they hurt my best friends, my family and me at such a happy time. They hurt the entire neighborhood, for committing such a crime.

It was a cold night; they had to drive all the way to Westchester, in a car with a broken window. My heart was broken for them, while all they were doing was coxing me and telling me how happy they are for attending my daughter's wedding.

When I got home the next morning, there was a message from Mrs. Heller, she said,

"Wynette, I know how angry you are about what happened. Please don't. These things happen everywhere. The insurance will take care of everything and the phone that was stolen is insured and the person who stole it can't use it anyway. Enjoy your happiness".

December 95, I got sick, very sick. I had pneumonia. I knew in my heart that I was not going to make it for another night. The children said that they are taking me to the emergency. I refused to go anywhere.

I remember giving Kim some important documents and instructions. I've been there too many times not to know the feeling of death.

I dreamt that I was in Guyana, going to the beach for a picnic with many of my cousins. I saw Richard standing on the other side of the deep and wide canal.- remember the canal that Datson took me across on his back? Then later left me on the other side? –

He was calling me to cross the narrow bridge over to him. I made an attempt to get on the bridge, when some of the male cousins grabbed me and asked if I was crazy? They said,

"If you cross over there, you will never come back"

The phone rang. Kim shout woke me up. She was in shock, asking Melanie whom did she hear that from? Melanie called to say that their father, Richard had died.

I lay in my bed, too weak to move but still alive. I wondered, 'Richard dead?

How could that happened? How could someone as macho and powerful as he, be dead?

How could a little thing like a mosquito kill a big man like him with malaria?

The same malaria that nearly killed me in Africa? Where he left me to die, rather than getting help? Why didn't someone get him help? Why he had to die so young?'

I had long ago forgiven Richard. I had much more important things to do.

It's my opinion, that until you forgive, you can never be free. My mother thought me.

Forgive but never forget. When you forget, you make the same mistake again.

The children went to Guyana to take care of their father's finial passage.

They discovered that their father had five other daughters from different women.

They went to the house and retrieved my mother's teapot and masala brick. The only two items I wanted from that house.

Later, Auntie Virgie told me she was at Richard's bedside at the hospital, minutes before he died. He kept asking her, "Where is my wife?" she said that she told him that his wife is by his side. He looked at his companion and said, "No, my wife, Wynette, where is she?"

Isn't it funny, two men whom I loved and craved for their love, used their last breath to call out for me? "Where is Wynette, my daughter?" "Where is Wynette my wife?"

At this stage I was in deep depression. I stayed in bed for days, lying in a fetal position, not caring that there is a living world outside my bedroom. No bath, hardly any food. The stench from Onyx and I made the apt unwelcome to living people. I actually felt like there were maggots crawling all over my body. I didn't even brush my teeth; even my septic breath didn't stop Onyx from licking my face when she needed to go out.

No one can put Humpty Dumpy together again. I felt sorry for myself. I felt as if I had put the mask for oxygen on everyone and when it became my turn to save myself, there was no more left for me. I was panting for breath. I had outlived my usefulness.

My two daughters were in a state of confusion too. There was nothing they could do.

I had nowhere to go, but within. It was hurting so bad.

I took my disabled, expired body, a little bag with some clothes, a sheet set that Daphne had brought for me from Norway, a towel, my meds, some cash and a debit card. Walking stick in hand, I informed my two daughters that I am going away.

"I don't know where, but I have to go away. Please take care of my pets. I will get in touch with you when I need to"

"But Mommy, how could you leave us without knowing where you are going? What if something happens to one of us? How could you leave us like this?" they were crying.

"You are big girls now. You have your homes and responsibilities to take care of.

I left you once to come here and pave a way for you. I did that, the three of you are well-educated adults, and you have good jobs. My task is over. Two of you are married.

One is already gone. I know when and how to let go when I have to. Now you let me go.

I need to do something for me. You will be OK I raised you well. I need to leave now, I'm doing this for me, I need to find myself. All my life I've been doing for others. I wanted so much to please everyone. Now I am pleasing me. I am leaving for me"

This gipsy was on the move.

It is too late for a 'Happy Childhood', but, I will be damned if I allow anyone to screw-up my 'Seniorhood'. I will give time time to heal myself.

My first stop was Puerto Rico. I found a family who lived in a small house close to the Rain Forest. All I needed was somewhere to rest my head at nights. During the day I spent all my time in the rain forest. I would buy bread with egg or salt fish, fruits and there were plenty water fountains in the park. At nights, Mrs. Cruz offers me some dinner. My stomach was very small from not eating for so long during the 'cold turkey'.

I took the local bus, which cost twenty-five cents. I visited the Fort, the Museum and went to the end of the bus line, walked around and return to my marked 'landmark'.

I spent most of my time in Puerto Rico, at the Rain Forest, it was healing and sousing.

I went to the Dominican Republic and did the same; I found a place to rest my head in Porto Plata. There were not many buses but motorcycle take you from place to place.

I spent most of my time by the water and getting to know the lifestyle of the people.

Moving on, I went to St Lucia. You see, I always speak to the local people wherever I roamed, because they know exactly what I am looking for; a cheap place to rest my head.

I spent one night at a Guesthouse in Castries, and then took a ride on a truck to Margot, found a place with a little old lady who treated me more like her family. I spent three months with Ms. Sally and walked the beaches and Parishes or Villages. In the evening, I sit with her in the moonlight while I tell her about my life and she told me about her's.

We went to the local market for fresh fish and provision. Boy Oh Boy could she cook?

In her outdoor kitchen on a coal-pot in cast-iron pots. She reminded me of Nana Sweetie.

I hopped to some other islands Martinique, Saba and Statia and St Kitts where my Uncle Bertram worked years ago. I mostly traveled in small boats. It was cheaper.

In my stops where the people didn't speak English, I made signs to explain myself.

This rolling stone was gathering friends and feeling very good about it.

I took a boat to St Maarten and went to see my friend Marie whom I met when Kim, Melanie and I went on holiday. She is a Postlady and she knows everyone and everything that goes on in both sides of the Island. Dutch and French.

She said I could stay in her home where she lived with her little son Reno.

I posted cards to my children from every stop, but this was the first time I spoke to them after about six months. My daughters cried just from hearing my voice.

One day Marie came home all excited, she said, "Wynette, there is a Dutch lady who lives up on the hill asked me if I know of any honest person whom she could leave in her home while she goes back and forth to Holland? She said that she has a separate apartment for a caretaker. If you wish, we could go to see her this afternoon"

I met Ms. Van de Pool, she said, "Once Marie recommends you, I will let you stay in the apartment. You will have to pay the electric and water bill and the gardener. If you want phone and cable, you will have to connect them yourself. If you think that you would be comfortable here? We have a deal" The view was to die for, the beach was minutes away.

"Thank you so very much. Could I bring my pets? Could my children or friends come to visit me here?"

"Sure, bring your pets, this yard could do with some animals running around.

You can have visitors; I am not looking for a hermit. I do not expect anyone to just sit and watch my house. Just make yourself comfortable" she looked at the cane in my hand and asked, "Are you sure you could stay here by yourself? Are you feeling OK?"

"Yes, I'm alright. How much rent do I have to pay?" I asked, hoping it was small.

"You have enough to pay for. The light and water bill can be high on this hill.

Once per month, go up to the main house, clean and air it out. That's it"

My three pets, Onyx, Snowflake, a black alley cat and Topaz, a gray cat, moved to St Maarten, the little island in the Caribbean, divided into two countries, Dutch and French.

I spent lots of time by the sea. I meditated most of my days. Little by little, I began to realize that there is life after raising three children. I have a little life left for me.

I wrote 'Thank You God' on a piece of paper, put it in a bottle, close it tight with a wine bottle cork, placed it on the beach and watch the incoming waves take it away.

I began to open up to strangers, starting with my neighbors, people along the streets and on the beach where I go everyday with my dog. It's truly a 'Friendly Island'

I sat on benches, on the streets in town or by the stores and chat with everyone who speared the time. I know I am not the only one who has a story to tell.

Marie and Reno visit me and took me out for drives and market on the French side.

I found peace and happiness. I found you Linda, and most of all, I found love.

Vera retired from the hospital and came to live with me in the paradise island.

I use my cane to draw a line on the sand, cross over and write 'I love me'. I stand and watch the waves take my words away to the deep everyday. I did it until I believe it.

It was at this stage, I began to love me. I began to see me as # 1 on my list.

All my life I put others above me. I gave them my bed and I slept on the floor. I fed them on my best china and crystal, and then wash and put away for when they come again.

I stood in the kitchen and cook and clean all day for visitors.

I changed all of that now. My bed is mine, no matter who comes to visit. I use my china and crystal as I please. When I cook, I no longer feed everyone first then eat what's left. I eat along with my visitors. It may be selfish, but alas I found me loving myself. I found myself in Paradise, loving me, enjoying peace, good health, and love from my growing number of pets, neighbors and friends. I have healed my dislocation. I love me. I am balanced at last.

As a young girl I remember hearing conversations between my mother and her female friends. They went like this.

"I think its that 'Change of Life' time" –Menopause

"You better stock up with plenty of barley, almond, soy and chana-chick peas"

"Those are the only things that will spear you from the terrible hot sweats"

I used their advice when my time came and I had no 'hot sweats' that I heard about.

Besides Vera, I had no family on this island, but, not too long after coming here, the whole island, Dutch and French, became mine and the islanders became my family.

I offered myself to them and they accepted me with open arms.

Once per month, I host a group of 'want-to-be' writers. We sit in a circle on my porch and read and critique each other's work. The group grew larger as time went by.

It was one of my activities that I really look forward to, because I steal a moment and their attention to tell them one of my childhood stories. They enjoy my stories.

There would be so many cars along the street, a nosey neighbor asked,

"What's happening in there every month that you have cars lining the streets?"

"Oh, once per month we hold a séances, we get in touch with the dead. Don't tell"

I forget to tell you this, remember I told you that I saved everything I placed my sticky fingers on from Guyana to Zambia to England and back to Guyana? Well I used that saving to make me a little more comfortable in St Maarten.

I also bought myself a new red Maharuti four door car made in India, for $3,299.

One morning, as I walked to the beach with my dogs Onyx and Leo, I saw a man sitting on a brick wall for the second day. I said hello and my dogs began to sniff him.

A man's watch, belt and shoes would tell you, without a question, who he is.

I saw that he was not a bum or a jumbee and he was not wearing a wedding ring.

"What are you doing here? Sitting in the same rock for two days? Are you alive?"

"Why should you care if I'm alive?"

"Because I don't want my dogs sniffing on no jumbee"

"No, I'm not a jumbee. I'm a sick man" he was trembling.

"If you are sick, you should go to the doctor, not sit here for two days"

"I went to the son-of-a-bitch and he wants to cut my balls out because I have prostate problem" he seems so helpless I needed to lift him out of his dept.

"So, because you have a lil peepee problem you want to swizzle and die on this rock.

Both my parents did not want me at birth. Compare that to your little peepee problem"

"Why they didn't want you?" he was looking at me, I saw his bloodshot eyes.

"Because I was born with green slimy teeth. They threw me out with the bathwater"

He got off the wall and began to laugh. He began laugh so hard my dogs began to bark. He walked close to the water and threw himself on the sand, feet in the air, he was laughing and kicking the air. He forgot for a moment that he had a medical problem.

I found love at the beach from a very handsome stranger.

We met every morning at the beach to listen to the quiet. He believed in mediation.

We sat together for hours, just listening to the waves from the Caribbean Sea.

He too use my cane to draw a line in the sand and write, 'I love you'

"Would you like to see the house in which I was born sixty-one years ago?" he asked.

"Are you married?" I asked.

"No, not at the moment"

"OK, I will go with you to see where you were born"

"Don't you want to know anything more about me?"

"No, when you are a fifth-three years old disabled, there aren't many questions to ask"

He took me to the house where he was born. It was a small one-room house, painted in bright Caribbean colors. The kitchen, latrine and bathroom were outside, a little distant away from the house. Just like it was in Guyana. He keeps it as a museum

He told me about his parents and showed me the large nail behind the door where his father kept a large leather belt named Brutus. He said his father only had to look at it.

He spent over forty years away from Dutch St Maarten. He lived in many parts of the world and graduated from two famous universities in the States. He was fluent with six languages. He was smart, bright, caring and very tall and good-looking.

He was a proud Caribbean man. He is insulted if I offer to 'go Dutch' at a restaurant.

I accompanied him to several doctors in Puerto Rico and the US where he was a citizen. The doctors recommended surgery for his prostate, but he refused. He said,

"When others may reject me, you embraced me. I am going to live everyday, from now on; as if it's the only day I have left to live. I will thank you and love you every day, for as long as I live, no surgery for me"

He knew all the words in the song 'The Power of love'. He sings it all the time to me.

Have you ever heard the saying, "Its never too late. That good things comes to those who wait?" I waited a whole lifetime to hear those words. It's better late than never.

We ate in every restaurant on the island. Drank in every bar happy-hour. Danced at every club. – St Maarten/Martin is only 39 square miles. – Went to the Jazz Café on Front St every Saturday night. Whenever there were visiting jazz artist, we would be present. Visiting spiritual gurus, we would be present. Special speakers such as

Dr Carson and other visiting dignitaries, we were there.

He was so bright, whenever the computer couldn't spell the word, he could.

I organized two Alexander Family Reunion in St Maarten in 1997 and 2003. He was with me every step of the way. All my family met him and loved him.

He was the best dancer. One of the most loving and caring men I ever knew.

We went to many States to attend spiritual conventions. He felt that if he would be healed, it would be through Spirituality. He believed in the Supreme Being.

We always race to watch the sunset on the French Side. "Look at it, if you live to be a hundred, you will never see this same sunset ever again. The same goes for the sunrise that you enjoy every morning" He took me to the 21 Club in NY for my birthday.

He treated me as if I was special. Whenever I went away, he tied yellow ribbon on the gate. He wrote poetry and posts them to me so that I would get mails from the mailman. He always made special and surprising arrangements for my birthdays.

We drank Champaign to celebrate the birth of five of my six grandchildren.

Sometimes he joins tourists taking pictures of me and my six dogs crossing the street.

When we met, I had a head full of soft black hair, ten years later, he was pointing out the gray hair that were invading my head. No matter how simple I look, he always says,

"You are so beautiful, I love you so much. You are one of the best things that ever happened to me" I say, "I am beautiful because you love me. You are one of my best too"

We never discuss our past. I promised long time ago, never to tell any about my past.

"Lets use all of today with peace and love for each other, tomorrow may not come"

Madam Sabrina joins us in 1998. From the time she arrived into our family, she took over. She made demands on me. She bit everyone who came near to me. She took over.

1999 I took her to Huston to visit Daphne. She took her frisky self outside and ran around the neighborhood. I did not know it then, but a poodle name Smoky raped her.

By the time we got back to St Maarten, the Princess was pregnant.

The vet assured me that she is having a healthy pregnancy. Her swelling belly did not stop her from behaving like the boss she is, chasing everyone else away from coming near to me. She had two puppies, Hidi and Smoky.

Kim got married to Dennis after her siblings. She too gave me the honor to give her away. Her roommate/best friend Lynn was her bride's maid, now Godmother to her son.

I visited Kim in NY. Lynn invited me to dinner. She said we are going to a small restaurant on the West Side. "Should I get dressed up or casual?" "Just be yourself"

I walked into a large banquet hall full of people, all shouting 'Happy Birthday'

There were friends whom I have not seen in over forty years. 'I'm glad I just peed'

There were Kim and Dennis; Rocky came from South Carolina, Melanie, Steve, Lauren, and Shelby came from Florida.

As I focus on the faces in the crowd I saw friends from Continental Biscuit Factory, Guyana Marketing Corporation, Colombia Presbyterian Hospital, family and friends from all over. Many flew in to New York for the grand occasion.

Mr. Stewart, my boss from GMC was one of the speakers who showered praises.

The Hellers were abroad; they sent a telegraph message of congratulation to me.

It was the surprise of my lifetime. I asked Kim, "How was this done? How you do it?"

"Mommy, it was a team work, your three children, Steve, Dennis, Lynn and Cheryl.

Seven of us have been working on this for over one year, mainly finding your friends.

Our mother live to be 60 years old, she deserves the grandest party"

When the Hellers returned home, they sent a limousine to take me and mine to their home for another party to celebrate my sixtieth birthday.

All their children and grandchildren were there with gifts and good wishes for me.

.

You know what they say? "God reward you with grandchildren, for not killing your own children" From 1998 to 2006 my three children gave me six grandchildren.

Vera went back to Guyana in 2000. She died in March of 2002. She was 70 years old.

She was my best friend and companion. We went through a lot together in New York.

Most of what I learned about the Alexander family, I learned from her too.

I am proud to tell you I know of none of my family ever been incarcerated.

I have family from both sides who have served and are still in the US militarily

I returned from Vera's funeral and noticed that Onyx was not as agile as usual.

I know from experience, that whenever I go away for a while, she would get an 'attitude'

But she would soon forgive me and be her sweet self once again.

This time, it was different. She was giving me a signal that I didn't need at this period.

That Saturday, I took her alone to the beach, leaving the five other howling so hard; I could hear them all the way to the beach.

I walked along with her as slowly as she was. She gave me that little lift whenever she wagged her tail, as if to say, "Don't worry Mommy, I can make it"

We reach the beach; she went as usual into the water and allowed the waves to wash her. I watched keenly, fearing that she was too weak to withstand the pull of the waves.

She sat on the beach for a while, and then she walked to where I sat and rest her head on my lap. I smooth her head; we looked into each other's eyes. I was looking into the eyes of my closest companion for fourteen years. She was the sweetest, caring friend.

She would allow Vera to hold on to collar while she climbs the steps.

She was so good with children, and thinks she was the mother for all puppies and kittens.

After a long rest, we began to head back home. When we got to the last climb on the hill, she just couldn't go anymore. I sat on the middle of road and cradled my best friend in my arms. I couldn't carry her the rest of the way up the hill because of my bad back.

A gardener helped me take her to her bed on the porch. The other five dogs gathered around. I think they knew what was happening.

She kept looking at me as if to say "Its OK Mommy, its time for us to say goodbye"

I went down and lie on her bed with her. I watch her chest move in and out. I was holding on for as long as I could. She could not hold on anymore.

I called her sisters and brother who grew up with her in our little apartment in NY.

As soon as they started to cry, I hand up the phone.

Since the death of my mother, I never cried for anyone the way I cried for my Onyxiepo.

She is resting under a daisy patch, on one of the highest hill in Dutch St Maarten.

Melanie had two of her three children. They were small and she needed my help.

I told all the friends and neighbors including the man who loved me unconditionally and had me pinched myself every day for ten year, that I was leaving to go help my daughter.

'I have promises to keep'.

The day I was leaving for the US, so many of my 'family' came to the airport.

I brought Sabrina, Smoky, Heidi and Snowflake back with me to the US. Prince and Asti, the larger dogs moved to Marie's, she assured me I too will have a home with her.

Some were crying, especially my Indian family, the Natram whom I met though their son Ganash, whom I adopted like my own son over the years, he still is my son.

The Connor's family from the French side, the Carters, Rogers, Van de Sar, Elveebel, Patricia, Van de Pool and many other friends and family that I met and lived with for ten years of roaming and gathering myself and friends.

I did my best to convince them that 'I will be back' as I kiss them goodbye.

Going through security, I looked back and saw him standing against the glass wall.

He was holding up the 'Ying n Yang' key chain that I had given him some years ago.

I held up the silver 'Heart' key chain that he had given to me. I pressed it against my heart and looked at him for a long tender moment for the last time. I said "Thank you"

[He passed away two years later.]

In the plane, a passenger asked, "What were those people crying for?"

"Its because I am going away" I said tearfully

"Who are you?"

"Just a drifter"

I came in time to be present and to hold my first grandson into my hands, fresh out of his mother, my firstborn daughter Kim's belly.

Kim is true to her craft. She is a real environmentalist. She refused to eat certain fruits. She said, "Mommy, they spray the field with pesticide while the workers are harvesting it. Those workers have children who are born with birth defect, brain damage"

She cuts all the plastic that hold soda cans together. She said, "Dolphins beaks get caught into them and they suffocate to death"

She never accepts plastic bags from the store. She carries her good-old canvas bag.

She said, "I know that I am not the only one who is doing these things for the good of environment and mankind, but what if I am? At least I am true to myself and belief"

Kim is the first in my family to graduate from High School then

Colleges, holding two Masters and many other degrees. She set the pace for her brother and sister to follow.

Many times she used her lunch break to bring home students winter gears to wash and dry. She uses her own money to buy school supplies for some of her students. She said,

"Mommy, they don't have the Jewish League of Women to help them.

She and Melanie are book snakes. Every spare moment they read and exchange books.

She placed her college ring on my finger and sends me a Father's Day card every year.

Rocky, my Shon was the pearl in the oyster. The girls and I treated him as such.

We were so close a family; we were the envy of some. He has an MBA

He was the man of the house and the protector of the women folks.

Lots of people thought he was my only child because they saw us together all the time.

He and I would drive around the neighborhood at summer time, closing all the open hydrants. He was Mr. Fixit and an inventor. He has one quarter of my heart.

He has two daughters.

Melanie thinks she is still a baby. She reminds us all the time that she is the sweetest, because she came from the bottom of the jar.

Steve, whom we met when he was fifteen years old, married my baby daughter.

He has all the quality of the best son, husband, father, and son-in-law.

I call him 'son' because he treats me with love and respect and I love him as such.

He allows me to share in raising their three children and to discipline them as I see fit.

She, Kim and their family plan their summer with me in mind.

They take me places where I couldn't afford to take them, such as Disney, Niagara Falls, cruise, camping etc.

She is an RN Specialty 2 in the emergency. She has become my childhood dream.

She has three children, two girls and one boy.

I saved my children's Christening clothes, first birthday outfit, every school report from kindergarten to their acceptance letters from colleges. Locks of their baby hair, pictures from baby to when they got married.

I presented my collection to my three children, as part of their wedding gift.

I went to the US Embassy in Guyana to get a visa for my brother David to come here in Florida, to spend some time with the family. He always asks if it is true that we live in a place as cold as ice? If we shiver all the time? I wanted him to experience winter and then take him back home. I took him away from Lancaster several times. To Georgetown several times, to St Maarten twice, to Suriname twice. Every trip, after 14 nights, he is ready to go back home. He is ready to go back to his community service where he goes around massaging people with stroke and other muscular pain, after the GMC closed.

I took my dumb, deft, and blind brother in to the embassy. I presented letters from my children, assuring the interviewing officers that my brother and their uncle will not be a burden to the country. The officer said, "Your brother do not have any asset to show that he will return to Guyana. I am sorry, I cannot give him a visa for the USA," I said,

"Sir, look at this man, he is 70 years old, and he is mute, deft and blind.

All his life, he has been mute and deft. Later he became blind. Would you have hired him to work in your office or your yard, so that he could acquire enough land, houses, and large enough bank account to qualify him for a visa to visit his family in America?"

"I am only doing my job," he said.

"Yes Sir, all I wanted was to take my brother for 14 days, because after 14 days, he would raise so much hell to come back to his cocoon, I would have to gag and take him to the airport. 14 is his number. He doesn't stay away from his home more than 14 days"

After taking David more than four different times to the US Embassy for a visitor's visa, each time we had to travel more than 180 miles to and back starting at 4am, on our last trip four months ago, as I led him out of the embassy, he grabbed me by the shoulder, pushed me against the wall, with his wide sightless eyes staring at me he, he sighed.

"Don't bring me back here. If they don't want me there, I don't want to go there"

I saw a story of an elderly brother name Hugo and his sister Rosa. Someone did the documentary in Europe, which took about three years in making.

It shows how the brother and sister lived together in a little farmhouse.

She did the cooking and he collected food and firewood from outside.

The story went on till their final days. I saw David and myself in that story.

I cried every time I saw that documentary of love and life of two old siblings.

Whenever David and I are together, we can't keep our hands off each other.

We sleep in the same bed, hugging each other, holding on to whatever time we have left.

On one of my visit to Houston because Daphne was not well, she suffered a heart attack. She was in a coma for days. I never left her side. It did not mattered that I had peed myself and did not wash or changed for days.

"Daphne, you have to open your eyes, you have to hear my voice. Squeeze my hand if you hear me. Remember it was your voice I heard that brought me back to you? Please my dear sister, don't go, come back to me"

After some days, a nurse whispered "I brought some clothes for you.

Follow me to the bathroom and take a shower. You don't want her to wakeup to the stench in this room?"

Daphne is fine and still bosses me around.

I have an unexplainable love for animals. All kinds of animals, I have the greatest respect for the elephant, whale, horse, cats and dogs. They have small eyes but once you look into them, they never forget you. Unconditional love is what you will get for your kind eyes. Lord Ganash, the elephant God is my favorite. He takes away sorrow and pain.

I have never been without animals. Today I live with my four small dogs, Heidi, Smoky, Duchess and Princess. I told you about Onyx, my faithful Lab? Labs are special.

I don't like snakes. Two of them bit two of my brothers. I could never like them.

One day, I took four of my grandchildren age ten to two to the dollar-store, I said

"Each one of you can get one item, no more, Grandma can only pay for one"

They all took baskets and began to pile things in like children in a toy store.

They lined up at the cashier looking at me. I held up my hand with my index finger up.

They emptied their full basket back into their right places and return with one item.

On our way home, they said to each other.

"I wanted all those things but Grandma only give me one, but she always comes into my bedroom, whatever is on the floor, she puts in an bag and take them to Guyana for children who need them. Whenever I see her coming, I pickup my things from the floor"

"Grandma never has money to buy everything we want"

"She needs to get a job. Grandmas buy everything, she pays for only one"

"She never had a job in her whole life"

"Ya, you are right, she needs to get a job"

I am judging my sustainability by what I had to give up in order to get it.

Not getting what I wanted could be a stroke of good luck.

I lost my taste for blood when I forgive all those who hurt me.

We are not paid to raise our children. We are 'village' people.

If my peace and happiness becomes someone's torment? So be it, I paid my dues.

Now I can stop in any deli and buy that muffin or cherries which I once longed for.

My mother, the Guardian, Protector, Shelter, Sustainer, Spark, Seed, the Embodiment

Of what Pure Love truly represents, is truly my hero.

They stuck her blueprint on me but I got to hold some grandchildren. She did not.

Now when Dhia's daughters ask about her, I say, "Look in the mirror and each other"

Because of my love for family togetherness, I was given the privilege to organize many of the Alexander Family Reunion in St Maarten, Barbados and other places.

Our last reunion was in California. I am working for our next in Antigua.

It was in Barbados, when my cousin Vera saw how hard I was working to make everyone comfortable and all the different activities that I arranged, she said,

"Wynette, I remember when you were the outsider, you were the brick the builder rejected? Now you have become the corner stone of our family whom you love so much"

I am telling this story for the very first time. You see my mother had a tattoo on her arm. As a child, I played with it and wondered 'how did they add so many different colors on the tattoo-painting on my mother's arm?' It was pretty and well exposed.

Many years later, I came to America and saw that the sign on my mother's arm was one of the most racist and bigoted sign. It is called a 'Swastika'

I kept that secret from everyone. I was ashamed that my mother was a Nazi?

Two years ago, I was at my cousin John's granddaughter wedding. She was marrying a man from India. I saw the same sign displayed on the floor. I was one confused soul.

I pull John aside and asked, "What is a Swastika doing at this wedding? It's terrible"

"No, its not. It's an Indian Arian sign. When the European came to India, they adapted it and use it to represent a certain group, but the origin of the Swastika is India"

"How come my mother had a Swastika tattooed on her arm?"

"Because, it was customary that when a girl gets married, she had to be branded- tattooed with her husband's sign-caste logo. Your mother's husband was an Arian from India, just like my grandson-in-law. But these days, we don't tattoo the brides anymore"

I am still not a good reader. I try very hard to read to my children and grandchildren when they are little. As they get older and can read for themselves, I don't risk the embarrassment. I let them read to me.

My respect for the $5 bill goes back a long way. Whenever possible, I do not use it for myself, but give it to charity and the homeless. I always remember how far the one that Uncle Bertram gave to me that early morning in 1963, took me. He called it 'Elephant'

My Mommy, Mahatma Gandhi, John F. Kennedy, Martin Luther King and Nelson Mandela are my heroes. Their strength and forgiveness sow the seed of 'hope' in me.

This is my recipe for making dhal. Boil a cup of yellow-green split peas in four cups of water until soft and smooth. In a saucepan heat some oil, add some cumin, garlic, pepper, curry powder and salt to taste, Sauté until its nice and light brown and the aroma spreads around the house. Add the spices to the peas and mix together.

You could have it on rice, roti, bread, salad, pasta or even drink in a cup.

Enjoy your liquid protein and daily regularity.

I love jazz and old movies. My all-time movie is 'To Kill a Mocking Bird' Boo reminds me of Nana Sweetie. I never miss a movie if Gregory Peck, Yul Brynner, Marlin Brando, Sidney Poitier Audrey Heburn or Betty Davis is the star.

I named two of my children after Kim and Omar.

I have two wishes, one, take away my constant companion, my back pain, so that could lift and bend and play with my grandchildren when they weigh more that ten pounds- Whenever I take the little one for a walk and he gets tired, he stands in front of me with his hands up for me to lift him. I can't do that, so I sit on the sidewalk with him until he is ready to walk again. This Grandma can't carry him and he does not understand why?

Two, let me bring my beloved David to America for a short visit, so that I could take him somewhere cold, because he can't imagine that people lives in the cold.

And to watch his face when I place a bushel of apples and box of grapes in front of

him and tells him that they are all for him. Yes for my David who never heard a human voice or say his name, who lives in a dark world with the widest smile on his face.

He sees no evil, hears no evil, and speaks no evil. Can anyone be purer than that?

I wrote this 'Thank You' note to God.

Your power spares me from the curse. Even though I was rejected from conception.

From a tender age, You give me the strength to hold on to my brothers.

The ants had their dance, until You stop the music.

You made no water deep enough to keep me down under.

You left me alone, to fight my own demons, made me wonder, 'Where are You?'

Only when I gave up, did You intervene and said, "I am not ready for you"

Every time I fall down, I quickly pick meself up, because I know You're watching.
For forgiving my oppressors, You rewarded me with six little angels.
No riches, no mansions do I have, but I drink from my saucer because I am
Contented and thankful.

Thank You for the people with humanity, whom I have halos for: -
My Mommy, who could've freed herself from the curse, but stuck with her mutes.
She taught me to 'listen to the quiet'. That 'I'm sorry' don't take back bad doings
Or sayings, only forgiveness erase the hurt and set you free.
My father, whose pain I was not responsible for, but paid the terrible price for it.
My brothers Datson and David, we were the tree rotten peas in so many pods.
But there is no measure for the love they gave to me and allow me to love them.
My brother Dhia, who refused to take his baby sister for the crab-dogs to feast on?
Aunties Chunu, Katy, Amoy, Pandu, Dull and the kind people of Whim Village.
Mrs. Moore, who taught me to pray. She assured me that I belong to both sides.
Mr. Reed, who taught me that there are good and bad in every race of people.
My Gramother, who taught me the importance of family, and how to hold on tight?
Nana Sweetie, whose 103 years old lap, I was allowed to rest my sorrow head.
Uncle Bertram and Aunt Eloise, who loved me as their own child, and then became
My 'Moses', set me free with an St Kitts canvas bag and an elephant to ride off on.

My stepsister Mine, who had conscience, in an unconscionable period of my live.

Sister Esther, who was there for me when I had no one else in the big city.

Cecil, who taught me that love and sex don't necessarily have to go hand in hand.

People like Clive, Stan, the Pereira's, Mr. Taharally, Mrs. Rogers and Ron who

Taught me that true love comes in different forms. It's like nourishment for the soul.

Richard, who truly loved me once, and gave me three beautiful children,

But when the fire went cold, he forced me to fly without wings.

Daphne, who saw something in me that no one else, not even me, ever thought I had.

Ada, Doreen, Cheryl, Noreen, Ed, Cedric, Sharon and others who played in my life.

I wish I could find the African lady who told me what to do to save my Melanie.

I wish I could meet the gentleman who gave me all his silver pieces at the airport.

When I arrived at in America, March 10, 1979, penniless, cold and homeless.

Vera and the entire Alexander family, who embraced and made me a part of them.

John, Mybee, Ram, Bada, Partab and their family who claimed our bloodline

Connection, even against their entire Hindu upbringing.

All of Kasy's bloodline who reached out to me and made me part of their family.

The Hellers who never stop loving me and mine. Who made us proud Americans.

Kim, Rocky and Melanie, who made me proud and easy to raise three teenagers

Into decent, respectful professionals in this blessed 'Land of Opportunity'.

Steve, Dennis, best husbands, father, son, and who allow me to call them 'son'.

Peter, who wouldn't stop the check even when I no longer worked for him.

Parc, who listened to the quiet with me? Who, for a decade, lit my life so bright?

Roy, Louise, Marie, the Connor family, the Natram family, Lasana, Patricia, Lelia,

The Carters, Van de Sar, Pool and all the other kind people from the Friendly Island,

Who encouraged me to write and surprised me with a huge party for my 65th birthday

All the kind people whom I met from island to island when I was finding myself.

They straitened my wilted self by every drop of love given to me on my adventure.

My six grandchildren who give me a reasons to stay afloat.

My cousins Ulric and Stanley for looking over my brother David.

Lammy, Onyx, Sabrina and all the animals I ever had and still have, for the privilege

of looking into their eyes and feel their love. They each had a character of their own.

They knew how to love me without conditions. Some said goodbye in my arms.

Linda, you spent so many years listening to my story. I know that there were times

When it was long and boring. I repeated myself many times, but I wanted you to hear

My story, from my ancestors from Monstaarat and India, up until today, my 68th

Birthday. Many times when I broke down, you put your arms around me and cry too.

Finally, me. As a child in Whim, my two brothers and I robbed the dog of his dinner.

Us in rags were the freaks and slaves for so many.

Whose mother could not call us by our Hindu given names for fear of reprisal?

I was kicked off the wagon, the bus, the church, the school and my home.

I heard so many times that I couldn't be anybody. No one would marry me. I would

Always is the 'gorilla' of the village. The dunce in school, the tramp on the street.

"If you swept me yard, fill me drum with water and wash me dirty dishes? Then I

Would play with you" "You are useless just like your two dummy brothers"

There is an ant in Guyana; we call it 'The Cob-cob ant'. You can dump a truckload of

Dirt on top of that ant, you can bet your life, that ant will see the sun again.

After meeting Daphne, Cecil, Hellers and all the kind people who reached out to me,

I think of myself as a Cob-cob ant. No one or nothing could keep me under anymore.

Lastly, I thank and forgive all my oppressors. They gave me strength to standup strait

And to be one of the strongest supporters for 'underdogs' all over the world.

I am drawn to 'mix breed' people, especially children. I pray they are luckier than

We were. I hope they never experience alienation and decimation like we did.

I am happy to see how diverse my family is in America. We just ignore the bigots.

I pray, my grandchildren never to see difference of people based of their color.

If I ever hurt or caused anyone pain, I apologize and ask your forgiveness.

Two weeks ago, my next-door neighbor asked, "Who is your house guess?"

"She is Mrs. Heller, the lady who sponsored us here thirty years ago" I said proudly.

"Are you telling me that your mistress who you work for thirty years ago, is spending time with you in your house here in Florida?" she asked, not believing a word I said.

"Yes, it's the truth. She is my best friend for as many years that I know her"

"I was sponsored too; the last time I saw or heard from my mistress was the day I left them with my belongings. What have you done to those people?" she asked curiously.

"Ask me what those people have done for us?" I said proudly.

At this moment in time, I think I can promise my six grandchildren what Mr. Reed promised me almost sixty years ago. I say, "By the time you grow up, things will be

different from how it was when I was a child. You are born in a different time.

You are Americans; you could be whatever you want to be. I kept 'hope' for you.

I will not fit you into my dark and ugly clothes. Yours will be bright and colorful".

After so many near-death experiences, I've become, 'simpler and contented'

I must have my tea with milk every morning in my large beat up enamel cup.

I was asked, "What do you want for your birthday?"

I reply, "Nothing, I have everything. I am alive with my soul and spirit intact ".

My two daughters destroyed my mother's blueprint when they gave me the honor and privilege to be present when they gave birth to their four children. I will not be true to myself if I did not tell you that my daughters made me so special, I have believe the other part of the saying, 'Your daughters are your daughters for the rest of your life'

I add to that. 'My daughters and my son will always be my children as long as I live'.

Whenever we need Rocky, even though he's far away, he'll be on the first plane to us.

They behave like children, trying to catch the past, while I cook their favorite dishes

Recently, my son Rocky, along with his sisters and their families went to Guyana for Uncle David's 70th birthday, he held me into his arms and said,

"Mommy, I am eternally grateful to you for my life and all that you have done for me"

"I am eternally thankful to all of you. You give me a reason to wakeup ever morning"

I told you of three generation of mothers who held their children so close, that no fire, water or brimstone was strong enough to separate us from our children.

'The cause of freedom is not the cause of a race or a sect, a party or a class.

It is the cause of humankind, the very birthright of humanity' says Anna Julia Cooper

"Who is more qualified to chronicle my journey, but me? Before I Forget?"

Wynette Eleyn Alexander-Greene

I dedicate my history to my beloved brother David
My six grandchildren,
And
In Loving Memory of
My Mommy, Datson
And
All those who touched my life with theirs

CPSIA information can be obtained at www.ICGtesting.com
Printed in the USA
LVOW06*1758051113

360112LV00019B/1482/P